*To my friend Arthur:*

# "Wrestlers Are Like Seagulls"

## From McMahon to McMahon

*The Leader of "The Four Horsemen" forever!*

# Other publications from Crowbar Press

**Inside Out**
by Ole Anderson, with Scott Teal

**Wrestlers Are Like Seagulls**
by James J. Dillon,
with Scott Teal & Philip Varriale

**Assassin: The Man Behind the Mask**
by Joe Hamilton, with Scott Teal

**"Is That Wrestling Fake?"**
by Ivan Koloff, with Scott Teal

**Bruiser Brody**
by Emerson Murray, edited by Scott Teal

**Wrestling with the Truth**
by Bruno Lauer, edited by Scott Teal

**The Solie Chronicles**
by Bob Allyn,
with Pamela S Allyn & Scott Teal

**Wrestling in the Canadian West**
by Vance Nevada

**Long Days and Short Pays**
by Hal West, edited by Scott Teal

**Drawing Heat**
by Jim Freedman

**ATLAS: Too Much, Too Soon**
by Tony Atlas, with Scott Teal

**The Last Laugh**
by Bill De Mott, with Scott Teal

**HOOKER**
by Lou Thesz, with Kit Bauman

**The Last Outlaw**
by Stan Hansen, with Scott Teal

**NIKITA**
by Nikita Koloff, as told to Bill Murdock

**The Strap**
by Roger Deem

**BRISCO**
by Jack Brisco, as told to Bill Murdock

**Mid-Atlantic Wrestling Memories**
by Mike Mooneyham

**"I Ain't No Pig Farmer!"**
by Dean Silverstone, with Scott Teal

**The Hard Way**
by Don Fargo, with Scott Teal

**Wrestling Archive Project, volume 1**
by Scott Teal

**Whatever Happened to
Gorgeous George?**
by Joe Jares

**"It's Wrestling, Not Rasslin'!"**
by Mark Fleming, edited by Scott Teal

— **The Great Cities of Wrestling #1** —
**Mayhem in the Garden:
The Battle for New York
Shoots, Works and Double-crosses**
by Scott Teal & J Michael Kenyon

**BRUISER
The World's Most Dangerous Wrestler**
by Richard Vicek, edited by Scott Teal

**The Mat, the Mob & Music**
by Tom Hankins, edited by Scott Teal

**BREAKING KAYFABE
Dinner with the Legends of Wrestling**
by Jeff Bowdren, edited by Scott Teal

**BATTLEGROUND VALHALA
The story of Finnish wrestling pioneer
Michael "StarBuck" Majalahti**
by Michael Majalahti, edited by Scott Teal

**Through the Lens ... Through the Ropes
#1
Southeastern Championship Wrestling**
Compiled by Scott Teal

— **The Great Cities of Wrestling #2** —
**The Greatest Wrestling Ever
in the History of Nashville, vol. 1**
by Scott Teal & Don Luce

**Wrestling Archive Project, volume 2**
by Scott Teal

**Through the Lens ... Through the Ropes
#2
Championship Wrestling from Florida**
Compiled by Scott Teal

— **Classic Arena Programs #1** —
**SLAM-O-GRAM, volume 1**
by Scott Teal

**Florida Mat Wars: 1977**
by Robert D. VanKavelaar, with Scott Teal

---

**MOVIES & ENTERTAINMENT**

**DURANGO**
by Herschel (Chuck) Thornton

**Charles Starrett**
by Herschel (Chuck) Thornton

# "Wrestlers Are Like Seagulls"

## From McMahon to McMahon

### by James J. Dillon
#### with Scott Teal & Philip Varriale

Gallatin, Tennessee

# "Wrestlers Are Like Seagulls"
## From McMahon to McMahon

Copyright © 2005 by James Morrison and Scott Teal

All rights reserved. No part of this book may be reproduced or transmitted in any form or by any means, electronic or mechanical, including photocopying, recording, or by any information storage and retrieval system, without permission in writing from the publisher.

Published by Crowbar Press
106 Tattnal Court
Gallatin, Tennessee 37066

http://www.crowbarpress.com

Book layout and cover design by Scott Teal

Library of Congress Cataloging-in-Publication Data

Dillon, James J.
   Wrestlers Are Like Seagulls / by James J. Dillon
        with Scott Teal and Philip Varriale

1. Dillon, James J.   2. Sports—United States—Biography.   3. Wrestling—United States—Biography.   I. Teal, Scott.   II. Title.

Printed in the United States of America
ISBN 0-9745545-2-9

First edition hardcover / June 2005
Second edition softcover / August 2014
Second printing softcover / February 2015
Third printing softcover / October 2017
Fourth printing softcover / January 2019

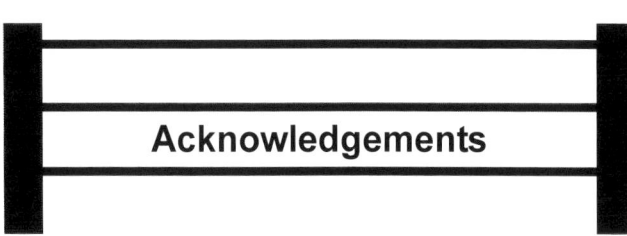

# Acknowledgements

Dedicated to my beloved children Pamela, Missy (Amanda), Geoffrey, and Nicole, and my grand-children Erica, Rebecca, and Meghan.

To my mother, Blanche R. Morrison, and my late father, J. Mitchell Morrison. To my sister, Joan, my nephew, John, my niece, Jill, and their respective families. To Mike McHugh, Collin, Kyle, and Lorrayne.

I would like to add a special "thank you" to Bruno Sammartino, the late Eddie "Sheik" Farhat, Pedro Godoy, and Art Nelson. Also, Anne and Bill Bowman, Les Thatcher, Jim Grabmire, the Cormier brothers, Dory Funk, Jr., Terry Funk, my mentor Eddie Graham, Ric Flair (the true "Nature Boy"), Tully Blanchard, Dusty Rhodes, Jerry Jarrett, Gene Okerlund, and Kevin Sullivan.

Thanks also to the Crockett family, Akio Sato, the Hebner boys, Terry Garvin, Pat Patterson, Priscilla, Ann, Dee and Vickie, Tony Schiavone, Bob Friedman, Chip Burnham, Ted Heath, the late Zane Bresloff, the late Jim Barnett, Georgiann Makropoulos, Bill Apter, George Napolitano, Steve Hisler, Harvey Brandwein, Jerry Turner, John Holland, "Mr. Mint" Alan Rosen, Mike Vettraino, and all the others who helped me along the way, including my three former spouses and Wayne, Rick, Mark, Stori, and Theresa.

May God bless you all!

# TABLE of CONTENTS

|  | Foreword | 8 |
|---|---|---|
|  | Introduction | 10 |
| 1. | The Dream | 13 |
| 2. | Living the Dream | 19 |
| 3. | Third Man in the Ring | 22 |
| 4. | The Bodyslam | 31 |
| 5. | Bruno | 36 |
| 6. | The Babyface | 39 |
| 7. | Nature Boy Dillon | 49 |
| 8. | West Texas Memories | 56 |
| 9. | The Cow That Ate the Cabbage | 72 |
| 10. | The Stomper and the Moondog | 78 |
| 11. | Chips Off the Old Block | 86 |
| 12. | The Giant and the Poofter | 92 |
| 13. | Closet Announcer | 97 |
| 14. | Border Crossing | 103 |
| 15. | Cable TV, My Toughest Opponent | 108 |
| 16. | Samurai and Cannibals | 115 |
| 17. | The Garden | 126 |
| 18. | Back to the Maritimes | 129 |
| 19. | Death of the Master | 132 |
| 20. | Cadillacs, Mercedes, and BMWs | 135 |

| 21. | The Four Horsemen | 141 |
| 22. | The Acquisition | 148 |
| 23. | Courted by the World Wrestling Federation | 152 |
| 24. | The Big Time | 155 |
| 25. | He Did It His Way | 159 |
| 26. | The Creative Process | 161 |
| 27. | Twins and a Miracle Baby | 171 |
| 28. | Dirtsheets | 172 |
| 29. | The Players | 177 |
| 30. | The Myth Becomes Personal | 188 |
| 31. | The Young and the Wrestlers | 191 |
| 32. | Resigned to Resign | 199 |
| 33. | The Obsession | 206 |
| 34. | ATM Eric | 214 |
| 35. | The Other Vince | 229 |
| 36. | Fire Sale | 242 |
| 37. | Total Nonstop Anxiety | 246 |
| 38. | Life After Wrestling (Yes, there is!) | 250 |
| 39. | Summary | 264 |
| Photo gallery | | 268 |
| Index | | 283 |

# Foreword

A girl loves her Daddy, and none more than I love mine. The older I get, the more respect and admiration I have for him and the life he leads. He is the kind of person that people like right from the start. He is warm and charming, and he makes the people around him feel good. He is passionate for the things he cares about.

Professional wrestling is something he has that passion for, and it was a better and more entertaining sport because of his contribution to it.

I didn't understand what my father did for a living until I was about 12 years old. What I knew of his livelihood was that his work involved a lot of travel. Based on the postcards, letters, and gifts I received, it was travel to interesting places. When he came to Pennsylvania to see me, he always seemed larger than life. I loved every minute I spent with him.

Thanksgiving 2004: Jim and his children
(front) JJ and Geoffrey
(back) Missy, Pam, Nicole

My first exposure to wrestling was in Dallas, the summer of 1980. I spent a few weeks with my father in Texas. During my visit, I attended my first matches, and saw James J. Dillon in action. I was impressed, not only by the fact that my father was notorious, but also by the amount of time that he put into the wrestling business. He worked harder at his job than anyone I knew, and he certainly had more enthusiasm. Mornings were spent at the office and nights were spent at the shows. On the days when the matches were local and there was time beforehand, we saw the sights. Other than that, time was spent on the road. I went to Amarillo and Lubbock, in addition to seeing the local matches at the Dallas Sportatorium.

The next few summers, only the territory changed. By then, I was spending the entire summer vacation with my Dad, going on the road when I could to spend as much time with him as possible. I knew his schedule by heart. I would not trade those summers for anything. They make up some of my happiest (and most colorful) memories.

It did not escape me though, even at a young age, that what the fans saw was very different from what happened behind the scenes. The fans saw glamour and drama in the superstars, whether in the form of platinum hair and fancy robes, or mysterious eyes behind a mask. The fans didn't see the often-friendly athletes (and they WERE athletes) performing the same match a couple of nights in a row to make sure that fans in multiple towns got to "be there" when history was made: when heels turned babyface, or vice versa, and when titles changed hands. Fans didn't see the strategic carpooling, when the guys regularly drove a few hundred miles to do what they loved for the fans who loved them back. I felt so fortunate to see that side of things.

Wrestling was more than a job for my Dad. It was a life. And it was a life my Dad loved. The stories he has from the last few decades are unsurpassed by any fiction. When he told me that he was working on a book, I was thrilled. How fortunate are his readers to have the opportunity to see things through his eyes. From the view in the dressing room to the view in the boardroom. From the perspective of someone who rode the roller coaster, right there in the front seat. From a gentleman who I am so proud to call my father.

**Pamela Morrison**

# Introduction

It is said that wrestling is the oldest sport in the world. This makes sense since wrestling embodies the bomost basic of confrontations "mano e mano," one on one, without weapons or armor.

I have been told that modern day professional wrestling evolved from the carnival days where it was a side show attraction. When the carnival came to town, the locals could challenge the traveling wrestler. If you could defeat the wrestler, you would win the prize money. I am certain that these early wrestlers were pretty tough men who could take care of themselves. If the wrestler lost and money was given away, the side show attraction would not have survived very long. When no local "marks" would take up the challenge, the pros would have to "work" with each other to keep the attraction alive.

By the time I discovered professional wrestling in the mid-fifties, it was an organized arena event shown on television.

This book is not intended to be a history of the wrestling profession. It is really the story of a wrestling fan who, from the time he was a 14-year-old boy, dreamed about finding a place in the wrestling world. Beginning with his early involvement on the periphery, his career in wrestling lasted over forty years and spanned five decades. He personally witnessed the many changes that took place in the history of modern wrestling, and he saw most of those changes taking place from the inside.

This is my story—the good and the bad, the highs and the lows, told "out of character."

I was first introduced to Scott Teal by Anne and Bill Bowman, life-long friends dating back to my first territory, the Carolinas, in 1971. Though I connected with Scott from our first conversation, the timing initially was just not right to undertake writing a book. That was eighteen months ago, and at the time, I was trying to get my personal life in order.

Over the next several months, the idea of writing a book persisted, but if I was really going to put my life on paper, I wanted to do it right, or not do it at all. During that time, Scott and I continued to communicate. As we discussed the process for a book project, the idea really grew on me.

As I went through my old photos and memorabilia in preparation for the project, I discovered my entire collection of "Week At A Glance" appointment books that I compiled every year during my career. I kept the daily records mainly for tax purposes and they dated all the way back to 1970. Each day, I listed the city, the mileage traveled (in those early days, we drove almost every trip), the name of my opponent(s), the outcome of the match, my "payoff," and the road expenses—all recorded for posterity spanning over twenty years in the ring. I have always been a detail person. Vincent K. McMahon (Junior) once remarked to me that whenever he asked me for the time of day, I would first have to tell him how the watch was made. Well, Vince. This time, it looks like my attention to detail has paid off.

I want to thank Scott Teal for his hard work and dedication, without which I could not have told my story. Through Scott, I was introduced to Philip Varriale, a very knowledgeable wrestling fan who appears to know more about my career than any other fan I ever met. Philip transcribed all of our recorded conversations, and without his efforts, we would not have met our projected schedule. I also want to thank Bruce Tharpe and Viktor Berry, who scrutinized the final text for any legal issues. Thanks to Jim Melby, Chuck Thornton, Pete Lederberg, and Philip Varriale, Eddie Cheslock for photo contributions.

Why would I want to write a book in the first place? As one ages, I am told that it is not uncommon for someone to search for the meaning of one's life. I realized that I had spent over forty years in sports entertainment, but what had I really accomplished? In 2003, I introduced www.jjdillon.com, intended as a marketing tool as part of my business plan to launch a real estate career in Georgia. After WCW had closed, I got my license, but a sudden, unexpected divorce derailed my real estate venture. However, my website remains up on the Internet, and it has been revamped by Scott. I still check the site from time to time, and I have been pleasantly surprised by the various messages left by visitors to the site, representative of fans from all over the world.

In 2004, I attended several "Legends" conventions in the Carolinas, and participated in several Q & A sessions with Jim Cornette, Les Thatcher, Tully Blanchard, and Baby Doll. These intimate gatherings allowed interaction with some of the most loyal wrestling fans that I had ever met. Individual fans, most of whom I had never met before, personally thanked me for the memories, and for taking the time to be there to meet them in person. I in turned thanked each one for attending, because in the end, I took away as much, if not more, from the experience then I had given. For the first time in my life, I felt a sense of satisfaction, that I had done something positive with my life. If during my years in the ring, I allowed just one person to laugh, or cry, or to vent their frustration, and forget their problems and troubles for a period of time, then it was all worth it. In fact, it reinforced my commitment to complete the book so that I could tell my story.

I hope you will read the whole book. I chose the title only to instill curiosity. To understand the meaning and origin of "Wrestlers Are Like Seagulls," you will have to read on. The title could just as well have been "The Dream," because I am reminded of that reoccurring theme throughout my career. I am so thankful that I was born and raised in the United States of America. Anyone that has traveled the world will tell you that even though we have our share of problems in America, this is still the greatest country in the world. This is truly the land of opportunity. I am also very appreciative that I was raised by loving parents who guided me well, and afforded me the opportunity to get an education.

When you finish reading my story, if you are left with only one thought, I hope that memory is "don't be afraid to dream." I was never the best or most talented, and I was not blessed with unique or exceptional skills. However, whatever I lacked in ability, I made up for in will and sheer determination. I encountered hurtles and obstacles that often tested my will and determination. In the end, I not only survived, but I made a good living in wrestling for many years. I am comfortable being the sensitive, caring person that is the real me, the direct opposite to the arrogance of the character "J.J. Dillon." I thought it best to try and always tell the truth. That is not so easy in the wrestling business, but in the end, it is the only way. If you run into someone six months after an initial encounter, you never have to struggle to remember "the story," because the truth will always be the truth. However, there is more than one way to tell the truth, and I did always try to be diplomatic. I try to practice the "Golden Rule" and I strive to be a man of principal. It may sound corny to some, but it is really the secret to my longevity in the wrestling business.

Remember; don't be afraid to dream because dreams can come true. I am living proof that they do.

# Chapter 1
## The Dream

Most kids grow up with a desire to be a fireman, or a policeman, or have a dream of joining the circus.

Me?

I fell in love with professional wrestling. From the day I discovered it, I knew that it was what I wanted to do with my life.

My family was originally from south Jersey, but my dad's father moved to Trenton, New Jersey, and became the Chief Probation Officer of Mercer County, the county in which Trenton is located.

My father's name was James Mitchell Morrison, but he always referred to himself as J. Mitchell Morrison. His friends just called him Mitch. My mother, Blanche, grew up on a farm in Delaware with eleven brothers and sisters. She moved to New Jersey to find a job when she was 18 years old.

That's where they met.

And that's where I was conceived.

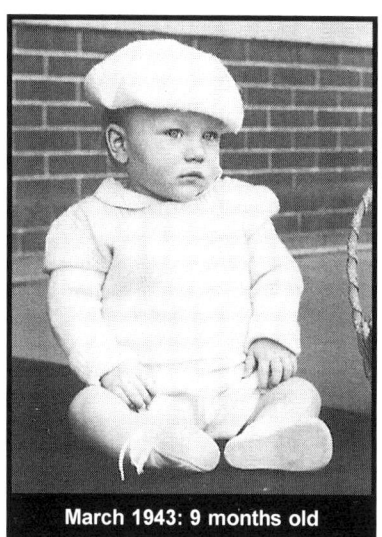

March 1943: 9 months old

My given name is James Albert Morrison. I was born in Trenton, New Jersey, on June 26, 1942, and spent the next eighteen years of my life there.

I first discovered wrestling when I was changing channels on the television. I had a passion for baseball, but when the Brooklyn Dodgers moved to Los Angeles, my interest waned somewhat. At that time, we didn't have the means of communication that we have today. We didn't have cable television or the Internet, so our only means of keeping up with the teams was in the morning newspaper. Even that was discouraging because, while the *Trentonian* and the *Trenton Times* newspapers carried the west coast line, due to deadlines, they were only able to report on the first couple of innings. What's the old saying? Out of sight, out of mind? As a result, my love for the Dodgers diminished pretty quickly.

On the other hand, the moment I laid eyes on professional wrestling, I was hooked. My immediate reaction was, *"Wow, this is great stuff!"* I was hooked right from the very beginning.

Every Thursday night, I tuned in to watch *Wrestling from the Capitol Arena* with Ray Morgan. As a television fan, you had a visual picture of the Capitol Arena that

## 14 • "Wrestlers Are Like Seagulls"

would make you think, *"What a magnificent place that would be to see the wrestling live."* In actuality, the Capitol Arena was a small, roller skating arena in a rough section of Washington, D.C.

The thing I remember the most about the shows were the interviews with great personalities like "Nature Boy" Buddy Rogers and his manager, Bobby Davis. Al Costello and Roy Heffernan, who wrestled as the "Fabulous Kangaroos," and their manager, Wild Red Berry, were also very colorful.

The cast of characters in that era was phenomenal. On Thursday night, I couldn't wait for the show to come on the air. From 8:30 to 10:00, I would sit in front of the television while the wrestlers did their angles. Sometime during the show, somebody would jump into the ring and involve themselves in someone else's match. While the wrestlers were involved in a big ruckus in the ring, the show would go off the air, leaving you in suspense. On rare occasions, you would even see blood shed.

During the show, the wrestlers also did their interviews. In essence, the television show was an infomercial for the upcoming arena show, giving the wrestlers an opportunity to talk about a big match coming up. It was just a fabulous medium of entertainment that captivated me.

When I learned that they had matches in Trenton, I begged my mom to take me. I wasn't old enough to drive, so she took me downtown to the old Trenton National Guard Armory for the monthly show.

My parents were always supportive of the things that I wanted to do. My father was an avid sports fisherman, and I remember going to boat shows with him. My mother and father met at a motorcycle club. They both rode motorcycles and took long trips around the country, so we went to motorcycle races at the Langhorne (Pennsylvania) Speedway. I also remember watching the Indy cars race there.

My parents also took me to a Brooklyn Dodgers game at Ebbets Field before the Dodgers left Brooklyn. I don't remember the date, but they took me because I bugged them so much. The Dodgers played the Boston Braves and our seats were around the third baseline. I remember watching Warren Spahn pitch. He had that big, banana nose and pitched with a high leg kick. I met Warren a few times later on in life. The last time I saw him, I was changing planes at Hartsfield Airport in Atlanta. As I stood in line in Sbarros, waiting to get a slice of pizza, I looked over and saw a man sitting by himself. I immediately recognized who it was. I walked over and said, *"Mr. Spahn! Hello, how are you?"*

He graciously asked, *"Would you like to join me?"*

Talk about reverting to your childhood! I sat down and talked to him for almost an hour. He passed away not too long after that on November 24, 2003.

So when I told my mom that I wanted to go to the wrestling matches, she simply said, *"Okay, if that's what you want to do."*

There was nothing like going to the Armory to see people like Argentina Rocca, Karl Von Hess, Dr. Jerry Graham, Professor Roy Shire, and Chief Big Heart. To the wrestling fans, the wrestlers were bigger-than-life characters. You didn't see men on the street with long, bleached blond hair, wearing flamboyant clothes, or being outspoken in the things that they said. In today's society, those types of people wouldn't generate any interest out of the ordinary, but they did in the mid- to late 50s. The wrestlers came to the ring dressed as cowboys, Indians, and all sorts of fantastic characters. When you met them at the arenas, or on the street, they were exactly what you saw on television. They were never out of character.

I had a friend named Gary Rittmann who lived a few houses down from me on Ardmore Avenue. He enjoyed wrestling, too, so in the months that followed, we would ride the bus to the Armory. It's been more than 40 years since I left, but he still lives in that same house. Years later, when I was in the wrestling business myself, he wrote me a few times when he saw my picture in a magazine, or when I would appear on television. I moved so much that it was difficult for him to follow my address changes, but I know that he always exchanged Christmas cards with my parents. He would usually include a short note to tell them that he had seen me on television.

During the time when I was growing up, the promoters didn't want the average fan to know how often the wrestlers wrestled. If a fan asked a promoter how many times a week they wrestled, he would probably say, *"Two or three times a week."* The fans took the answer at face value because they really didn't have any way of checking up on the promoter. More than likely, their response to the promoter's answer would have been, *"Two or three times a week? That has to be physically demanding!"* What we didn't realize was that the wrestlers wrestled seven times every week, and on some days, especially when they had a TV taping, they wrestled two and three times a day.

The fans in New York knew that Bruno Sammartino would be defending the WWWF title in Madison Square Garden. What they *didn't* know was that Bruno also defended the title against that same opponent in Boston, Baltimore, Philadelphia, Washington, and Pittsburgh—all during that same month. They didn't have the Internet, or cable TV, or any of the communication methods we have now, so the fans didn't hear about those matches.

What the fans *did* have was fan clubs. The promoters didn't like the fan clubs because they were a source of information that they didn't want the fans to have. The fan clubs would publish newsletters and print the results of matches from as many of the towns as they could find. I have always been a free spirit. I wasn't worried about what the promoters thought. All I knew was that I wanted to be a part of the professional wrestling business, so in 1958, I started a fan club for Johnny Valentine.

Johnny Valentine

When Johnny Valentine came into the New York territory in 1958, he became a huge star. I can't explain it, but there was something about Johnny that I admired. When he came into a territory, he took several weeks—sometimes months—to get over [develop a reputation]. He was very slow and methodical in what he did in the ring, but he was always very, very believable. When he smacked his opponent in the chest, sweat would fly into the air, and you could hear the sound of the blow in the balcony. If you didn't hit him back just as hard, he would gobble you up. Johnny was also as proficient at ring psychology as anyone I ever saw. He would keep one hold on his opponent for twenty minutes. If he did that today, the people would yell, "boring." In that era, though, Johnny worked that hold until he had the people eating out of the palm of his hand.

I had membership cards printed and I published a periodic newsletter with news of

16 • "Wrestlers Are Like Seagulls"

Johnny's run in the territory. Even though I was his fan club president, I only met with Johnny a couple of times. He was busy and didn't have any time to offer input into the club. I had a page filled with questions about his background, so after his match one night, we stood in a corner of the Trenton Armory. I asked my questions, jotted down his answers, and then we took a few pictures. One of those photos is reprinted on this page. That's me standing next to John.

John and I made plans to meet one other time, when he invited me to spend an hour or so with him at his house in Wilmington, Delaware. I took a train from Trenton to Wilmington, and a cab to his house. Unfortunately, something came up and Johnny had to leave before I arrived. His wife was very gracious and didn't want my trip to be for nothing, so she invited me in. She pulled out a stack of photo albums and told me some stories about John's career.

My newsletter was a short-lived venture because I was more interested in the wrestling business as a whole. I ran it for a year or so, but it was tough trying to find enough information to fill a newsletter, especially when John would leave the New York territory for several months to wrestle elsewhere.

At the time, you could join fan clubs for many of the wrestlers. One of the hardest working fan club presidents was Georgiann Makropoulos. I've known Georgie since 1957, when she ran a fan club for Bruno Sammartino. She was promoting and running fan clubs forty-eight years ago, and today, she's still active in the wrestling business on the Internet. Georgie has been good for the wrestling business because she treats the business and the wrestlers with a level of respect that most people don't show today.

In 1959, I met Larry Simon, a wrestler who lived in New Jersey. I had driven to the matches in Highland Park, New Jersey, one night. Larry was on the card that night and we struck up a conversation. I don't know what prompted it, but he invited me to visit with him and his wife at their home after the matches. The three of us sat in his kitchen, talking and eating pizza. His two young sons, Dean and Joe, who would later become wrestlers when they grew up, were already in bed. When we finished eating, Larry showed me photo albums of his career, including a photo of when he wrestled as Otto von Krupp.

Three years later, Larry went on to make a big name for himself in the business as *The Great Malenko*.

Once I discovered that wrestling was held in other cities, I started to make short trips. Newark was an hour ride from Trenton. When they had matches in Philadelphia, I took the train. You could make the trip for a couple of dollars, then walk from the station to the Philadelphia Arena on 46th and Market.

As a teenager, one of my big goals in life was to get my drivers license. Let's be honest. There are two reasons why teenage boys can't wait to get their drivers

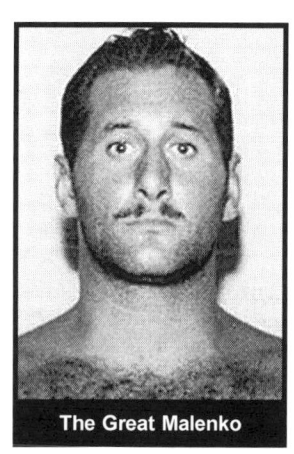

The Great Malenko

license. One, they want to drive themselves to school. Two, they want to take girls out on dates.

Not Jim Morrison.

I only had one reason to get a drivers license.

I wanted to be able to drive to other cities to see professional wrestling.

I eventually met the man who handled the arena programs in Trenton. When he started to see me at the matches in various towns almost every week, he asked me if I'd like to help sell the programs. In return, he would get me into the matches for free and I would make a few dollars. That was my first official job in the wrestling business—and I was as proud as a kid who got a job working in a candy store.

I would drive to Newark, Elizabeth, or Highland Park, and he would bring me in. He would hand me a stack of programs and I would walk around the arena. The program wasn't very informative. For ten cents, you got a single sheet of paper with the matches printed on one side, and a picture of a wrestler on the opposite side. Even so, they sold a lot of those programs.

That job led to others. If one of the ring crew didn't show up, or if one of them quit and walked out, I took his place. I would carry the planks in when they set up the ring, and help tear down the ring after matches. Most of the time, I did it for free, but on occasion, someone would give me a couple of dollars. It didn't matter to me. I was happy just to be a part of the wrestling business, no matter how small that part was. All I wanted was the opportunity to get in and watch the matches—and just be around it all. Those jobs made me feel like I was a part of it.

My life took an unexpected turn when I met a wrestler named George Bollas, who was from Warren, Ohio. From 1948 until 1963, George wore a mask in the ring and called himself the Zebra Kid. There were many Zebra Kid copycats over the years, but he was the original. None of the imitators were as successful with the gimmick as George. He traveled the world extensively and was a very big card in Japan and England.

I used to collect pictures and autographs of the wrestlers. One day, I found a picture of the Zebra Kid. I also found a picture of George Bollas without the mask.

I don't know what led me to do it, but one afternoon, I went to the TV taping in Philadelphia and took the pictures with me. When the Zebra Kid walked in—wearing the mask, of course—I confronted him with both of the photos. He barely even glanced at them. He kept walking and didn't acknowledge them one way or another.

The Zebra Kid

I was no different than any other die-hard wrestling fan. I knew that the wrestlers would come out the front door of the TV studio, cross the street, and walk into an underground parking garage. They made their exit from the garage one street over, which was out of sight of the studio. When the matches were over, I exited through the front entrance of the studio and watched the Zebra Kid walk across the street and into the parking garage.

I ran around that block to the opposite side of the parking garage, to the point where the cars exited. As he drove up the ramp to the street, he had to stop for traffic.

*And he wasn't wearing his mask!*

He had the window down, so I started out with, *"Mr. Bollas. How are you today?"*

## 18 • "Wrestlers Are Like Seagulls"

I'm sure he was thinking, *"Oh, sh—,"* but he was a gentleman. We struck up a conversation and, based on that simple encounter, became friends.

George and I corresponded by mail after that, usually by something called airgrams, blue pieces of paper that you would write on. When you finished your message, you would fold the pages over and over into an envelope sized packet and put postage on it. When you received one in the mail, you would open it out flat and you would have a two-page letter.

George used to write to me when he was in Japan and England. When I wrote and told him that my dream was to get into wrestling, he wrote back asking if I had any amateur experience.

I had never seen an amateur wrestling match. At that time, they didn't have an amateur wrestling program in the state of New Jersey—high school or collegiate. They did at one time, but when a wrestler suffered a serious injury, they discontinued the program.

George continued on to say, *"Look, if this is really what you want to do, my suggestion to you is to go to college and get your education, because they can never take that away from you, and you never know when you'll need it. Go out for the wrestling team and learn the fundamentals of wrestling. At that point, if you still want to pursue a career as a professional wrestler, then go for it. You'll have all the tools you need to set out on a wrestling career, but you'll also have an education to fall back on."*

Based on that advice from George Bollas, a man who made a living wearing a zebra-striped mask, I decided to further my wrestling aspirations by going to college.

Jim and the Zebra Kid

# Chapter 2
# Living the Dream

Although I wasn't able to participate in amateur wrestling during my time at Trenton Central High School, I did take part in other sports. I was always tall and I tended to be on the lean side, so I played baseball and competed with the swim team. I can't say that I excelled in either sport. I did it for the enjoyment of it. When I was in junior high school and high school, I went to an academy and studied judo for five years. I really enjoyed that. Learning how to fall in a controlled manner served me well once I got into wrestling. It came very natural to me, in terms of being able to protect myself and minimize the situations where I might have otherwise been injured.

In 1960, I left home to attend Albright College in Reading, Pennsylvania. I had only two goals in mind—the first being an education. I didn't care what field of study I was going to pursue. I just wanted to get my diploma with a degree in something that interested me, then pursue my second goal, which was to become a professional wrestler.

Even though I had no amateur wrestling experience, I went out for the wrestling team. Albright was a small school, and not many students went out for the team, so if you made the effort, you were almost guaranteed a spot. I made the team and learned the basic fundamentals of amateur wrestling, which, combined with my judo training, also served me greatly years later in my professional career. Many of the things you did as a professional were based on balance and logical things that an amateur would do. I wrestled on the team for two years.

During the summer of 1962, when I was in Philadelphia, I met a referee named Lou Super. Lou ran a small gymnasium and taught self defense to the Philadelphia police force. I used to hang around the Philadelphia Convention Hall, which is where they had wrestling when they moved from the old Philadelphia Arena. One afternoon, Lou invited me to come down

**1963: Albright College**

to his gym. Lou really didn't do anything in terms of training wrestlers. He just ran the gym and tried to hustle customers. He had a ring in the gym, but it wasn't what you would call a working ring. He simply placed mats on the floor and surrounded them with makeshift ropes attached to stanchions that were anchored down with sandbags. You couldn't bounce off of the ropes because there was no tension on them. There was nothing to hold them in place.

Generally, the wrestlers were good people. If they knew that you wanted to wrestle, they would be there to help you, if only for an instant. They all knew that I wanted to wrestle, so when I stayed over in Philly one night after the matches, Dominic DeNucci and Professor Tanaka invited me to join them for a workout at the YMCA gym. The YMCA didn't have a ring, either, but they had wrestling mats. That was a heady time for me. I wasn't even in the business yet, and two of the big stars were going to teach me a few things.

Al Costello, who wrestled as one of the Fabulous Kangaroos, also offered to show me a few things. I remember Al standing in front of me and saying, *"Kid, show me how you lock up."*

I lowered my head, closed my eyes, and locked up. He said, *"No, no, no, no, kid! That's not how you do it. Think about what you just did. When you drop your head down and rush in like a bull, do you know what you're going to do? You're going to crack your head against your opponent's. Keep your head up, look your opponent in the eyes, and lock up. Now, lock up with me, kid."*

That was how I learned to lock up.

Lou Super had a few other guys who wanted to become wrestlers, one of whom was Juan "Hawk" Rodriguez, a Puerto Rican boy who grew up in Vineland, New Jersey. Juan knew Bill Nocco, the local promoter in Vineland. Nocco, who was either the owner or the manager of the Vineland Speedway, had booked an outdoor wrestling show at the Speedway. In south Jersey in the summer, there were a lot of migrant workers who worked the produce farms, so Nocco wanted to have a local, Hispanic wrestler on his card. He knew that Juan and I knew each other, so he asked me if I would like to wrestle on the card against Juan. I could only come up with one answer.

*"Sure!"*

Juan and I worked out together in the gym, then wrestled at the Vineland Speedway on July 11, 1962. This was four years after Johnny Valentine's first appearance in New York, but he was still a big drawing card in the territory. I thought so much of Johnny that I used the name Jim Valence for that first match.

That was the first time I wrestled in front of people—and I had no training whatsoever. I'm sure that it showed in my performance. In fact, I know that it did, because I still have an old 8mm film of the match. But it was a milestone in life for me.

> **WRESTLING**
> **VINELAND**
> **SPEEDWAY**
> Route 47, Delsea Drive
> WED., July 11, 8:30 P.M.
> WINDUP—3 out of 3 FALLS
> **MIGUEL PEREZ**
> PUERTO RICAN CHAMP
> VS.
> **HANS SCHMIDT**
> GERMAN BOMBER
> TAG MATCH—2 out of 3 Falls
> **Gene & Tommy Marin**
> VS.
> **Skull Murphy &**
> **Danny McShain**
> 30 MINUTE BOUTS
> PETE SANCHEZ vs.
> JOE QUIONES
> JUAN RODRIGUEZ vs.
> JIM VALENCE
> Tickets On Sale at
> DeLuxe Taxi Stand
> (Sun Ray Drug Corner)
> General Admission $2.00
> Reserved Seats ... $3.00

The main event on the card that night featured Miguel Perez, who used to be Argentina Rocca's tag team partner, against Hans Schmidt. Years later, during one of my trips to Puerto Rico, I wrestled Miguel, but it was very late in his career. In fact, by that time, his son Miguelito was wrestling. I also wrestled Hans Schmidt a couple of times on television in 1970 when I was wrestling part-time. But I'm getting ahead of myself.

I was paid $50 for my appearance on the Speedway show, so I was regarded as a professional. That $50, of course, put an end to my amateur wrestling career. When the promoter handed me the $50, it seemed like a lot of money, but as I drove home, I remember thinking, *"Jeez, I thought these guys got paid a lot more than this."*

That's a subject that I'll deal with later on in the book—an aspect of the business I call *The Myth*.

When the promoter booked a return match at the Speedway, I wrestled again—once again against Juan Rodriguez. Nothing else opened up after that, so I went back to Reading for my junior year of college.

It was an exciting time for me. I met famous wrestling stars like Buddy Rogers and Antonina Rocca. Pedro Martinez promoted Philadelphia for a time, so we saw people like Bronco Lubich, Angelo Poffo, and the Gallagher Brothers — people who wrestled primarily in upstate New York, who we didn't usually get to see in our neck of the woods. That was when the original Gorgeous George came through Philadelphia, but it was late in his career. I had taken a train from Trenton to Philadelphia for the matches. That train would stop at Trenton, then go non-stop to New York City from Philadelphia. I was walking through the cars of the train, looking for an open seat, and there sat Gorgeous George with his valet. I talked to George and he signed a picture for me.

July 11, 1962
Jim relaxes (?) in the dressing room before his 1st match

I had the privilege of meeting many of the movers and shakers of the wrestling business. I met Jack Pfefer when he came to New York. Argentina Zuma was under contract to Pfefer, so when Rocca left, Pfefer brought Zuma into New York. I met Toots Mondt and Kola Kwariani. I came into the business when they were the power people. I never met Jess McMahon, the father of Vince McMahon Sr., but I knew Vince Sr. very well.

In 1964, I met Hans Mortier, whose real name was Jacob Grobbe. Hans was a big star in the Montreal territory wrestling as Tarzan Zorra. He had married a French girl named Yolaine and they had a son.

Hans lived in Paulsboro, New Jersey, which was the ideal location for wrestlers in the territory to live in at the time. They avoided the high expense of living in big cities like Philadelphia and New York, but they were close to the turnpike and parkway. It was a good midpoint of the territory. Smasher Sloan, Baron Scicluna, Wild Red Berry, and many others lived there. Gorilla Monsoon had a home in Willingboro, which was also close by.

Hans and I hit it off and we became good friends. One night, he invited my girlfriend Lynda, my college sweetheart, and me to their apartment for dinner. During the course of our conversation, he told me, *"If you want to get started in the business, I have all kinds of connections with promoters in Europe. I'll help you get started over there if you want."*

I didn't take Hans up on his offer because other events forced me to change my plans.

# Chapter 3
## Third Man in the Ring

In 1963, they filmed the local wrestling show on Wednesday in a tiny studio in the basement of Channel 3 on Walnut Street, the NBC affiliate located in downtown Philadelphia. This was the same TV studio where I had first confronted the Zebra Kid years earlier.

The studio was set up as if it was designed to be a movie theater. The ring was set up on a stage and the seating for the studio audience sloped upwards. I think the ring was stored in the building, but the man who set the ring up was named Bruce Brumbaugh. Bruce was also from Reading. I would hang around the studio all the time, so we got to know one another and we became friends. When he would drive to Philly from Reading, I would go along to give him a hand with the ring.

After the ring was set up, I would put on a plain, colored T-shirt and follow the wrestlers to the ring. When they took their ring jackets off, I would carry the jackets back to the dressing room. That was kind of cool because my college buddies would see me on TV. The show didn't air until Saturday, but they would kid me about it the next day.

That is what I would consider to be my first "official" employment in the wrestling business.

Sometime in the winter of 1963, Philadelphia was hit with a horrendous snowstorm. Bruce and I were able to get from Reading to the studio in downtown Philadelphia to set up the ring. Enough of the wrestlers made it to go ahead with the show, but no referee showed up. It was strange that Bruce and I were able to drive in from Reading, but the referees, who all lived in Philadelphia, weren't able to make it. I don't remember who was in charge, but somebody looked around and said, *"Well, we need somebody to referee."*

It was spontaneous, but if you had seen it in a movie, it couldn't have looked more staged. Everyone turned at the same moment and looked directly at me.

*"Hey, kid. Can you referee?"*

*"Oh, yeah. Sure I can."*

The wrestlers seemed to like me, so they were all for having me as the referee, even though I was a green kid who had never done anything in the business other than sell programs and set up the ring.

After somebody found a shirt for me to wear, I walked up the aisle, climbed up the ring steps, and stepped through the ropes into the ring for the first match.

*"Ladies and Gentlemen. Your referee for the evening ... Jim Morrison!"*

I was so excited that it was happening, I don't remember asking a lot of questions before that first match. I don't even remember what they told me. The only instructions

I can recall were, *"Just walk around three sides of the ring and keep your ass out of the camera."*

I refereed for the entire hour. Obviously, my instincts kicked in and I did exactly what they wanted. I had watched so much wrestling that I was smart without being smart, and I instinctively knew what to do.

I was in heaven, but before I knew it, my hour of glory was over. That was the shortest sixty minutes of my life.

I wasn't smartened up that day. "Smartened up" is a euphemism used in the business for educating someone about the *realities* of pro wrestling. In fact, I was *never* smartened up—at least not in the conventional sense where someone sits down with you and explains the inner workings of the wrestling business. It was like, after you've been hanging around for so many years, everyone just assumes that you're smart. Obviously, if you have to referee a main event match, they give you a finish [plan for the ending of a match], but if you're working the opening matches, you don't have to know a whole lot. Through the whole process of breaking into the business as a referee, I became smart without having it explained to me.

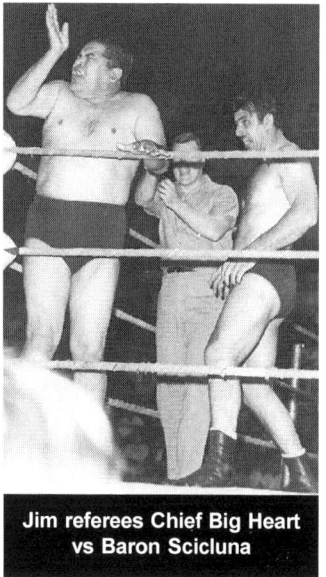

**Jim referees Chief Big Heart vs Baron Scicluna**

I was young and energetic, so they were happy with me. I don't remember who it was, but someone said, *"We'd like to get you on the staff here in Pennsylvania as one of the referees."* That's how I ended up being on the commission list of referees in Pennsylvania. Getting jobs as a referee on the house shows [live, non-televised, arena show] was a political thing. They would run Philadelphia every third or fourth week. It would rotate around and I would get the odd assignment. I certainly wouldn't get them all, although if it were in my power, I would have refereed every match.

That was the beginnings of my career as a referee. I was still going to college, but I was refereeing whenever I could get a shot.

In those days, they used to run the old Philadelphia Arena, which was an old, decrepit building in a tough section of town. Adjacent to it was the TV studio where Dick Clark telecast the original *American Bandstand* show when it was aired live from Philadelphia. A lot of times, I wouldn't be assigned, but I would still go to the arena on the off-chance that they would need someone to referee. I always took my gear with me.

Arnold Skaaland and Angelo Savoldi used to handle the backstage details for the wrestling office. Vincent J. McMahon, who is most often referred to as Vince McMahon Sr., would be there quite often, but I don't remember him coming to every show. I don't recall when it started, but after a while, at the end of the night, Skaaland would walk up, shake my hand, and palm me a twenty-dollar bill. He would say, *"You're not working tonight, but Vince wants you to have this."* To a poor college kid, twenty dollars was a *lot* of money. Because of that showing of kindness, I have fond memories of Vince, Sr.

Willie Gilzenburg, who was the promoter in New Jersey and the president of the WWWF (World Wide Wrestling Federation), was at a Philadelphia show one night when I was refereeing. He asked somebody who I was. *"Oh, he's a kid who goes to college in Reading. He's from Jersey."*

Somebody introduced us and Willie said, *"I'd like to have you referee some of my shows in New Jersey."*

## 24 • "Wrestlers Are Like Seagulls"

That was my opening to getting a job as a referee in New Jersey—and that opened several other doors. While refereeing in a town in Jersey, I asked Vince McMahon if he ever needed any referees for the Capitol Arena in Washington, D.C. *"Yeah, kid. Any time you want to, let me know."*

So, I called Vince a few times and asked for work. *"Yeah, kid. Come on down this Thursday night."*

It wasn't big money. I would get twenty-five bucks, or whatever the payoff was at the time, but I looked at the Capitol Arena as a plum job because of the exposure and prestige. When I thought about where I started, selling programs in Trenton, and now I was working on television in the Capitol Arena in Washington, D.C., that was pretty heady stuff for a young man who was still in college.

There was even an exciting moment one night when they had some time to fill. They took me aside and told me they wanted me to do an interview with announcer Ray Morgan—on the air! He asked me what it was like to be a referee. I talked about what a thankless job it was, and how people got mad at you when you didn't see everything.

Eventually, I was able to referee on a regular, steady basis. I was in the ring with people like Bruno Sammartino, who held the WWWF world title, Gorilla Monsoon, Baron Scicluna, Professor Tanaka, George "The Animal" Steele, and Crazy Luke Graham.

One night, I was going to referee a match between Johnny Valentine and Killer Kowalski. A few minutes before we were going to walk out to the ring, Valentine said to Arnold Skaaland, *"Quick, Arnie. Make me one!"*

I didn't have the foggiest idea of what they were talking about, but Skaaland immediately started fumbling in his bag and pulled out a package of Gillette razor blades. He removed one blade from the package and broke off one corner of the blade. He said, *"Here, hold this,"* and handed me the corner piece. He then looked over his shoulder at the dressing room door, and back at me, as if to say, *"Keep an eye out."* I kept an eye out, but I didn't know what I was keeping an eye out for. I then watched in amazement as he began putting tape on the edges of the blade, leaving only a sliver of the sharp corner jutting out. I suddenly knew what he was doing, but I was seeing it done for the first time. I didn't tell Arnie, but that was my first visual exposure to what we called a "gig," or a blade, a device that wrestlers used to cut themselves when they were required to bleed.

Arnie was obviously in a hurry to finish his project. In the process, he speared himself in the thumb with the corner of the blade and blood started to drip. Somehow, he finished what he was doing, but blood was all over the floor.

The first time I was asked to use a blade on myself, I was still living in Reading, Pennsylvania. I was refereeing part time, and working for a department store—hating my job. One day, from out of the blue, I got a phone call from Arnold Skaaland. *"Hey, kid. We need a referee for a match between Kowalski and Bruno in Boston."*

Arnold laid out a finish where I would get hit on the head with a chair, bleed profusely, and get carried out on a stretcher. *"You've got to ... well, you'll need to bleed a little bit. Can you do that?"*

Even though I had never done that before, I said *"Oh, of course! Absolutely! What's the date?"*

Since I didn't want to show my ignorance by asking somebody, I had to figure out how to do it. I remember making a blade and kind of practicing with it—whining the whole time. *"Ohhhh! That hurts, but when it comes down to it, I'm gonna have to do it."*

I carpooled with Gorilla Monsoon and a couple of others from New Jersey to the Boston Garden. If I remember correctly, the stipulations of the match were *"To a*

Ref Jim Morrison tries to control the Beast

*finish, no count out, no disqualification."* Those were the standard stipulations of the blowoff match [final match of a series of matches when two wrestlers are feuding] when they needed to have a definitive winner.

When it was time to go to the finish, Kowalski went to the floor and threw a chair into the ring. Bruno was down on the mat, selling [enhancing the drama of a beating, or a painful hold, by using exaggerated facial expressions and body movements, in order to convince the audience that the wrestler is in trouble]. As Bruno struggled to his feet, Kowalski picked up the chair and began to stalk him. The three of us were all moving around in a circle. At some point, Bruno stepped between Kowalski and me. As Kowalski threw the flat of the chair toward Bruno's head, Bruno ducked, and the chair hit me squarely in the face. I knew it was coming, so I was able to partially block it. I went down and poked the blade into my forehead, then slowly came to my feet. I'm sure that I didn't bleed profusely, but there was some blood on my forehead. I stumbled around, acting like I was knocked out on my feet. I made a 360-degree circle, staggering like a drunk, so that everybody could see the blood. Then I collapsed and didn't move.

The other wrestlers ran from the dressing room and filled the ring. The babyfaces [good guys; clean wrestlers] grabbed Sammartino, while the heels [bad guys; villains] grabbed Kowalski. Even the cops were in the ring. Eventually, order was restored and everyone left the ring. I was still laying there, motionless. They brought a stretcher into the ring, put me on it, and carried me out.

Now, the fans were all looking at each other. This was the big match where *there had to be a winner.* And yet, there was no winner. It was the eventuality that none of the fans could have predicted. Since the referee was knocked out, and there had to be a winner, they had to have *one more* return match. If memory serves, I think they brought Archie Moore or Two-Ton Tony Galento in as a special referee for the *final* match. In the minds of the fans, either of those two guys were tough enough to ensure that there would be a finish. What happened to me wasn't going to happen to them.

I had worked a few of the larger cities outside of the Philadelphia area. On the bigger shows, you would be paid $100. After the matches in Boston that night, either Arnold Skaaland or Angelo Savoldi handed me $100. I didn't say anything. I just took it.

A week later, I saw Bruno and told him the whole story of what had happened. I said, *"They called me, asked me to bleed, and I thought it was something above and beyond what would normally be asked of a referee. Don't get me wrong. I was happy to do it, but by the same token, I was a little disappointed in how I was compensated. Nobody said I would get any extra, but I was still disappointed."*

Bruno said, *"Yes, you're absolutely right. Let me*

Camden, New Jersey
Argentina Apollo vs
Frank Hickey

*handle it. Don't say anything to anyone else."*

Ten days later, they had an outdoor show—in Reading, Pennsylvania, of all places. I was living there, so I went to the show, but I wasn't the referee that night. Again, it was the political matter about who gets assigned where.

Vince McMahon had three partners who had a small interest in the WWWF promotion—Gorilla Monsoon, Arnold Skaaland, and Phil Zacko. Zacko, an old promoter from Baltimore, was running the show that night in Reading. He used to chomp on a cigar. When he saw me, he said in that gruff voice that he was known for, *"Kid! Come over here!"* He peeled out $200 from a wad of bills that he took from his pocket. *"Here, kid. This is for you."*

It was like all the money in the world to me. I thought, *"Oh, my God."*

I saw Bruno two days later and he said, *"Has anybody seen you yet?"*

I said, *"I saw Phil Zacko the other night. I couldn't believe it."*

*"Were you satisfied with that?"*

*"I'm more than satisfied."*

*"Okay."*

*"Bruno, I can never thank you enough."*

*"Don't worry about it, kid. That was just the right thing to do."*

Phil Zacko

To this day, I have a warm spot in my heart for Bruno. I was once told that situations like that caused a lot of the friction between Bruno and Vince Sr., which then carried over to Vince Jr. Bruno would get involved in situations with other talent—always on behalf of the talent—and as the champion, he had a lot of clout.

I think Vince, Sr. resented the fact that Bruno, while making all the money that he was making, whatever it was, would intercede and stick up for other people. Vince didn't think that his dealings with the talent were something that Bruno should concern himself with. Vince never told me that, but I heard it from several other sources that a lot of the heat was brought about by Bruno sticking up for the boys [wrestlers; talent].

Bruno took the time to stand up for me, when he just as easily could have said, *"That's a hard lesson to learn, kid. You'll have to learn to stand up for yourself."*

He could have said *anything* that he wanted to say, but instead, he chose to go to bat for me.

There were some guys who weren't comfortable carrying the blade while they wrestled, like George Steele, but George wasn't the only one. There were many others. In this example, I was the referee for a cage match between George and Bruno. They needed blood that night, so George made up his blade and gave it to me. I folded a handkerchief over it and put it into my pocket. A few times during the match, I would pull the handkerchief out, pat the perspiration from my forehead, and replace the handkerchief in my pocket. When the time was right, it was natural and easy for me to get the blade out of the handkerchief and slip it to George.

I remember Baron Scicluna using a gimmick [an object commonly referred to as a *foreign object*, used to gain an unfair advantage] in his tights for a finish in those days. One common gimmick used for a disqualification finish was a roll of quarters. When Scicluna hit his opponent with the roll of quarters, the roll would break, and quarters would scatter everywhere. The referee would find the loose quarters in the ring and that would be grounds for Scicluna's disqualification.

It would be difficult for Scicluna, or anybody for that matter, to wrestle a whole match with a roll of quarters in his tights, so I carried the roll of quarters. They would split the roll in the dressing room, and use a piece of tape to hold the wrapper together. At the right time, when the wrestlers were ready to go home [end the match], I would have to go into my pocket, get the roll of quarters, and pull off the tape. As I searched Scicluna for illegal objects, I would pretend to search him, but as I did, I would drop the roll of quarters into his tights. When I told them to resume wrestling, Scicluna would go to the finish with them.

I always took pride in the knowledge that I was a proficient referee, but another name that comes to mind is Tommy Young, who refereed in the Carolinas. Tommy was a fan, too—and he remains a fan to this day. He always took tremendous pride in what he did.

A good referee is someone who is there, but also someone who is *not* there. They take steps to be sure they don't become the focus of attention. A good referee is worth his weight in gold, because he knows how to give the impression that he's somebody who is really trying to make a good faith effort to catch the heel at breaking the rules. He also tries to position himself so that he is not the object of the heat [anger from the fans], which is the worst situation, because people don't buy tickets to see the referee.

The New York territory featured big cities, big shows, big venues, and once-a-month type of extravaganzas. An example of the booking style there would be to feature Bruno against Waldo von Erich. Their program [series of matches] would run a three-match cycle in Madison Square Garden. After the first encounter at the Garden, that same series of matches would go around the territory to all the major towns. At the same time, they were building Bruno's next opponent up underneath, having him win an earlier match on the card.

That was the pattern that worked for the WWWF at the time. If you were a main event wrestler coming into the territory, they would tell you how many shots you were going to get against the WWWF champion in the Garden. They would also give you the stipulations. *"Your first match will end with a disqualification, so the return match will be a 'No Disqualification' match, and your program will end up in the cage."* Rarely would anyone get a fourth match against the champion.

The midgets were another highlight of my years as a referee. I loved working with the midgets. When I refereed in Pennsylvania and New Jersey, the midgets would come through the territory on a regular basis.

Sky Low Low

Many of the commissioned referees had day jobs and weren't really into the business. It was more of a political appointment. I, on the other hand, loved the business, and I was a mark for both the midgets and their high spots [exciting action move or series of moves]. Their spots required a fifth guy who was willing to interject himself as part of their routine. Since I knew all of those spots by heart, the midgets loved having me work their matches.

I remember doing a routine with midget legend Sky Low Low, who I thought was the best heel midget. When the babyface midget draped his body across Sky in an attempt to score the pinfall, I would get on my hands and knees, lining up head-to-head with Sky. As I counted 1-2, Sky would kick out and catapult the babyface off and into the air. As the babyface came down, I looked up and caught him in my arms. I would then toss the babyface right back onto Sky and begin my 1-2 count again.

We did that three or four times in a row, much to the amusement of the audience. Eventually, Sky Low Low would struggle out from underneath his opponent and get into my face, screaming at me for throwing the babyface back onto him. He pantomimed to me, so the audience understood what he was saying. *"You idiot! Don't you understand that when you catch him, you're supposed to throw him AWAY from me—not on me!"*

I pantomimed my understanding. If that's what he wanted, that's what I would do. The match continued until Sky covered his opponent for the pin. The situation was now reversed. I got into the position for the count and started out with 1-2. When the babyface kicked out and sent Sky into the air, I caught Sky and threw him across the ring, just like he had demanded I do. The audience would howl with laughter. They loved it. Sky Low Low would lay there like he was dead, then groggily get up and threaten to fight me—all because I did what he told me to do. We had a lot of fun with those matches.

I have very fond memories of my refereeing days. My time spent as a referee served me well for my future career because I never had any formal training as a wrestler. I actually learned to work by being the third man in the ring.

I spent a total of four years at Albright College, going home each summer to work odd jobs. During the school year, I continued to referee at the wrestling cards throughout eastern Pennsylvania and New Jersey.

Lynda, who was a year behind me at Albright College, was my first and only serious relationship there. In July 1964, one month after I graduated, we were married in the college chapel. Hans Mortier was the best man in my wedding, while his wife, Yolaine, was one of the bridesmaids. I promised Lynda's father, Earl (who later was called "Grandy"), that I would make sure that Lynda finished college and got her degree.

As a side note, a few months after Scott Teal and I began working on this book, I got an early morning phone call from Scott. He gave me an overseas phone number to call, but he wouldn't give me any details or tell me anything about it. As I hung up the phone, I thought it was one of the strangest things that anyone has ever asked me to do. Regardless, I dialed the number. When the person on the other end of the line answered, I had no idea who it was, and he gave me a hard time for a few seconds. What a wonderful surprise it was when he told me it was Jacob Grobbe— Hans Mortier. Evidently, he had conspired with Scott earlier that morning. It was very heartwarming and I was thrilled to be speaking with Jacob for the first time in over thirty-five years.

I graduated from college with a degree in Sociology, but during my final year of college, I didn't attend any job fairs and I didn't look for employment. My very first job after graduating was with a department store, but I hated it and soon got my name on a list to work as a substitute teacher in Reading, Pennsylvania. I wasn't giving up on my dream of wrestling. I was simply doing what I had to do to put bread on the table while Lynda finished school. I was called periodically to fill in until one of the teachers had a heart attack and was forced to stay out for the remainder of the school year. Even though I didn't have a teaching certificate, the principal asked me if I was willing to work as an on-going, permanent substitute. I agreed and taught $7^{th}$ grade English and Math for the entire school year.

Within a year, Lynda was pregnant, but early in the pregnancy, she had a miscarriage. I don't know why, but we both had tremendous feelings of disappointment and guilt over it. As a result, we tried again and Lynda was pregnant within a few months. On August 28, 1966, my daughter, Pam, was born.

When I took on the responsibilities of being a father, my goal of pursuing a career in wrestling was derailed. It was a very frustrating time for me in my life. It seemed to me like, all of a sudden, I was out of college, I was a father, and my whole dream of where I planned to go was turned upside down. All the plans of my lifetime had ground to a halt because I was married and I had the responsibility of taking care of a child. It was beginning to look like my dream was only that—a dream—but I wasn't willing to give up on it. Although I continued to referee during that time, I was merely on the periphery of the wrestling business, and that was not what I had dreamed it would be.

I quit teaching and found work through an employment agency. They assigned me to several different jobs. After a few months, I took a job selling a specialized life insurance program for a company based in Dallas. They sold insurance to college seniors and deferred the premiums until they graduated. I don't remember the exact pitch we used to sell it, but I sold a million dollars worth of insurance that first year. Even with my success, I hated it as much as I hated the job at the department store. From there, I became a claims adjustor for Allstate. Needless to say, I didn't enjoy that, either. I then went to work for Jones Motor, a trucking company, which was located on the outskirts of Philadelphia.

My wife, Lynda, was very supportive of my dreams. She said, *"I'll support you in whatever you want to do. I'll go with you to the ends of the earth."*

In reality, she was happiest when she was at home, close to her mother and her family. That was understandable. As I look back, the two of us, unfortunately, were never meant for each other. I certainly contributed to the failing of my marriage. In fact, I contributed more than my share. I had a beautiful child, but I was not mature enough to understand what a blessing that was, or to appreciate not only the responsibility, but everything else that goes with it. I was not a faithful husband, either. I'm not bragging about that. I'm just stating a fact and I'm not proud of it. It was just part of my immaturity and the things that you go through in life as you grow up. We were divorced in 1968.

Lynda then married Bill, her high school sweetheart. Shortly after the wedding, they asked me for permission for Bill to adopt my daughter. I was still consumed with my dream. I wanted to move away and travel the world. Perhaps the best thing for my daughter was to give my consent—which I did.

As time went by, I often thought, *"Did I do the right thing?"* But as I look back, I know that I did. If for no other reason, it was in her best interest at that time.

Pam is, and always will be, *my* daughter. After her mother and I were divorced, I would see Pam on weekends, and when I relocated and began to travel extensively, I always stayed in touch with her. "Nana," Pam's grandmother, used to write and send photos regularly. Once Pam was old enough to fly unaccompanied, I would fly her in to visit with me during the summer.

Pam even made some road trips with me to wrestling events, and so she, unlike my younger children, had some exposure to my chosen profession and the lifestyle that went with it. My oldest daughter is a lot like me—a free spirit—but she has both feet solidly on the ground. She is a wonderful person and a loving mother. Pam has blessed me with three grandchildren: Erica, Rebecca, and Meghan. Erica and "Becca" are older than my three youngest children, but Meghan is younger than my youngest (Niki) by about three months. In 1994, I was an expectant father and grandfather at the same time! It may sound a little confusing, but we are one big, happy family. Pam went through a divorce and is now with a guy named Mike, who has two young boys, Collin and Kyle. I am thankful that I have Pam and I feel closer to her now than ever before in my life.

I am grateful that Bill treated Pam as if she was his own daughter, even though Lynda and Bill had a son of their own named Steve. I don't know if I ever properly thanked Bill for being the father to Pam that I never was during those years, so I'll go on record now and say, *"Bill, thank you ... from the bottom of my heart."*

Through the years, Lynda and Bill would drive down to Delaware to visit with my parents, who treated their son, Steve, as if he was their grandchild. They have had a wonderful relationship and my mother remains close to Lynda and Bill to this day. When my father passed away five years ago, I lived in Marietta, Georgia. The first two calls my mother made were to my sister, Joan, and me. After that, she called Lynda. Lynda dropped what she was doing and drove for 2½ hours from Reading to Delaware. She knew that neither I nor my sister, who lived in Charlotte, North Carolina, could get to Delaware as quickly as she could, so she wanted to be with my mother to help her get through that first day until we arrived.

When I moved to Delaware in August 2003, my mother and I went to Pennsylvania to visit Pam and we saw her grandmother, Pearl, for the last time. When she got ill and passed away soon after that, I went to the viewing in Reading and saw Lynda and Bill there. It was a sad day, but life goes on. Today, Lynda is a schoolteacher. She is a member and the choir director of the same church that she attended when we met.

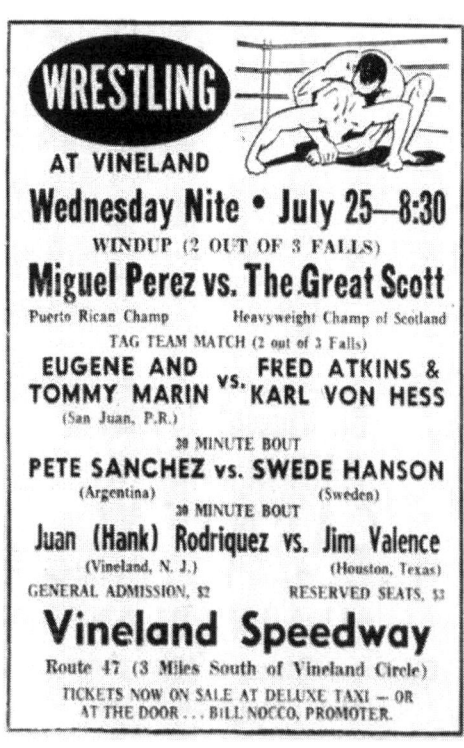

# Chapter 4
# The Bodyslam

In 1967, the original Sheik, Eddie Farhat, came into the New York territory and I refereed a few of his matches in Pennsylvania and New Jersey. Very few of the fans realized it at the time, but the Sheik was the promoter of the Detroit, Michigan, territory. The Sheik's nickname to the boys who knew him well was "Zib," or "The Zib." I talked to him one day and told him about my dream of wrestling. He said, *"Man, if you ever want to travel my way, I'll book you. You can work."*

I said, *"What do you mean? Do you mean come out there and referee?"*

*"No, man! I said work. If you want to work, you work."*

I was speechless for a moment or two. It was the door that I had been looking for—an opportunity to spread my wings and do what I had been wanting to do for over a decade.

I had to wait until December 1968, when I had a week's vacation coming. I called Eddie Farhat in November and told him, *"I have some time off next month. If you have an opening, I'd like to take you up on your offer."*

**The Sheik of Araby**

My parents drove me from Reading, Pennsylvania, to Dayton, Ohio, and they sat in the audience. The date was December 6, 1968—a date I'll never forget. The show was held in a small studio—actually, the building was more like an oversized garage—with about two rows of chairs for the small contingent of fans who attended. The ringside commentator was Ernie Roth. Ernie worked as the Sheik's manager, calling himself Abdullah Farouk. In later years, he would see his greatest fame in the WWWF as *The Grand Wizard*, during which time he managed talent such as Stan "The Man" Stasiak and Billy "Superstar" Graham.

For my character, I chose a western motif, so when Ernie asked me where I wanted to be announced as being from, I picked a town that sounded interesting.

Provo, Utah.

Don't ask me where that came from. I suppose it sounded interesting and, to my knowledge, no one else had ever been announced as being from Provo.

My first match was a tag team match. My tag team partner was Ron Sanders and we wrestled the Hell's Angels, Ron Dupree and Chris Colt. Chris had quit the wrestling business for a short time. He had gone to England and drove a tour bus for Joe Cocker, who was, and still is, my favorite music artist. I don't remember much about

## 32 • "Wrestlers Are Like Seagulls"

the match, but I do consider it to be my first professional match. I don't count the two matches at the Vineland Speedway.

Later that night, somebody said, *"We can use an extra guy for TV tomorrow in Pittsburgh,"* so I volunteered. A wrestler named Johnny Carr offered to give me a ride and told me to be at a certain exit at a certain time the next morning. I had my first singles match at the Channel 11 studios in Pittsburgh. I wrestled Killer Kowalski and I thought I was going to die. He was in tremendous cardiovascular shape and he never stopped to catch a breath.

The next day, I went back to Detroit and wrestled three times on TV in Bay City, Michigan. Arnold Skaaland and I wrestled the Hell's Angels in a tag team match, then I worked with Ron Sanders and Killer Karl Kox in singles matches.

Needless to say, as Arnold Skaaland's tag team partner, I did a job [lost] in every match during those three days, except for the match with Ron Sanders, and that was a draw. I think the Sheik ran in and attacked both Sanders and I, so the match was stopped and called a draw. I was always a businessman, so winning and losing didn't have great significance, but those three days were my first real exposure to working as a wrestler.

**June 1969
Cowboy Jim Dillon**

I used the name Jim Dillon when I wrestled in Detroit, but I don't know if I used that name during my first match in Dayton. I wish I had a great story about how that name came about, but I don't. I had a brother-in-law whose last name was Dillon, but that wasn't where I got it. It was just a name that seemed to grab me.

After the matches in Bay City, I returned to my home and continued to work on my regular job at the trucking company.

In May 1969, when my next vacation rolled around, I called the Sheik again. This time, he booked me for the whole week, and not only did I wrestle on the TV taping, but I was booked on the big house shows in Toledo, Cincinnati, and Detroit.

Back then, if you had a positive, respectful attitude, the older guys would help you. I had that kind of an attitude, and I think that's why many of them gave me good advice. During that week, I had three matches with a wrestler named Pedro Godoy. As I said earlier, I had never had any formal training, so at that stage in my career, I had never bodyslammed anyone.

My first match against Pedro was in Toledo. Early in the match, he called for a bodyslam, so I attempted to do it based on what I had seen others do. In the process, I almost dropped him onto his shoulder. In fact, I thought that I *had* dropped him onto his shoulder and hurt him. I was scared and I worried about what he was going to say when we got back to the dressing room.

After the match, Pedro walked into the dressing room and said, *"Come here, kid. Let me show you how you should bodyslam somebody."*

He picked me up and said, *"Do you see how I have your body positioned?"*

He walked me through the process of how you hoist someone up, while keeping your center of balance. *"When you get your opponent into the correct position, you hold their head and flip them over,"* he instructed. *"The important thing is to make sure that your opponent lands flat. Now, you try it."*

I was hesitant to try it. The floor in the dressing room was concrete, so it didn't have the give that a ring does, but Pedro encouraged me to give it a shot. After his patient instruction, I picked him up, and once again, almost lost my balance with him. He didn't give up on me. He had me pick him up three or four more times. After I had the knack of picking him up, he said, *"Now, once you have me in the correct position, just take your hand and push out. Gravity will bring me down. I will tuck my head and protect myself at that point."*

I proceeded to comfortably pick him up, all the while keeping control of his body, and set him back down on his feet. After a few more attempts, the move felt almost natural, but I still had not properly slammed anyone in the ring.

On the next night, I was booked on Dayton TV, and who was I going to wrestle?

Pedro Godoy.

When we locked up, the very first thing he called for was—a bodyslam. I picked him up and slammed him beautifully. That gave me confidence.

The most important thing that I learned was, where someone else would have said, *"This kid's getting nothing because he almost broke my neck,"* Pedro realized that I didn't do it intentionally. He showed me how to do it the correct way, knowing that I had to get my failure out of my mind, which is why he called for the slam at the beginning of the match. I did it correctly, and that did wonders for my self-esteem.

The next time I saw Pedro Godoy, it was years later in Florida. He was wearing a mask and wrestling as the Red Shadow. I will never forget Pedro or what he taught me.

By the winter of 1969, I had been with the trucking company for almost a year, and they transferred me to Detroit in a trial situation. I thought, *"Oh, boy. I'll give the Sheik a call. I'll let the company move me out there, then I'll quit and ask the Sheik if I can start working for him."*

My father, who worked for General Motors, had also been transferred to Detroit, so I had a place to stay. As soon as I got to Detroit, I phoned the Sheik and told him my story. He said, *"Look, kid. I'm just gonna be straight with you. Business right now is not all that good. I have guys working full-time, who do this to put food on their table. I can't very well book you regularly, or full-time, because it would take bookings from them. You're fortunate that you have a job. Keep your job and I'll give you what work I can, then if things change, we'll work something else out."*

I did get a handful of bookings that year, but there weren't many. I appreciated his honesty, but I was somewhat discouraged because my dream seemed to be just out of reach. It was nine long months before I was able to venture out again.

On February 5, 1970, the Sheik booked me on television in Walled Lake, Michigan. I wrestled Hans Schmidt, who worked so realistically that it was painful. He stomped me with the boots so hard that it knocked the wind out of me. We referred to wrestlers like Hans as being stiff as a board.

In addition to Detroit, the Sheik also had an interest in the Toronto promotion, and the two promotions swapped talent back and forth. The Toronto promotion taped their television in Hamilton, Ontario, so the Sheik sent me up to do jobs [lose] on TV for Bull Curry, Chris Tolos ... and my new friend, Hans Schmidt.

After my match against Schmidt in Walled Lake, one of the wrestlers told me something about Schmidt. *"When he hits you hard, hit him back just as hard or harder. He will like you and respect you for it."*

I wasn't sure if I was being set up for a rib or what, but I took it upon myself to talk with Hans before our match in Ontario on February 27. I told him, *"The only reason I'm here is to do a good job for you. I'll do anything you want, but if you stomp me and knock the wind out of me, I can't do the best job that I can for you."*

Whatever the reason—I didn't whine about it, so it might have been the manner in which I told him—he worked differently with me after that. I worked hard to do a good job for him.

I also worked with Bull Curry. Bull was a real character and I saw something one night that I will never forget.

Bull had a specialty that he used in every match. He would grab a handful of your hair and put your head under his left armpit in a headlock position. With his right hand, he would punch you, but when he did, he would slap the right arm against his side to make a loud popping sound in his armpit. The sound gave the impression that he had really clobbered you with his fist.

Bull Curry

On that afternoon, Bull was working with a young wrestler. When Bull pulled him into the headlock position, the wrestler did what everyone had the tendency to do when they were in a headlock. He slid his right arm around Bull's waist and rested it just above Bull's waist on the right side. That would be fine in a regular situation, but it kept Bull from being able to do the armpit pop. Bull Curry took the kid's arm, flipped it down from his waist, and threw the punch. It was comical to watch if you knew what he was doing, and he did it many times during that week.

There was quite a difference in the way wrestling was presented in the various territories. New York featured a laid back style, with a lot of holds. Detroit, on the other hand, was just balls-out wild. The Sheik used pencils on his opponents, and threw fire when he found himself in a tough situation.

I watched a main event between Bull Curry and Tex McKenzie. I don't know if Tex had been injured, or if there was another reason, but Bull went to the ring first and started ranting and raving on the house microphone. All of a sudden, the lights dimmed and the spotlight came on. A tall guy walked out, wearing a trench coat and a cowboy hat pulled down low over his eyes. He kept his head down as he walked down the aisle to the ring, waving from one side of the audience to the other. He looked just like Tex McKenzie. He dragged his entrance out and took his time. Bull Curry, at the same time, was leaning over the ropes, facing the regular entrance aisle, yelling insults at the guy in the cowboy outfit. *"Come on, Tex. Come on! I'm gonna kill ya!"*

In the meantime, the "real" Tex McKenzie had entered the arena from the other side of the building. He was actually tip-toeing up the other aisle and carrying a folded chair. Tex climbed up onto the ring apron, got into the ring behind Curry, and tip-toed across the ring. He tapped Bull on the shoulders and ... *splat!* Bull went down and Tex covered him. *1-2-3.* The bell rang and the match was over.

I don't remember who was under the hat. There were a lot of tall guys on the card, but whoever it was, of course, took the hat off and waved to the crowd.

*"The winner of the match—Tex McKenzie!"*

In most territories, a 30-second main event would kill a town, but it seemed to work for the fans in Detroit. For one thing, Tex was really over [popular], even though he was clumsy. He would trip over the ropes and fall flat on his face as he got into the ring.

None of that mattered to the fans, though. They loved him.

On a few occasions in 1970, I had matches with various partners against a tag team known as The Outlaws: Dusty Rhodes and Dick Murdoch. They were one of the toughest teams out there, almost like the Road Warriors of their era. I first faced them on March 1, 1970 in Walled Lake, Michigan. I didn't know it at the time, but both Dusty and Dick would, at separate times, go on to play big parts in my career, and I would be strongly linked to both of them.

Since Detroit was such a heavy union town, and because of the strict union rules, I wasn't able to do anything at my full-time job. After three or four months, my boss called and said, *"It's a waste of time to keep you there, so we're going to transfer you to Warren, Ohio"*

I moved to Warren, but I looked at it as being in the middle of nowhere. Although my wrestling bookings with Farhat had been few and far between, at least I had the opportunity to work occasionally. Now I would be far removed from the mainstream of Eddie's territory, so I had to give serious thought to a new plan if I was ever going to make a career in wrestling.

---

**INDIANA LIONS CLUB**

# Wrestling Show

**2 TAG MATCHES**
**SAMMARTINO & VeNUCCI**
VS.
**STEELE & PROF. X**
PLUS
**4 GIRL TAG MATCH**
PLUS
**DR. BILL MILLER vs. JIM DILLON**

# INDIANA

J. S. Mack Community Center 8:30 p.m.

**JULY 4**

ADVANCE TICKETS ON SALE
- Waxlers
- Jo-Kays
- Indiana News
- Barclays

Indiana, Pennsylvania • July 2, 1970

# Chapter 5
# Bruno

In 1970, Bruno Sammartino was running a territory spinoff of the northeast [New York] territory. He promoted shows in the area around Pittsburgh, which would be western Pennsylvania, eastern Ohio, and a few towns in West Virginia. Warren, Ohio, was only 70 miles from Pittsburgh, so I thought Bruno might be able to give me some work on weekends.

When I called the wrestling office, which was run by Ace Freeman and Rudy Miller, Ace answered the phone. This was in April 1970. When I told him that I wanted to get word to Bruno, I got the compete runaround. I was certain that they weren't going to pass my message along, so I sent a letter to Bruno at his home address and told him about my situation.

*"Wrestling is still my dream. I have some experience. I worked for the Sheik. I'll do whatever and take whatever you have available. I really want to do this."*

Yada, yada, yada.

I took the letter to the post office, but I didn't hear anything from him. After a few weeks went by, I decided

Bruno Sammartino

to drive to the Pittsburgh Civic Arena for the next show, which was held once a month. A week before the show, I sent Bruno a second letter to let him know that I'd be there. *"I'll be at the Civic Arena next week in the hopes that I can have a couple of minutes with you. Maybe you can give me some advice and tell me what to do."*

I drove to the Civic Arena and told the guard at the back door that I wanted to talk to Bruno. When the guard returned, Ace Freeman was with him.

*"Who are you?"*

*"I called you at the office last month and asked about talking to Bruno."*

*"Oh, yeah."*

*"I wrote Bruno a letter. I think he knew that I'd be here tonight."*

*"All right. Wait here, kid."*

A few minutes later, the door opened and Ace Freeman stood there with a surprised look on his face. He motioned for me to come in and took me to Bruno's dressing room. Bruno stood up and gave me the biggest hug. It was like we were long-lost brothers. He apologized for not answering my letter, telling me that he had been on the road.

And then he said something that made me want to do a backflip.

*"I would love to have you working here."*

He looked at Ace and said, *"I want him booked starting this weekend. I don't know where you can put him, but find a spot for him. After today, I want him working at least two or three times every week."*

I worked on the TV show in Pittsburgh that next Saturday, April 25, 1970, against Bobby "Hurricane" Hunt. Later that night, in Hubbard, Ohio, I wrestled Frank Durso. For the remainder of the year, I worked on all but four weekends. Bruno booked me on the spot shows around Pittsburgh, in places like Johnstown, and occasionally put me on the big show at the Civic Arena.

Every now and then, when I would go back to Detroit to visit with my parents, I would pick up the odd show for the Sheik. There was heat between Bruno and the Sheik, for whatever reason, but Bruno knew that I worked for the Sheik. He didn't have a problem with me working for him. When I knew that the Sheik had a Cobo Hall show coming up on a Saturday, I would call him a month in advance and ask if there was a possibility that I could work. If I did, I would stay over and do TV the next day.

May 25, 1970: Pittsburgh TV

The Sheik booked me almost every time I called. I would go to Bruno and ask, *"Can I work just Thursday and Friday this week? I have an opportunity to pick up Cobo Hall and the TV on Sunday."*

*"No problem, kid."*

By that time, I was 28 years old, so I wasn't a kid any more, but I didn't mind being called "kid." I would love to hear someone call me "kid" today, although that's not likely to happen, unless I visit a nursing home.

Three or four times in 1970, I worked the two days in Pittsburgh, then got into my car and drove to Detroit. I would stay with my parents, work the big show in Cobo Hall, then do the TV on Sunday.

I had the privilege of working with a regular group of guys who lived in the Pittsburgh area and worked locally—Frank Durso, Johnny DeFazio (who I think is still involved in the union there), Frank Holtz, and John L. Sullivan, who later became Johnny Valiant.

Thanks to Bruno, I became what we called a "weekend warrior." Bruno booked me almost every weekend. It was the first time that I was booked with any kind of regularity, so I was always excited to know that I had a couple of matches coming up. I also knew that the learning curve had to do with how much experience you had under your belt.

It was during this period of time that I met Jim Grabmire. Jim was somewhat of a loner. I think he still lived with his mother in Springfield, Ohio, at that time. He would work around his home territory during the winter months. In the summer, he would go to the Carolinas, where they ran outdoor shows and did much better business. He would work there for six months, then go back home.

Jim Grabmire

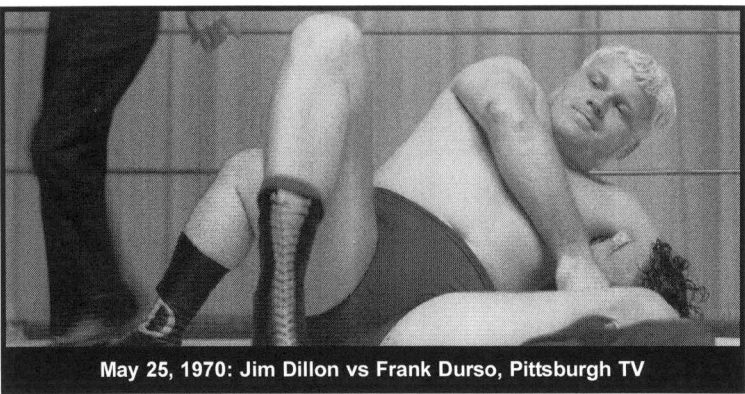

May 25, 1970: Jim Dillon vs Frank Durso, Pittsburgh TV

I lost track of Jim's whereabouts, but there is one thing that I remember the most about him. There were some guys in the business whose punches and kicks *"looked like sh— and hurt like hell."* If I had only one memory of Jim Grabmire, that would be my memory. That fact notwithstanding, he was a wonderful person. In fact, if I had a list of people to thank for helping me get started in the business, Jim Grabmire would be near the top of that list. When we made some trips together, I shared my dream with him. Before he left for Charlotte in April 1971, he said, *"Give me some of your publicity pictures. I"ll take them to Charlotte and put in a good word for you with George Becker, the booker."*

Two weeks later, he called and said, *"If you're interested in wrestling here, you have a starting date on May 3rd."*

At the time, I had no money. I was living paycheck to paycheck. I was living in Warren, Ohio, in the home of someone who rented out rooms. I lived in the basement, because it had a larger living space and a shower, and I paid a very reasonable $15 a week.

I had been with the trucking company for almost two years, and my worst fear was that when I gave my boss my notice, he would simply say, *"You can leave right now. You're no good to us for the next two weeks."* Then I would be out of work for two weeks with no income.

My starting date in Charlotte was on Monday, May 3, 1971, so I finished the week out by working on Friday. Before I left work, I typed a letter giving my two weeks notice. I was worried that the terminal manager would keep my last two checks, so I had to tell a few fibs in the letter. I told him that the promoter called on Saturday with the job opportunity, which was my dream of a lifetime. The promoter had said that one of the wrestlers had been injured, so he needed me there on Monday. If I wasn't there on Monday, he would give my spot to someone else. My plan was to drive to Charlotte, then call the terminal manager on Monday morning and apologize.

I took the letter with me and drove to Pittsburgh. The following day, I worked on Pittsburgh TV, then wrestled on a house show in Beaver Falls, Pennsylvania. After the show, I left Beaver Falls and drove back to Warren. I went to the trucking company and slid my notice under the door of the terminal manager's office. On Sunday morning, I woke up and drove the 650 miles to Charlotte.

When I called my boss, he was very gracious about the whole situation, which made me feel guilty about the subterfuge. He asked for my new address so he could send my check from the week before—since there was a week's lag time from the time you worked until you got paid—and my final check. He ended the conversation by wishing me a heartfelt, *"I wish you the best of luck, Jim."*

That made me feel even worse.

# Chapter 6
# The Babyface

When I pulled away from my home in Warren, Ohio, I had never been further south than Richmond, Virginia. I had no idea of what I was getting myself into, or where I was going. I had a map, I was by myself, and I had everything I owned in my beat-up, old Chevy Impala.

Jim Grabmire had told me to go to the YMCA when I arrived in Charlotte. It was an inexpensive place to stay. The amenities included bunkbeds, a gang shower, and a gym where the boys could work out. Several of the guys went there to play handball. Most important, the Y was only two blocks away from where the wrestling office was at the time—1111 East Morehead Street. After I had been in the territory for a few weeks, I rented an apartment with Joe Furr, who was Grabmire's nephew, and we shared expenses.

My first booking was on May 3, 1971 at the Charlotte Park Center against the legendary Gene Anderson. For most of my career, I had always worked as a heel, so George Becker took me aside and said, *"We have you booked as a babyface because we're short on babyfaces."*

I wasn't going to argue, so I just said, *"Well, I've never been a babyface before, but that's okay."*

As it turned out, I was a babyface the whole time I was in the territory. I had never worked babyface in my life, but since I had been a heel, I understood how to be a better babyface. Generally speaking, in underneath matches—and I had always been in an underneath match up to that point in time—the babyface went over [won the match]. That way, when the heels won the important matches, it meant something. The exception to that would be when an established heel wrestled a babyface in an underneath match. But in most cases, the babyface went over.

In the Park Center, the heels and babyfaces had separate dressing rooms. I was wrestling Gene Anderson, who I had never met before, and we were supposed to go between 6 and 8 minutes.

We went fourteen.

We didn't finish at eight minutes because the match was really going well. I didn't know it at the time, but Gene was having a good time and wanted to see what I could do.

When I went back to the dressing room, one of the referees came over from the other side and said, *"You did great, kid. Gene is in the other dressing room, saying things like, 'That kid's got it. He's gonna be good.'"*

That was music to my ears. Everybody seemed to like my work, so I was confident that I would finally have the opportunity to do what I had dreamed about all my life.

# "Wrestlers Are Like Seagulls"

To me, Charlotte was such a contrast to the northeast. When I arrived at the Park Center, I was surprised at how small the venue was. Most of the arenas were smaller than what I was used to in the northeast. The Carolinas had small towns and small wrestlers. There was a marked difference between George Becker and the bigger-than-life characters in the New York territory.

I was also surprised to see the blacks all sitting in one section. In 1971, the south was not that far removed from segregation. Even though the south had been integrated by that time, the blacks had been sitting in that one section for so many years that they continued to sit there, even though they were allowed to sit wherever they wanted to sit. I also saw signs over the water fountains that said, "Whites Only." That was quite a shock to this young man who went to a high school in Trenton where 30% of the students were black.

Charlotte, North Carolina vs Gene Anderson

They didn't have liquor by the drink in Charlotte at that time, either. Everything was brown bag. You brought your own bottle of liquor in a brown bag, and you paid for a pitcher of ice and a cup.

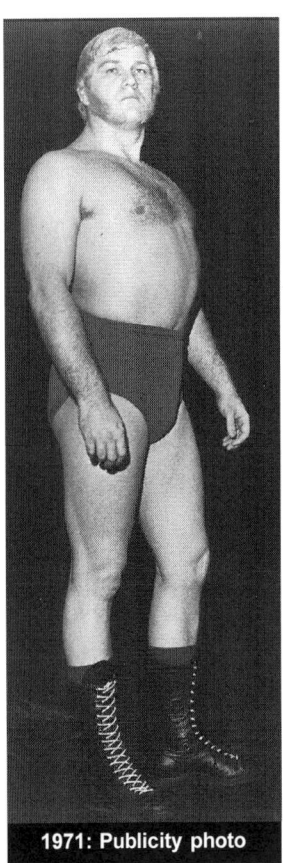

1971: Publicity photo

I also remember coming back from a town and turning on the television. There was nothing on the air but a test pattern. In New York, we had all-night television, or at least late, late-night television. At eleven o'clock at night in Charlotte, they played the National Anthem and they were off the air, with nothing to watch but snow.

It wasn't that long ago, and it was normal living for the people in the Carolinas, but to a northeastern boy like me, it was all a surprise.

There was one thing that didn't vary with my change in location, though. During that first year, I was still living paycheck to paycheck. I only averaged about $270 a week in the territory, but as long as my check was big enough to cover my share of the transportation, rent, and food, I was happy. I had no other responsibilities and I was living my dream. I was able to live on what I was paid with the hope that it would get better.

I worked hard and I had a good attitude, so I was booked every night, and it did get better. In 1972, my second year in the territory, I averaged $360 a week, which was up about $90 a week from the previous year.

One thing that many people don't know is that you didn't always get paid to wrestle on TV. Some promoters paid when you wrestled on TV, but only when you did a job. If you won your match, they considered it to be advertising for your career. I think we were paid $10 to $15 for doing TV in High Point, but they didn't pay you anything for Charlotte TV. However, your appearance on TV would normally guarantee you a spot on the Park

Center house show, so you would get a good payday without having to go out of town.

We did TV interviews, or what we called promos, in Raleigh, North Carolina. When I first went into the territory, though, at my level, I didn't do promos. I only did promos when I was involved in a main event, and I only had a handful of those during that time, usually in a small town like Lynchburg, Virginia. I would be in a tag team match with someone like Les Thatcher against a team like Rip Hawk and Swede Hanson. The main events that I had at that time were few and far between.

Les and I traveled together a lot since we were tag team partners quite often. I made trips with many other wrestlers, including Art Nelson, Johnny Weaver, Luther Lindsay, Abe Jacobs, and Frank Hester.

The only problem I remember having with anyone came about on July 11, 1972 in Columbia, South Carolina, when I wrestled George "Two-Ton" Harris. George was not a small man. In fact, his average weight was somewhere around 325 pounds. He was a big, heavy man. George spent most of the match leaning on me, to the point where I thought he was being deliberate. I don't remember how I handled that situation, but whatever I did, I never had that problem again.

I was able to survive those early, lean years thanks to people like Art Nelson, who not only helped me in the ring, but in other ways, too. Art came across as being a roughneck, the type of guy that people avoid. He was kind of blustery. You might compare him to someone like Ole Anderson. He had no time for anybody who didn't take the business seriously. I got to know Art real well and he liked me, I think, because I was serious and committed to my trade.

I had my first pair of custom boots made in Hamilton, Ontario. They were cut up high and the leather was thin. They were a good pair of boots, but they weren't very durable. Art had his boots made by Clifford Macias, a well-known, reputable bootmaker in Houston. Clifford hand-crafted a beautiful boot with heavy leather. If you sent him a tracing of your foot, along with your ankle measurements, he would make them to fit.

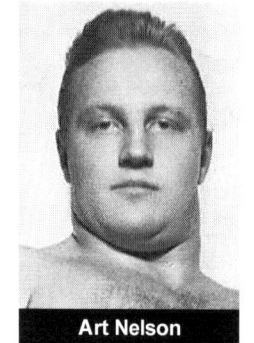
Art Nelson

As it turned out, Art and I wore the same size boot. Art was meticulous about his gear, his car, and everything else in his life. When his boots started to look worn, he would have them resoled and refurbished. During the 2½ years that I was there, he gave me two or three pairs of boots. He would never let me pay for them, and I know he had some money invested in them—the money he originally paid, and the money he paid to have them refurbished.

I remember one match with Art in particular—a battle royal in Greenville, South Carolina. The finish stuck in my mind and I would later use it throughout my career because I liked it so much.

I was a mid-card babyface at that time, so it would have been a long shot for me to win a battle royal, but in this case, the battle royal was down to me—the mid-card babyface—and two heels, Art Nelson and Ole Anderson. The two of them took turns having their way with me, so I was pretty well beat down. It was just going to be a matter of time before they eliminated me, but they were going to have their fun until they did. Since I was already written off, Art came to the realization that if he was going to win, he would eventually have to deal with Ole, so after Ole did something to me and had his back turned, Art attacked Ole. I was just laying in the middle of the ring like a dead fish.

The only way you could win a battle royal was to throw your opponent over the top rope, so Art took Ole to the side of the ring and was struggling to dump him over. In the meantime, I struggled to my feet and threw a desperation dropkick that hit Art in the back, propelling both of them over the ropes. I collapsed in the middle of the ring and was declared the winner.

It was a feel-good type of finish for the fans when an underdog babyface, who has no chance to win, overcomes all odds and wins that kind of a match. It was a really great finish and I never forgot it.

I didn't particularly enjoy—still don't and never will—going to the gym and pushing weights. That was never my thing, but I did get some exercise in the Carolinas when I started working with Art Nelson. Art did isometric exercises with a rubber strap that had a handle attached to each end. He even used surgical hose at one time. I would sit in the dressing room and do chest pulls, but I didn't push myself too hard.

Working with that rubber strap was as close as I ever came to working out on a regular basis. The truth of it is, to this very day, I hate to work out. I have never worked out in the gym in my life. I never took steroids, either, so what I had was natural weight. My weight wasn't quite 220 pounds, but I was tall, about 6'2, so my height gave me the appearance of being bigger than I actually was. Of course, with age, your body compresses, so now I'm closer to 6'0.

I looked at working out like this: Let's say that you worked for a grocery store, and your boss said, *"The produce truck driver left fifty 100-pound bags of potatoes by the back door. We need to take them back to the storeroom."*

I could justify picking up those 100-pound bags of potatoes, carrying them back to the storeroom, and stacking them on a pallet. But I could never see the logic of being in the gym, picking up a 100-pound barbell, pushing it up into the air, and putting it right back where it started.

You might say, *"But that would have been an investment in your career."*

Yeah, maybe so, but not for me. I never looked ripped, but I had enough of a body that I could get by and get some respect as a wrestler. The fans focused more on the things that I said and did.

I had my first exposure to steroids when I was in the Carolinas. Someone offered to get me some Dianabol to help me bulk up. I didn't want any part of it. It was a personal decision. First of all, I had a fear of putting something in my body that I couldn't control. But most important, for steroids to do what they're supposed to do, you have to work out—and I wasn't going to ruin my reputation as the anti-gym-rat by doing that.

> **Dillon Wins Main Event**
>
> The winner of the main event Monday night at Memorial Auditorium was Jim Dillon. He survived an over-the-top, battle royal against nine other wrestlers.
>
> In individual matches Jim Grabmeyer topped John Heidman, Gene Anderson bested Nick Ruco, Brute Bernard downed El Gaucho, Missouri Mauler beat Joe Furr, and Art Nelson stopped Jim Dillon.
>
> In a girls match, Tami Jones defeated Belle Starr.
>
>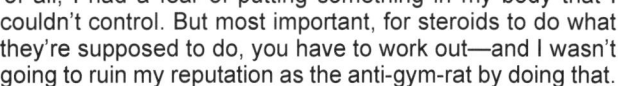
> Greenville, July 5, 1971

The man who promoted the Carolinas and Virginia was Jim Crockett, Sr. Jim was a typical southern gentleman, but he commanded respect. When he talked to the boys, they answered with, *"Yes, sir,"* and *"No, sir."*

Jim was a big, stout man who made a lot of money promoting wrestling, but he told me that he never drove a car more expensive than a Buick. He could have afforded a Rolls Royce, or a fleet of them, but he had a good reason for his stance. He knew that his core audience, the people who came to the Park Center every Monday night, were predominately blue collar workers. He didn't want them spending their hard-earned money to buy tickets to see wrestling, and see the promoter's Cadillac parked behind the building. Jim thought a Buick was comfortable and roomy, but it wasn't the type of car the fans would look at and say, *"That's what*

Jim Crockett

we're paying for every week." That's exactly the way he thought. Along those same lines, his office was situated in an old house and it wasn't very fancy.

Jim didn't go to the TV in Raleigh, but the Charlotte TV was his baby. He would always sit in the back with his hands draped across his stomach. If he got nervous about something, he would roll his tie up from the bottom with his fingers. If we saw Mr. Crockett rolling his tie, we knew that he wasn't happy.

One of the wrestlers that I have to mention is Luther Lindsay. I really liked Luther. Luther was a wonderful, wonderful man who could beat just about anybody in a real wrestling match, but I don't think he ever reached his true potential—because he was a black man in the south.

When I met Luther in 1971, the other wrestlers told me that Luther was a shell of the man that he had once been. He had been in an automobile accident and almost died when he went through the windshield. As it was, he was badly scarred.

Since Luther lived between Charlotte and Norfolk, Abe Jacobs and I would pick him up on our way to Norfolk. We would wrestle in Norfolk, then Richmond on the following night. On the return trip, I would drop Luther off at his home.

One day, Abe and I left early because Luther had invited us to his home to have dinner with his family. While we were there, we met his daughter, who was an Olympic caliber swimmer and a great, all-around athlete.

Luther Lindsay

On December 9, 1971, when I stopped by his house to pick him up, Luther was sick with the flu, but he insisted on going. He wrestled in Norfolk that night, and stayed with relatives after the show. Before he left, we made arrangements to meet the next day to go to Richmond. When we picked him up, he was so sick that he was shivering. He made the trip underneath a blanket in the back seat of the car.

They used to pay us cash in Richmond, so when we arrived at the Richmond Fairgrounds, I told the promoter, Joe Murnick, *"Joe, Luther is very sick. It wouldn't be right to expect him to wrestle tonight. I'll work twice in his place, but I want you to give Luther his envelope."*

After taking Luther's place against Frank Morrell in the second match, I went back to the dressing room to prepare for my next match—the one I was originally scheduled for—against Tony Romano. They had given Luther an envelope, but they had also put an extra $20 in mine. When we got out to the car, Luther tried to give me his envelope. He said, *"I didn't earn this money."*

I said, *"Luther, I did that for you because we're friends. If the situation was reversed, I know you would have done the same thing."* What I did for Luther was certainly no big deal. I just felt good that I was able to do something for him.

On February 21, 1972, Abe Jacobs and I were scheduled to wrestle Gene and Ole Anderson in the Park Center. Luther was wrestling Ronnie Paul before us, so I was watching the match. Luther wasn't very tall. For his finish, he would push down on the bottom rope with one foot and catapult off, high up into the air. As Luther came down, he would give you a headbutt, then cover you for the pin. And that's what he did that night. He went up, hit Ronnie with a headbutt as he came down, and covered him. 1-2-3.

For several seconds after the referee counted three, the two men just laid there. There was an uncomfortable pause. Finally, Ronnie tried to kick out, but when he did, Luther didn't come up off of him in the traditional way. He just laid there, until Ronnie finally managed to struggle out from underneath him.

Luther finally sat up with his arms extended, as if he was struggling against something, until he finally collapsed backwards. We quickly called the emergency medical team, who went into the ring and gave him oxygen. At some point, they took the two bottom ropes down and carried him out to an ambulance.

Nobody seemed to know what was wrong, so we were told to go to the ring for our match. Our match was scheduled to go thirty minutes, but it seemed to last for an eternity, with me standing on the ring apron most of the time. Abe, who was Luther's closest friend, didn't want to stand on the apron and think about Luther, so he stayed in the ring for 28 minutes of the 30. The match didn't suffer, and the fans wouldn't have known that anything was wrong, but there was no communication in the ring. The four of us just went through the motions because we were all thinking about Luther. When Abe finally tagged out, I went in and the Andersons took the fall on me.

We immediately bailed out of the ring and went back to the dressing room, which is when they told us that Luther had been pronounced dead. The cause of death was determined to be a heart attack. Luther was 48 years old when he died. I lost a good friend that night.

I'd like to rewind and move back to 1969, when I met a woman named Jeanette. She was a hostess at a bar in Pottstown, Pennsylvania, and was five years older than I was. She was divorced and had three sons: Mark, Rick, and Wayne. When I met Jeanette, they were 9, 11 and 12 years old. Jeanette and I lived together for a while, and got married on Christmas Eve, 1971. I spent the night at home, then left the next morning—Christmas morning—to work the Christmas day show at the Charlotte Coliseum against Bobby Kay. Christmas, Thanksgiving, and New Years Day were big Coliseum shows back then.

I took Jeanette with me to every territory I worked, even Japan and Australia, and helped to provide for and raise her boys.

In that era, it was not uncommon for wrestlers to work occasional shots in other territories, usually when one promoter sends you in as a favor to another promoter. While I was in the Carolinas, I made trips to Florida in 1971 and 1972. On the second trip, I teamed up with Buddy Colt and Phil Robley against Eddie Graham, his son Mike Graham, and Don Curtis in Orlando on July 31, 1972. I remember my first year as a referee, being in the ring with the Sheik, Bobo Brazil, Haystack Calhoun, Arnold Skaaland, and Killer Kowalski, and how I was in awe of them at the same time. Even though I had watched Eddie when I was a kid, as well, I don't remember being in awe of Eddie that night when we were in the ring. I'm not saying that the magic ever wore off, but as I gained more experience, and got more matches under my belt, my focus shifted to the importance of the match that night, and not on the fact that I was rubbing elbows with one of my childhood idols.

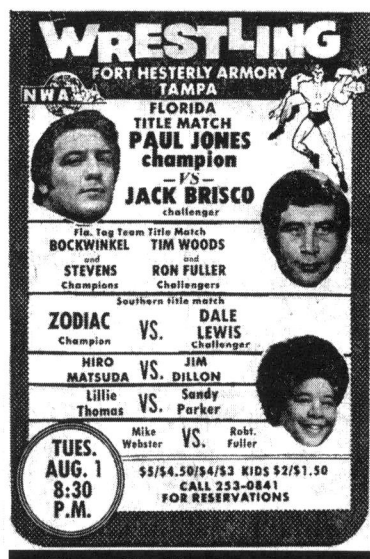

Tampa, Florida • Aug. 1, 1972

Two things happened during my time in the Carolinas that I consider to be lucky breaks. The first break was being given the opportunity to wrestle Dory Funk Jr., who held the National Wrestling Alliance (NWA) world heavyweight title.

The NWA world heavyweight champion would usually come into a territory for a week to defend the title in the major towns. By that time, George Becker was getting up in years, and he just wasn't a suitable opponent for the champ. Johnny Weaver was usually the one who chased the title, so he was booked against the champion in most of the towns, including Richmond, Virginia.

In those days, the promoters didn't want the fans to know that they booked the same matches in several towns. Richmond and Norfolk were only 90 miles apart, so Mr. Crockett couldn't book the same match—Dory Funk Jr. versus Johnny Weaver—in Norfolk.

Weaver finally came to me and said, *"We have an idea. Dory will be here in September, but we don't have anybody for him in Norfolk. We'd like to make an opponent for him ... and we'd like it to be you. We want to book you and Dory on Raleigh TV in a one-fall, non-title match. To a degree, Dory will basically make you [go out of his way to make you look good to the audience] before he catches a quick fall. We'll do an interview with you the following week and show clips from the match.*

*"Your story will be that this was the first time that you ever wrestled a world champion, even in a non-title match, and you had butterflies because it was the highlight of your career. Even though Dory is the world champion, you were able to stay with him, step for step. You think you might have a good shot at possibly beating him in a 2-out-of-3-fall match. You have nothing to lose, so why not try it?*

*"We think that will make a story that the people will relate to and get behind. You're somebody that's difficult for Dory to prepare for because you're new, and he doesn't know what to expect from you. You got his attention in the TV match and you proved that you could stay with him. And now that you're over your initial butterflies, the result of the match could be a whole different story."*

Using that scenario, Dory and I wrestled on Raleigh TV on July 5, 1972, and our rematch was scheduled for September 7, 1972 in Norfolk. Three nights before our rematch took place, I wrestled in Greenville, South Carolina, with Big Boy (Luke) Brown as my partner, against Gene and Ole Anderson.

Ole did a spot where he would demonstrate his power. He would pick you up and press you way up into the air. He would then pivot, as if he lost his balance, and fall back with you on top of him in a pinning position for a quick 1-2 near fall. On that Monday night, when he pressed me up, I pushed myself up off of his shoulders. At the same time, he had already started to pivot and fall back with me. I was much higher than I normally would be, so when gravity took over and began to bring me down, I wasn't coming down with my weight across his upper chest. I was coming down onto his face and head. At the last second, I broke my fall with my wrist and the tips of my toes. It felt like I broke my ankle.

Later that night, I went to the hospital and the doctors took x-rays. By that time, my leg had blown up like a balloon. The x-rays showed that it wasn't broken, but I had a severe strain, so they put ice on my ankle and wrapped it tightly.

It was difficult to walk without limping, but I didn't miss a booking. I worked in Raleigh on Tuesday, Asheville on Wednesday, and Thursday was my world title shot—another one of my dreams. On Thursday morning, I took a handful of aspirin and re-wrapped my ankle.

Dory Funk Jr. showed just how good he was that night because he carried a cripple to a respectable match.

We had a good house that night, but I can't take credit for it. My match with Dory was the marquee match, but in my opinion, the true main event, Jerry Brisco and Thunderbolt Patterson versus Rip Hawk and Swede Hanson, with "Playboy" Gary Hart as their manager, was what really drew the house. You might say that we were co-main events, but the tag match was what carried the card into the following week.

Regardless of who drew the house, it was an honor just for me to be there.

As a result of working through my injury, and the reaction we got from the crowd, Dory took me off to the side in the dressing room. He said, *"When you're done here,*

## 46 • "Wrestlers Are Like Seagulls"

*I'd like you to come to Amarillo. We'd like to use you on top there."*

What an honor *that* was—the NWA world heavyweight champion telling me that he wants me to come work on top in his territory. To me, going to the Carolinas from Michigan seemed like a great adventure. Now I had an opportunity to go to Texas, which to me, was like the other side of the world.

Two months later, we had a show in Greensboro, North Carolina. Dory Funk Jr. and his brother, Terry, were wrestling Jack and Jerry Brisco in a co-main event. Dory asked me to meet them at their hotel before the show. I had met Terry before, but that was my first opportunity to meet their father, Dory Funk, Sr.

Dory Sr. told me that he was excited about me coming to Amarillo. It was basically the standard promoter sales pitch about how *you'll love Amarillo.*

I told Dory, *"I'm going to Halifax, Nova Scotia, next April, but it's a short season and it ends in October. I really don't have any plans after that."*

As it turned out, that was the only time I ever talked to Dory Funk Sr. The following year, while I was still in Halifax, I got one of those middle-of-the-night phone calls that you don't expect, but you always remember. Dory Funk Sr. died on June 3, 1973.

Going to Halifax was my second stroke of good fortune. It all came about when I met the Cormier brothers, who promoted Halifax, Nova Scotia, Canada, or what we called the Maritimes territory. The four brothers were—Leo Burke (Leonce Cormier), The Beast (Yvon Cormier, who was given his name, the Beast, by Jim Crockett Sr.), Rudy Kay (Jean-Louis Cormier), and Bobby Kay (Romeo Cormier), the youngest brother.

The Cormiers always opened their territory in April and shut operations down in October. When the season ended, the Cormiers, Freddie Sweetan, and Mike Dubois, would all go to Charlotte to work through the winter months. There were a lot of guys who wanted to come into the Carolinas during the summer because Mr. Crockett ran a lot of outdoor shows and business was good, but the territory tended to drop during the winter. However, even though business was down, it was good for the Cormiers because it gave them somewhere to work during the winter months. Mr. Crockett always booked them, even knowing that they would be returning home in the summer.

Johnny Weaver and Leo Burke were the best of friends. I don't know if it was due to them having worked the Charlotte territory together during the winter months prior to that, but they were already the best of friends when I arrived in Charlotte. Weaver, who was a mainstay in the Carolinas, wrestled in the Maritimes during the 1972 season. Johnny was scheduled to return to the Maritimes to work as Freddie Sweetan's tag team partner for the closing week of the season. In the meantime, one of Crockett's wrestlers had to quit due to an injury, so Johnny couldn't get away for the week.

Since he felt responsible to fill the position for the Cormiers, Johnny asked me if I would be interested in taking his spot for the week. He told me that the Cormiers would reimburse me for my airfare when I got up there. I thought that would be a great opportunity, but I had one small problem. *"John, I know they'll reimburse me for my plane ticket, but I don't have any money to buy it."* Johnny suggested that I talk to Mr. Crockett.

After making a few calls and getting a quote of $238.52 for the airfare from Charlotte to Halifax, I went to the office to see Mr. Crockett. *"Mr. Crockett, I have a chance to go to Halifax for a week, but I don't have money to pay for the plane ticket."*

He didn't hesitate and he only asked me one question. *"How much is it?"*

When I told him, he reached into his pocket, pulled out a stack of bills, counted off $240, and said, *"Here's the money for your ticket. They'll reimburse you and you can repay me when you get back. I wish you good luck."*

I was in the Maritimes from October 9-14 and I wrestled the Beast, Yvon Cormier, every single night that week—Monday through Saturday.

He also beat me every night that week. I must have made a favorable impression because they invited me back for the next season. *"Would you come back next year for the whole season?"* they asked. I couldn't accept their offer fast enough. I thanked them over and over. They paid me for the week, reimbursed me in cash for my plane fare, and I flew back to Charlotte. For that week in Canada, I went from making $300+ a week to my biggest week in the business to that point—$690.

I consider that to be the biggest break of my career, not so much for what happened that week, but for what it would mean for my future.

As soon as I got home, I went to the office to see Mr. Crockett. I walked in, plunked the $240 down on his desk, and said, *"Mr. Crockett. I would like to give you my six month notice. The Cormiers invited me back and gave me an April starting date."*

Mr. Crockett said, *"That will be fine. You can stay here until it's time to go up there. If you change your mind, or if you go up there and want to come back, you'll always have a home here."*

He died on Sunday, April 1, 1973, a month before I left.

Mr. Crockett was very well respected in the community and his funeral was a major event in Charlotte. The night before, I wrestled in Spartanburg, South Carolina. We didn't wrestle on Sunday in those days, but they cancelled the matches at Park Center on Monday night. I met Terry Garvin for the first time at that funeral. Terry was a well-known wrestler who, along with his "brothers" Ronnie Garvin and "Gorgeous" Jimmy Garvin, held several regional tag team titles.

The Carolina territory was a family affair. Mr. Crockett had three sons—Jimmy, Jackie, and David—and a daughter named Francis. Jackie Crockett was the main TV cameraman. I saw very little of Jimmy in the early days, and virtually nothing of Francis, who was busy running the Charlotte O's minor league baseball team. David Crockett was an announcer, so he was more hands-on. David also had a brief career as a wrestler under the name David Finley. I think he had been trained by Johnny Heideman, and I would imagine that Gene Anderson worked with him,

1972 • vs Sandy Scott

too. If memory serves me well, Finley had been his mother's maiden name. David's career was brief, but he had a great attitude and he really wanted to learn. Like most promoters' sons, he was held to a higher standard by the wrestling community. David and I were both babyfaces, but we wrestled against each other in Charleston, South Carolina on September 29, 1972. During the match, we messed up a spot and collided in mid-air. I can't say for sure that it was anyone's fault in particular. We were just two young guys giving their all. It was one of those, *"I thought you were jumping over ME when I dropped down."* We both recovered and finished the match. I wound up with a black eye. If you look closely at photos where I wrestled Sandy Scott a few days later, you can see that I have a shiner. David and I also teamed together twice, with our most notable match being against Freddie Sweetan and Mike DuBois at the Greensboro Coliseum on Thanksgiving night, November 23, 1972. The annual

## 48 • "Wrestlers Are Like Seagulls"

Thanksgiving shows were always Mr. Crockett's biggest shows of the year. Years later, the event would be renamed *Starrcade*—which actually predated *Wrestlemania* as the annual wrestling event. My payoff for the night was $250—my biggest payoff for one night at that point in my career.

With the passing of Mr. Crockett, it looked as if John Ringley, who had married Francis, would be the heir apparent to run the company. His bad judgement altered those plans when he bought an airplane and got caught flying his girlfriend around. It wasn't too long before John and Francis got a divorce, and John was pushed out of the company.

Jimmy was the oldest of the boys, so Ringley's ousting created an opportunity for Jimmy to step in and run the company. I had the feeling that David may have harbored some resentment over that. He never said anything to me personally, but from what I observed, there seemed to be some underlying jealousy between the two brothers.

Joe Murnick was Mr. Crockett's partner in the Virginia end of the territory, so he continued to run that end. Joe's sons, Carl and Elliott, took over when their father passed away.

Four weeks after Mr. Crockett's death, I left the territory. Shortly after that, Jimmy Crockett brought George Scott in to book the territory. George brought a lot of new talent into the territory and they did great business.

My last match in the Carolina territory was in Danville, Virginia, on April 24, 1973. I teamed up with the Haiti Kid, a midget wrestler, against Phil Robley and Frenchie Lamont, another midget.

Four days later, I had all of our worldly goods packed into a U-Haul trailer. Jeanette, her three boys, and I, drove to Moncton, New Brunswick ... ready for new adventures in a new territory.

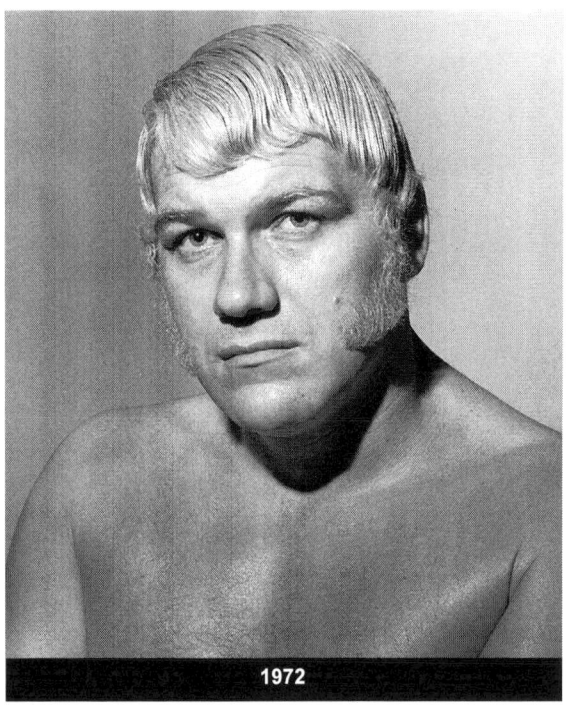

1972

# Chapter 7
## Nature Boy Dillon

My early years in the business were an exciting time for me, but going to the Maritimes was the highlight of my career.

It was my good fortune that circumstances got in the way of the Cormier's scheduled program for the season. Stan Stasiak was booked for the season as the new monster heel. However, shortly before the season started, he got a call from Vince McMahon Sr. Vince wanted Stan to keep his schedule free, beginning in August 1973, for a run on top in New York. If Stan had an opportunity to work on top in New York, the Cormiers weren't going to hold him to a commitment to work for them.

Unfortunately, there was nobody else scheduled for the season who hadn't been there before, and the Cormiers didn't have time to find somebody else to fill the spot. They were in a panic.

While still in Charlotte, I was making a trip with Leo Burke, and we were throwing ideas around. I said, *"Leo, this might sound crazy, but it's an idea that I hope you'll consider. Each year, you bring in a monster heel, like Stomper and Killer Karl Krupp. You're always on the lookout for someone bigger than the guy you used last year. Your deal with Stasiak fell through, so you're in a bind.*

*"I'm already committed to come up there. Have you ever given thought to using somebody different—somebody with a totally different style and look—who, instead of being a monster on a rampage, was a wrestling heel. Why not work your program in reverse? Instead of having a new heel come in to wrestle you, Bobby, and Rudy, before getting his title shot with the Beast at the end of the season, why not run your whole season in reverse.*

*"Why don't you have a wrestler like me come in and win the title from the Beast immediately. I would cheat to do it, so the fans would think I was stealing the title from him. I would be a coward and a braggart who uses gimmicks, or does whatever I have to do to win my matches. Then I could do a program with you, Bobby, and Rudy. Since I'm a chicken sh— wrestler, the people would believe that all four of you could kick my ass. That would give your territory a fresh look. After that, you can bring in Stomper and the other monster heels. At the end of the run, you could bring the Beast back to kick my ass."*

It was one of those moments where you have a beer or two (or six), and you start throwing ideas out.

The next day, Leo called and said, *"I told Rudy about your idea. At first, he thought it was a crazy idea. However, after thinking about it, he called me back and said he loves the idea. What we need to know is, are you sure you can handle it?"*

*"Absolutely."*

When I hung up the phone, I had a brief moment of panic. *Could I really handle the job?* The feeling of apprehension passed quickly. I just knew that it was going to be my big break.

Before he hung up, the last thing that Leo said to me was, *"You need to bulk up."* My size, or lack of it, was one of the Cormier's main concerns. They wanted me to fill out a little bit. They called me every day. *"You've gotta eat more, and Rudy wants you to get into the beer."* But there were several problems that stood in the way of that goal.

For one, once I started to work on top every night—wrestling longer matches than I was used to, and putting out a lot of effort—I would sweat a lot. That was especially true in the summer months. It was hot in the Maritimes, and we wrestled in a lot of hockey arenas that weren't air conditioned. I would make it to 225, but then I would lose it, even when I tried to put the fluid back into my body.

And at night, there weren't any eating places open. Those factors made it a challenge to keep up my weight. At the time, I might have averaged 220 pounds when I was soaking wet. For most of my career, though, I stayed right around 230, and I was comfortable with that. Later in life, when I was in my late 30's, my metabolism changed and the struggle went in the other direction. I was struggling to keep my weight down.

I had been told that I would be billed as "Nature Boy" Dillon. Rudy Kay told me, *"The fans all know that Buddy Rogers was from New Jersey, so we want you to be Nature Boy Dillon."*

I was also billed as being from Atlantic City, New Jersey, because it was a much more recognizable name than Trenton, not to mention sounding more glamorous.

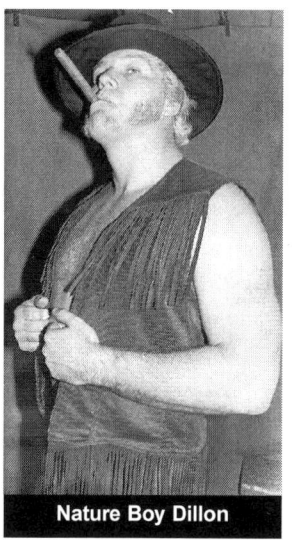
Nature Boy Dillon

For the previous two years, I had worked as a babyface, but I had done my homework and prepared an image for myself. I created a character that wasn't patterned after anyone else. Before I left Charlotte, I went to a second-hand clothes store and bought several outfits that were outrageously colorful. On my first night in the Maritimes, I wore a pair of red, corduroy pants to the ring, along with a leather hat.

I also bought a big box of cigars. When I was a kid, I remember seeing older men sitting back in their car, smoking a big cigar. I don't know what it was about nicely-attired men who smoked cigars, but that got a lot of heat with the general public, so I bought a box of the biggest, cheapest cigars that I could find.

My gimmick was that I would walk to the ring with a cigar in my mouth. I didn't light it. I just walked to the ring with it hanging from the corner of my mouth. When it was time for my match to begin, I would take the cigar out of my mouth, break it in half, and throw the pieces away.

Smoking a big cigar would get you heat, but when you take a perfectly good cigar, break it in half, and throw it away, that gets you double heat. There were many people in the audience who were barely making a living—just like I was, although they didn't know that—so to throw an *expensive* cigar away was wasteful, and most people don't like waste.

That was just one aspect of the character that I created.

Everything was built around our interviews. The setup was to wrestle at the Halifax

Forum on Tuesday night. The next morning, we would film live TV, during which time we would each do one generic interview, which was applicable to every one of the towns. We were only given one shot to do our interview, so we had to get it right. I remember laying awake when I went to bed at night. I would lay there for hours, going over the interview in my mind. By the time I was in front of the camera, I could disassociate my mind from the camera and do my interview as if I was talking to my opponent.

When it came to doing interviews, I didn't talk about how tough I was. I talked about my opponents.

There are two ways to do an interview. You can talk directly to the audience, telling them that they're fat, ugly, toothless, and in need of a bath. To me, that was cheap heat. The fans were the people who spent their hard-earned money every week to buy a ticket. The real Jim Morrison is actually a very sensitive, caring person. I never did like making fun of someone else, because you don't know what they're going through until you walk a mile in their shoes.

So instead of demeaning the fans, I would talk about the Cormiers, and the Beast, in particular. I talked about the Beast, who worked in the woods all day long, having big, black flies buzzing around in his beard. I talked about the grime on his body, and how his body odor would make me sick. *"Do you think I want to climb into the ring and have my body touch that?"*

I was insulting the Beast, and yet, in a sense, I was insulting the people, too. I didn't address them directly, but I let them come to their own conclusion. *"The Beast is one of us! We work hard and smell when we come home from the woods, too!"*

I let the people make the connection by insulting them indirectly. To me, that was good heat, because I singled the Beast out and made it personal between the two of us. The people could connect the dots and realize that I was ridiculing them, too.

That gave the Beast the opportunity to tell the people that he was proud to be a Maritimer. *"Dillon, you never worked a day in your life! You don't know what it's like to struggle to make a living."*

Now our storyline was rolling along.

We started the week off on Monday in Moncton, New Brunswick. I rented a small house in Moncton, so the drive to Halifax, Nova Scotia, our Tuesday night town, was about 175 miles one-way. We stayed over in Halifax that night so we could make an early Wednesday morning TV taping at the CJCH-TV studios. That was the only night we stayed over. On the other nights, we would drive back to Moncton after the shows to spend some time with our families.

After shooting TV, we all piled into our cars and drove from Halifax, past Moncton, and on to St. John, N.B., a total of 265 miles plus another 90 miles back home after the show. The Thursday through Sunday towns were—Fredericton, N.B. (215 miles round-trip), Bridgewater, N.S. (480 miles round-trip), New Glasgow, N.S. (300 miles round-trip), and North Sydney, N.S. (600 miles round-trip).

The regular Saturday night town, New Glasgow, was almost halfway to North Sydney when starting out from Moncton, so on rare occasions, I would stay overnight. It would save about 300 miles when compared to driving the entire 300 miles from Moncton to North Sydney on Sunday, passing right by the town we worked the night before.

I worked underneath during the first four weeks. They were building me up for a program with the Beast. My first match in the territory was on Monday night, April 30,

## "Wrestlers Are Like Seagulls"

1973, in Moncton. I wrestled Willie Trembley.

On Tuesday night, I wrestled in Halifax ... against Willie Trembley.

The next morning, I worked with Willie Trembley on Halifax TV.

That night, in Saint John, New Brunswick, I was in the opposite corner of the ring from ... Willie Trembley.

Willie and I both had the day off on Thursday.

On Friday night, the fans in Bridgewater, Nova Scotia, saw me square off against Willie Trembley.

We had a day off again on Saturday, but on Sunday, I faced my toughest opponent of the week.

Willie Trembley.

We followed the same schedule every week. Whatever your match was on Monday, you had the same match around the horn for the entire week.

One of the toughest things to do in the business was to go into a new territory and get over. It was even tougher in the Maritimes because it was a short-season territory. Our success or failure during those first four weeks would either make or break the territory. The Cormiers didn't have time to push somebody for four weeks, then decide, *"Well, this guy isn't working out. We need to try somebody else."* There wasn't enough time to start over. If I was going to be in a position to take off in a program with the Beast at the end of those four weeks, I had to get over. Rudy Kay knew what to do to get me over, and I had to just listen and execute. Once I got over, I did all of my own promos and, in my opinion, the promos were the key to my success.

I had my work cut out for me. The fans in that territory were tough, hard-working people. They could buy into the big monsters who came there every year, but were they really going to buy into a guy who was smaller, a coward, and who had a big mouth? I was convinced that it would work, but to accomplish that, I had to do everything I could to make sure that it did. I didn't want to get to the end of four weeks and think, *"I wish I had done this,"* or *"I wish I had tried harder."*

Fortunately, I never had time to think those thoughts because everything turned out well. After the initial four weeks were over, I had a great three-week run on top with the Beast.

The main title in the territory was the North American heavyweight title. I won that title from the Beast, who was the champion going into the season. After I won, the Beast acted frustrated on his interviews: *"Dillon won't stand up and fight me!"*

The Beast

In order to keep the Beast strong when I beat him for the title, I used a chain to knock him out. The Beast wanted me to cut his head open with the chain, which is what we called a hardway [not using a blade, but actually drawing blood by hitting your opponent with your knuckles or an object], so that he could go to the hospital and get stitches. When the time was right, I pulled out the chain and hit him twice.

The chain left two pink marks on his forehead, but no blood.

I whispered, *"Ohhh, man! I can't do this. It's just not me."*

He growled back at me, *"Just clobber me, man!"*

I hit him a third time and busted his eyebrow wide open. It was what the Cormiers wanted, but it was sickening. He went to the hospital that night and got stitched up.

When I saw him at the TV taping the next morning, I immediately started apologizing.

*"Ahh, it's good for the business,"* he said, brushing my apology aside.

That's how tough that family was.

Me? I wasn't tough. I never claimed to be tough. In fact, I wasn't even tough enough to do it to someone else. But that's what they wanted me to do. Unfortunately, I had to give him three whacks before I got the job done because I was too squeamish to hit him as hard as I should have.

My program with the Beast was followed by a four-week run with Leo Burke. Leo was the classic wrestler. I would describe Leo as a cross between Pat O'Connor and Dory Funk Jr. He could do anything. He was just a great mat technician. When my focus moved from the Beast to Leo, the program was reversed. Where the Beast would complain that I wouldn't stand and fight toe-to-toe, that was okay with Leo, because his specialty was wrestling.

Bobby Kay & Leo Burke

Our four-week program built up to a match with my title on the line. They didn't want to take the title off of me because they wanted to program me with Eric Pomeroy. To get out of it, they had Leo and I do the logical thing—go an hour broadway [wrestle to a draw] in the cage. That way, I kept the title and Leo didn't get beat.

As I said earlier, the match was the same every night, so I wrestled four one-hour draws with Leo Burke during that one week. In two of the matches, we went the hour without either of us taking a fall, and a couple where we split falls. It was the standard, I go out and get my ass kicked in the last five minutes, and just barely hold on until the bell rings. I don't remember the reasoning behind it, but we did change the finish in two of the towns and I went over [won the match].

I followed that with three weeks with Eric Pomeroy, who also wrestled as Stan Pulaski and Stan Vachon.

Once I had gone full circle with the program, Rudy came to me and said, *"I have a problem. I have nobody new left for you to work with, and I don't want to go back and rehash."*

Rudy had an opportunity to get Killer Karl Krupp back midway through the season. He said, *"I'd like to bring Krupp back, and I'd like you to put him over. After a three-week run with Krupp, I'll immediately put the tag titles on you and Freddie Sweetan to finish out the season. I'll also pay you a main event split of the money. In other words, you'll be giving up your spot, because we don't have much of a choice. But in that position, you'll do well and we will take care of you."*

In my opinion, he did just that. In one sense, it was a decision that I wasn't thrilled about, but I tried to be objective about it. I understood the position that Rudy was in. And at that point in my career, it would have been foolish to make threats about leaving.

Krupp was a real character. Years later, I worked with him in Amarillo. He was an older guy who worked his gimmick well, but was very clumsy in the ring.

True to his word, Rudy gave me my three-week run with Krupp (during which time I lost 17 straight matches and the title), then threw in a final week on top with Archie Gouldie, the Stomper.

I had nothing to complain about in regards to money, either. Starting with my fifth week in the territory, my pay went from an average $450 a week to $1,285, up to a high of $1,655 for my final week with Krupp.

I spent the next four weeks as Freddie Sweetan's tag team partner. Freddie was the perennial tag team champion, with a new partner each year. They would program

Jim Dillon & Freddie Sweetan

Freddie and a partner against Bobby Kay and somebody else. This time, they programmed Freddie and me as the North American tag team champions against different combinations of Bobby, the Stomper, and the Beast.

My last match in the territory was on October 4, 1973. Finishing up the season with Freddie was enjoyable. Freddie's real name was Fred Prosser, but he started wrestling as Sweetan early in his career when he teamed up with Bob Sweetan. Freddie was a big man and a credible worker.

Freddie was also a heavy smoker. On July 26, 1974, less than one year after our run together, he passed away at the young age of 36. Contrary to reports that he died in a freak accident when his gas grill exploded at a family cookout, Freddie died alone in a hunting cabin. I spoke to Freddie's girlfriend after it happened. Freddie drank his share of beer. It was surmised that he had a few and fell asleep while smoking. The hunting cabin caught fire and Fred never woke up. He was found seated at a table, badly charred, with his head resting on his arms, which were folded on the table.

Fred was a good guy and a friend.

When I started wrestling part-time, I never thought about what my signature move might be because I didn't need one. I never won any matches! When I got to Charlotte, they gave me a small push, so they wanted me to have a finishing hold [hold or move used to win matches] that the fans could associate with just me. Johnny Weaver came up with the idea of having me use a chicken wing crossface—a submission hold. Bob Backlund, the great WWWF champion, used the same hold with great success.

One of the first times I tried to use it, I was working with Larry Hamilton—The Missouri Mauler. Larry was so bulky that when I slid my left arm under his left arm (in a hammerlock position from behind him), and stretched my right hand across his face, I couldn't reach around far enough to lock my hands together. The closest thing I could get to it was to put my right hand under his chin without ever locking both hands. Larry danced up and down as if in extreme pain, and waved his right hand in the air as a sign that he submitted. The referee called for the bell, the crowd cheered, and I released Larry, who collapsed to the mat in a heap.

Well, to be honest, that only happened in the first or second fall of a best-of-three fall match, but it was exciting, nonetheless.

When I went to the Maritimes, the Cormiers wanted me to have a finishing hold that was more suitable for a heel. I'm not saying that heels never used a submission hold as their finishing hold, but if they did, they were the type of moves where a babyface would visually fight against it. If the heel won the match with the hold, it wasn't because the babyface gave up. It was because the babyface passed out, or was subdued enough that the heel was able to get a three-count for a pinfall. The chicken wing crossface was not that type of a hold. The problem with the chicken-wing was that once the heel has the hold applied in a shoot [real; legitimate] manner, the babyface has no leverage to even give the impression that he is fighting it. It wasn't a hold that allowed the babyface to make it look like he was fighting his way out of it. It jams his shoulder and neck, and causes great discomfort across the jaw or bridge of the nose, depending on the height and build of the person to whom the hold is applied. Since the head is drastically twisted to one side, any attempt to fight against the hold usually causes the opponent to lose his balance. If he falls to the left, which is usually what happens, one can easily fall on the shoulder of the arm in the hammerlock position, and do serious damage to the shoulder or the neck. Believe me, the chicken wing crossface is nothing to play with. Nobody other than a trained professional should apply it to anybody because somebody will get hurt.

The Cormiers wanted me to use the elbow drop. As a fan of Johnny Valentine, I remembered how he used that move. He would stand over his prostrate opponent and drop down, bringing all of his weight and his elbow down across his opponent's chest. In later days, Greg Valentine did that move as well as anybody in the business.

At the time, I weighed 218 pounds soaking wet. I didn't have a lot of bulk on me, so I had to exaggerate the drop by hitting the mat hard. For the first couple of weeks, every time I hit the mat, I jammed my right hip. I was in excruciating pain. The whole cheek of my butt turned black. I remember telling Rudy Kay, *"Rudy, that move is killing me. We've gotta do something else."*

The move looked effective, so we didn't want to completely scrap the idea. *"Why don't you try coming off the ropes with some momentum,"* Rudy suggested. *"That way, you'll be moving forward as you come down, and your hip won't go straight into the mat."*

That's what I did—and it worked. I would hit the ropes, rebound off, and smash my elbow down onto my opponent's chest. Of course, it took a few attempts to get my timing right, so that I knew when to leap into the air. Occasionally, in order to make it look like I was being overly vicious, I would do it two or three times.

When I left the Maritimes and went to Amarillo, the figure four leg lock became my finish. Jack Brisco had a lot of success using that hold in Florida during his feud with Dory Funk. It was a natural hold to use against the spinning toe hold, which was Dory's signature move. There were a lot of things that Dory could do with the figure four: escape from it, fight against it, block it, or convert it into a spinning toe hold.

Later on in my career, when I started managing, a signature move became a non-issue, but it was a very big issue when I got my break in the Maritimes.

That summer was the most memorable time of my career, because it was the first time that someone had given me an opportunity to work on top. I had the satisfaction of knowing that I was living my dream, and I was being pushed as a main eventer in a territory, doing a program that had been my idea. I worked very hard and capitalized on the opportunity, and I think people looked at my run as a success. Personally, I have a great feeling of satisfaction about what I accomplished there.

I would be remiss if I didn't take this opportunity to thank the entire Cormier family because they had a lot at stake. They gave me the opportunity to succeed—an opportunity to succeed that would have cost them dearly if I had failed—and we did incredible business that summer.

I had a phenomenal summer and made $23,515 for the 23-week run, at a time when the Canadian dollar was almost par to the American dollar. I even went back for two weeks the following year—June 29 to July 11, 1974—and worked a program on top with the Great Kuma.

# Chapter 8
## West Texas Memories

We had maintained a grueling schedule for the entire summer, and I was physically exhausted, so after driving home to Pottstown, Pennsylvania, I took two weeks off. Before making my debut in Amarillo, I made some shots in the Charlotte and Georgia territories. One of my most notable matches was in Atlanta on October 27, 1973, against NWA world heavyweight champion Jack Brisco. He had won the title from Harley Race on July 20 in Houston, Texas.

The whole Maritimes experience did wonders for my confidence and self-esteem. It gave me the confidence I needed when I went to my next territory—Amarillo, Texas.

While the Maritimes was memorable in regards to launching my career, Amarillo was the territory I remember as being the most enjoyable. I enjoyed my summer in the Maritimes, but working on top was new to me, and I had a lot to learn, so it was very hard work.

My first match in the Amarillo territory was on November 1, 1973. The caliber of talent in Amarillo was outstanding from the top of the card to the very bottom—Ciclon Negro, Nick and Jerry Kozak, Alex Perez, Killer Karl Kox, and Karl von Steiger. They were all just fantastic athletes and performers. Even the Beast, Leo Burke, and Killer Karl Krupp came in for a few weeks. I met Andre the Giant for the first time while I was in Amarillo.

During my career, I met most of the big names in the business, and many of them came through Amarillo. I had heard so much about Lou Thesz, perhaps the most widely-recognized NWA world heavyweight champion of all time. The first time I met him, he was brought into Amarillo as a special referee for a match between Dick Murdoch and me. When I put a short arm scissors on Murdoch, Thesz sidled up to us and said, *"Kid, that used to be my specialty."* It was part of the casual conversation that occasionally happens in the course of a match, but it was memorable because it was the first time I had the opportunity to meet the legendary Lou Thesz.

We wrestled on the Amarillo house show on Thursday night, then went to the studio to do promos on Friday morning. We had plenty of time to get to Lubbock for the Friday night house show because it was only a 100-mile trip from Amarillo.

The Saturday morning TV taping in Amarillo was

Jim Dillon in Amarillo

handled much like the taping in Charlotte. The only guys who got paid for TV were the guys who did jobs. If you worked on top on TV, that was your opportunity to promote yourself. You didn't get paid for promos, either.

The Funks would have somebody personally deliver the tape to the studio in Albuquerque. Albuquerque was the only town where you would go to the studio and do your promos live. The promos for every other town were inserted into the tapes between the matches, but in Albuquerque, we would do the cut-ins live in the studio with Mike London, the local promoter. We would sit in the studio and watch the show (that had been recorded in Amarillo) as it aired in Albuquerque. If there were any local commercials, they were few, so we went out during the breaks between the matches and cut our live promos.

Mike London was a strange character. You could be right in the middle of a monologue, and he would suddenly break your chain of thought by asking you a stupid question.

Nobody could *ever* accuse London of being a high-pressure announcer, either. When he gave information on how to get tickets, he would read in a monotone, with no expression or excitement in his voice. *"Tonight at the Civic Auditorium, so-and-so against so-and-so, so-and-so against so-and-so. Opening bell at 7:15. Tickets on sale at the end of this broadcast."*

That was the extent of his promotional skills on the mic.

Other than the live TV promos, which were aired on Sunday morning, London did no publicity leading up to the house matches on Sunday night. And yet, he had the biggest drawing town in the territory. I don't know if the success of the town was due to Mike London's style of promoting, but whatever it was, it worked for him. The city of Amarillo may have had 125,000 people in 1974. I don't know what the population of Albuquerque was, but it was a much bigger town than Amarillo, and it was a hot town for wrestling.

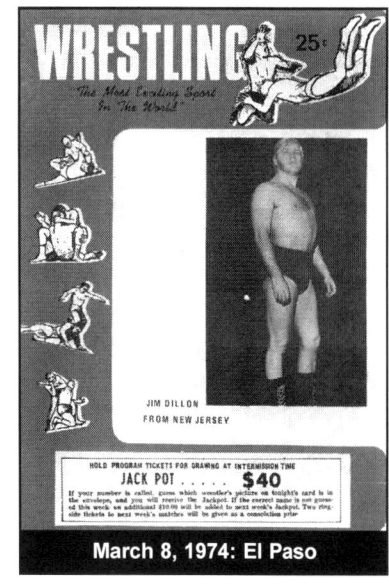

March 8, 1974: El Paso

We would be worn out when we arrived in Albuquerque on Sunday morning. The Amarillo TV taping was held on Saturday morning. That night, you were booked in either Colorado Springs or Pueblo, a drive of 310 and 290 miles, respectively. When the show was over, you made a 325 to 340-mile trip to Albuquerque. If you were lucky, you got in around four in the morning, but most of the time, it was five or six o'clock. A good day's sleep wasn't an option. You had to be at the studio by nine o'clock to do the promos for that night's show.

There were a lot of Mexicans and Indians who watched the show in Albuquerque. Ricky Romero was a huge star in Albuquerque, New Mexico, more so than anywhere else in the territory. He had name value in places like Amarillo and Lubbock, but he had been there so long that he didn't mean as much as he did at one time. In Albuquerque, though, the native American people related to him.

I was booked to wrestle Romero one night, so during my promo, I started to talk about riding to the studio that morning, and how I almost didn't get there.

*"On the way to the studio this morning, one of the wheels fell off my limousine. A mechanic jacked the limo up and said it was a wheel bearing. Can you imagine what*

**WRESTLING TONIGHT** . 8 P.M.
**DOUBLE MAIN EVENT**
THE WINNER TO MEET WORLD'S CHAMPION JACK BRISCOE IN ABILENE, JUNE 28.

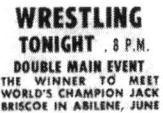

**TERRY FUNK**
—vs—
**JIM DILLON**

SPECIAL REFEREE,
**BOB MILBURN,**
SPORTS EDITOR OF SAN ANGELO STANDARD-TIMES.

**BLACK JACK MULLIGAN**
6'6", 320 LBS.
—vs—
**DORY FUNK JR.**

**GIRLS! GIRLS! GIRLS!**

TEXAS LADIES' CHAMPIONSHIP
**MARIE LAVERNE**
—vs—
**KAY NOBLE**

**THE LAWMAN**
—vs—
**VICTOR VARGA**

**AKIO SATO**
—vs—
**ALEX PEREZ**

**SAN ANGELO COLISEUM**
LAKEVIEW DRUG
2934 N. CHADBOURNE
PHONE 653-3321
Ringside ............... 3.00
Gen. Adm. ............. 2.50
Kids 3-11 ............... 1.00

**July 21, 1974**

it's like to find parts for a car on a Sunday morning? The guy who owned a parts store happened to stop by. He said, 'I have a wheel bearing, but I don't have any grease to put on it.' A bunch of Mexican kids were standing around watching, so I grabbed one of 'em by the neck and rubbed the bearing through his hair several times. That bearing slipped right onto the wheel after that. And now, here I am on time!"

You would have thought that I had insulted the president of Mexico! I thought I was being a smart ass, but the ensuing backlash from the audience resulted in the station manager threatening to cancel the show. The following week, I had to go on the air and publicly apologize.

There are so many memories of that territory, like on May 25, 1974, when I was legitimately knocked out while wrestling Terry Funk in Albuquerque.

Except for the luchas [Mexican wrestlers], most people here, in Japan, and in Europe, all worked from the right side. In other words, you always worked on the left arm, and punches were always thrown right-handed. I suppose it's because most people are right-handed, so you always worked from that side, rather than taking an arm bar with the right hand, which someone normally throws a punch with, or writes with.

Terry Funk, on the other hand, was naturally left-handed. I don't know if he wasn't thinking about what he was doing, or didn't anticipate what he was going to do until the last second, but I remember coming off the ropes in some kind of a spot. When I did, Terry hit me with a big forearm smash to the chest—and he threw it left-handed. Terry, of course, is a big, burly guy. His forearm caught me right across the heart. The shock of it knocked me out for two or three seconds. It was a momentary thing, but I was unconscious for that brief time. That was the only time in my career when I was legitimately knocked out.

In San Angelo, Texas, Bob Milburn, the sports editor of the *San Angelo Standard Times*, wrote a column that knocked wrestling. He basically said that anybody who watches wrestling was a fool and an idiot. Terry Funk called him to task. *"I challenge you to come down and referee a professional wrestling match. Then, when it's all over, you can write anything you want."*

When Milburn took Terry up on his offer, Terry booked himself against me in the main event for June 21, 1974. Terry told me ahead of time, *"We can't talk in the ring. We can't say ANYTHING! We're going to have to be much more careful than we normally are."*

That wasn't going to be a problem. Wrestling is like dancing. We had both been around for a long time, so we didn't have to talk. Even with the referee standing right in front of us, there were subtle ways we could communicate with each other.

Before the match started, I stood toe-to-toe with Milburn and said, *"I don't like what you wrote about us, but I respect you because you're the referee. I won't touch you, but don't lay your hands on me, either. When Terry's shoulders are down, I expect you to count to three, and I don't want to hear any bullsh—!"*

Terry and I had a knock-down, drag-out match and we both bled.

The next morning, the original, negative article became a positive when Milburn retracted what he had said earlier. He wrote an article that was unbelievable. He wrote, *"I was WRONG! I was in the ring with them. I SAW! I HEARD! I FELT!"* As proof, our attendance picked up the following week and several people told us that they came because of his retraction.

Stan Hansen was just breaking into the business. He was a big boy. When he started wrestling, he already had bad knees from playing football at West Texas State University. Stan was also deaf in one ear, and he couldn't always understand you when you talked to him.

I worked with him many times. He would hurt you in the process of locking up. It got to where I would tell him, *"Don't do anything unless I tell you to do it."* I told him that out of self-preservation. I didn't want him to do something on his own and hurt me.

Stan tried out for the World Football League's Detroit Wheels and got invited to camp, so we had a big sendoff for him on the Amarillo TV show, wishing him well on his venture to the new, successful franchise. Stan went to training camp, got hurt during the first week, and they immediately sent him home. The next week, when Stan returned to Amarillo, announcer Steve Stack said, *"Joining us today is the former star of the Detroit Wheels ... Stan Hansen!"*

Then he blindsided Stan by asking him, *"What can you tell us about your storied football career?"*, and shoved the microphone in his face. Stan was mortified. There was a deathly silence for about five seconds, and then Stan stormed out of the studio. I'm glad I wasn't the first person in front of him because I think he wanted to kill somebody. Terry Funk had orchestrated the whole thing. We were all backstage on the floor, laughing so hard that tears were rolling down our faces.

Ted DiBiase had his first professional match with me. He was well known because his father, "Iron" Mike DiBiase, was a wrestling legend in the area. Ted was going to West Texas State University at the time and was the special referee for one of my matches. I punched him and we set up a match for June 7, 1974, in Abilene, where he would make his debut. I teamed with the Patriots (Bobby Hart and Bob Griffin) to take on Ted, Terry Funk, and Dick Murdoch. One week later, again in Abilene, Ted and I met in a singles match.

One night in Abilene, I did something underhanded, so Terry Funk came in to help my opponent. If you're a wrestling fan, you probably know that Terry does things that are a little bit off-the-wall. He brought a 50-gallon, metal drum to the ring and heaved it over the top rope. He came into the ring, nailed me, picked the barrel up, and turned it upside down over my head. He actually knocked me down and stomped on the can, smashing a big dent into the side. When I finally wriggled out, I had tiny flakes of rust all through my hair, in my ears, and in my eyes.

Karl Kox was watching the whole thing. Five nights later, we were in Lubbock, and Kox was scheduled to do a run-in on me. He did the same thing that Terry did. He picked up a trash can and brought it into the ring.

That gave me an idea. I said to Kox, *"Why don't we have a trash can match? We can put trash cans behind the ringside seats. The only way the match can be settled*

## 60 • "Wrestlers Are Like Seagulls"

*is when one man picks his opponent up, carries him to the back, and physically dumps him into the trash can."*

That was right down Kox's alley, so that's what we did.

The following week, before the matches started, Kox came out and cut a promo for our match. *"Last week, I took that trash can and I put Jim Dillon in there, and that's right where he belongs! He's at home in that trash can with all his friends. But there was one thing missing. There was no trash! I want you women with babies to take their dirty diapers and put 'em in that trash can! You guys who are dippin'! Don't throw your spit down the toilet. Put it in that trash can!"*

When it was time for the main event, not only was the trash can filled and overflowing, but a 6-foot area of the floor surrounding the can was littered with everything you could possibly imagine.

Of course, when Kox got into the ring, he said, *"You're going back in the trash can, pal! You'll be right where you belong—with all the garbage!"*

The match itself was insignificant. It didn't mean anything, because no matter what we did in the ring, the fans knew that the match would not end until someone was in that trash can. What was the sense of trying to pin each other?

Kox used a move called the brainbuster. He made it look like he dropped you right on the top of your head. It looked devastating. It scared my parents when they saw him use it on me. They were really worried that I would be paralyzed from the impact.

Sometime during the match, Kox picked me up, gave me the brainbuster, and I sold being out cold. He really had to struggle to haul me to the ring apron because I was dead weight. He jumped down to the arena floor and picked me up over his shoulder, like a fireman's carry. My head was hanging to his rear.

Kox took his time, because he wanted to give the people a logical time frame for my recovery. As he carried me up the aisle, with my legs in the front, he staggered. At that point, I started to come to. The fans could see me shaking the cobwebs loose, but Kox couldn't because he was looking towards the trash cans. When he got to the trash cans, he set me down on my feet and tried to manipulate me into the can. As he did, I reached into my tights, pulled out a pair of brass knuckles, whacked him one time, then scoop slammed him head first into the trash can.

Kox and the trash can both fell over. I picked up the trash can, dumped the contents on top of Kox, and staggered back to the dressing room. Just before I went into the dressing room, I turned around and saw Kox sitting on the floor with a banana peel draped over the top of his head. I don't know how he managed to get that banana peel to stay there when he sat up,

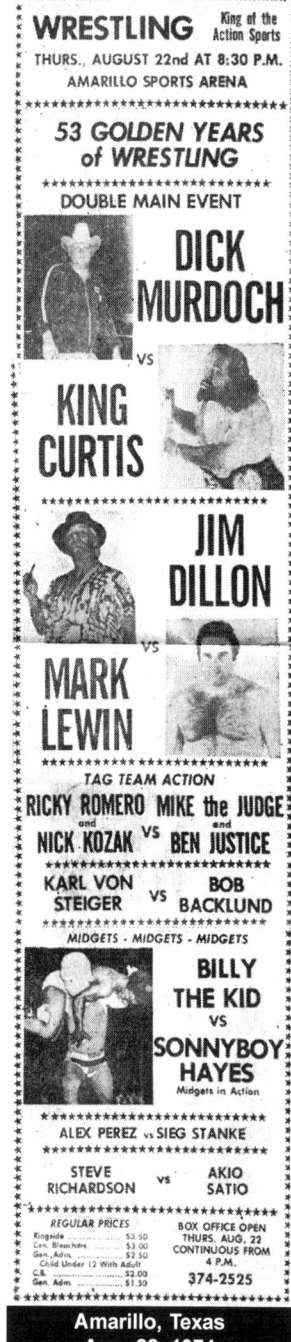

but what a worker he was. He had tobacco juice running down the side of his bald head, and he was sitting in every type of garbage that you can imagine. To top it all off, the fans were saying, *"Killer! We're sorry!"* They were apologizing for the disgusting things they put into the trash can.

Killer Karl Kox was such a great character. I'm not taking anything away from Mick Foley, because nothing is original, but when I saw Mick Foley talking to Mr. Socko, I immediately thought, *"That's what Karl Kox used to do."*

Only Karl wasn't talking to his hand. In the early '70s, Karl Kox was talking to Alex—his imaginary friend—who sat in the rafters. The people would actually look up into the rafters and think, *"That man is crazy."*

That was a good example of the saying, *"Nothing is original in the wrestling business."* Dick Slater was very successful, but he was a clone of Terry Funk. There were a lot of people who took ideas from others. If they were smart, they developed their own style by using bits and pieces of many different people—names, monikers, and signature moves. But *everything* has been done somewhere or someplace.

Kox and Dick Murdoch bought a Volkswagen van together. They were going to use it for trips to towns. It was economical and they could make a little trans money from the boys they took along with them. They slowly came to the realization that it was a bad choice for a vehicle. In a front-engine Volkswagen van, you can only go so fast. In fact, if you were fighting a headwind, you would lose speed. The heater wouldn't work, either, so it was cold in the winter.

We used to bring souvenirs across the US-Mexican border from Juarez, Mexico, to El Paso. There was a hand-blown glass factory where you could observe items being made. Some of the items were nice, some were junk. It all depended on your individual taste. We bought "authentic" sombreros, leather jackets, hats, boots, and hand-painted pictures on velvet (everything from pictures of Elvis to naked women). Liquor was very cheap in Mexico and you could bring back one liter every thirty days. With a van load of the boys, you would be amazed at just how much "junk" we bought in Mexico. As with anything, one man's junk is another man's treasure. We would keep the items in our hotel rooms at the El Paso Airport Holiday Inn until we were ready to leave for Odessa on Tuesday.

On one particular day, we were all cold, so someone said, *"Look, there's no heater in this thing and it won't go faster than 45 mph. Why don't you just torch it? That way, your insurance will pay for it and we can rent a car. Otherwise, we're gonna freeze to death in this van before we get home."*

We stopped at a motel in Odessa, took out everything of value, and put it all into our room. We drove the van to the building where we wrestled in Odessa. Kox crawled underneath the van, unscrewed a fuel line, and got a cup of gas. He reattached the fuel line, opened the engine hatch, and threw the gas onto the engine.

For the next twenty minutes, he stood in front of the van, striking matches. Try as he might, he couldn't make it ignite—and it never did.

We had to go back to the hotel after the matches, load all of our stuff back into the van, and drive the 235 miles back to Amarillo at 45 mph. We still had no heat, and we were stinking and saturated with the smell of gasoline.

One of the things that I loved about the Amarillo territory was that the talent was constantly thinking about angles and ideas. There were times when we had to fly by the seat of our pants, but we tried new things from week to week. Many of them worked and were successful.

*"What can we do next week?"*

*"How can we get another week out of this program?"*

Dick Murdoch and I worked together so often that we would always ask, *"What are we going to do this week?"*

Occasionally, when the babyface makes a big comeback and kicks the heel's ass, the heel takes a walk and gets counted out. The natural thing was to come back the next week with a lumberjack match, followed by a cage match. Dickie and I wanted to do something that accomplished the same thing, but with a different twist.

A lot of Murdoch's buddies were calf-ropers. The week after I got counted out, Dickie said, *"I'm gonna kick Dillon's butt next Thursday night. If he tries to walk, one of my championship calf-ropin' buddies will be waitin' for him at each of the four aisles. He'll hog tie Dillon and bring him back to me, all trussed up like a Thanksgiving turkey."*

I liked the idea. I just didn't trust his buddies. Not that they would intentionally hurt me, but they were all marks [diehard fans who take wrestling very seriously], and I was horrified to think that they could rope me, take my legs out from under me, and drag me up the aisle, while the fans kicked the hell out of me as I slid past them.

Dickie had it all figured out. He picked the least confident of the group and told me to not worry. *"He'll be more scared of you than you are of him. I'll be there and I'll tell him to just throw the rope over you and cinch it up. Then I'll walk over and drag you back."*

That would give the audience what we advertised, but in a somewhat controlled environment that wouldn't get me killed.

Before the match started, I walked down the aisle, got within a foot of each guy, and said, *"Look, I'm not afraid of you. If I decide that I want to take a walk, then you'd better be somewhere else. Get my gist?"*

At the opportune time, Dickie made his big comeback on me. I was bleeding as I staggered up the aisle and walked past the calf roper we had chosen to use. Dickie came up from behind, nailed me, and the guy threw the rope over me. Dickie carried me back to the ring and we went to the finish.

That was one of the many storylines that were unique to West Texas.

I could talk about Dickie Murdoch all day long. Dickie was a couple of inches taller than me and he weighed 280 pounds. I was just 225 and all mouth, and yet I could talk about him being a redneck, driving a pickup truck, and how tobacco juice stained the corners of his mouth. Again, I made fun of Dick Murdoch, and not the fans. It was important that you didn't run down the people, or belittle them, because they were buying the tickets. You could get quality heat by running Dickie down for all those character traits, and let the people make the association. In essence, I was running them down, even though I never said so directly. That formula worked for me throughout my career. That gave Dickie an opportunity to do a promo and say, *"Hey, I'm proud to be a redneck."* That was true. Dickie personified those traits.

Terry Funk, Dory Funk, Tully Blanchard, Ted DiBiase, Dusty Rhodes, Barry Windham, Stan Hansen, Bruiser Brody, Manny Fernandez, Tito Santana, and Bobby Duncum all went to West Texas State University. Dickie Murdoch never went to West Texas State, but he told everyone that he did, and nobody ever called him on it.

One time, Dickie came to the ring accompanied by West Texas State football cheerleaders. They did a *"Dickie, Dickie, he's our man"* chant up and down the aisle with their pom-poms, and then parted as Dickie walked through. I liked the idea, so I talked to Terry Funk about me getting my own cheering squad. Terry jumped right on it. *"Ooooh! Great idea! We'll hire a band, too."*

The next week, I went on television and said, *"I've seen goats that were better looking than Murdoch's girls. I was a hero at Trenton Central High School, and I'm going to fly in the entire cheerleading squad, plus the school band."*

Later in the week, I ask Terry if he had the band lined up. Terry said, *"Well ... not* yet. *Do you have any idea what it costs for something like that?"*

I didn't know, and I really didn't care. All I knew was that I had already done the interview. I had put my foot in my mouth by telling everyone that I would have a band. Now Terry was telling me that he doesn't have the budget to hire a band!

As it worked out, my parents were in Amarillo for the week and were coming to see me wrestle that night. My mother and father were always very supportive throughout my career. They would come see me once or twice a year.

So what was I going to do about the band? Bob Griffin's wife offered to help me and we found a pan, a spoon, and some garbage pail lids. On the night of the match, I went out to the ring and said, *"The jet that I personally chartered, with the band and all of my cheerleaders, left Trenton early today. But someone called in a bomb threat and the flight was diverted to Newfoundland. I blame Dick Murdoch and the Funks for trying to embarrass me! But I'm not about to be undone, so I got on the phone and put together a new band!"*

At that point, my mother and a couple of the boys' wives came out banging on pots and pans with spoons.

That was just one of the memories I have of the fun we had. There are so many more.

Bobby Hart and Bob Griffin were in Amarillo, wrestling under masks as the Patriots. They were managed by Percival A. Friend. We made a trip together one night. When we arrived in Odessa, we pulled up to a restaurant. As we were getting out of the car, I saw a goat walking around. A few minutes after we were seated in the restaurant, I said, *"I left my wallet in your car,"* so Percival gave me his keys.

I went outside, caught the goat, put it in the car, closed the door, and went back into the restaurant. After we finished eating, we walked out. As Percival walked to the car, he said, *"Well, look at that. Somebody played a joke on me and put a dog in my car."*

As we got closer, he yelled, *"That's no dog. It's a goat!"*

When Percival opened the door, the goat jumped out, but he left quite a few presents behind. He had crapped all over the car and left hundreds of tiny pellets.

I started 1974 off by going to Japan for a month. To explain my absence, the Funks booked Dick Murdoch and me in a chain match on December 13, 1973. Murdoch took one end of the chain, wrapped it around my head, and leaped off the top turnbuckle with the chain on my head. The announcers told the fans that he had broken my jaw.

Percival A. Friend

Before I left the arena that night, I rubbed my cheek with a wet towel to scrape off the first two layers of skin, and then I stuffed tissue into my mouth to make it look swollen. It didn't hurt at the time, but it did the next morning.

When I started wrestling, I set several goals for myself, the overall goal being to work in every state in the United States. But I also had three specific goals. I wanted to wrestle in three places—Japan, Australia, and Madison Square Garden.

I achieved one of those goals in January 1974 when I made my first tour of Japan.

In 1961, I saw Shohei "Giant" Baba wrestle in New York. Thirteen years later, he was the owner of the All-Japan Wrestling Alliance promotion, and he wanted me to wrestle for him.

Baba had a great roster of talent, both native Japanese and American wrestlers. The American wrestlers on that tour were Dick Beyer (who wrestled as the masked Sensational, Intelligent Destroyer), Jerry Brisco, Harley Race, Dory Funk, and Terry

Funk. Since Americans were the foreigners in Japan, we were always considered to be the heels. The one exception to that was Dick Beyer, the Destroyer, who had become somewhat of a cult figure in Japan.

I can't remember if I had met Harley prior to that trip, but I teamed up with him in Nagoya. When it came to taking bumps, people compared me to Harley. Harley was classic in every bump he took in terms of always landing perfectly. I was, too, if for no reason other than self-preservation. I was always very careful about protecting myself when I fell.

The Japanese wrestlers were Masio Koma, Thunder Sugiyama, Mitsu Hirai, Motoshi Okuma, and Akio Sato. Even more noteworthy than the active Japanese wrestlers were two young boys who I met while on the tour.

Tomomi "Jumbo" Tsuruta, who would become a big name in Japan, was just getting started. "Tommy" placed seventh in the Super Heavyweight division at the 1972 Munich Olympics. As a pro, he became the first Triple Crown heavyweight champion (unifying the Pacific Wrestling Federation, All-Japan United National, and All-Japan International titles) in 1989, and was a former A.W.A. world heavyweight champion (defeating Nick Bockwinkel) in 1984. Many people refer to him as the "Japanese Ric Flair."

The second boy was Atsushi Onita. Onita was one of the young boys who packed Baba's bags, and scrubbed Baba's back in the baths every night. On August 4, 1990, Onita became a cult-figure in Japanese wrestling history when he pushed the limits of extreme wrestling stipulations. He wrestled against Tarzan Goto in the first No-Ropes, Barbed-Wire, Electrical, Explosives Death Match.

I am such a big fan of Japanese wrestling. If there was one wrestler that I wish I could have met, it would have to be Rikidozan. I met legends like Baba and Antonio Inoki, but Rikidozan was the father of professional wrestling in Japan.

Rikidozan, whose real name was Kim Shinraku, was born in Korea. In the '50s, the Japanese hated the Koreans, so Rikidozan passed himself off as Japanese and called himself Mitsuhiro Momota. As a sumo wrestler, he should have been promoted to the rank of Grand Champion, or Yokozuna, but he wasn't—probably due to his origins—so he left sumo and started wrestling in 1951.

Rikidozan became a mainstream celebrity in Japan, with high profile matches against the tag team of Mike and Ben Sharpe, and a match against NWA world heavyweight champion, Lou Thesz, before 27,000 fans at Korakuen Baseball Stadium. The match with Thesz drew an 87.0 rating, the highest TV rating pro wrestling is believed to have done anywhere in the world, even to this day. By contrast, on February 28, 1983, the final episode of *M\*A\*S\*H*, which is the highest-rated program ever in the U.S., did a 60.2 rating. The famous *Who Shot J.R.?* episode of *Dallas* on November 21, 1980, *only* did a 53.3.

On December 8, 1963, Rikidozan was stabbed in an Akasaka night club, in what was purported to be a gangland hit. Two mob gangs were fighting for control of the pro wrestling promotion in Japan, and Rikidozan was aligned with one of them. Legend has it that his assailant, Katsuji Murata, a major figure in the opposing mob family, urinated on his knife before using it on Rikidozan, in the hopes that it would cause an infection. After being stabbed, Rikidozan beat up Katsuji and threw him out of the club. He failed to get immediate medical attention and contracted peritonitis. He had to undergo major surgery, but died on December 15, 1963, from complications.

I met two of his sons—Yoshi Momoto, a ring announcer who wrestled later on, and young Riki, who also wrestled, but wasn't very big. I wrestled both of them during subsequent tours of Japan.

I always wondered what it would have been like to meet Rikidozan. To this day, they revere him in Japan.

When I returned to Amarillo on January 31, 1974, I snuck into the arena through the back door with a towel over my head. I didn't want the fans to see me because I wanted my appearance to be a surprise. At an opportune time during Murdoch's match, I barged into the ring and pearl harbored him. (In wrestling, to "pearl harbor" your opponent means to sneak up and attack him from behind.)

Jim Dillon was back in Amarillo—and we were off and running again.

On October 14, 1974, Mike Dubois, Greg Watson (the son of the legendary Whipper Billy Watson), and I were booked in El Paso against Ricky Romero, Dory Funk, and El Santo. They wanted me to drop the fall to El Santo. I hate to admit this, but I pitched a fit. Looking back, I can only explain that this was during my learning curve time in the business. I had been working a program on top with Murdoch, and I had worked with Romero in towns like El Paso, so I could understand the logic of dropping the fall to Romero, who I had been programmed with. But why should I lose to this El Santo guy, who was just coming in for a short time? Not only that, but he looked so tiny and frail. What was that going to do for my credibility?

I remember them giving me the finish. *"Romero will slam you in position and he'll tag out with Santo. Santo will climb up onto the top turnbuckle and do a diving headbutt onto your midsection, then he'll roll across and get the pin. Whatever you do, don't let Santo miss. If you have to catch his head and pull him in, do it. Just don't let him break his neck in this town!"*

I remember thinking, *"Ugh! Not only do I have to drop the fall to this guy, I've gotta worry about catching him so that he doesn't kill himself."*

I didn't understand what the name "El Santo" meant to the people in that part of the country. I understood later, and came to realize that it was an honor for me to even be in the ring with him. El Santo was like a God to the Mexican people. For me to drop a fall to him would have *no* impact whatsoever on my career. But at the time, I didn't understand it.

El Santo

I did the job that night for El Santo, and I did it to the best of my ability, but for me to complain about it showed the immaturity on my part. Later in life, when guys would question things they were asked to do, I would shake my head in disgust. And then I would remember, *"Hey, you did things like that when you were young, too."*

When you're young in the business, you question the logic of decisions you don't understand, but if you have a little patience, you will usually come to understand the reasoning behind the situation. Nobody's perfect, and I wasn't either, but the times where I said things out of immaturity were few and far between.

I also went to jail when I was in the Amarillo territory. In fact, the only time I ever went to jail was in Juarez, Mexico.

After the matches in Albuquerque, we had a 250-mile trip down to El Paso, one of my favorite towns. I loved to go there. They had a lot of restaurants to choose from. We would get to our motel, the Holiday Inn near the airport, at about one o'clock in the morning. The boys had a deal where they could come in late. The guy at the desk would give us a key to our room and let us wait to check in when we got up the next morning. In essence, they let us stay there for two nights and only charged us for one. They also had a good buffet at the motel, and the boys really took advantage of that.

One night after the matches, Ben Justice, Siegfried Stanke, Karl von Steiger, and I stopped to have a drink before going back to the motel. Ben Justice was not a drinker, but we talked him into drinking a small glass of wine. When he tasted it, he said, *"This tastes good!"* Someone said, *"Let's go across the border!"*

*"Come on, Ben. Do you want to go across the border with us?"*

*"Yeah!"*

We went to a club that had floor shows and we ordered a few drinks. As soon as any of us took a sip of our drink, Justice would reach over, grab it, and chug it. It was like a monster had taken over his personality. I finally said, *"We need to go before we get into some kind of trouble."*

Steiger wanted to stay because he had some kind of drinking competition going with Justice, so Stanke and I left to get something to eat. We went down a narrow side street to one of my favorite hole-in-the-wall restaurants where they made great tenderloin, with crushed garlic and butter, and served it with fresh garlic bread. While we were waiting for our order, Stanke said, *"Maybe I ought to go back and check on those two. I was hoping they'd join us."*

Stanke left and came back about ten minutes later. *"I couldn't drag them out of there. They're in bad shape. One of them never made it to the john, and I think he went under the table."*

Just as the waitress brought our steaks to the table, a policeman walked in. They came right over to our table and stopped. *"Get up, pay your bill, and come with us."* They put us in the back of their patrol car and we headed towards the police station.

As we parked in front of the jail, another car pulled up in front of us, and out staggered Steiger and Justice. They could hardly walk. I was stone-cold sober by this time. As we walked in, Justice whispered, *"How far is it to the border? I think we should make a break for it."*

I said, *"Do whatever they tell you to do and keep your mouth shut."*

They took our wallets and personal items, and walked us into an open-air compound with cells along the perimeter. They herded us into the first cell, which is where they put non-natives. As we walked in, a big guy stood up and said, *"I know who you are! You wrestlers think you're coming in here to take over."*

Steiger threw a punch and knocked the guy on his ass. All of a sudden, the guy became our best friend. He told us that he was a sportswriter for an El Paso newspaper and that he had been there for ten days.

The guards were looking in at us, so I said, *"Will somebody please tell Gory Guerrero that we're in here, and tell him to get us out of here."* Gory was the local promoter in El Paso. Gory has a son, Chavo, who wrestled, and a grandson, Eddie, who still wrestles. I used to see the Guerrero kids almost every Monday night when they were growing up.

One of the guards said, *"If you're in here past midnight, you don't get released until the next morning. You're here for the night."*

Our cell was nothing more than a cold, cement slab. There was no chair, bench, or bed. If you wanted to sit down, you had to sit on the floor. You couldn't lay down because the cell was absolutely filled with prisoners. At night, it got cold, and you were sitting on cold cement. There were several flattened, cardboard boxes strewn across the floor, but the prisoners hoarded them like they were gold.

After you took a leak, you had to pinch a small faucet with your fingers and fill an empty Maxwell House Coffee can with water. When you had enough water in the can, you had to dump it into the toilet to get it to flush.

Every hour, you would hear a whistle as the guards walked around on the four walls. I guess that was the signal that all was well on the hour. We were in there all night, and I didn't sleep a wink.

Just before the sun came up, they brought us a big, open vat filled with some kind of soup. I wasn't going to eat any of it. For all I knew, they killed pigeons and threw them into the pot.

When nobody came to get us by eight o'clock, I began to worry. Eight became nine. Nine became ten. At eleven o'clock, the guy from the El Paso newspaper got released. He told us that he'd get word to people for us. I had the feeling that he was mad at Steiger for punching him, so I wasn't putting any money on him coming through with his promise.

At 11:30 a.m., somebody opened the cell door and motioned for the four of us to come out. We collected our belongings and walked to the main building. There stood Dory Funk and Gory Guerrero. Dory said, *"Keep your mouth shut and walk out the door."*

He didn't have to tell us twice. We walked out, got into Dory's car, and headed for the border.

Dory told us that the club we had been in was owned by the Chief of Police. He had become furious when somebody had taken a leak underneath our table. In all the commotion, his pregnant wife, who was at the club, was knocked down. The Chief of Police was going to make an example of us for, (1) assault on his pregnant wife, (2) insulting a Mexican movie star, who was the emcee, and, (3) a list of trumped-up charges that was a mile long.

Apparently, when Stanke went to check on Justice and Steiger, the police followed him back to the restaurant. Thinking that he had been with Justice and Steiger the whole time, they arrested him. I don't know why they arrested me. I suppose I was guilty by association.

It cost the Funks $500 to buy our way out. I was in the main event in Odessa that night, so Dory took us to the airport and bought us plane tickets to Odessa. Ben Justice stayed in El Paso and drove my car back to Amarillo.

That's a story that I will never forget. Even if I did, Dory would remind me about it. He still jokes about getting me out of jail that night. In fact, he has something about it on his website.

Abilene was our Friday night town. It was a horrible 250-mile trip each way with virtually no house, but we had to go there. The first year I was there, for whatever reason, there was a group of people from Dice Air Force Base who took a liking to me. That may not seem to be out of the ordinary to fans today, because it has become somewhat cool to cheer the heels, but in those days, the people always cheered the babyface and booed the heel.

These, however, weren't conventional fans. It started out with a small number of military personnel, and grew until they filled a whole section of seats. It got out of hand when some of the locals tried to run them down with their pickup trucks, and shot over their heads. It became a dangerous situation, but the interaction with the fans was one of those spontaneous things that you couldn't have planned. It just happened, so you ran with it.

I began to acknowledge them each week on television, which helped the number grow and kept them coming back. I would talk about how the promoter wouldn't treat me right. One night, I decided to stage a protest, so I asked the entire section to come up and we marched up the aisle of the Taylor County Coliseum.

On the way back to the ring, someone in the group reached out and thumped me on the back of my head with his knuckle. It really hurt! I didn't know which one it was, but I thought to myself, *"You stupid idiot. You asked for it when you invited these marks out."*

The matches in Abilene were held on a huge basketball court. The fans would walk back to where a rope cordoned off the dressing room area. The dressing rooms were in the corners of the building—heels on one side, babies on the other. To get to the dressing room itself, you walked through one door for about ten feet, then through a second door.

Normally, when I came in after a match, I would take my trunks off first, and then I would unlace my boots. One night, I heard a loud rumbling noise coming from the arena. I was unlacing my boots and didn't think anything about it. All of a sudden, I heard the first door opening. Then the inside door opened. There stood Dory Funk, Terry Funk, and Dick Murdoch—babyfaces in the heels' dressing room.

The fans egged them on after they ran me off at the end of our match. *"Go back into the dressing room and get him!"* So, that's what they did. The fans stopped at the ropes, but Murdoch and the Funks marched right back to my dressing room.

By the time they walked in, I was stark naked, except for one sock. Dory was the last one in. Terry started walking around a long table on one side of me. Murdoch started walking around the other side. Dory said, *"Guys! What are you doing? No, guys. I know what you're thinking. You can't do this! You'll kill the town!"*

Finally, he gave in. *"Oh, what the hell."*

They grabbed me, still stark naked, carried me through the first door, through the second door, and threw me across the floor. I was still sweaty and wet from my match, so I slid along the parquet floor. When I looked up, the whole arena was staring at me. I just stood up, turned around, and walked back through the doorway.

Art Nelson booked Amarillo during one of my runs there. He got really angry with Don "The Lawman" Slatton, who promoted Abilene. I think Don is still a bail bondsman in Abilene. He was well-connected locally. Art was angry because the office had sent posters to Abilene, and they found them laying in the back of Lawman's truck. *"No wonder that town can't draw!"* yelled Art. *"The lazy sonofabitch didn't get the posters out."*

I said, *"Art, if you want me to cut a promo on Lawman this week, I'll do it."*

"Cut a promo" means to talk derisively about someone (usually your opponent) on television.

Art said, *"Go for it."*

I knew that the Lawman's wife collected dolls and dressed them up, so that gave me a subject to talk about. I said, *"Do you people think the Lawman's tough? I went by his house the other night to call him out. I yelled and yelled, but nobody would come out, so I went up to the house to see if anybody was home. When I looked in the window, there was a room full of dolls. There were dolls everywhere! Every size, every shape. And there's the Lawman, Don Slatton, wearing a frilly apron. His wife was standing there saying 'Now, Donald. I want you to take the dress off this one and put it on this one!'"* It was one of those promos you do to entertain yourself.

Don Slatton

I had never met Slatton's wife and I didn't have a clue as to what she looked like. Unbeknownst to me, she didn't see the humor in my interview. She was afraid that people, knowing about her valuable collection of dolls, would break into their home. Of course, Slatton called and complained, but Art stood up for me.

The following week, I went to Abilene. As I was waving to my Air Force base contingent, a woman stood up in the front row and dumped a bucket of water over my head. For the first time in my life, I came very close to punching a woman.

Luckily, I didn't. It was the Lawman's wife.

Unless you're someone like a Ricky Romero, or a Dick Murdoch, it was very hard to stay in a territory for more than a year when you work week after week. It was especially tough if you were a heel. I was very, very fortunate. Except for the four weeks I spent in Japan, I worked in Amarillo from November 1973 until December 1974.

On December 12, 1974, I made my last shot in the town of Amarillo before leaving for the Christmas holidays and a January tour of Japan. I worked with Killer Karl Kox in a cage match. He ended the match by dropping me with a brainbuster. Black Jack Mulligan had just come into the territory, so to get him involved, they interjected him into our match. Mulligan walked down the aisle, ripped the door off the cage, took a bottle of black ink out of his tights, and threw it into Kox's eyes.

I had blood all over me, so I left the ring first, with Mulligan walking behind me. From the bleachers to our left, someone with a cowboy hat pulled down over his eyes came running towards us at full tilt. He ran right by me, as if I wasn't there, launched himself into the air, and hit Mulligan with a dropkick.

Blackjack Mulligan

It all happened so fast. I didn't know if the guy had a knife or something, so as I turned around, I was in self-preservation mode. I started to kick at him. I never got anywhere near him, but I was kicking away.

Mulligan is a huge man. At the time, he stood 6-foot-9 and weighed 340 pounds, so the guy's boots only got high enough to hit Mulligan on his belt buckle. The guy fell onto the concrete floor on his back.

Mulligan reached down, grabbed him by his neck with one hand, and his belt with the other. He picked him straight up into the air over his head — and slammed him down onto the concrete floor. Mulligan picked him up again — and slammed him again.

The guy laid on the floor, motionless, with blood trickling out of both ears.

Someone finally said, *"That's enough! You guys get back to the dressing room!"*

Mulligan stepped over the guy and we went back to the dressing room as we were told.

The mark turned out to be a 17-year-old kid whose father was very well-known—and well-connected—in town. He had a *lot* of money, too.

On December 16, Jeanette and I went home to Pottstown, Pennsylvania, for the Christmas holidays. While I was there, I got a call from Dory, who told me that the kid was going to sue Mulligan and me. I never touched the kid, but the story had taken on a life of its' own, as stories usually did whenever we got involved in a fracas with the fans. The kid claimed that Mulligan had beat him up, then I had kicked him when he was down.

It had the potential to be a huge lawsuit, so Dory said, *"Maybe after Japan, you shouldn't come back to Amarillo."*

I was originally scheduled to stay in Amarillo for one more month after Japan and do blowoffs, after which time Dory had me booked to wrestle in Florida beginning in March. Dory said, *"When you come back from Japan, it wouldn't be a good idea to come through town, even to pick up your trailer. Just go directly to Florida and have somebody else do it."*

I took Dory's advice. I stayed in Pennsylvania for the holidays, then left for my second tour of Japan. Bob Backlund, Bulldog Bob Brown, Red Bastien, Harley Race, and Anton Geesink were also on that tour. Geesink was the first non-Japanese to win the World Judo championship. As a pro wrestler, he wore a judo gee when he worked. The Japanese people loved him because of his judo background, but he was a horrible worker.

## 70 • "Wrestlers Are Like Seagulls"

Halfway through the tour, the two "Bobs" and I made a trip to Okinawa and wrestled there four times. On the way to Okinawa, we wrestled on a small island off the tip of Okinawa called Okinoerabu. There were no major industries on Okinoerabu, and it wasn't the kind of place that tourists and businessmen normally visited, so when we arrived, the natives of the island came out of their homes and gawked at us.

Joe Higuchi, who was the wrestling office-appointed referee/interpreter/babysitter for the American wrestlers, took good care of us, but the guys used to drive him crazy. The poor guy. It was a thankless job. Some of the guys would whine constantly — *"Joe, I need this. Joe, I need that"* — so I didn't bother him unless I absolutely needed something.

Joe knew that I really liked Japan, so when we would go to a town, I would ask Joe, *"Is there anything of particular interest in this town that I should see?"* He would tell me about the parks, the shrines, or anything of particular interest. He would get me maps and directions, or call a cab for me, and I would visit whatever sights I could.

One example was Hiroshima, which has a huge park commemorating where the bomb was dropped. Nagasaki, on the other hand, only has one statue to commemorate the event, but I went to both of them.

Joe caught our interest when he told us a story about the mongoose and the habu snake. On that particular island, the natives were famous for promoting fights between the mongooses and snakes. They didn't have cobras on the island, but they had an indigenous, poisonous snake called the habu (pronounced "hahboo"). Of course, once Joe told us about the fights, we had to see one, so he made arrangements for a taxi ride to the other side of the island.

I was amazed that Joe was able to communicate with the taxi driver. There are so many different dialects in Japan, but Joe managed to let him know where we wanted to go. After driving for twenty-five minutes through the jungle on bad roads, I began to wonder if the driver had really understood Joe. All of a sudden, we pulled into a clearing in the middle of nowhere.

Article from a Japanese wrestling magazine

We walked into a small arena that had a plastic enclosure—about six feet long, six feet wide, and four feet high—in the center, with a sliding partition like a guillotine. Along the perimeter of the arena, on all four sides, were three rows of bleachers. There was also a display that featured jars of mongooses, cobras, and habu snakes in formaldehyde.

A Japanese man walked out, but he didn't speak English. We did the best we could to make ourselves understood, until he finally shook his head. There were no fights scheduled for that afternoon. He must have realized that we had gone out of our way to see it, so he offered to give us our own private showing.

After putting a mongoose into one end of the enclosure, he pulled a habu snake from a cage. Since mongooses were hard to come by on the island, and snakes were plentiful, he didn't want to take a chance of the habu getting lucky and nailing his mongoose, so he milked the snake while we watched.

When he put the snake into the other side of the enclosure, the mongoose immediately began gnawing at the plastic partition, trying to get through to the snake. When the man pulled the rope that lifted the partition, the mongoose shot through and hit that snake faster than we could follow with our eyes. The mongoose grabbed the snake by the neck and shook it violently. A second or two later, we heard, "*crunch, crunch, crunch.*" The mongoose devoured half of the snake before the handler could get to him.

I have the whole thing on 8mm film.

I love Japan. It's probably my favorite country in the world. I love the culture. I love the people. I love the respect the people have for their elders and for authority. Most of all, I love the respect their fans have for the wrestlers.

After spending four weeks in Japan, I flew back to the States.

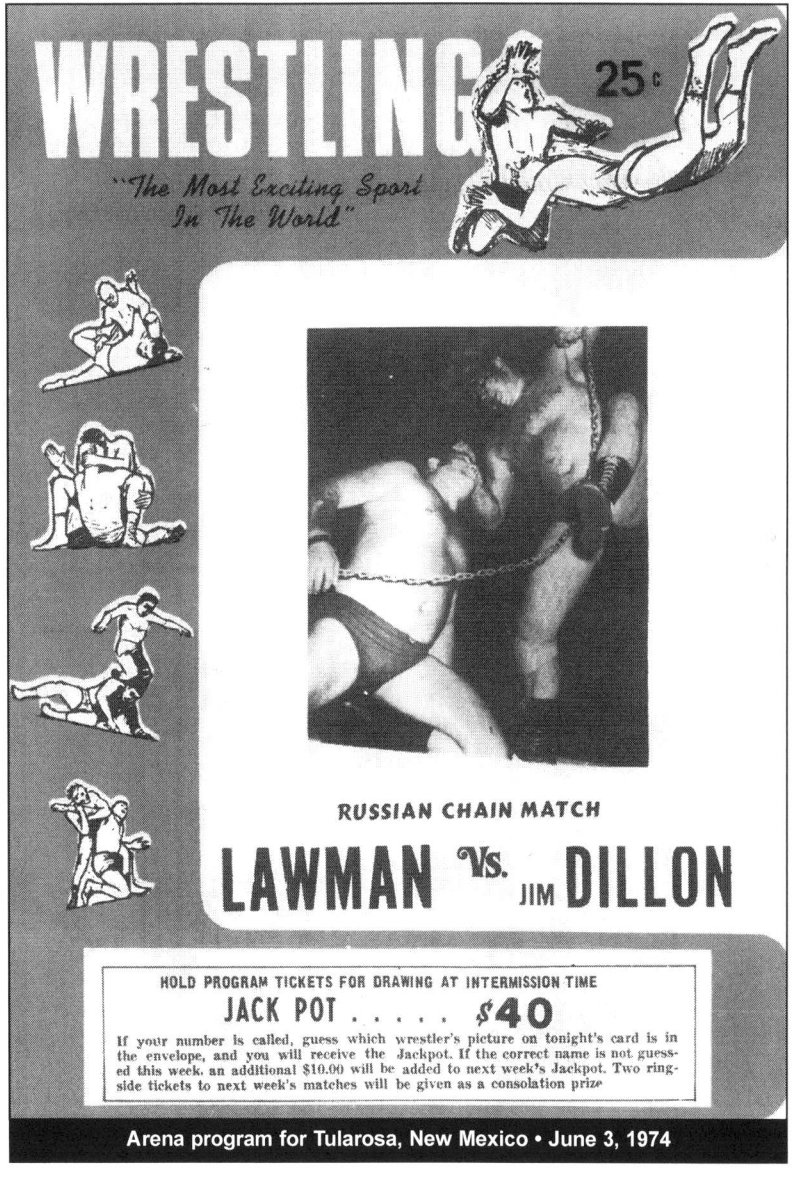

Arena program for Tularosa, New Mexico • June 3, 1974

# Chapter 9
## The Cow That Ate the Cabbage

I had wrestled in Florida twice before, but never on a full-time basis. I had three matches in the summer of 1971, and two in the summer of 1972. When I was a kid, I had watched the Graham brothers—Dr. Jerry Graham and Eddie Graham—wrestle in Philadelphia. Eddie was now the owner of the Florida territory. I know I keep talking about my dream, but working in Florida for Eddie Graham was another dream come true for me. Eddie Graham had been a big star in New York before I started to referee.

Jeanette and the boys stayed in Pennsylvania until I could get settled in. I had no place to live and it was expensive to stay in a hotel. "Baron" Mike Scicluna shared an apartment in Tampa with Bruce Swayze. Talk about the odd couple. I knew Mike from my years as a referee in New York, so he said, *"You come stay with me."*

Mike took the mattress off of his bed and put it on the floor in a huge, walk-in closet. For the next three weeks, until my wife got there, Mike slept on the box spring and I slept on the mattress in the closet. What a wonderful experience it was being around Mike. He is just a wonderful, wonderful guy.

When I got to Florida, Bill Watts was just winding down his run as the booker. Watts was hot-shotting the cards [booking an excessive number of "hot" matches] with all of his blowoff matches, and there was a concern that the territory would die when they were done.

Eddie was bringing Bobby Shane back from Australia to take the booking job. Since 1971, Bobby's nickname was the "King of Wrestling." Even though Shane wasn't responsible for bringing me in, because of my relationship with the Funks, and in turn, their relationship with Eddie, I went in knowing that I would have a good spot and would make a good living.

Bobby Shane

On Tuesday night, February 18, 1975, I teamed with Bobby Shane in Tampa. On Wednesday, we went to Miami. Buddy Colt, who was the top heel in the territory at the time, had just bought his own airplane—a single-engine, Cessna 173. He flew to Miami after the afternoon TV tapings in Tampa, taking Bobby Shane, "Playboy" Gary Hart, and Dennis "Mike" McCord with him.

Dick Murdoch, Bob Roop, and I chartered another small four-passenger airplane with a professional pilot. We left from the private aviation center at Tampa International Airport and flew to Miami. Bob Roop, the Mongolian Stomper (Archie Gouldie), and I wrestled in a 6-man tag team match against Bill Watts, Dick Slater, and Chris

Taylor that evening.

After the matches, we all returned to the airport around the same time. I remember looking out the window of our airplane as we sat, waiting for clearance. As Buddy Colt taxied his plane past us, I saw Bobby Shane waving at us. They took off before we did.

In the meantime, a line of storms had moved into Tampa.

Murdoch, Roop, and I spent the flight shooting the bull and drinking beer. As we got closer to Tampa, the storm picked up steam and the plane started to rock around. The fog was so thick that the pilot couldn't see anything. It got so bad that they closed Tampa International, the main airport in Tampa. Fortunately, the air traffic controllers at Tampa told our pilot that he would be able to land at Peter O. Knight Airport on Davis Island, which had been Tampa's original airport before they moved operations to the big airport in the '40s.

We heard on the radio that 456-BC, which we knew was the number of Buddy Colt's plane, had gone in ahead of us on its final approach, but the people at Tampa International Airport hadn't received confirmation of its' landing.

I could hear our pilot getting his landing instructions from the control tower. *"Turn so many degrees, maintain this altitude,"* and so on. After a minute or so went by, we heard somebody say, *"Forget 456-BC. We have a report that they're down in the bay."*

All of a sudden, there was dead silence in our cabin.

A few moments later, our pilot began his landing pattern and we dropped through the bottom of the cloud level. It was as if we were in the Twilight Zone. Right in front of us, we could see a city, all lit up. There was a drizzling rain, but we had clear visibility and we were lined up perfectly with the runway.

The whole time we were landing, nobody said a word. As we taxied over to the buildings, we saw two or three people who had been listening on police scanners. Surprisingly enough, they were wrestling fans. They said, *"We heard there was a plane crash and we heard wrestlers were on it."*

Our cars were over at the Tampa Airport, so we asked, *"Could we get a lift with you?"*

The fans motioned for us to get into their cars, so we got in and they drove us to the other side of the island. Between the airport and Hillsborough Bay, there was a row of houses on the inland side, then a street, and more houses on the bay side. When we drove down that street, we saw ambulance lights.

Gary Hart was lying on a stretcher in an ambulance. They had already taken Dennis McCord to the hospital. Somebody directed us to an area between two houses where Buddy Colt was lying on the ground. His one ankle was turned at an unnatural angle and the paramedics were treating him. They asked us to help get him off the ground and onto the ambulance. Dick Murdoch got on one side, I got on the other, and we hoisted Buddy onto the stretcher.

Meanwhile, helicopters were hovering over the bay, with searchlights criss-crossing over the water. They were still looking for Bobby. We eventually left and got rides back to Tampa International Airport, where our cars were parked. From there, we went straight to the hospital and checked on Buddy, Gary, and Dennis. Gary had a lump on his forehead that looked like a big gourd. It looked like somebody had taken a lemon, cut it in half, and stuck it under the skin. It was blood red and horrible looking. He was a mess.

On Thursday morning, we went to the wrestling office. Somebody told us that they had found the wreckage of the plane. They found the engine in one spot, and a piece of wing in another. The main fuselage looked like the Incredible Hulk had reached into the cockpit and pulled the wires out of the dashboard.

Bobby Shane was still strapped into his seat. When the divers cut his seat belt, he just floated up and out.

When Bobby was examined, the medical examiners came to the conclusion that he drowned after being knocked out on impact. That was backed up by the fact that there was no sign of a struggle. When people are underwater with their seat belt fastened, they try to get the seat belt loose. When they are found after drowning, their fingers are lodged underneath the belt. Bobby's arms were floating, which they said was consistent with someone who had been knocked out on impact. I also heard that the impact had been so great that he had been cut in half at the waist by the seat belt, but that story was not true.

On Friday morning, I flew to Houston, Texas, to work a shot [one match] against Red Bastien. My wife had flown back to Amarillo to get our trailer, which had been stored at Karl von Steiger's house. They hooked it to our car and she drove it to Houston. We met at the motel where I was staying and we drove back to Tampa together. The events of the week were weighing heavily on me, so it was a long drive.

Harley Race came in to take Bobby Shane's place as the booker and he did a good job. I held the Florida TV title. I always wondered if Harley gave me the title as a rib. When you were the TV champion, you didn't get a belt. You got a trophy. That trophy was as tall as I was—maybe a little taller. I always thought it was a joke on me because nobody wanted that title. When you defended the title, you had to lug that trophy along with you. It was a royal pain to keep up with. It was hard to make myself look upset when I lost it to Rocky Johnson in Jacksonville. I got a $60 payoff for that match. If they had only known that I would have paid them to let me lose it.

My impression of Rocky Johnson was that he was lazy. You always had to push him to be Rocky Johnson. He had a bird tattooed on each of his pecs. I assumed they were targets, so whenever we wrestled, I would hit him hard with forearm smashes. He would squeal every time.

I also held the Florida tag team title with Roger Kirby. I had heard Roger's name many times when I teamed up with Les Thatcher in the Carolinas. Les talked about him constantly. Roger had been a big draw in Kansas City, Missouri, and Portland, Oregon. He had a waxed, handlebar moustache and was a very slow-www talker.

Roger Kirby & Jim Dillon • Sept. 19, 1975

Roger made a trip with me to Melbourne. The last leg of the trip was a two-lane highway with nothing but marshes on either side of the highway. Another car came up behind us at a pretty high rate of speed. When they passed us, I wasn't surprised to see that it was Terry Funk, who was in the territory for a couple of weeks. His passenger was Rick Martel. It wasn't long before they were out of sight.

After driving several more miles, we realized that a car in front of us was traveling at a very slow rate of speed. As we drew near, I saw that it was Terry. He was weaving back and forth across the center line to keep us from passing, and eventually came to a dead stop. There was no other traffic coming in either direction at the time. The passenger door opened and out stepped Rick Martel — stark naked! He strutted around the rear of Terry's car like a bantam rooster, wearing nothing but a big smile. When he got around to Terry's side of the car, Terry locked the car doors and sped away. The smile instantly disappeared from Rick's face and a look of panic replaced it. He knew that Kirby and I were his only salvation. I wasn't going to let him down too quickly, though. I shifted the car into gear and tried to ease past Rick, who ran alongside my car, still naked (with his clothes in Terry's car) holding on to my outside mirror. As I sped up gradually, Rick's hand slipped off the mirror and he fell onto the highway. From the way he fell, Kirby thought Rick was dead, so we stopped the car and went back to check on him. He was shaken up, but there wasn't a mark on him. A few minutes later, Terry drove up and we all had a good laugh.

Then again, I don't remember Rick laughing.

Before he got back into the car, Rick said that a cat's eye, onyx pinky ring had fallen off. *"Don't worry,"* Terry assured him. *"I'll buy you a new ring. How much is it worth?"*

*"A hundred bucks,"* answered Rick.

Terry paused for a second, then suggested that we should look for the ring. Rick got dressed and the four of us tried to retrace our route. As we searched, a sudden storm came up and we all got soaked. Just as we were about to give up, I found the ring at the edge of the road.

Florida was a major promotion, and from a wrestler's perspective, it was a desirable place to be booked because of the reasonable trips (back home almost every night), beautiful weather (compared to working in Minneapolis, for example), and the beaches. However, it also had a bad rap for mediocre pay-offs. Wrestler logic was to get booked in Florida to enjoy all the fringe benefits, but don't plan on making big money.

After Terry Funk had been in the territory for a couple of weeks, he got his paycheck for the previous week's work. In some of the towns, the babyfaces and heels dressed in the same dressing room, but they were well out of sight of the fans. Terry looked at his check, looked up, looked back down at his check, then muttered loud enough for everyone to hear, *"I wonder where the cow is that ate all the cabbage?"* Dusty Rhodes was within earshot in the dressing room that night. Everyone knew just who Terry was referring to.

I had a good run while Harley Race was there. I enjoyed working for Harley and respected him for his work in the ring. He did a good job with the book, even though he had to step into a tough situation on very short notice.

Tallahassee and Ft. Lauderdale were the towns that ran on Friday night. 95% of the time, I was married to Tallahassee. In wrestling parlance, "married" means working on a regular basis in a particular town, or against a specific opponent. Everyone seemed to look at Tallahassee as the "B" town. It wasn't as glamorous as an "A" town, such as Ft. Lauderdale, but it gave me a chance to work on top, and even though I did not work in the office, it became my town to oversee. Harley would give me the rundown of the finishes he wanted for the town each week. I was there every week it ran, and it was a great experience for me.

When Harley was booking, he brought in Larry Hennig, his old tag team partner from Minneapolis. By this time, it was late into Larry's career, and he was moving out of wrestling and getting involved in real estate. He didn't want to travel that much, but he was anxious to go to Florida and get out on the road with his friend, Harley.

We were usually booked in West Palm Beach on Monday nights. A local guy, who owned a karate studio, started to attend the matches. Every week, he would stand up in the bleachers and challenge the heels as we walked back to the dressing room. He would really bad mouth us. As the weeks went by, he became more and more obnoxious. He would unbutton his shirt and act as if he was going to take it off.

Harley Race

If you know anything about Harley Race, you know that he would only take so much. One night, he was wrestling Ciclon Negro. When Ciclon made his comeback at the end of the match, Harley bailed out of the ring and headed up the aisle. As usual, the guy stood up, peeled his shirt open, and called Harley a no-good, chickensh— coward.

It was the wrong night to challenge Harley.

Harley stopped dead in his tracks, walked back to the front of the aisle, turned around, looked at the guy, and hooked his finger. *"Come on, pal."*

Here we go.

Several of us were in the dressing room, but word filtered back to us immediately. Everybody scrambled. The guys in the shower ran out and pulled a pair of pants on. Nobody was going to miss this one.

As I stood up, I saw Larry Hennig pull a tube sock and a hockey puck out of his bag. I don't know where he got the hockey puck. I suppose that everybody from Minnesota carries a hockey puck in their suitcase when they travel. Larry dropped the hockey puck into the sock, wrapped it around his fist once or twice, and headed out into the arena.

By the time we walked out, Harley was already in the ring. The mark was on the ring apron, climbing through the ropes. As he stepped through, he kept a close eye on Harley, especially Harley's right hand.

But he was watching the wrong hand. Harley is left-handed.

*Boom!* Harley jabbed him and the guy went down.

It was over before it started. There were all kinds of people jumping into the ring, yelling and hollering, but there was no more fight from the mark. The wrestlers all jumped into the ring to make sure nobody else tried anything stupid.

I don't know if someone shoved Larry on purpose, or if he was just jostled, but Larry turned around and swung the sock at someone.

Now, get a mental picture of this. As he swings the sock overhand, the guy moves. Due to the weight of the hockey puck in the bottom of the sock, it stretched out to twice its normal length. As Larry's arm dropped down, the sock pivoted around, came back up, and hit Larry right in the back of his own head.

His legs started to buckle, and his eyes were rolling like a slot machine, but he didn't go down. When he regained his composure, he immediately went back to the dressing room. He had a huge welt on the back of his head.

That was one of the funniest things I ever witnessed. If I thought about someone I wouldn't want to have a fight with, I would put Larry Hennig somewhere near the top of that list because he's like a bear. But when he swung that hockey puck and hit himself on the back of the head, I thought I'd die from laughing so hard. He didn't touch anybody, and nobody touched him, but he had a lump on the back of his head as a souvenir for the night.

I was always able to talk my way out of bad situations with the fans. We had a situation in Orlando one night when we had an open enrollment battle royal. The fans were allowed to participate, but they still had to buy a ticket. There were three Hell's Angels there that night who made a lot of noise about entering, and (like an idiot) I was taunting them, inviting them to come in, but they didn't take the bait.

After the matches, I pulled my van up in front of a liquor store near the Orlando Sports Stadium. I stayed in the van while Bob Dellaserra and Don Kent went in. Lo and behold, who pulls up right beside my van and makes eye contact with me? It was one of the three bikers. He was *huge*. He walked over to my car with a serious expression on his face, so I put him over by saying, *"Hey, man. I'm glad you changed your mind about entering the battle royal. You would have been a handful."*

I remembered that Swede Hanson was real tight with the Hell's Angels in Charlotte, so I threw Swede's name out, and told the guy that I had met a bunch of his buddies from the Charlotte chapter. All of a sudden, he was my best friend! We talked until Dellaserra and Kent came out, then we left. It could have turned ugly real fast, but it didn't.

I have two vivid memories of Eddie Graham. If you were a heel, you would occasionally pull your opponent's hair. If you pulled Eddie's hair, he would pull yours while fighting back in a selling mode, and/or during his comeback. When he grabbed *your* hair, you had to be prepared to react quickly and go down, or he would pull clumps of hair out of your head. Eddie also threw one hell of a punch. He wouldn't hurt you, but when his punches landed, you knew that you had been hit ... and so did the fans. *Temporary suspension of disbelief.* I wrestled Eddie at an outdoor stadium in Freeport, Bahamas, on April 19, 1975. During the course of our match, I pulled his hair ... and lost quite a bit of my own as a result.

We also wrestled at an outdoor show in Plant City, Florida, on March 8, 1975. Plant City is known as the Winter Strawberry Capital of the World. In early March for the past 70 years, they have held the Florida Strawberry Festival. The harvest is in and you can buy flats of fresh strawberries, as well as anything that is made with strawberries. The wrestling office often sold a live show to be part of the festival. My first time at the Festival, I was in the main event with the Mongolian Stomper against Eddie and Mike Graham. On that night, I did reflect back to my early days as a fan in New York. I was in the main event with Eddie Graham.

# Chapter 10
# The Stomper
# and the Moondog

In the fall of 1975, I got a phone call from Archie Gouldie. Archie, as I already mentioned, had been in Florida, but I first met him in the Maritimes. Archie had been a huge drawing card in several territories, including Calgary, Alberta, Canada.

In August 1975, Archie went to work in Tennessee with Bearcat Wright as his manager. After a few months, they parted ways. When he called me, Archie said, *"Bearcat and I are done. I have to leave Tennessee because I don't have a manager. I've been doing my own promos here and it killed my gimmick. I've got a chance to go to Dallas and work on top, but I need a manager. Have you ever given any thought to managing?"*

Archie had seen me doing promos in the Maritimes and Florida, so I think he felt that I would make a good talker for him. I said, *"I've never thought about that. I don't know why I couldn't. I would need to make an investment in some clothes."*

I agreed to do it. We got a starting date of November 10 from Red Bastien, who was the booker in Dallas, and I finished up in Florida on November 7. On the night of our first match, Red took us aside and said, *"I'm trying to figure out how to bill you. The Stomper with Jim Dillon. Jim Dillon is too plain. We need something else."*

Before we went out to the ring, Red came up with the name *J.J. Dillon*. Red said that it sounded more like a business name, or like an executive of a corporation.

I didn't wrestle at all during my first three months in Texas. I confined my activities strictly to managing. After that, I would wrestle occasionally. I didn't mind doing that. In fact, I enjoyed it. I had people ask if it bothered me that the office only paid me once, and not twice, since I was both managing and wrestling in one night. No, it didn't. I was already in the town and I had incurred the expense. I looked at what my total compensation was for the week, and for the most part, I was happy with my deal. In a lot of cases, managers were paid preliminary pay, or something just above that. I always had the understanding that I would get the same amount of money as the guy that I managed. I felt that I deserved as much money as the guy I was managing because I had proven myself as a worker. I don't say that to demean a manager who never wrestled, but somebody asked me to be a manager. It wasn't a position that I sought out, so if I was going to do it, I was going to make what my charges were going to make. And since I wrestled *and* managed, I had confidence as to what I could do with my character, and what I meant to a promotion.

The Stomper

On April 13, 1976, Stomper and I had a match in Dallas with Rocky Johnson, who was a big card in Texas. The match was one of those angles where I agreed to wrestle, but I added a stipulation: *"Sure, I'll wrestle, but I get to pick your (Rocky's) partner."*

I picked Cowboy Lang, a midget wrestler, to be Rocky's tag team partner.

We did a watered-down version of what we originally planned because Fritz von Erich, the Dallas/Fort Worth promoter, was afraid we'd have a full blown riot if we did what I wanted to do. I wanted the midget to do a stretcher job.

Of course, Stomper and Rocky were in the ring most of the time, while I spent my time on the ring apron, taunting the midget. When Stomper would get Rocky down, I acted like I wanted to get into the ring so badly. I would tag in, but as soon as Rocky started to regain an advantage, I would run over to Stomper and tag out.

Eventually, we got to a situation where it looked like Rocky was beaten down for good, so I started gloating and taunting the midget. I strutted around the ring, posing and acting like a real jerk. I was so wrapped up in myself that I didn't realize that Rocky was back on his feet—and between me and Stomper.

When I realized the trouble I was in, I tried to escape, but Rocky caught me and made his big comeback. He did everything he could to me. To add insult to injury, he tagged Cowboy Lang, who came in and took up where Rocky left off. Lang even kicked me in the ass and covered me for an attempted pinfall. Stomper ran in and made the save by pulling him off by the leg. Rocky came back in and began to fight with Stomper as they worked their way to a neutral corner with the referee.

Cowboy Lang got up and started to cheer and encourage Rocky. In the meantime, I sat up and, looking around, saw the midget with his back to me. The referee was trying to break Stomper and Rocky up because the midget and I were the two legal guys in the ring. I staggered to my feet, grabbed the midget, turned him around, picked him up, bodyslammed him, and covered him. When the referee turned around, he counted *1-2-3*.

The best part about the finish was the bragging rights that I got out of it. To me, that was good heat. The finish that I originally pressed for was to drop the midget with a piledriver. Fortunately, Fritz said, *"No, that's too much. We'll have a riot. Just slam him and cover him. That'll be bad enough."* Fritz was correct in his decision. There was a thin line between good heat and cheap, or distasteful, heat. It was one of those finishes where people could understand the logic of what had happened. Lang and I were the two legal men in the ring, and I took advantage of it.

Archie had his personal problems, most of which were self-created. He had a track record of going into a territory and, after a short period of time, coming to the conclusion that, *"They're not gonna do anything with me. This is a waste of time. I can't stay here."* Whenever that would happen, Archie would just disappear without a word to anyone. He would pack up his bags and go back to work for Stu Hart, the promoter in Calgary.

Archie had the same problem when we were in Dallas. He would repeat over and over, *"They have no plans for us. This is a waste of time. I can't stay here."* I was told that Archie was a manic depressive. I seem to remember him taking medication to manage it. I don't know if it was because he would get off the medication, but he could be his own worst enemy.

In this case, when he decided to leave, somebody caught wind of it and called to ask me if I had seen Archie that day. I gave them an honest answer. *"No, I haven't talked to him."*

I immediately got on the phone and called him at the house he had rented, but nobody answered. I drove to the house and looked through his windows. The house was empty! I then called the office and told them, *"Archie didn't call me or tell me anything, but he's gone."*

Fritz von Erich used to run spot shows on Saturday nights in high school gymnasiums. Most of the big names and managers refused to work them. I didn't care where the shows were or how small the venues were. I was interested in making money and doing what was right for the business. I told Fritz, *"I would be glad to work on Saturdays. In fact, if you have an opening, I'd like to wrestle on the card."*

November 1975
First publicity photos

The towns booked by Fritz were Dallas, Fort Worth, and the Saturday spot shows. San Antonio and Corpus Christi were booked by another promoter, Joe Blanchard, and those are the towns where I wrestled the most. Since he had control, Joe got me more involved. In fact, I wrestled Joe Blanchard once in Corpus Christi where we fought outside the ring, out the front of the building—which was a beachfront coliseum—across the street, through traffic, over the boardwalk, and down the beach. Joe finally hit me with a big knockout punch that sent me staggering back about five steps, and I took a big bump back into the ocean.

Once again, those were the kinds of things I did as much for my own pleasure as for that of the fans. And yet, the fans would be saying things like, *"Oh! This is the greatest thing we ever saw!"*

On May 15, 1976 in Austin, I wrestled Joe's 21-year-old son, Tully Blanchard, for the first time. We would wrestle many times during my stay in Dallas, and ten years later, we would leave our mark in wrestling history. But again, I'm getting ahead of myself.

When I went into Dallas, I had been told that one of the challenges you face was not only the plans that the Dallas office had for you, but in getting the assurance that Paul Boesch, the promoter in Houston, was willing to use you. If you worked on top in Dallas, but you weren't figured in on the Houston shows, you didn't make a very good living. Paul Boesch was one of the better payoff people in the business, so your success in Texas, at least in regards to money, was based on Paul using you in Houston. Fortunately, when I talked to Bastien about it, he assured me that Paul had plans for Archie and me.

As a rule, Paul was a good businessman. On the few occasions when my payoffs were not what I expected, I would call Paul and he would usually make things right. Every now and then, however, Paul would get a wild hair up his butt about something, such as the time when Archie left. When those things happened, I had to make Paul understand that I still had value to him and could manage someone else.

I did something one night, about halfway through my run in Texas, that got me some heat with Paul. The story going around was that Gino Hernandez was Paul's illegitimate son. I don't know if that was true or not, but I do know that Paul really took Gino under his wing. In spite of all the demons that Gino had, and the bad decisions that he made, Paul liked him and tried to help him.

On April 9, 1976, I was booked on a card to wrestle Gino in a two-out-of-three fall match. I had only worked a few times that year, so I wanted to have a tremendous match with Gino and call upon the skills I had used when I worked with Dick Murdoch and Leo Burke.

We had what I thought was a great match, but when I got to the back, Paul was fuming. In hindsight, I understand the point he made, but I didn't understand it at the moment.

That was one of the few times in my career when I let my ego get the best of me. I went to the ring that night to show the other boys, and the fans, that I was a quality worker. I felt like a lot of the guys had forgotten that I was a pretty fair worker in my day. It wasn't something that I dwelled on, but deep down, it really bothered me. I wanted to show everyone that I was a good worker, and it was the wrong thing to do—for the match, for the town, and for my career as a manager.

What I lost track of was the fact that the wrestling fans in Houston didn't see me as a wrestler. They saw me as a loudmouth, not-so-hot, chickensh— manager. The things that I did in the ring with Gino—high spots, bumps, and timing—were not consistent with the character that I had developed, or what I was portrayed to be.

If I had been the great worker that I thought I was at the time, I would have gone out and worked like a manager. I would have used the skills that I was blessed with in that type of a match. Instead, I went out and let my ego get the best of me. I tried to have a great match and steal the show. It was stupid on my part. As I look back on it now, I can see that it made no sense. Paul Boesch was 100% correct.

That was one of the things I did that took me a while to get right with Paul again. I lost sight of what my role was, and I promised myself that it would never happen again. It was a valuable lesson learned. To me, every match was a challenge, and I wanted to get the most out of it. I think a lot of that had to do with the fact that I never stopped being a wrestling fan. I loved wrestling. From that point on, though, I concentrated on doing things that a manager would do, even to the point of making a total fool of myself. I never lost my passion for working, but I learned from that experience.

On the other hand, were there nights when I went out and had fun?

Absolutely, but I also had a tremendous amount of pride in that, no matter who I worked with, I went into the ring with the goal in mind of getting the absolute most out of whatever scenario I had to work with. I'm not drawing a comparison between me and Ric Flair, but one of the things I admire the most about Ric as the champion— and I always knew him as the champion—was that regardless of how big the town was, how many people bought tickets, or who he had to work with, Ric gave every match his best.

Ric never said, *"I'm tired,"* or, *"I've got a double shot tonight, so I'm going to take it easy,"* or, *"The house is way down from the last time I was here, so I'll just go through the motions and give the people a 12-minute match."*

Ric always gave the fans their money's worth. If it took 25 minutes to get the job done, that's what he did each and every night.

There's another thing that I respect about Ric. Ric Flair's gimmick was ... Ric Flair!

Ric always lived his gimmick. He always looked and dressed the part. I don't ever remember seeing him without a shirt and a tie, no matter how small or insignificant the town. I adopted that same philosophy before I met Ric Flair, so it's not something that I picked up from him, but he took it to a level that no one else ever did. He paid for his own limo, hired the driver, bought the suits, and lived the life he portrayed on television. He was a great wrestler and a credit to the business.

When Archie left, I didn't know what I was going to do, but Fritz told me, *"I want you to stay because you're over."* The office solved the problem by putting me together with Lonnie "Moon Dog" Mayne.

JJ Dillon & Lonnie Mayne • 1976

Lonnie was another great guy with a fabulous character, but Lonnie had a drinking problem. I'm not talking out of school because it was well known by everyone.

I had a big, customized Dodge van at the time. It had a lot of room, so Lonnie would ride with me. We made one trip from Corpus Christi to Houston with Lord Alfred Hayes. Alfred and I were sitting in the two captains chairs up front, talking and solving all the problems of the world. Lonnie was laying on the couch seat in the back.

You could buy shrimp at good prices from the roadside stands, so I would take a cooler filled with ice and stock up during the trips. When we stopped at one of the roadside stands, which was sitting in front of a strip mall, Lonnie said, *"I'll be right back,"* and walked over to a liquor store. When he got back, he went right to the back of the van and laid down. It was more than 200 miles to Houston, so we got right back out onto the road.

When we reached the city limits of Houston, I heard a snoring sound coming from the back of the van. Lonnie was sound asleep. Alfred went back to check on him and found an empty liquor bottle on the floor.

We went directly to the hotel and I checked in, while Alfred got a thermos full of coffee. We were going to force it down Lonnie's throat because he was working on top that night against Jose Lothario. We didn't want Paul Boesch to know that he had been drinking. Lonnie always smelled the same, whether he had been drinking or not. He also had a glassy look in his eyes, so you could never really be sure.

As soon as we arrived at the Sam Houston Coliseum, I told Lonnie, *"Don't say anything and don't talk to anybody. Just avoid everybody. I'll get the finish and I'll go over it with you before your match."*

That is exactly what happened. I gave Lonnie the finish: *"It's a 2-out-of-3-fall match* with Lothario. *Lothario takes the first fall, you take the second, and Lothario takes the last."* That was all there was to it. It was no more complicated than that.

Lonnie asked me at least ten times that night, *"What was that finish again?"*

Things got worse from there. We had to walk to the ring at a snails pace because Lonnie could barely walk. He had to rest his left arm on my right shoulder just to steady himself enough to get to the ring.

As soon as we got him into the ring, the bell sounded. Lonnie's adrenaline kicked in and he did just fine. I'm not saying that he did very much, but it was passable. I remember Jose looking at me and rolling his eyes after taking the first fall.

Lonnie used to do a move where he would have his opponent laying on the mat in the middle of the ring. He would then climb up onto the turnbuckle, but before he could get turned around, his opponent would get up, grab Lonnie by the back of his trunks, and give him a tug. Lonnie would take a hellacious bump backwards into the ring.

He decided to do that during the second fall.

After working Lothario onto the mat, Lonnie started to climb the ropes. It seemed to take an eternity for him to make the climb. I kept expecting him to slip and fall, but to his credit, he didn't. When he reached the top, Jose stood up, grabbed him by the back of the tights, and Lonnie took a huge bump in the center of the ring. When Jose covered Lonnie for the false finish, Bronco Lubich, who was the referee, counted, *"1 ... 2 ..."* There was a pregnant pause as Bronco's arm went back up for the third count. He brought his arm down as slowly as he could, trying to hold on until Lonnie kicked out. If you were paying attention—and believe me, I was—it looked like Bronco was in a slow-motion replay. His arm slowly lowered down to the mat, until he finally had to count, *"3."*

When the bell rang, Lonnie still didn't move. Lothario stood up and looked around, trying to decide what to do. He looked at me, as if asking me for my advice, and I just stood there, like, *"Well, what can I do?"*

I got into the ring and started to talk like a ventriloquist, trying not to move my lips as I chewed him out. *"You dumb sonofabitch! You just lost two straight falls."*

I kicked him in the ribs, but got no response.

I got down on my hands and knees, and peeled back his eyelids. I saw nothing but the whites of his eyes.

He was out cold.

Houston, after eating dog food • Aug. 6, 1976

I don't remember how I did it, but I got him back to the dressing room. Nobody said anything because it looked like one of those bumps that went bad. That can happen to anybody in any match.

Everybody was sitting around, waiting for Paul Boesch to come around with the payoffs. When Paul walked in, he started to hand out the envelopes. As he got to Lonnie, he said, *"Lonnie, this is your payoff. You had a wonderful match tonight. There is a little extra money in there for tonight's performance ..."*

Then he added, *"... in spite of your manager."*

He handed Lonnie his envelope and walked over to me. He had a little smirk on his face when he handed me my envelope, then he left.

Nobody said anything. Nobody said anything in the car, either.

We were staying overnight because we had to work in Austin the next night. When I got to my hotel room, I looked in my envelope. It was a good payoff. Houston was Houston. It was good money. All of a sudden, I heard a knock on the door. When I opened it, Lonnie stood there, bleary-eyed and holding his envelope up in the air. He said, *"I want you to take this. You deserve it."*

I said, *"Lonnie, I didn't take it personal. Paul Boesch thinks he's so brilliant, but the dumb sonofabitch didn't know any better! Don't worry about it. I'm happy for you. Nobody needs to know."*

That's a true story. Perhaps Paul thought I had given Lonnie the wrong finish, or blamed me for instructing Lonnie to take the bump that knocked him out. I don't really know what Paul was thinking, but I do know that he didn't respect managers. He thought he was being cute by making a smart-ass comment. *"Your manager gets in your way ..."* That kind of thing. It was meant to be a tongue-in-cheek remark. *"It was a great match in spite of having to carry him, too,"* is what Paul was saying.

There was a tragic ending to the life story of Lonnie Mayne. In 1978, he was involved in a head-on collision in southern California and, apparently, laid in a coma for several days. Until he passed away on August 13, nobody even knew he was missing. He was 34 years old.

My run in Texas ended in September 1976. I answered the phone one day and it was Archie Gouldie. He immediately started to apologize. *"I'm so sorry. I don't know what I was thinking. I never should have left, but before I did, I should have told you what I was gonna do. We had such a good thing going and I realize that I made a mistake. I talked to Verne Gagne about bringing us into Minneapolis. He's thinking about it, but there's a spot in Atlanta — a spot on top — and that always pays well. I always got along with Jim Barnett* [the promoter in Georgia]. *He said that he'd love to have us, so if you're interested, he gave us a start date."*

I was ready to make a move, anyway, so I agreed to it. I told him to call Barnett and accept his offer. The next day, Verne Gagne called and gave me a starting date for Minneapolis. Verne owned and promoted the American Wrestling Association [AWA]. I met Verne when I was in Japan. He was booked on one of my tours and I got to be around him for a week. I said, *"Verne, I would love to come work for you, but I already made arrangements to go to Atlanta. I gave them my word and that's what I have to stand by. That's the way I've always done business, even if someone offered me more money."*

Verne was very indignant that I wouldn't jump on his offer of a start date, no matter what the circumstances. I told him, *"Verne, if I had given you my word, I would honor it, too. I've already confirmed my start date and given them my word. Now I have to be good to my word."*

My last two weeks in Houston were spent doing blowoff matches. One of the matches came about when Paul Boesch "tricked me" into signing an open contract during a TV interview. *"I have an open contract on you, Mr. Dillon. I found an opponent who can't wait to wrestle you next Friday night."*

On September 3, 1976, my opponent was Victor, the wrestling bear.

I had never seen the bear work before. I had been told that their trainer gave them a bottle of Coke before and after a match to make them happy, but you have to be careful because they'll whack you with their snout. They have incredible power. The worst thing you can do is try to take their Coke away. I had been forewarned, so I didn't fall for the trap, but the first thing the trainer did when I got into the ring was say, *"Take his Coke away from him."*

I remember the bear standing up on his hind legs and locking up with me. When a bear does that, there is no way possible for a man to get behind him. If you wrestle a person, you can raise one of his arms up and do a go-behind, but you can't raise a bear's paw up once they have it on your shoulder. No matter which way you go, they go with you.

It was an interesting experience. I don't remember much about the match, other than being embarrassed and humiliated by the bear, but on the following week, I was going to get my revenge on the man who perpetrated it all.

Paul Boesch.

Paul was 65 years old, so the only thing we could really do was a gimmick match. The gimmick he chose was a bathtub.

*The first person to get thrown into the bathtub loses.*

I watched as they brought out a huge washtub, muscled it into the ring, and filled it with water. We both climbed into the ring and we were off to the races. The match was almost as much fun as the midget matches that I remembered from my early days as a referee.

The first thing Paul did was take me down with a leg sweep. He pulled my shoe off and dunked the shoe in the water. While I was pitching a fit about that, he poured the water over me, then waxed me with my own shoe. Next, we locked up over the tub, got down on our hands and knees, and he forced my hands down into the water. All of a sudden, he flipped a handful of water into my face. I came up spitting and sputtering.

The match didn't go too long because there really wasn't a whole lot that we could do. We pushed and shoved, trying to pull each other over to the tub, and blocked and resisted being thrown in.

We ended the match by having Lonnie Mayne come to ringside and distract Paul's attention. I snuck up behind Paul and clobbered him, then I hooked his arms and took him over to the ropes where Lonnie stood. Lonnie pulled his arm back for a big haymaker. He swung, Paul ducked, and Lonnie hit me. I staggered backwards, with my arms windmilling, and managed to catch my balance just before I fell into the bathtub. I let out a sigh of relief ... just as Paul came over and hit me with a big chop. I fell backwards into the bathtub and water splashed everywhere.

My last match in Texas was on September 14, 1976. One week later, my family and I moved to Atlanta, Georgia.

# Chapter 11
# Chips Off the Old Block

I was never formally introduced to Ted Turner, but I saw him quite often when I was wrestling for *Georgia Championship Wrestling*. Every Saturday morning, we would tape the TV show at Ted's studio on Techwood Drive. We never knew when Ted Turner would pop in. He would show up with a beautiful girl on each arm after being out partying all night. His favorite line was, *"These are my rasslers!"*

Archie and I made our debut in Atlanta on September 18, 1976. I enjoyed my stay in the territory, but my time there was rather uneventful. I went in as Archie's manager, but I was also given more opportunities to wrestle, which suited me fine. Archie stayed around longer than he normally did, and when he finally did leave, they delegated me as Abdullah the Butcher's manager.

Abby and I got along well. One night, Abby was supposed to drop the Georgia TV title to somebody that he had issues with. An hour before the show was scheduled to start, everybody was in the dressing room at the Omni ... except for Abby.

Ole Anderson, the booker, was in full Ole Anderson mode. *"Somebody tell that sonofabitch to get down here or I'll go over there and kick his ass!"*

Eventually, Ole mellowed down to, *"I've got to have that belt tonight."*

JJ, Stomper, and Freddie Miller

When I called Abby, his girlfriend answered the phone. I said, *"It's me. Would you put Abby on the phone?"*

As soon as Abby got on the phone, we both started to laugh. I said, *"Abby, I understand where you're coming from. I have no problem with you not wanting to come down here tonight, but business is business. Since I'm your manager, they'll just send somebody out with me to drop the belt in your place."*

*"I don't have any trouble with that,"* he replied. *"What do you want me to do?"*

*"I need to get the belt because we need to do it tonight."*

Abby and I agreed to meet at a bar in downtown Atlanta. We sat down and had two or three drinks, with the belt sitting on the bar. It was getting close to match time, so I said, *"Abby, I've gotta get back with this."* He gave me a big hug and I left with the belt.

When I got back to the Omni, I told Ole, *"I don't know how I managed to talk him out of the belt, but I did it. Here it is."* I'm not positive, but I think it was Les Thornton who took Abby's place and dropped the belt that night.

Just as I did in Texas, I also wrestled frequently. During that run in Georgia, I held the Macon title. The Macon title was a lot like the Florida TV title. Nobody really wanted it. The Macon title was represented by a belt, so you didn't have to lug a trophy around, like you did with the Florida TV title, but it still presented a problem. It meant you had to defend the belt in Macon for Fred Ward, and there just wasn't a lot of money to be made there.

Shortly after the incident at the Omni, Abby was scheduled to leave for Japan. Abby had stroke with Baba, so before he left, I said, *"Will you see if you can get me on your tour?"*

*"I'll get you booked,"* he assured me. *"Don't worry."*

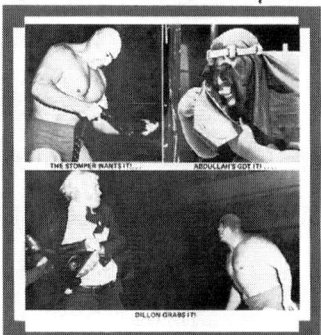

*Over the TV Championship Belt*
Atlanta • Feb. 18, 1977

And he did. That was strictly a gift because I certainly was not a big card in Japan. The two times I had been there before, the Funks had sponsored me. In all, I did seven tours of Japan. I enjoyed being on the tours with Abdullah because I liked him as a person. I have nothing but good things to say about Abdullah. He was very, very good to me.

I finished up in Georgia on April 4, 1977, and left for Japan.

Dick Beyer, who wrestled on my first tour of Japan, was a huge star there. He actually lived in Tokyo and even appeared on a weekly TV comedy show. Dick was an American, of course, but he dressed and wrestled on the Japanese side. He wore a mask when he wrestled and called himself the Sensational, Intelligent Destroyer. Whenever he went out in public, he wore the mask. It was a very rare situation when he didn't wear the mask. I can't imagine anyone in America, even before 9/11, wearing a mask in public.

I knew that Dick and Baba liked cigars, so I took two boxes over with me. I did that on each subsequent trip. I don't know if it was on my second or third trip to Japan, but Baba's wife invited my wife to accompany me on my next tour so she could experience the Japanese culture. I paid for her plane fare, but the wrestling office took care of our hotel (larger suites) and transportation around Japan.

Dick took us out for sushi one night as a way of saying thank you for the cigars. When he came to pick us up, he wasn't wearing the mask. That was really a surprise for me, but when the public saw him without the mask, they had no idea who he was.

Sumo was one of the things that I really took an interest in. Sumo has a history that goes back more than 300 years, and it seems to be Japan's national sport, although baseball is probably more popular. They hold six major sumo tournaments a year, each of which lasts 15 days. Depending on your win-loss record in the tournament, you either move up in rank or move down in rank for the next tournament.

The ultimate honor is to be awarded the rank of Yokozuna, or Grand Champion. As I write this, only 68 wrestlers have been promoted to that level. Once you reach Yokozuna status, you're never demoted from that ranking. When your skills begin to wane, you retire.

On one of my tours, one of the Grand Champions was named Kitanoumi Toshimitsu. He was huge. He must have weighed close to 500 pounds. Another one was Wajima

Hiroshi, who wasn't nearly as big, but something about him intrigued me. I enjoyed watching him wrestle on TV, so I went to see him wrestle on several live sumo tournament dates. For some reason, after retirement, Wajima was banned from the Sumo Association, and he went to work for Baba's All-Japan Pro Wrestling. They sent him to Kansas City to train with Pat O'Connor.

I never took much time off. When I made a trip to Japan, I would usually work the night before I left, even knowing that I had to get up early to fly all the next day to Japan. When I returned to the States, I would fly all day and work that same night. That was my commitment to the business.

Terry Funk was in Japan when Abby and I went over together. Terry had watched Abby over the years, so he asked if we could all meet together in private. When we did, he said, *"The Amarillo territory is on its ass and we're starved for talent. We've got to do something to pop the territory."*

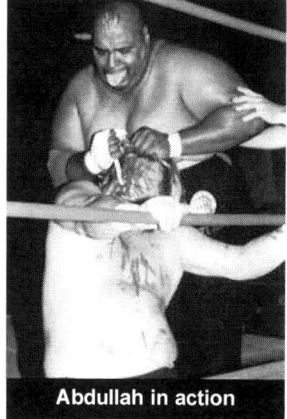

Abdullah in action

Since I had been a big card there, the Funks thought the combination of Abdullah and myself would be what the territory needed. The promoters — Terry and Dory Funk, Jerry Kozak (Amarillo), Mike London (Albuquerque), Pat O'Dowdy (Odessa), Nick Roberts (Lubbock), Don Slatton (Abilene), and Gory Guerrero (El Paso) — had pooled their money and gave us a guarantee. If I remember correctly, Abby and I got weekly guarantees of $1,000 and $700, respectively. It wasn't a lot, but at least we had a guarantee going in at the beginning.

Before we left Japan, the Funks had me cut a promo for their television show. I stood in one of Baba's rings and said something like, *"I'm sending this message from halfway around the world to the wrestling fans in west Texas. I have some good news ... and I have some bad news. I'll give you the good news first. I'm retiring from active competition in wrestling. Dick Murdoch, Ricky Romero, Terry Funk, and Dory Funk Jr. You can all sleep at night because you don't have to worry about me any more.*

*"Now for the bad news. I'm coming back to Amarillo ... and I'm bringing my black specimen ... Abdullah the Butcher."*

The people were chanting, *"BUT-CHER! BUT-CHER!"* When the music cranked up, Abdullah exploded from the dressing room and roared down the aisle. The people in the audience scattered in every direction. Chairs were tipped over, people were trampled. Abdullah came into the ring like a wild man, while I stood there and laughed. *"My black specimen! My black specimen!"*

They aired the promo several times before we arrived on June 2, 1977.

When Abby and I went to Amarillo, Dory was working big shows in the Detroit territory for the Sheik. Abby got his start in the business in Windsor, Ontario, during a time when the Sheik was a big name in that part of Canada, so the Sheik was Abby's role model. He wanted to be the black Sheik. When Abby began to make occasional trips to Detroit with Dory to wrestle for the Sheik, I said, *"I'd love to go up and work, too."*

I had worked for the Sheik when I started wrestling, so it was somewhat exciting to think about going back. And that's just what I did. In fact, on September 3, 1977, I was booked in Cobo Hall with Moose Cholak, one of the legends of our business. I had heard stories about how big, strong, and reckless he could be. The last thing I wanted to do was to go to Detroit for a one-shot deal and wind up getting hurt, so Dory took Moose aside and said, *"You'll enjoy working with Jim, but I'd like you to* make sure that he doesn't get hurt. He's one of our key people in Amarillo and he's doing us a favor here tonight. You know how you work with Baba?" And he reached out and touched Moose very gently. *"Well, that's how I want you to work with Jim."*

"Sure," said Moose. *"No problem!"*

As a rule, wrestlers worked very gently with Giant Baba. For one thing, they really respected him. The other reason was because he was older.

When I walked into the Cobo Hall dressing room, I saw Moose on his hands and knees, with a monstrous moosehead sitting on the floor in front of him. He had a harness that fit over his shoulders to help hold it in place. The moose horns were detached. He used automotive hose clamps, that he would tighten down with a screwdriver, to fasten the horns to the head. Once he got it all together, it was huge.

Moose Cholak

I went to the ring first. I watched as Moose walked down the aisle. He looked ten times bigger than life with that apparatus on his head. As he climbed up the ring steps and onto the ring apron, he pushed the top rope down and stepped over it with his right leg. I looked on in disbelief as I saw the headpiece begin to lean backwards. His arms were windmilling as he lost his balance and plummeted to the ring floor. I was thinking, *"Oh, my God. When he gets up, he's gonna be mad, and there's only gonna be one person he can be mad at. What's gonna happen to me? If I could get away with going down there and helping him up, I sure would do it."*

I don't know how he got out of the moosehead, but when he came into the ring, he was literally snorting. When the bell rang, he ran right over to me. The match didn't seem to go all that long before it was time for the turnbuckle. Moose's standard finish was to whip you into a corner of the ring, bellow like a moose, and run at you like a freight train. It was a lot like a Stan Hansen squash-in-the-corner. I thought, *I'm just gonna close my eyes and hope I survive this car wreck.* To his credit, I never felt him hit me. He covered me, 1-2-3, and I thought, *I had an angel on my shoulder today.*

The guarantee that the Funks gave us stroked Abdullah's ego, and he was happy to know that they wanted him to work on top, but Abdullah did not understand how long the trips were in the Amarillo territory, and how they would affect him. For one thing, Abby has sleep apnea. He would pull to the side of the road during a trip, leave the engine running, and go to sleep. He also had a serious problem with hemorrhoids that developed from sitting in the car for long periods of time. After a few months, he said, *"I can't take this any more. I'm satisfied with the way the Funks are treating me, but I can't take the trips. I need to move on."*

Abby is a wonderful person. He was a great success in the business and is like a God in Japan. When he went to Japan, he had the stroke to get me on the tour and make sure I got a nice payday. One night, we went out to a nightclub in Tokyo. Abby and I both liked to drink rum. After a couple of drinks, Abby got up to leave, but told me to stay, relax, and have a good time. For the next hour, women would come to my table, fuss over me, and pour drinks. When I asked for the bill, they said, *"Mr. Abdullah has taken care of everything."* Abby was very, very kind.

When Abby left, I assured the Funks that I would stay, so I managed Brute Bernard and The Angel (Frank Morrell). I knew Brute from my early days in Charlotte. He was a hard-worker and one of the true characters of the business. He also reeked of garlic. He ate garlic on everything.

The best interview I ever did was entitled *"Chips Off The Old Block."* I used to brag constantly about being from New Jersey, and put Murdoch down for being a hillbilly from Texas who drove a pickup truck loaded with hay. I would say, *"You'll always know Murdoch's truck when you see it. It's the one with dried tobacco juice all over the side."*

We couldn't run in the Amarillo Fairgrounds, our regular venue, during the week of the State Fair. On television that week, I said, *"While Amarillo is having their little fair, I'll be traveling to New Jersey for their State Fair, where the feature of the whole attraction is a display that I built."*

I actually built a display for the following week's show. I asked the Funks, Murdoch, and Ted DiBiase, to each give me a pair of their personal cowboy boots. They all wore different styles. Terry raised cattle on his ranch, so I also asked Terry to bring me some large, fresh cow chips from his field. Of course, Terry wasn't going to get *his* hands dirty, so he had his wife, Vicki, fill two or three paper bags with cow chips. Vicki had to run some errands that afternoon, so she said she'd leave them right inside the garage. When I got there to pick them up, I got out of the car and went into the garage to get them. Their pit bull growled at me the whole time I was there.

In addition to their boots, I asked for a hat they had worn. Dickie usually wore a baseball cap.

I then painted *"Chips Off The Old Block"* on a piece of wood, and made a nameplate for each of the wrestlers involved. On top of the boots, I put paper plates filled with cow manure, and covered the manure with the hats. Before I went out for my interview, I draped a sheet over the entire display.

JJ, Brute Bernard & The Angel

I started off by saying, *"I just came back from the New Jersey State Fair. It was a huge success. Everyone back home was so excited to see me, and happy to hear that I'm ruling the wrestling world out here in west Texas. They don't understand why you haven't embraced me, though. While I was at home, I made this display as a salute to you people here in west Texas."*

When I unveiled it, the studio audience saw *"Chips Off The Old Block,"* and four pairs of boots with hats on top. Then, as I lifted the hats exposing the cow chips, I said, *"Isn't this great? Chips off the old block! These chips over here are Dory Funk and Terry Funk — chips off of Dory Funk, Sr! Look! Here's the next chip, right off of 'Iron' Mike DiBiase. It's Ted DiBiase!"* As I picked a hat up off of another pair of boots, I said, *"The last one was Frankie Hill Murdoch, and his chip off the old block is Richard 'The Rube' Murdoch! The people in New Jersey thought it was the greatest thing they ever saw, and I won first place!"*

I held up a big, blue, *first place* ribbon, then I start laughing. All of a sudden, Murdoch came running out, but I managed to escape. Dickie just stood on the set, with his hands on his hips, and stared at the display. He talked about how I had trashed the memory of men like Dory Funk Sr., "Iron" Mike DiBiase, and Frankie Hill Murdoch, all legendary west Texas wrestlers who had passed on. We got tremendous mileage out of that.

Fans used to throw coins and batteries at the heels. I remember one horrible incident with Karl von Steiger. I was very close to Karl and his wife, Pat. Karl did a run-in on a match in Albuquerque, New Mexico. That town was so hot that we used a series of ramps to get in and out of the ring. The ramp was just a table, about four feet wide and level with the ring apron, and it didn't feel stable under your feet, but you had to walk down that train of ramps to get into the ring.

This was a particularly hot finish, and someone in the balcony had taken the arm rest from their chair. The arm rests were quite sturdy and made out of metal. Someone had rocked theirs back and forth until it snapped off the frame, threw it from the balcony, and hit Karl on his cheek. The force of the blow shattered his dentures and pierced his cheek. He had to have the wound sutured. That's the worst memory I have of injury caused by a fan throwing something.

Another time, in the Sportatorium in Dallas, I was in front of Abdullah as we walked back to the dressing room. A fan pulled an ice pick from his pocket and jabbed it at me as I walked by, but he ended up sticking it in Abdullah.

One night, Dory invited Jeanette and me to his house for a few drinks. A few drinks turned into a half gallon of rum. All of a sudden, it was five o'clock in the morning. I said, *"Oh my God! If we're going to make the Albuquerque show on time, we have to leave now!"*

Dory said, *"What do you mean we?"*

He didn't have to go!

The drive from Amarillo to Albuquerque was 300 miles and we had to be there at nine o'clock a.m. The trip was all open highway, so we could drive 80 mph. Fortunately, we also changed time zones on the trip, so we picked up an hour, which gave us just enough time to reach Albuquerque.

Jeanette said she'd go with me and we could keep each other awake. We fought sleep all the way to the New Mexico state line. At one point, I pulled over into a rest stop so I could close my eyes for just five minutes. At the time, we owned a blue, customized van. As we lay in the back of our van, we heard a sharp rapping sound on the window. It was Ted DiBiase, who had stopped to see if I was okay when he recognized my van. When I told him what happened, Ted told the person driving his car to go on ahead. Ted climbed into my van and drove to Albuquerque, while Jeanette and I slept in the back.

In Amarillo, we drove to the towns, but there were a few occasions when we flew. Dory's brother-in-law had a pilot's license, so he flew us to a show in Salt Lake City, Utah. We also flew to a show in Tucson, Arizona. On that trip, I was on the plane with Dick Murdoch and Kay Noble. Not only was Kay one of the greatest women wrestlers of all time, but she was a fun person to be around.

Dickie came onto the flight with a case of beer under his arm, so God only knows how much weight was on the plane. The three of us drank beer after beer ... until Kay had to use the bathroom. This was a small, private plane, so there was no bathroom onboard. We rearranged our seats so Kay could get as far to the rear of the plane as possible. She used a plastic Hefty bag and said, *"If either one of you turns around and looks, I'm gonna kill ya!"*

I made many life-long friends while I was in Amarillo. Stanley Blackburn was a wonderful man. The Blackburns were one of the founding families in Amarillo. At one time, their family owned half the town. Stanley would send me a birthday card every year. Cletis Smith was another good friend, and a good person, as well. She worked in the Lubbock box office for Nick Roberts. She also worked for Continental Airlines. Whenever I needed to fly somewhere and couldn't get a flight, Cletis was always someone I could call on for help. She helped a lot of the guys with their flights.

In March 1978, I was invited to wrestle in Australia. As I've already mentioned, Australia was the second of the three specific goals I set for myself when I got into the business. But not only was I going to wrestle in Australia, I was given the opportunity to do the booking.

## Chapter 12

## The Giant and the Poofter

My impression of Australia was that it was like the United States, but fifteen years behind in terms of development. They say it's a man's country, and to a degree, I think it is. The Australian men work all day long. Before going home, they go to the pub and get looped. When they get home, they expect their wife to have their meal on the table. That seemed to be the mindset. You can see a little taste of that in the current Foster's Beer commercial.

The Aussie people were wonderful. When they are your friends, they are your friends forever through thick and thin. I met a group of guys who owned a detective agency. One of them owned a fishing boat and he took Brute Bernard and me fishing when we had a day off.

Australia is a huge continent. We made two trips to Perth, on the coast. That would be like going from New York to Los Angeles, a five to six-hour flight.

Most of the boys lived in Sydney. If I had to compare Sydney to an American city, it would be New York City. It was an exciting place. Melbourne, on the other hand, was very grey, and the weather seemed very different. It was more like London. The American soldiers spent their R&R time in Sydney during the Vietnam war. In fact, most them stayed at the Texas Town and Country Tavern, the same hotel where I stayed. It had bars on three different levels, one of which stayed open every night until five o'clock a.m. The specific section of Sydney where we lived was called King's Cross, which was similar to the Times Square area, an area replete with strip clubs, nightclubs, and other adult entertainment.

Ron Miller and Larry O'Day (also known as Larry O'Dea; real name Larry Davies), who I had met in Florida in 1971, owned the wrestling promotion in Australia when I was invited over.

The first person to successfully promote wrestling in Australia on a large scale was Jim Barnett. He sold the promotion in 1973 to Eddie Graham and Buddy Fuller. They, in turn, sold the business to Tony Kolonie, who owned a chain of laundromats, but knew nothing about the wrestling business. Miller and O'Day manipulated Kolonie for little or no money and wound up owning the business.

At the same time, another promotion was trying to run in Australia, using Bruno Sammartino and Waldo von Erich as their big names. They didn't have TV, which is a necessity, so they only lasted six weeks before the promotion folded. Waldo had worked for Ron Miller in the past, so he called Ron and they brought him over.

My first appearance in Australia was on March 22, 1978. When I first went in, I managed Brute Bernard. They brought Brute in and shipped Bruiser Brody out (you can draw your own conclusions about their perceptions of talent) a couple of weeks after I came in. He (Brody) met his wife, who worked as a receptionist, in Australia.

She went to America with him, they got married, and had a family.

Brute had been a commodity back in the early days when Barnett was promoting, so in Miller and O'Day's eyes, it was, *"Oh, boy! We can get Bernard!"* Even though it was towards the end of his career, and he was badly crippled up, Brute was a hard-working man. I also managed Waldo von Erich when he came in.

I faced several obstacles that made it difficult to promote successfully. Part of the problem I faced was that I didn't have any talent depth. I was booking for a population that had seen the best of the best—Dusty Rhodes, Dick Murdoch, Killer Karl Kox, King Curtis Iaukea, Mark Lewin, and Red Bastien, among others. Most of the big names had appeared in Australia at one time or another.

Larry O'Day was featured, but Ron Miller and Mario Milano were the nucleus of the promotion. Milano had been there for a long time. He retired at one point, then he came back. He lived in Australia and he still had name value, but he was no longer showcased at the level he had been years before. I tried to do an angle with him, but it just didn't have any legs to it. Ron Miller, the main babyface in the territory, was not a huge man. He was comparable to Chris Benoit in size. Ron was not very flamboyant. He was bland, colorless, and his interview skills were lacking.

Miller kept the Austra-Asian title on himself for more than two years. He didn't want to give the belt to anybody else because he was afraid they'd walk out and take it with them. From a business standpoint, I had worked for enough offices to understand the logic. Promoters were always fearful of putting stock in an outsider, especially a foreigner coming through their territory, and then having them leave on short notice. Ron Miller was acceptable as the champion. We could have made a lot more money with others, but since he was one of the owners, nobody could say much about it. It was also a time when business in the States was fairly good, so I couldn't get anyone to travel halfway around the world for the same kind of money, or less, than they were already making.

Another problem we faced were restrictions by the TV station. There was a lot of focus by the government on violence on television. If there was such a thing as being over-censored, that's what was happening. I had to do angles to get heat, but if I did anything in the studio that the station management considered to be violent, they would refuse to air it. The same rule held for any angle I might have taped in the arena to air on the show. There was an extremely thin line between what was acceptable and what was not. At the studio show in Melbourne, we used sandbags to hold down set scenery. We also used sandbags on the corner of the ring posts to give them extra stability, so the ring wouldn't shift during a match. When Waldo von Erich picked up one of the sandbags and whacked his opponent in the stomach with it, the censors wanted to stop the show!

I did one angle that I had seen in another territory. Mario Milano was slated to leave for Japan, so I did an angle with Mario and Brute Bernard in the Melbourne Arena. I went into the ring, lit a cigar, and stuck it in Mario's eye. When he got to Japan, he cut a series of promos while wearing a patch over his eye. He vowed to come back and get revenge. When he returned to Australia, he wore the patch for a few weeks.

I don't know how we got that one by the censors, but we did. Unfortunately, once they realized what we had done, they wouldn't allow us to air it a second time. We got what mileage we could out of it. We did the best with what we had to work with. Again, we were working with Mario Milano and Brute Bernard, both of whom had been there a long time, and as you age, there are limitations to what you can do.

With limited talent, and not being able to work any hot angles, it was a struggle just to get through that period of time.

Wrestling in Sydney was actually held in a town called Flemington, which was out about 20 miles. The matches were held on land that was used as a wholesale produce

Fishing with Brute Bernard & Australian friends

farm during the week, in an open-air, tin shed that was open on the sides and closed on the ends. They didn't have bleachers. They brought in folding chairs and used 12-foot boards laid on construction stanchions to make aisles.

Andre the Giant came in for two weeks in June. For the first week, I wanted to do something that would lead to Andre coming back against Brute on the following week. I told O'Day, *"During the match, Andre will end up with a bearhug on Brute. When I realize that all hope is lost, I'll roll into the ring, take my shoe off, and whack Andre with it."*

Larry didn't like the idea. *"Oh no, mate."* he said. *"That's too much like a poofter."* In Australia, *poofter* is a slang word for homosexual. In Larry's mind, using my shoe was too effeminate.

I said *"Larry, trust me on this one. I'm not gonna hit him in an effeminate way. I've had great success with this, and it will look good. You watch."*

He very reluctantly agreed. Sure enough, when Andre put Brute in the bearhug, I rolled in, took off my shoe, and used it like a baseball bat. Andre dropped to one knee. He stood back up, with blood pouring down his face, and bellowed like a wounded moose. Brute and I each took one punch from Andre and we rolled out.

And then came the audience.

It was a very ethnic audience, mostly Italians and Greeks. They started their "protest" against my cheating ways by throwing chairs over the top rope. When they ran out of chairs, they stormed the aisles, tossing the construction stanchions around like Lincoln Logs, the construction toy that children played with years ago.

Before long, the aisleway had disappeared ... and so did our escape path. The former aisleway became an obstacle course. If you tried to step over the 12-foot boards, the people would pull them up and crotch you. If you tried to go under them, they would kick you in the head. It was a bad situation and we fought every inch of the way to the dressing room.

Ron Miller, Larry O'Day, and all the other boys ran out from the dressing room, knocking people out left and right, trying to clear an aisle for us to run through. I was in front of Brute, but I still got speared with a chair that left a strawberry-colored welt on my back.

Brute, who was completely bald, got hit in the head with something. When we got to the back, we saw that he had blood running down his face. Whatever the object was, it had cut a deep gash in his head. We put a whole roll of gauze on it to stem the bleeding, then went back to our hotel, the Texas Town & Country Tavern. Brute had an old flame there who nursed him. Of course, he insisted on having a few beers to take the edge off. Unfortunately, that thinned his blood and the wound started to ooze through the bandage.

When he woke up the next morning, the wound was still bleeding, so we called a doctor. He invited us to stop by his office so he could take a look at it. The doctor had a great deal of trouble getting the gauze off of Brute's head. The blood and puss had dried and the gauze seemed to be a part of the wound itself. Brute was relatively calm and peaceful at that point. When the doctor finally got the gauze off, we all looked at the wound. The gash was laid open to Brute's skull. The doctor didn't do much for Brute's peace of mind. *"Oh, my God! What have they done to you?"*

At that point, Brute was getting scared. He looked at me and said, *"How bad is it?"*

*"It's not that bad,"* I lied. *"The doctor will be able to take care of it."*

Brute had to get stitches inside the wound, and another layer of stitches on top, to keep the wound closed. It was a stupid thing to do, but Brute continued to work that week. In fact, on the night after the riot, Brute and I worked in a handicap match against Andre. The whole week was geared around Andre, Brute, and Waldo von Erich. I had to watch Brute and keep him subdued so that he didn't rip the stitches out.

By far, that was the worst riot I have ever been caught up in, but our matches with Andre spiked business.

Brute and Waldo left when we ran out of ideas for them. When they left, we had trouble finding talent to take their place. We finally talked to Ox Baker, who had a style similar to Brute's, and convinced him to come in. There really wasn't a top spot for Ox in the States at that point in his career, but he could come to Australia and capitalize on his name. I also used Butcher Brannigan and King Curtis. Nothing against Ox or Brannigan, but it was tough to build the territory around them. It was like making chicken salad out of chicken sh—. We also had a cash flow problem. Miller and O'Day didn't have any money. If they did, they certainly didn't want to spend it. They were very frugal.

Terry Garvin came to Australia while I was there. There was a strip club in Kings Cross called Le Girls. On a prior trip to Australia, Terry met a cocktail hostess named Chris at the club. His main reason for returning to Australia was to take her back to the United States and get married. He later helped Chris get her U.S. citizenship. They had two children and she became a nurse.

I stayed in Australia from late March 1978 through October, and lived by myself. Initially, at the hotel, I met a girl named Irene, who was from Scotland. She knew that I was married, but we became very close, and there was a point when I thought I had fallen in love with her. I even entertained the thought of giving up everything and starting a new life with her.

When my stepchildren got out of school, and my wife was going to come to Australia, I was at crossroads. Irene was a tremendous friend and a good person to be around. I do sometimes wonder, *"Where is she? Is she married? Does she have a family of her own?"* And of course, *"What would have happened if ...?"*

When Jeanette arrived, we stayed at the Texas Tavern until we got our apartment. I put out the word: *"My wife is staying in the hotel. I don't want any stories getting out."*

I was on the road every weekend. When I came home on Monday after the first weekend, we were eating breakfast. Jeanette casually said, *"I met one of your girlfriends this weekend."*

I almost choked. *"You what?"*

*"I met one of your girlfriends this weekend!"*

Apparently, Jeanette was in the bar at the hotel when a drunk girl walked up to her and said, *"I know who you are. I'm in love with your husband! If I can't have him, you can't either. I'm gonna kick your ass!"*

Fortunately, the fight never transpired. I played innocent and told Jeanette, *"These Australian women are crazy! I have no idea who she was!"*

For the record, the girl who approached Jeanette was not Irene. She never would have done that.

I finally parted with Miller and O'Day's company. They were looking for ways to cut costs. At that point, they had given me every opportunity to succeed. With the talent I had to work with, and the conditions that I had to work under, I had done everything that I possibly could. I didn't want to stay there just to collect a paycheck, so I gracefully bowed out and made my final appearance on October 31, 1978.

I enjoyed my time in Australia, and I loved the country, but it was time for me to leave. From there, I went to work for Steve Rickard in New Zealand. I had met Steve years before in Amarillo. When I called him, he was happy to have me come over, and gave me a starting date of November 2, 1978. Basically, my ticket was already paid for, so he got a name with a fresh face to come in and work, without the expense of having to fly someone in from the States.

When I went to New Zealand, I let my hair grow, and actually grew a beard for the first time in my life. My hair was darker, too. I started bleaching my hair around 1970, when I was working for Bruno and the Sheik. Since my ex-wife's mother was a beautician, I would get the chemicals from her in bulk. Eventually, I started to use the Clairol products that come in a box, and Jeanette would put it to the roots so that I didn't burn out my hair. I've seen guys smear it on their hair. That works, but over a period of time, it damages the hair. Jeanette wasn't with me in New Zealand, and I didn't want to slop it on and possibly damage my hair, so I let my hair grow out to its natural color. I also wanted to let my hair have a rest from the chemicals. I must admit that I was curious to see what color my hair really was. I had colored my hair for so long that I didn't even know what the actual color of my hair was at that stage of my life.

Brute Miller, who also wrestled as Butch Miller, and later wrestled with Luke Williams as the Bushwhackers, was in the territory. His partners were Sweet William and Mad Dog Martin. The Bushwhackers were born, raised, and started their wrestling careers in New Zealand. Mad Dog Martin, who later wrestled for the WWF and did some managing as Frenchy Martin, was working on top when I got there. The babyfaces were Rick Martel, Les Thornton, and my old friend, Leo Burke. On February 14, 1979, I was in a tag match with Mad Dog against Martel and Leo. When Leo hit the ropes, the ropes gave way and he fell over the ropes, backwards. He hit his head on the floor and was knocked unconscious.

The match had to be stopped and they had to call an ambulance to take him to the hospital. I was very close to Leo and it was a scary situation, but he recovered quickly.

New Zealand • Nov. 1978

# Chapter 13
## Closet Announcer

I went back to Amarillo for the month of January 1979, and worked out a deal where I would return full-time in April. I returned to New Zealand in February and finished up with them on April 8, 1979. I also managed to get booked in Hawaii.

When I returned to Amarillo on April 12, Dick Murdoch and Black Jack Mulligan owned the territory. They had bought it from Dory and Terry Funk. Not only did they want me to wrestle, but they wanted me to book the territory, as well. Terry Garvin was also working in the office, trying to promote a few towns.

I was very surprised when Dory and Terry opted to sell. I remember having a conversation with Terry Funk, who I always respected because of his insight into the wrestling business. He was always on the front end of the curve. When the Funks sold the territory, I said, *"Terry, when I came into the business, I would have died to be in your position, to be a second-generation wrestler, and have the experience of working with my father. When he passes on, my brother and I get the territory. I would've thought you were set for life. You're a promoter. You own the towns and the territory. Why did you sell? Why did you get out?"*

I had similar conversations with Dory. Looking in from the outside, I just didn't understand the amount of work that was involved, or the financial risk. They told me that at the end of the year, in addition to what they earned working in their own territory, their financial reward for their percentage of the profit was $30,000 apiece. When you consider everything that was involved—the work, the responsibility, and the financial risk—that wasn't a huge amount of money. The bulk of their income didn't come from the promotion. It came from their efforts as performers in the ring.

Terry Funk

When the United States went through the gas rationing in the '70s, you can imagine being in a territory like Amarillo, where you drove 2,000 miles a week, and then being told that you could only buy gasoline on odd or even days. Gordon Nelson wanted to be sure that he had enough to get to the towns, so he had an auxiliary tank installed in the trunk of his car.

Terry saw gas rationing coming, and even though that eventually passed, he knew the price of gas was going up. He realized that gas was not always going to be 40-cents a gallon. Other road expenses were going up, too. You could no longer stay in the El Paso Holiday Inn for two nights for $18.

Terry also recognized the dramatic changes the business had coming with the advent of cable television. Cable TV was making inroads in all parts of the country.

Fans in west Texas now had access to *Championship Wrestling from Georgia*, the hot wrestling show on Ted Turner's WTBS Superstation. All of a sudden, the fans started to ask, *"When are we going to see somebody new?"*

Dick Murdoch, Dory Funk, Terry Funk, Black Jack Mulligan, and Jim Dillon were all yesterday's news. The fans wanted to see the wrestlers who appeared on the Superstation—"Wildfire" Tommy Rich, "Mad Dog" Buzz Sawyer, Ole Anderson, Ivan Koloff, Dick Slater, Thunderbolt Patterson, Tony Atlas, Wahoo McDaniel, and Ernie Ladd. With cable television being installed in many homes, those wrestlers were being seen on television every week, but not live in our towns.

Due to cable television, I don't think wrestling will ever go back to the territorial system. Before cable television allowed wrestling promotions to be seen by people worldwide, most cities had one product, so there was no comparison made between two or more promotions. If you lived in Florida, wrestling was Eddie Graham, Jack Brisco, Jerry Brisco, and Dusty Rhodes. You knew that the Funks were going to come in every so often. Terry would tape outrageous promos in Amarillo and send them to Eddie. When they came into Florida, they were the despicable villains and the Briscos were the babyfaces. In Amarillo, wrestling was Dory Funk Sr., Dory Funk Jr., Terry Funk, and Dick Murdoch. Every so often, the Briscos would come in from Florida, and the shoe would be on the other foot. The roles were reversed and the Briscos were hated in Amarillo.

The really astute fans in Amarillo watched the TBS show and thought, *"That's strange. In Georgia, the Funks are bad guys."* They started to realize that wrestling was a business that was choreographed and manipulated.

Michigan was the stomping ground of the Sheik, Bobo Brazil, and the Mighty Igor. As far as wrestling fans in Dallas were concerned, the world revolved around the Von Erich boys. The fans thought they were nationwide stars, and yet, until the 1980s, very few people outside of Texas even knew who the Von Erichs were. There were many other territories, and they all had their stars. That was how wrestling had been presented for decades.

That was when I finally began to understand that professional wrestling was a talent-driven business. It didn't matter how good a worker you were, or how over you were, or how hot your angle was. After a period of time, the fans wanted to see new faces. They had seen me, Murdoch, and the Funks, every week for years. They wanted to see Tommy Rich and Tony Atlas.

Terry Funk saw the writing on the wall and felt the time was right to get out. Terry and Dory wanted to get out while they could still get a little something for the territory. In time, it wouldn't be worth anything, because financially, it wouldn't be feasible to continue to run it.

I don't think there was any malice on the part of the Funks in selling it to Dickie and Black Jack. Terry and Dory were both up-front with them and told them where they thought the territory was headed. It's not unlike selling someone a stock that you think has reached its peak and is going down. If somebody else sees an upside to the stock, and wants to buy it, that's a logical business decision on both parts. Dickie lived in Amarillo, and owning a promotion was something that he always wanted to do.

Dory and Terry didn't get as much for the territory as people thought they did. They were paid $10,000 apiece as a down payment on the territory, and were supposed to be paid the rest in installments, but that never materialized.

Jerry Kozak promoted Amarillo. Jerry was a good figurehead for the promotion because he had wrestled, and he developed a good reputation by going to Better Business Bureau and Chamber of Commerce functions, but business-wise, his wife, Edie, was the driving force behind the success of the promotion. When Edie contracted cancer, we all watched her wither away, until she finally gave up the battle. Jerry tried to make a go of it by himself, but it would never be like it was.

Murdoch, Mulligan, and I all worked together in the office. I was the one who put the ideas to paper, but they were involved in the booking process and ultimately approved or disapproved them.

The territory was struggling. Since Dallas and Fort Worth were within driving distance, we made a deal with Fritz von Erich to use our talent in those two towns. We reciprocated by booking his boys in Amarillo. It was an economic decision that gave both offices a broader base of talent to work with, and also allowed us to supplement our pay.

Gary Hart, who booked the Dallas territory for Fritz, was very smart. He was a businessman. He knew the territory, had a good working relationship with Fritz, and worked well with Fritz' sons. Gary, like me, was also a working manager. Many times, when a new manager came into a territory, it put the local managers on the defensive. That has always been the nature of the wrestling business, or any business, for that matter. If somebody new came into a territory, everybody worried that the new guys were coming in to take their job. Gary didn't look at it that way. Gary was smart enough to recognize that he could bring me in as the invading, heel manager.

Gary Hart

Gary had been in the territory for a long time, and was established, so it would be easy to turn himself babyface. Gary would remain a heel when he was managing his own men in other matches, but when they faced my men, Gary and I would have confrontations. Other bookers, who were less knowledgeable and understanding in the business, might have resisted that and fought against me coming in, but Gary had enough business savvy to use my talent to his own advantage. He didn't feel threatened in his position by having me come in. Most bookers would have looked at me as a threat and fought against me.

"Playboy" Gary Hart was the rich kid, while I was the brash, loud-mouthed kid from the east who thought he was better than the hometown boys—the good ol' boys who raised cattle, drove pickup trucks, wore baseball caps, chewed tobacco, and drank beer.

Terry Garvin and I did whatever we had to do to make the Amarillo promotion a financial success. We wore many different hats. Concession is a big part of the income that keeps a promotion going, so Terry would get huge bags of popcorn, 2-liter bottles of soft drinks, and bags of ice, at wholesale prices, and the promotion would sell them. I even pulled a microphone into a closet in the back of the arena one night, and surreptitiously did the ring announcing. When I say that I've done it all, I mean it. I've done it all!

We had a power outage at the Lubbock Coliseum one night, in the middle of the card. At the time, I was the International heavyweight champion, and I was in the main event. We opened the roll-up garage doors, brought in eight pickup trucks, and aimed their headlights at the ring. That's how we lit the main event.

On May 17, 1979, I teamed with Black Jack Mulligan to wrestle Dick Murdoch and Dory Funk Jr. in Pueblo, Colorado. When I hit the top rope, it buckled, and I did a cartwheel in mid-air over the rope. The next thing I knew, my feet hit the arena floor and I collapsed. I wasn't hurt, but it looked bad enough to scare Dory. He came out of the ring to pick me up (making it look like he was picking me up to continue punishing me) and whispered, *"Are you all right? It looked like you killed yourself."*

That was the only time I had a rope break on me. We used to tie each others heads up into the ropes. It was easier to do in the large rings because the ropes are longer. In the shorter rings, the ropes are tighter and have less mobility, which is logical if you think about it. There were some guys who had the ability to go over the top rope, and in the process, tuck their head under the top rope, grab the top two ropes with their hands, and tie themselves up—all in the same motion.

Dick Murdoch and I drew a lot of money together. He was the hometown babyface. I was the brash, loud-mouthed heel. That being the case, Dickie and I went to great lengths to kayfabe [protect the secrets of the business] in that territory, as did everyone else. If I was in a restaurant in Amarillo, and Dickie walked in, or vice versa, one of us would turn around, walk out, and find another restaurant. Those were the lengths we went to in order to protect the business. The towns in that territory were small, and we couldn't afford to expose the business. It would have devastating effects, so I never socialized with any of the babyfaces.

If we weren't booked in Albuquerque on a Sunday night, we made a trip from Clovis, New Mexico, to El Paso, Texas, on Monday. For some reason, on one particular week, Dickie and I were the only two people making the trip to El Paso and around the loop. Since we were always on opposite sides of the fence, that was the only time that Dickie and I made a road trip together while we were in Amarillo.

The trip was all back roads and late at night, so one of the boys dropped Dickie off on a deserted stretch of highway. A few minutes later, I pulled up and he jumped in. A short while later, as we were driving through the mountains, my car broke down when the water pump stopped working. Dickie and I knew there would be few cars on the road, but we also knew that Barry Windham would be along shortly. Barry, the son of Black Jack Mulligan, had just graduated from high school. He was in Amarillo for the summer, so his dad put him to work hauling the ring from town to town. Since he had to be in the towns early to set up the ring, Barry usually traveled by himself, and took his dog along with him.

Dickie and I stood by the side of the road. We didn't think a pickup truck hauling a ring would be difficult to spot. When we saw it, one of us would flag it down. We also tried to flag down the few cars that happened to drive by. At this point in time, we were still trying to kayfabe, and we didn't want the general public to see us traveling together, so whenever we saw a car, either Dickie or I would hide in the bushes. There weren't many cars on the road at that hour of the night, and the few that went by refused to stop. Dickie weighed 280 pounds and I weighed 230, and we both had blond hair. Two strange-looking individuals in the middle of the desert between Clovis and El Paso. Would you stop to give either one of us a ride?

Eventually, we saw the ring truck. We both stood on the side of the road and waved as Barry roared past us. He must have been driving in a daze because he never saw us. We picked rocks up and heaved them at the truck, but it was a futile attempt because the truck was long gone before we had thrown the first rock.

Dickie and I were in the desert, in the middle of the night, and our only chance of a ride had driven right past us.

Five minutes later, another car appeared in the distance, so I hid in the bushes. This time, the driver slowed down. He didn't stop, but he did slow down enough to allow Dickie to say, *"My car broke down. I tried to flag my buddy down as he went past, but he didn't see me and kept on going."*

The guy told Dickie to get in and they took off, hoping to catch Windham. An hour later, Barry and Dickie pulled up. Dickie drove the ring truck and I sat on the passenger side. Dickie stuck Barry in the bed of the pickup with his dog. It was the middle of the night, and it was cold! Dickie made him stay there until we got to El Paso. All because he had driven by us and didn't stop.

Barry Windham was connected to Murdoch at the hip. Murdoch always had an entourage of people following him around. *"Let's go to the honkytonks and get drunk!"* Barry was a natural fit into Dickie's entourage. They had a good time together and Dickie loved him. They were like two brothers.

Somewhere along the way, we broke Barry into the business. He had his first match with me in Odessa, Texas, on November 27, 1979. He was just a skinny kid at that point, but he was tall, and we were certain that he would fill out. Barry had God-given, natural abilities that you could see even then. He evolved from a skinny kid to one of the great performers of our business.

Dick Murdoch never seemed to change. He always looked the same, and he was always a happy-go-lucky guy. In total, we had 196 matches against each other. On top of that, I must have managed wrestlers against him another 200 times. We were also tag team partners twice—once in Tampa and another time in St. Louis. I personally felt that Dick Murdoch would have made a great world champion. There's no arguing the fact that he had the talent, as much as anyone I ever worked with in all my years in the business. He was a naturally big guy, too, but like me, Dickie hated to train, and he had a belly that pooched out. The promoters also got frustrated because Dickie liked to clown around in the ring. He was one of the few who could get away with it, but even so, the promoters resented that side of him.

Those are the only criticisms I ever heard of Dickie, and that may have been the reason why he was never considered to be a world champion. Perhaps they felt that he would do silly things in the ring and tarnish the reputation of the title.

**Dick Murdoch**

Jack Mulligan was in the office every day. When it came to running the business, he was a very hands-on person, unlike Dickie, who was the type of person who didn't like to be cooped up in an office. Mulligan had a good run in the Carolinas while working for George Scott. When he bought the Amarillo territory, he transferred $25,000 into a bank account in Amarillo. He planned to use that money for his daily living expenses until the company could turn a profit. It wasn't intended to be a business account.

One day, Mulligan got a phone call from the bank manager, who told him his account was empty. *"Wadda ya mean there isn't any money in there?,"* Jack questioned. *"I put $25,000 in there when I came here."*

*"That's true,"* the bank manager replied, *"but it's all gone."*

All of a sudden, Jack realized that he had been there for a long period of time, and he had depleted the account in an attempt to keep the business running. He called George Scott and said, *"George, I've gotta go back to work and I need to earn some money."* George was thrilled to hear from Jack and immediately took him back. Jack got a starting date in the Carolinas and left rather abruptly.

With Mulligan back in the Carolinas, it fell on Dickie's shoulders to take on the office duties, but Dickie Murdoch was not suited to doing the things it took to run a business. That was when the business really started to fall apart. We did whatever we could to hold everything together. In addition to aligning ourselves with the Dallas office, we also began working with Bill Watts' Mid-South territory. However, when you sense that a ship is beginning to sink, you begin to make plans.

My last match in the territory was on November 6, 1980, in Abilene, Texas. I wrestled Yaqui Joe. Terry Garvin was still there when I left, but I don't think they were in business for very long after that.

Amarillo was a tough territory to work, and the trips were long. We averaged more than 2,000 miles a week. That's a lot of time to sit in a car. And yet, of all the territories I worked, Amarillo was where I had the most fun. You were encouraged to be creative, and the Funks listened to your ideas. If you had a good angle, they would do it. They also allowed a lot of the top guys to book their own angles.

I have such respect for Dory and Terry Funk as workers. They made me feel special when they recruited me to go there. They brought me back several times and told me they would always have a spot in the territory for me. They also followed through on every promise they made to me. I have nothing but great memories of the territory.

Unfortunately, everything that Terry Funk predicted would happen to the wrestling business came true, and the territory struggled as a result of those changes. Expenses went up and creativity was difficult because of the impact of cable television. Eventually, all of the territories fell by the wayside. The territory that survived the longest was Memphis, Tennessee, and the promoter, Jerry Jarrett, managed to sell it before it fell apart.

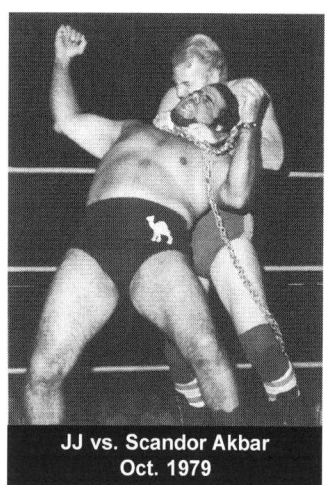

JJ vs. Scandor Akbar Oct. 1979

# Chapter 14
# Border Crossing

I was scheduled to return to Japan in January, so after leaving Amarillo, I started to look for something to do during November and December. Les Thornton, who was booked on a tour of Germany, took some of my pictures with him and gave them to the promoter, Nico Selenkowitsch.

I had always wanted to go to Europe. I had never wrestled in England, but by that time, the guys who worked there traveled long trips every night for little or no money. France didn't even have a wrestling promotion. That left Germany as the only viable place to work.

The promoter booked me for a six-week tour—November 13 through December 17, 1980—as Cowboy Jim Dillon. Dick Murdoch, Ed Wiskowski, Phil Mercado, Tony St. Clair, Eddy Steinblock, Geoff Portz (under a mask), Bob Dellaserra, Moose Morowski, and Barry Douglas were also on the tour, as well as German regulars like Otto Wanz and Wolfgang Saturski. Kevin Sullivan was supposed to be on the tour, but decided to cancel out at the last minute. I also met Stephen Wright there. Stephen, who wrestled until he was injured by Fit Finlay, is the father of Alex Wright, who later wrestled for WCW [World Championship Wrestling].

The trips in Germany were short. In fact, they were very, very short. We wrestled in Bremen, Germany, every night of the week, for the entire six weeks! There were a couple of nights when I didn't even wrestle. We would go to the arena and get dressed, just as if we were wrestling. We marched out in parade fashion while circus music played. We marched around the ring, up the ring steps, and everybody would be introduced. They would then announce who was wrestling against who. If you weren't wrestling, you would sign autographs in the ring area at intermission. After that, you were done for the night. You were paid a set fee for the week, and you wrestled five or six times a week.

The atmosphere at the wrestling shows in Germany was very different from shows in the United States. Wrestling was quite an event, so the fans would all dress up. It made you feel like you had traveled back in time. The men in the front row wore white shirts, ties, and jackets. The women were dressed to the hilt, and even wore fur coats.

The action in the ring was very tame when compared to that in the States. While our country had gone the route of violence—blood, punching, and kicking—the German promoter refused to allow it. He said that when wrestlers in the U.S. get punched, they don't bleed, and their eyes don't swell up. Murdoch threw as good a punch as anybody in the business, and yet, they didn't even want to see him do it. In their eyes, if somebody threw a punch like Murdoch did, the recipient should be knocked out, or at the least, incapacitated. It was an eye-opener on where we had gone as an industry in the United States.

Germany • November 1980

If one of the wrestlers threw a temper tantrum and pushed the promoter out of the way, the wrestler was reprimanded and threatened with arrest. I could see the advantages of being able to promote your business under that system.

For American fans, it's hard to understand how they could draw a crowd in the same building, in the same town, night after night. However, you have to remember that Bremen only saw wrestling for those six weeks out of the year. The matches were promoted in a tournament system and they kept track of wins and losses. During the week, the house might be half full. At the beginning of the tournament, you would draw three-fourths of a house on Friday, Saturday, and Sunday. By the end of the tournament, the championship matches would be held on specific nights, usually on weekends. They would also build to having the world heavyweight champion come in for the final week of the season.

Many of the European wrestlers lived in small campers that hooked onto the back of their vehicle. They would lease them by the week. They were big enough for one person to have a hot plate for cooking basic meals. There would be a line of the campers behind the arena, with power cords running from each into the building. They would use the toilet and shower facilities inside the arena.

The promoter put the Americans and wrestlers from other countries in hotels and boarding houses. I was one of the lucky ones who stayed in a boarding house which had a shower stall in my room.

My most vivid memory of Germany was the system of fining wrestlers for rules violations. If someone refused to break a hold, or choked their opponent, the referee would hold up a yellow card, similar to what we see in soccer, and he would levee a fine for a specific number of German marks, depending on the severity of the infraction.

The people were educated to assist the babyface with any fine he might incur. If a babyface made a comeback, and in the heat of the moment, did something that would earn him a fine from the referee, the fans in the audience would run down to ringside and pay his fine! For instance, if a babyface was fined ten marks for a rules infraction, you would see some guy in the bleachers, or the ringside seats, get up and run down to the announcer's desk. The announcer would say, *"His fine has been paid!"* The person who paid the fine would get his name announced. When that happened, the people would all cheer.

At the end of the night, the promoter took the fine money and divided it among the boys.

You can imagine how easy it would be to milk that to the breaking point, and eventually kill it, but they never pushed it too far. It was like found money. The money from fines would give everyone a little extra cash to pay for the beer that night. There would be nights when the fines didn't amount to much, but if one of the big stars was fined, it could be a considerable sum. A big star could push the referee and get a "double fine," and the fans would respond in the same fashion.

At night, after the matches were over, you would hang your wrestling gear and boots up in the arena. The arena would be locked up overnight and your gear would be there when you returned the following night. Following the event, we would go to Nico Selenkowitsch's bar/restaurant for delicious, home-style meals.

After that tour, Nico came to the United States and met with Bob Geigel and Pat O'Connor in Kansas City. He wanted to set up a talent exchange, but it never got off the ground.

Bob Geigel, Nico Selenkowitsch & JJ Dillon

I left Germany a week before Christmas and spent the first three weeks of 1981 in Japan with Abdullah.

I didn't have any bookings scheduled when my Japan tour ended on January 22, 1981. It was the only time in my career that I wasn't scheduled to go somewhere. I'm not saying that I was a commodity, or in big demand, but that was kind of scary because I always had someone interested in me. My next move was always planned out before I finished up in a territory. I always had a place to go.

I talked to George Scott, but there was nothing available in Charlotte. Art Nelson had a lot of stroke in the Carolinas, but he couldn't help me because he was booking for Ripper Leone in California, and they didn't have any openings for talent there, either.

I always hoped that before my career ended, I could say that I wrestled in every state in the United States. I also wanted to work in every territory. If I had an opportunity to work someplace like Montana, even if for only one shot, I would jump at the opportunity. When my career did end, I had only missed a few states: New Hampshire, North Dakota, South Dakota, and Alaska.

Mr. (Kazuo) Sakurada was working in Japan for Giant Baba when I was there in 1981. Mr. Hito (Adachi), his tag team partner, lived in Calgary, Alberta, Canada, where he owned an Asian restaurant. I had managed Sakurada and Mr. Hito when I was in Dallas, and the two of them were working in Calgary at the time. Since I didn't have anything scheduled when I finished up in Japan, I flew into Calgary with Sakurada. I had heard so much about Stu Hart, the promoter in Calgary. I had met him once before, but I wanted to see the Hart mansion, and the infamous "dungeon" in his basement that everyone talked about. I also wanted to meet Stu's wife, Helen, and their TV commentator, Ed Whalen.

When I arrived, Stu put me to work. I was there for 10 days—from January 23 to February 1, 1981. That gave me time to get on the phone and see what I could get going.

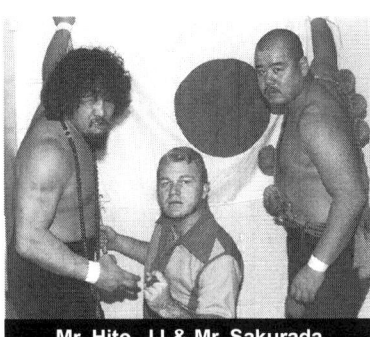
Mr. Hito, JJ & Mr. Sakurada

One morning, I went over to the Hart's mansion. It was a beautiful house that sat on top of a hill. I was told that at one time, it was the only house in the area for miles, but over the years, they sold the surrounding property and a subdivision had been built around it.

I remember seeing a ring and a ring truck in the yard as I walked up to the house. When I walked up the front steps onto the porch, I saw a beautiful staircase with huge pillars reaching up to the second floor. In the living room, they had 2-foot by 3-foot portraits of their twelve children that were taken when they were 9 years old.

Their kitchen had a huge, commercial-sized stove, and pots hung down from the ceiling. I made sure that I arrived after breakfast was over. I had heard the stories about Stu making eggs in the kitchen. When the cat crapped on the kitchen counter, he used the spatula to scoop up the turds and flip them into the trash can, then went right back to flipping the eggs.

I also went down to the basement to see the dungeon. It was nothing fancy—just a room with holes in the wall, where people's heads and elbows had been dashed. If the walls could talk, I'm sure the stories would be incredible.

Stu Hart told the same stories over and over again, stories about Archie "Stomper" Gouldie, George Gordienko, Luther Lindsay, Wilbur Nead [ex-Iowa State star], and Gorilla Monsoon. Those were a few of the guys that Stu couldn't manhandle in the dungeon. The list of those he couldn't manhandle was very short, so he had a great deal of respect for them. He held them in high esteem and talked about them constantly.

When the wrestlers were required to make a long trip, the office supplied a van and everybody rode together. While I was in Calgary, we made one trip to Montana for shows in Billings and Butte. Six or seven guys were in the van, with Jim Neidhart doing all the driving. We had wrestled in Canada earlier that night and it was late as we approached the US-Canadian border. When we were about a mile from the U.S. border, I watched as one of the boys reached into his suitcase and took out a cast. He wedged his arm and hand into the cast, put a sling around his neck, and leaned his head on the window, as if he was sleeping.

If you were a Canadian citizen, you had to have a green card or work permit if you were coming into the United States, and the guard knew that we were wrestlers. It became obvious to me that the guy with the cast didn't have the documentation he needed, or the authority to work.

I was used to going to major border crossings like Tijuana, Mexico, and Windsor, Ontario, Canada. The border into Montana was situated on a back road and the guard was stationed in an old shack. When we pulled up to the border crossing, the guard walked out of the shack and shined his flashlight into the van. *"Does everybody have a work permit?"*

I held up my passport, showing that I was a U.S. citizen. Somebody said, *"That guy in the back broke his arm tonight and can't wrestle. He's still traveling with us because we have no way of getting him back to Calgary."*

That was good enough for the guard. He said, *"Okay, go ahead,"* and we drove into Montana.

Shortly after that, we ran into some bad weather and the temperature dropped. As we drove into town, the transmission went out. After having the van towed to a garage, we were told the repairs would cost $700. One of the boys asked, *"Does anyone have cash?"*

When you leave Japan, they pay you in cash, so I had almost $3,000 in cash with me. When I told him that I did, he asked, *"Would you pay for it? When we get back, Stu will reimburse you."* I paid the bill and was reimbursed as soon as we got back to Calgary. Everybody slept that day while the van was being repaired, and we left in time to get to Billings.

I didn't know it, but the boys had a rib going on behind my back. While I was in Calgary, I spent a lot of time on the telephone, talking to Eddie Graham, to see if he was successful in hooking me up somewhere. I had spoken to Eddie Graham during the holidays, before I left for Japan. *"I have a full roster right now,"* he had said, *"but let me see what I can get going for you. Call me when you get back from Japan."*

As soon as I had arrived in Calgary, I called Eddie. *"I still don't have anything,"* he said, *"but I want to help you. Let me make a few more calls. Call me tomorrow."*

Every time I called Eddie, he told me to call him back. *"I'm working on something for you."* That went on and on, so whenever I had an opportunity, such as when we stopped the van for gas, or to get something to eat, I went to a pay phone and called him.

Meanwhile, the other boys in the van were telling Neidhart that every time I had a chance, I was running to the phone to report to Stu on what they were doing. Neidhart, who didn't know me from Adam at that point, was a nervous wreck. He was on pins and needles, worrying about what I might be telling Stu. Neidhart was always nervous, anyway. He was high strung, and he knew that I was making more than the normal number of long distance phone calls that someone would be making.

I don't remember how the rib ended, but by the end of the week, Eddie said, *"I'd dearly love to have you come here, but I don't have anything right now. I do have a friend who is in dire need of help. I told him you're the man and I want to send you there."*

The man he was talking about was Bob Geigel, who was a partner in the wrestling promotion in Kansas City, Missouri, with Pat O'Connor and Harley Race.

Jeanette & JJ, Nico Selenkowitsch & wife AnneMarie, in Kansas City

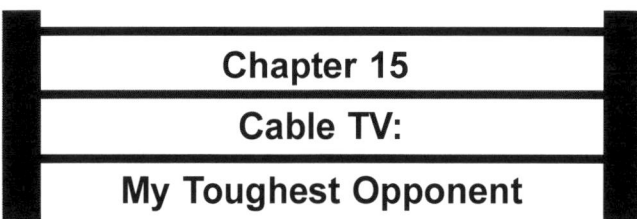

# Chapter 15
## Cable TV:
## My Toughest Opponent

Before we finished our conversation, Eddie Graham said, *"I've arranged for you to do more than just work in Kansas City. You'll also do the booking. It will be good experience for you. You won't have a whole lot of talent to work with, but they need the help and you'll get some experience."*

To me, Kansas City sounded a lot like Australia, but I did want the booking experience, and my choices were somewhat limited, so I was happy to accept. When I called Bob Geigel, he said, *"Yeah, Eddie called me. Based on what he told me, we'd love to have you."*

I was told later that my old friend, Terry Garvin, who was running some towns for Geigel, was a supporting factor when Eddie called Geigel. Terry said, *"It would be good for business if you brought him here. I worked with Jim in the Amarillo office."* He told Geigel about my work ethic, and my passion for the business.

Geigel didn't offer me huge money, but it was a decent salary. I averaged about $800 a week to wrestle, book, and work in the office. For the kind of business that the Kansas City territory was capable of doing, it was a fair amount, and it was a salary. I started working there on February 5, 1981.

The position also gave me the opportunity to work for Sam Muchnick in St. Louis. As a rule, if you worked the Kansas City territory, you got to work in St. Louis, but they were separate operations. Geigel, Pat O'Connor, and Harley Race were partners in the Kansas City office, but Muchnick owned St. Louis.

I was excited about wrestling in St. Louis. After all the stories I had heard from my friends, I was thrilled at the thought of being able to work in the old Kiel Auditorium, and to do TV at the Chase Hotel. They were two of the most famous venues in wrestling.

I was wrestling in a new territory, getting an opportunity to book again, and wrestling in St. Louis. With those three factors on my mind, I went in with a very positive attitude.

As far as the booking went, I had a free hand in regards to coming up with ideas. That was probably the reason I got the job. They were starved for new ideas. Since Harley Race was the NWA world heavyweight champion, he was on the road, defending the title, and he didn't have time to involve himself in the day-to-day operations of the business. Harley was very supportive. He would call me periodically and I kept him informed about things that were going on. A few times, he intervened in support of ideas that I wanted to try by calling Geigel himself. To this day, I respect and appreciate Harley for that. Pat O'Connor was in the office every day, but creativity was not Pat's forte. And Bob Geigel was Bob. Geigel was the NWA president at the time and he ran the office. He walked around in flip-flops and went to a lot of the towns. Bob was a man's man. I never had the opportunity to be around Dory Funk Sr., but I always thought they were cut from the same mold. They were as tough as iron and good guys. I have very pleasant memories of Bob Geigel.

Booking is a tough job. Very few guys wanted to be in the office all day long, and then work the towns at night, which is what you had to do, but it was a side of the business that I had always been fascinated with.

I always tried to do things that were consistent and logical, which was not always easy to do when you're trying to be entertaining at the same time. When you were in a small territory, and you didn't have the diversity of talent available that the large territories did, you had to take what you were given and figure out how to get the absolute most out of it. If I was able to book someone who was passing through, or if Geigel called Dick the Bruiser and got him to agree to work a date or two, I made the most of those opportunities. But it was tough to get talent to commit to a lengthy stay because they could get more money in several other territories. That was just the reality of the business.

We had the mainstay wrestlers like Bulldog Bob Brown and Rufus R. Jones. They both lived in Kansas City, so they weren't going anywhere, and they had been there for a long, long time. Bob Sweetan, a long-time heel, was there as a babyface. He had also been in and out of the territory for many years.

I had worked with Bob Brown when we were both in the Maritimes, and we became friends, but once I got to Kansas City, our relationship became very strained. As a booker, I resisted putting him over every night. I didn't want to focus everything around him because the territory was starved for something fresh, but he was Bob Geigel's best friend. I can't tell you how many times I heard, *"We can't take the title off of Bob Brown."*

In Bob Geigel's mind, he had a logical reason for keeping the belt on Bob Brown. He knew that Brown would never pull up stakes in the middle of the night and leave with the title belt. There was a level of comfort in knowing that Brown was loyal to him. Geigel also saw Brown as being more of a drawing card than he really was. That was a part of how the business was, and how it is to this day. I understood the situation, and even though I didn't like it, there was nothing I could do to change it.

It was difficult and frustrating, and I desperately needed fresh faces, but there was no upside to not use Geigel's regulars. At the same time, I tried to weave other people in with some fresh ideas. It was a tough challenge.

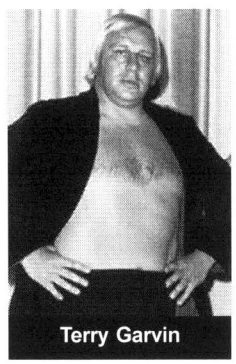
Terry Garvin

Terry Garvin was a notorious ribber. He could be a vicious ribber, too. In Kansas City, we worked in a lot of high schools, so we showered and changed clothes in the boys' locker room. Terry would test the locks on the lockers, trying to find one that wasn't locked. When he found one, he would take it off and lock it on the handle of one of the wrestler's suitcases. Nobody knew who was doing it, but it was a serious rib, because they had to get heavy-duty bolt cutters to remove the locks. There were times when there would be five or six locks on one guy's bag.

I never had the reputation of being a ribber. It wasn't that I didn't like to have fun. I was just very serious about my job, and I didn't think about ribbing. My feeling was, if you rib, you're going to get ribbed back, and I never wanted to get into that vicious circle. I saw it going on all around me, and I laughed just as hard as anybody else, but it was not my thing.

There were a few times when I ribbed, but they were very few and far between. One night, I made a trip with Terry to a town he was promoting. While I was sitting in the locker room, Terry put his briefcase down, and walked out. I wasn't really conscious of doing anything, but when I looked up, I saw a locker with a lock that wasn't latched. I reached up, took it off the locker, and locked it on Terry's briefcase handle. I casually stood up and left the room.

That night, we had a battle royal, so there were a lot of boys in the dressing room. Everybody went out to the ring, did what they had to do, and came back. When the matches were over, Terry and I went out to his car and left.

Terry didn't say one word for thirty minutes. He finally said, *"I'm going over in my mind which one of those bastards put a lock on my briefcase. I know you don't rib ..."*

He continued talking, going through everybody on the card, one by one. He totally discounted me. I wasn't even on the play list. For the rest of the week, he drove himself crazy trying to figure out who might have done it. It was a question with no answer. He had too many possibilities.

Later that week, we went to another town with a similar situation. We were in a high school, in a locker room, and we had a battle royal.

As soon as everybody had evacuated the dressing room for the battle royal, Terry barged into the room, carrying an 8-foot section of heavy chain. He pulled everybody's bags into the middle of the room, threaded the chain through the handles, and locked them to the radiator. He turned around, looked at me, and said, *"I don't know which sonofabitch it was, so I'm gonna get even with all of 'em!"*

One by one, as the boys were eliminated from the battle royal, they came back to the locker room. Terry said to every one of them, *"I don't know which one of you put the lock on my briefcase, but whoever it was, I got you back!"* They all had to wait around until someone from maintenance brought a bolt cutter. I never told Terry the truth, because he was the kind of guy who would have to get even.

While we were in Kansas City, Jeanette's sister died a tragic death at an early age. She had two daughters, Stori and Theresa, and the circumstances at the time were such that their father could not take them in or provide for them. Jeanette's oldest boys were out of the house with families of their own, and the youngest boy was in the Navy, so we offered to raise the girls.

Buzz Tyler and I were tag team partners and we held the North American tag team title. Buzz, who was originally from South Carolina, was married to a girl wrestler named Sandy Partlow. There was also a red-headed girl wrestler in the territory at the time named Shirley Black. Buzz divorced Sandy and married Shirley. Later on, after he divorced Shirley, she married wrestler Mike George. It had all the makings of a soap opera.

Buzz was a lot of fun to be around. He worked very hard and was a credit to the business. We made a lot of trips together, including one noteworthy trip to Garwin, Iowa for a 4th of July matinee show promoted by Terry Garvin. After our match, I made the rounds to the local bars with Buzz and a referee named Larry Dwyer. In a small town like Garwin, that was a big deal because wrestlers enjoyed celebrity status with the local people.

After doing a moderate amount of drinking, each of us fell in love with one of the local girls and paired off. Larry met a young girl and asked if he could borrow the keys to my Dodge van. They were looking for some privacy. Several hours went by and he hadn't returned. We didn't know where he was or how we could get in touch with him. Buzz was angry. He felt that if we got into trouble with the locals, we wouldn't have any way of getting out of town.

When Larry finally came back, he told us that he had been driving around, got lost, and almost ran out of gas. Since it was a holiday, he never found a gas station that was open for business. Enough time had gone by that we had sobered up, so we left the bar and I drove. We were lucky to find an open gas station before the tank went dry. Buzz was in the passenger seat and Larry was in the back. As we drove further into Iowa to our next booking, Buzz was yelling at Larry: *"You are so stupid! You could have gotten us killed! If things got bad at the bar, we had no way to leave! We didn't know where you were ..."*

On and on and on. The more Buzz talked, the angrier he got. Larry was still a kid, so he wasn't saying anything. That seemed to make Buzz angrier. Finally, Buzz said, *"I oughta kick your ass and teach you a lesson."* Buzz reached over, jerked the steering wheel, and the van swerved to the shoulder of the road as I slammed on the brakes. Buzz was screaming, *"I'm gonna kick your ass!"*

Before the car stopped completely, Larry opened the door and jumped out. What he didn't realize was that we had pulled up beside a cement culvert with a drainage ditch that went under the road. After Larry took four or five steps in the pitch darkness, we heard a scream. It sounded like he had fallen into a well. He took a 10- or 12-foot drop into the culvert. It was a miracle that he didn't land on his head and kill himself, or at the very least, break a bone or two. He was sore, though. We got him back into the vehicle and went on our way.

I was in Kansas City on the night when Ric Flair beat Dusty Rhodes to win the NWA world heavyweight title for the first time—September 17, 1981. It was a very emotional night. I first met Flair in Amarillo when the NWA was farming him out to the territories to give him exposure. They were building him up so he would be perceived as a national star. I didn't know him very well when he came to Kansas City that night, and nobody told us that the belt was going to change hands, but I could sense that something big was going to happen. When people brought their wives to the matches in a town like Kansas City, you knew that something was up.

In Amarillo, I became acutely aware of the impact that cable television was having on the territorial system of wrestling, but my time in Kansas City was when I experienced an entirely different problem caused by cable television.

The Kansas City station that produced our wrestling program was KBMA, Channel 41. Saturday (or Sunday) was the traditional day for TV wrestling in that era, but we taped on Thursday nights in Memorial Hall, which was the live house show in Kansas City. Rather than produce a weekly TV show in a studio, we had a remote TV truck come to Memorial Hall and record a simple, two-camera shoot, which is referred to as "live to tape." We were fortunate that our flagship station owned their own remote production truck that was readily available on Thursday nights. Based on an attractive cost and the advantage of having an arena show ambiance, the shoot from the arena made the most sense at the time.

I had a new backdrop made for our opening, breaks, and interviews, and shot those with one camera, which pivoted 45 degrees on the stage of the auditorium. We would close the stage curtain when we shot the opening, and opened it when we used the same camera to shoot the ring. The other camera took care of our close-ups. It was a basic, static setup. We didn't even have a hand-held camera shooting the action in the ring.

Due to the shortage of talent in the Kansas City territory, and to peak interest and keep ratings up, we would often have to show some, or all, of the "main event." The alternative would have been a studio wrestling show. However, a studio show comes with its own set of problems. When you're in a studio, you lose the atmosphere of the live arena. You have the logistics of finding a day, time, and location that worked into the schedule. There was also the issue of finding and paying additional talent.

In the early '80s, TV wrestling was usually arranged through a barter agreement with the television station. The deal with KBMA had to be different than the other markets due to the expenses associated with the "live to tape" production at Memorial Hall. In all the other markets, each station would be given a one-hour show, with open commercial spots that were sold locally by the station. In addition to getting air-time for their show, the wrestling promotion usually retained two of the commercial spots. The wrestlers would record two different 2-minute, local promos for each market to promote the next local event. Each week, the promos for all of the markets were recorded in Kansas City, usually in a TV studio in front of a set, at a specific time, and on a prearranged day.

Television technology was not what it is today. The shows then were recorded on 2-inch video tape. The tape would roll continuously for one hour, and there was no post-editing. During the allotted commercial time, the tape was black, or "dark." There would be pauses in the live, arena show during the commercial spots, which allowed time to clear the ring after one match, and to get the next one into the ring. Two days later, when the show aired, someone in the KBMA studio would run the commercial spots from separate tapes in place of the "dark" spots.

In Kansas City, after the local wrestling promos had been edited into the one-hour show, Bob Geigel personally took the tapes to the bus station, where they were shipped to the various towns in time to air during the coming weekend. The schedule was tight, so bad weather and lost tapes were problems from time to time. If a tape did not arrive to air in a local market as scheduled, it spelled doom for the house show that week. Due to the cost, the Kansas City promotion used minimal newspaper advertising, and no radio spots. Our live event success was directly correlated to the TV show that aired that week.

Unfortunately, the process was archaic. However, you couldn't change "the system" and stay current in every market. There was not enough time to make multiple dubs of the Memorial Hall show, or to insert all the different promos, and get them to the stations on time. In today's world of satellite TV feeds and technology, it would be a piece of cake.

One of the programs that comes to mind featured Pat and Mike Kelly, twin brothers, who worked under the hoods [masks]. After a period of time, the Kelly brothers were unmasked. Of course, they were identical twins. They looked so much alike that at a pivotal point in a match, they would do a switch without a tag, and get the win. The same thing happened the following week. On the third week of the blow-off, the babyface team brought out a box with a lid that contained "the secret" that would prevent the Kelly's from getting away with their illegal tactics.

During the early stages of the match, the Kellys would try, unsuccessfully, to steal the box, but as the match settled down, the box was forgotten. Near the end of the match, one of the faces opened the box and took out a can of spray paint. One of the brothers was on the mat in a controlling rest hold, facing away from the babyface corner. While his brother argued with the crowd, with his back turned toward the action in the ring, the babyface crept up behind the Kelly twin in the ring and, without him knowing, painted an "X" on the back of his wrestling trunks. He crawled back to his corner and replaced the paint in the box.

The referee noticed the "X", so he was now able to differentiate between the two of them, but neither of the Kelly twins noticed the marking. The match continued until the Kellys reached a point where they made the illegal switch and got the babyface in a pin position. As the referee counted, *"1 ... 2 ...,"* he suddenly saw the "X" on the illegal man in the ring, and knew they had made the switch, so he stopped the count and ordered the twins to trade places. When the other Kelly twin, looking confused, came into the ring to continue, he immediately got rolled up for the pinfall.

That was a simple idea that got over well, but when we bicycled the introduction of the angle around the territory, a problem developed. The cable feed originating from Kansas City would always conflict with regular broadcast TV in the individual markets.

The house shows in the territory were all booked off of the Kansas City tape. The system of circulating the tape to the TV stations was similar to the system I was familiar with in Amarillo. Each show ran a five-week cycle. After the show aired in Kansas City, the tape was bicycled around the territory to Wichita, Topeka, Des

Moines, Sedalia, and Cedar Rapids.

As an example, after the tape aired on Saturday in Kansas City, it would have two "fresh" interviews inserted for *"this coming Monday night in Wichita."* The tape would be shipped to the local Wichita station to air the following Saturday. After airing, that same tape would be shipped back to the Kansas City office and two "fresh" interviews would be inserted for *"this coming Wednesday night in Topeka."* Once again, the tape would be shipped out, this time to Topeka. The Topeka fans saw the tape two weeks after it was taped and aired in Kansas City. After the tape aired in Topeka, the whole process was repeated in the other markets. This is what we called "bicycling" the tape, and as the booker, you booked the card in each town based on what actually aired in the town on the Saturday TV show.

KBMA was the first channel in the heart of America to be picked up by cable companies, so when the tape of the first match aired in Kansas City, it was also picked up by cable companies throughout Kansas, Missouri, and Iowa. By the time the fans in Topeka saw the tape from the first match on their local broadcast TV station, they also had the opportunity to see the third-week blow-off to the angle, or at least, a specific reference to the angle, on cable from KBMA in Kansas City.

When people saw the blow-off on cable, the surprise was gone. I could no longer book in the traditional fashion, which was to follow our tape around the circuit. We promoted the matches on local TV, with the interviews, specific to the individual towns, inserted into the tape. The people in Topeka would hear the babyface team say, *"We have a secret in this box that will keep you from getting away with your shenanigans,"* but earlier that morning, they watched the blow-off from Kansas City. They knew what the box contained, and they had seen the blow-off for free.

I can use the TV show "24" as an example. "24" is one of the few television shows that I really enjoy. I try to be at home on Monday nights to watch it. It's different from a lot of the other hit shows because most TV shows are complete stories in and of themselves each week. "24" is unique because it is episodic. Each week's episode opens with a recap of what happened in the previous episode. The episode consists of sub-stories that happen within the context of a 24-hour time period, and the shows usually ends with a cliffhanger and a teaser of what you'll be seeing in the next episode.

Does that sound familiar? It should, because that's how wrestling was presented. To draw the similarities, let's say you live in Philadelphia and you watch "24" on the FOX network, which is a station carried by your cable company. You really get into the show and become a regular viewer. One night, you're surfing the channels and you notice that the FOX station in New York is airing "24," but it's two episodes ahead in the story. Now, which station are you going to watch? Are you going to watch the show that you've been watching every week that originates from Philadelphia, along with the local commercials, or are you going to watch the New York broadcast that is two weeks ahead. If it were me, I would be watching the FOX New York show because they're ahead of the story by two weeks. I would no longer watch the Philadelphia station because I already knew what happened with the cliffhanger.

If we were talking about wrestling in the Kansas City territory, and not "24," the results would be the same. Let's use Topeka once again as an example. More than likely, when you start to watch the Kansas City (New York) show, you would quit watching the show on the local Topeka (Philadelphia) station. Since the promos for the weekly wrestling shows in Topeka were only shown on the Topeka station, and you stopped watching that version of the show, you wouldn't know who was wrestling locally that week in Topeka. In time, you would lose interest and would quit watching and/or attending the local matches. That's exactly what happened to the Kansas City wrestling promotion.

Cable television affected all of our towns. It also exposed the fact that the same match was being held more than once. We didn't have a depth of talent, so we didn't have any choice other than to work return matches. Even if we changed the finish of the returns, to some degree, it was still the same match with the same wrestlers.

The exposure by cable TV was a problem that there was no solution to, and sad to say, Bob Geigel just didn't understand what the problem was. *"Well, then we need to do something else, something with more heat!"*

He refused to recognize the gravity of the problem. It wasn't a matter of the talent, and it wasn't a matter of the finishes. It was the circumstances and the presence of cable television that spelled doom for his territory. The impact that cable television had on the territory was frustrating. I even suggested, and tried to implement, getting out of Memorial Hall and going to a studio show, and giving the audience generic matches. Geigel finally relented and we moved to a studio, but that still didn't solve the problem. Even though the viewers weren't seeing the angles before they took place, the new format watered down the product, and I still had the problem of the interviews for the Kansas City house shows airing on cable. The interviews still gave away the results of the matches, even if the viewers no longer saw the actual finish. There was no solution to the problem. It was impossible to book the territory.

As a footnote, I had a similar situation seven or eight years earlier in the Maritimes. The big difference between the Maritimes and Kansas City was that the entire region [Nova Scotia and New Brunswick] was covered by one central network feed, which was boosted by local relays that had the capability to insert and broadcast local commercials. Our TV show aired simultaneously throughout the Maritimes on Saturday night. The wrestlers did one generic interview, and it was applicable to every town for the week. We referred to one opponent and the specific match stipulations for that week. We always said, *"This week ..."*, and we never mentioned the name of a town. The local relay would air billboard-type ads on the screen following your generic promo, which is where the date, building, and time would be mentioned. There was some cross-over in some areas, but it was very minimal, and the entire operation worked for the territory.

I eventually reached a point of desperation, to where I had to get out of Kansas City, just to maintain my sanity. My top talent was Bob Brown and Rufus Jones, and I couldn't build the territory around them any longer. I left, but I left on good terms with Bob Geigel because I had worked hard, even in the face of insurmountable odds.

My time in Kansas City was directly attributed to Eddie Graham's persistence in getting me a job. I was grateful that Eddie went to great lengths to help me find a place to work so that I could make a living. When I took the booking job in Kansas City, I wanted to succeed, if at all possible, because I was hopeful that someday, I would get a chance to book Florida for Eddie.

# Chapter 16
## Samurai and Cannibals

Call it fate, luck, or whatever you like. Just about the time I was at my wit's end in Kansas City, Eddie Graham called and asked me about coming to Florida to assist with the booking. Jody Hamilton was booking at the time. Eddie said, *"Jody's been doing a good job, but we need some new ideas."*

Initially, he was going to bring me in as Jody's assistant, but when I got there, Eddie told me that I was going to replace Jody. I'm a very sensitive person, and I knew that he hadn't yet told Jody about his plans, so it put me in an awkward position. When Eddie finally told Jody that he wanted me to take his place as booker, Jody handled it well, and I thought the world of him for it. Jody had been down that road before, and he knew that it wasn't anything personal between the two of us.

I was so excited to be going back to Florida to work under Eddie Graham. I suppose the stars in my eyes blinded me to the situation that I was walking into. I was in a situation that mirrored that of Kansas City. Once again, I had very little talent to work with, and it was hard to get talent to come in because business in Florida was down. I started in Florida on October 6, 1981, but continued to wrestle in Kansas City until October 23.

In Florida, my top heel was Don Jardine, who wrestled as the Spoiler. Jardine stayed there for a while after I got there, but when he got an opportunity to go to another territory for more money, he took it. I can't blame him for that. My other top heels were Eddy Mansfield, Avalanche Tyler, and "Hangman" Bobby Jaggers. Jaggers was a great guy to be around, but he couldn't tell the truth even if the truth was a better story. He embellished stories to the point that we would just stare at him in disbelief.

My babyfaces were Charlie Cook, Mike Graham, Eric Embry, Ox Baker, and Bugsy McGraw. In his book, *Ric Flair: To Be The Man*, Ric wrote about me convincing him to do one-hour broadways around the circuit with Charlie Cook because we had nobody else to work with. That was the truth. I also tried to do something with Eric Embry, but he just wasn't big enough to build the territory around.

The Spoiler, Barbara Clary, and JJ

That was a frustrating time for Ric because he didn't have the marquee talent to work with. Florida was still a major territory and Eddie owned it, so Ric had to make his cycle through the territory. Eddie wanted the champion in there every few months so he could increase ticket prices. The problem was, we didn't have a hot Jack Brisco, or a Dusty Rhodes, for Ric to work with. We were so short on talent that the logical guy for him to work with was Charlie Cook. Charlie was a wonderful human being, and I hate to use the analogy, but in the ring, he was as exciting as watching paint dry.

Ric also wrote about going to Florida when I was the booker and pouring rum and coke down my throat. Early in my career, I was not much of a beer drinker. I would get indigestion after drinking one beer. I developed a taste for it, but to this day, I don't drink American beer because of the chemicals. When I do drink beer, it's either Corona, a Japanese beer, or a beer imported from Germany. Even then, my limit is around four bottles. It's almost impossible for me to drink a six-pack. It used to amaze me to see somebody like Harley Race drink a case of beer during a trip. Instead of beer, I would drink Bacardi light rum. I would take a cup, a cooler of ice, a half gallon of Bacardi light rum, a couple of liter bottles of Pepsi, and large bags of pre-popped popcorn. That was my fuel to run down the highway. Whenever we went out after the matches, my drink of choice was rum and coke. That's what Flair was referring to.

When Flair went out to bars, he got a perverse pleasure from trying to get everybody ripped to the point where they made fools of themselves, or so they couldn't stand up. That always entertained him. The more, the faster, the better for Ric. He would order 151 proof and pass it around, but I could smell the difference immediately. He knew that I caught on pretty quick, too.

The effect of cable was hitting Florida, too, just as it was every territory. The New York and Georgia shows were both seen in Florida. Granted, cable didn't have the same impact on the booking in Florida that it did in Kansas City because the local Tampa show wasn't being seen statewide, but it did exacerbate the same problem that I had faced in Amarillo.

Dusty Rhodes

Eddie and Mike Graham, Jack and Jerry Brisco, and Dusty Rhodes had all drawn huge money in the past, but they were no longer looked at as being special because they had been overexposed in Florida for more than ten years. Again, the people wanted to see wrestlers who appeared on WTBS, the Atlanta Superstation. They also wanted to see Bob Backlund, Pedro Morales, Jimmy Snuka, Sgt. Slaughter, Hulk Hogan, and the other wrestlers who wrestled for the WWF.

I needed some marquee names to come in. Of course, when they did agree to come in, they wanted extra compensation. I booked for a couple of months, but it was an impossible task to turn business around.

There was something else that I learned about booking while I was in Florida. Booking is more than just having ideas and being able to execute your ideas. Successful booking entails having the ability to convince main event talent that, with their help, you *can* turn things around. Many bookers also had their own network of "my guys" who they had a successful run with in other territories.

Take Dusty Rhodes, as a for-instance. When Dusty would come back to Florida, the roster would be enhanced by his presence alone, because the people looked at Dusty as a superstar-level main event talent. Not only that, but when Dusty came into a territory, he had a circle of guys who came with him. He had a track record of not only making money for himself, but making money for the people who worked with him, so they would drop what they were doing and come in to work with him. It didn't matter how bad the territory was doing. They knew that Dusty drew money, and they wanted to get a piece of the pie.

That was a part of what many successful bookers brought with them, and it was something that I didn't have. I wasn't a superstar-level, main event wrestler. You could say the same thing about successful bookers like George Scott and Louie Tillet, but they booked during a time when they had an abundance of main event talent to work with. I didn't have a crew of guys that I could call and say, *"Look, we're gonna get the territory turned around. You're figured in if you choose to come in."*

I did the best I could with what I had, but when I was booking in Australia, the territory was on the heels of Jim Barnett's glory days. When I booked Amarillo for Murdoch and Mulligan, it was during the twilight years of the territory. Kansas City was hampered by the problem of cable television. I'm not making excuses. Those same factors played a big part in the downfall of every territory. And it wasn't like I was fired for being incompetent a month after I took the job. Each time I took a booking job, I kept the job for a considerable amount of time, so somebody must have thought that I was getting the most out of what I had to work with.

Eventually, Eddie Graham asked Terry Funk to replace me as the booker. Terry wanted the job, but he didn't want to be shackled to the office every day, so they brought Dory in to work in the office and communicate with Terry on the telephone. When Dory and Terry walked into the office, their first order of business was to ask Eddie if there was some way that I could stay on board. Eddie was happy to accede to their request because I was the type of person who took care of even the smallest of details. His solution was to offer me the position of assistant booker. I was happy to accept the offer because I would still be paid a salary, although it wasn't quite as much as before, and it allowed me to stay in the territory. It was unusual for something like that to happen. In a left-handed way, I think it said something about what I was contributing.

After a few months, Dory became restless and didn't want to remain there full-time, and allowing Dory and Terry to run the territory by telephone just wasn't a viable, long-range solution.

One day, Eddie took me aside and said that he was talking to Dusty Rhodes. Apparently, Dusty had suddenly become available and was coming in to book. It was something that Dusty had always wanted to do. As the booker, he would be getting a salary and he would be working on top.

Many times, when a new booker comes in, he brings his own crew of guys with him, but Eddie wanted me to stay on, and Dusty was thrilled to have me. That was when my relationship with Dusty really began.

Due to that whole series of events, I was able to stay in Florida for 2½ years.

In addition to working in the office, I was still working on the road as a wrestler and a manager, even winning the Florida heavyweight title at one point. There always comes a time when talent gets frustrated with business because they're not making any money, and since I was still around the boys, I became a sounding board for them when problems cropped up.

Whenever Dusty was booking, he was on top, so the younger babyfaces always had him under scrutiny. They would come to me and say, *"Dusty's holding me back!"*

Most of the talent never saw the big picture. Some of the top boys had the ability to manage their own character and their own match, but the difficulty for the promoter/booker was having to manage not just one match on a card of seven, but every one of the seven matches. You had to determine how each match would affect the others. You had to watch the flow of the show, and time the matches so they started and ended on time.

When the wrestlers arrived at the arena, they didn't have to think about the intricacies of a show. They wanted to go directly to the dressing room and play cards, or go out and talk to the girls. They wanted to have their match, take a shower, get a beer, and go home. In territories that enforced the rule where the guys had to stay until all of the matches were over, the promoters almost had rebellions. Again, the guys wanted to do their thing and leave.

Ole Anderson enforced that rule. He was an in-your-face type of personality, who was apt to have confrontations with talent. I was more of a *"Let's talk about it"* voice of reason, or, *"I know how you feel, but can you understand where I'm coming from?"* I was usually able to talk things out, which is why I stayed in the business as long as I did and held the positions as long as I did. That was my personality. I had the patience. The guys would ask me, *"How can you sit there and listen to that? I'd just tell 'em to hit the road!"* It was just my personality and way of doing things.

October 1982

The first time I knew that Eddie Graham had confidence in me was when he openly talked to me about Dusty Rhodes' shortcomings. I was Dusty's assistant, and Eddie and I were alone in the wrestling office. Eddie walked into my office, sat down on the sofa, and expressed his frustrations with Dusty.

*"What am I going to do with Dusty? He just doesn't get it. He wanted to have an extravaganza, so he booked a big show in Tampa Stadium, but without regard to expenses. He spent a huge sum of money on searchlights and they didn't even add anything to the show! He never puts any thought into the expenses that go into those shows.*

*"And for Dusty to run a show like that, it's not just about how much it drew that night, but what its effect is on the backside. Yes, Dusty drew a huge house, but my business was dead for the next four months! When I averaged it all together, I would have been better off without the big show. When business dropped off, I lost whatever profit I made on that one big show many times over. But with Dusty, his ego gets all wrapped up into that one show. He looks at it as 'Dusty's big show' and keeps adding people, gimmicks, and expenses."*

Eddie confided to me that, in effect, he would use Dusty's own ego to manipulate Dusty. In other words, when he saw Dusty was reaching the point of being uncontrollable, he would call Vince McMahon, or another promoter, and say, *"I need you to call Dusty and give him a few shots in your territory. Tell him how badly you need him."* Vince would call Dusty, then Dusty would go to Eddie, who would say, *"Well, gee, Dusty. If he needs you that badly, I guess we can get by."*

The whole scenario was orchestrated by Eddie! That shows how shrewd Eddie was, and how Eddie used Dusty's vulnerability, his ego, to manipulate him for the good of his business. Eddie would manipulate Dusty out for a while, and then he would manipulate him back. When business was bad, and the territory had a rest from Dusty for a while, Eddie would bring Dusty back. He would embrace him and treat him like a savior. Dusty would bask in that kind of attention. He had a huge ego, and still does to this day.

When I was welcomed into Eddie Graham's inner circle, that was, to me, a measuring stick of what I had accomplished in the business, and it gave me the opportunity to work closer with Eddie Graham than I would have otherwise.

Even though I discussed it earlier in the book, blading was a subject I never talked about until recently. I always had a hang-up about exposing the business, and blading was one of the topics that I resisted exposing the most.

I had the reputation of bleeding freely throughout my career, especially as a manager. On my website forum, somebody asked me a question about how I used the blade. That person had watched old matches on videotape, and even when he played them in slow motion, he couldn't figure out how I did it. I take pride in the fact that even after my career was over, somebody watched my matches and couldn't see me do it. I also take pride that I was proficient enough that people would ask how I did it. Whatever technique I used, I was good at it—good enough to do it unnoticed. I have seen the other extreme—sloppy jobs—where guys on live TV were so clumsy with the blade.

Terry Funk used a different technique, and even to this day, he is one of the more proficient people in the business to use a blade, but in all my years of blading, I have never had stitches. I bled easily, so I didn't have to cut deep. I was able to jab the blade into my skin and pump the blood out. If I clotted too early and needed more, I would gig [cut] myself a second time.

Before a match, I would take an aspirin to thin my blood. Art Nelson was the first person to tell me about another drug that the guys took called Niacin, or Niacinimide. It would make your face flushed by causing the capillaries on the surface of your skin to become engorged with blood. You only had to take one, but boy, did it work!

JJ & Jimmy Garvin

The American version of Kendo Nagasaki was created by Terry Funk when he was still booking the Florida territory. While we were sitting at Tampa TV one afternoon, Terry said there was a character in England named Kendo Nagasaki. Terry decided that we needed our own version of Kendo Nagasaki in Florida, so he went out and bought the whole Kendo outfit—chest plate, sticks, and head mask. Terry then took poor Mr. Sakurada, my old friend from Dallas and Calgary, who didn't have a whole lot of hair to begin with, and shaved the top of his head. After adding some face paint, Sakurada was Kendo Nagasaki, and I was his manager.

When we were trying to get Kendo over in Tampa, we booked him with Mike Rotunda on a big show in the Sun Dome. Kendo was going to do the "karate to the throat" gimmick and Rotunda would throw up blood. Of course, regardless of what people think, there was no such thing as blood capsules, but we got inventive. I'm sure it had been done before, but it was the first time that I had been involved in anything of this nature.

I don't remember who it was, but somebody volunteered to donate their blood. We used a syringe to draw blood from his vein and put it into a condom. The package was about the size of a golf ball. We tied the condom off, dropped it into a cup of warm water, and left it there until the very last minute so it wouldn't coagulate. The match wasn't going to go very long, so there wouldn't be a problem of the blood drying out before we needed it. Just before we went to the ring, somebody handed me the condom. It would be obvious that I was holding something in my hand, and I didn't want to put it in my pocket and take a chance on having it break, so I put it into my mouth.

When Kendo and Rotunda were ready to go home [end the match], Rotunda took a bump and fell out of the ring and onto the concrete floor. With the audience distracted, I moved the condom from my mouth to my hand. While the referee gave Kendo a warning about rules infractions, I walked over to Rotunda and grabbed his hair with my right hand. With my left hand covering his mouth, and picking him up as if in preparation to punch him, I transferred the condom to Rotunda's mouth. Just before I punched him, the referee turned around and I backed off. *"I wasn't gonna hit him. I was just helping him up,"* I said, acting innocent.

When Mike rolled back into the ring, Kendo attacked him, whipped him into the ropes, and kicked him in the solar plexus, setting him up for the big thrust to the throat.

Well, everything worked fine up to that point.

The plan was for Kendo to whack Rotunda with a karate chop to the throat. Rotunda would bite down on the condom and fall to the mat. Blood would pour out of Rotunda's mouth and he would act like he was hemorrhaging.

Unfortunately, when Kendo kicked him, the kick landed so solidly that it knocked the breath out of Rotunda. The condom flew out of Rotunda's mouth and skimmed across the mat.

JJ & Kendo Nagasaki

I was horrified! Before anybody had a chance to realize what happened, I scampered into the ring, tripped myself on the bottom rope coming in, dropped face first on top of the condom, covered it with my arms and face, and sucked it into my mouth. As I rolled out of the ring, Kendo did something to Rotunda and the referee counted to three.

It had all happened so fast that nobody seemed to notice. If they did, it was along the lines of, *"What was that? I thought I saw something fly across the ring!"* If they noticed anything, they probably thought Rotunda spit up a big honker, and I tripped when I was getting into the ring.

It was a tremendous amount of planning and preparation for an effect that backfired.

Only in professional wrestling.

As I reflect back on that story, it's hard for me to comprehend that I would do something as disgusting as putting a condom filled with somebody else's blood in my mouth, let alone AFTER it's been in another man's mouth, AND lying on a dirty ring! As crazy, dangerous, and gross as that sounds to you—and I agree—those were the lengths that I was willing to go to in order to entertain the fans and to protect the business. At the time, it all seemed normal to me. It was just another day at the office.

For a big show scheduled at the Bayfront Center in St. Petersburg, we brought Jerry Lawler in from Memphis to defend the Southern heavyweight title against Kendo. When he arrived, Lawler said, *"Our business is dead in Memphis. Instead of just doing a title defense, I'd like to work an angle while I'm here."*

Eddie agreed to do it. Kendo would screw Lawler for the title in the Bayfront Center, with the match to be taped and shown on the Memphis TV program. In the hopes that it would pump up their territory, the rematch would be held in Memphis.

We did the screwjob finish and Lawler took the tape to Memphis. He later called me and asked, *"We have the tape with Kendo. Would you do me a favor? As his manager, would you cut a promo for the Memphis match?"*

Even though I wasn't accompanying Kendo to Memphis for the match, I agreed to do it and cut the promo in Tampa. *"I'm so confident that Kendo Nagasaki is going to annihilate Lawler that there's no need for me to be there."*

Well, the show did great in Memphis. I don't want to say the house doubled, but they got a huge house out of it.

I sent another promo to Lawler. *"You took the title from Kendo, and you embarrassed me. I got there late because you did something to divert my flight. When I walked into the arena at the end of the match, I heard the bell ring and I was nearly trampled by the fans rushing out of the building."*

That explained my absence from the match.

*"I recently went to Africa, where I captured a savage in the jungle. I was keeping him under wraps until I could teach him the ways of civilized man and help rid him of his primeval instincts. But Lawler, you've made me so mad that I don't care. I'm unleashing him this week. Be prepared to face ... Kimala, the Ugandan Giant."*

Kimala did huge business and defeated Jerry Lawler for the Southern heavyweight title on June 7, 1982, at the Mid-South Coliseum in Memphis.

The promotion kept calling me back and asking, *"Would you do one more promo?"*

Jerry Jarrett, Lawler's partner in Memphis, finally called and said, *"Jim, the people are calling and asking, 'When are we gonna see JJ Dillon?' When can we get you to come in?"*

We had done several big angles, introduced several new characters, and I had cut countless promos for their television. Even with all of that, which included having two of my men win the heavyweight title, I had never actually appeared live in Memphis. I said, *"I don't know. You're gonna have to talk to Eddie about that."*

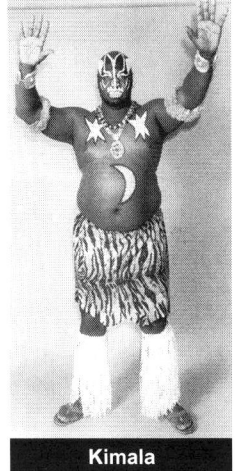

Kimala

Jerry Jarrett called Eddie and explained the whole series of events. He told him that I had cut promos for Kimala, but we had never seen each other, and yet, we were the hottest thing they had going in the territory. *"Is there any way you could let Jim come to Memphis for just one Monday night?"*

Eddie agreed and I managed Kimala in Memphis for the first time on July 19, 1982. Due to having several weeks of high-profile television exposure, and the fans demand to see me live, I walked into the arena like I was a star. They treated me very, very nicely. After the first night, they called Eddie and asked for another date. He gave his okay and I was booked in Memphis on the next four consecutive Monday nights—not only as a manager, but as a wrestler. I also worked in several other cities in the territory, including Louisville and Lexington, Kentucky, Evansville, Indiana, and Jackson, Tennessee. My stint in Memphis was so successful that I would continue to work there sporadically until April 12, 1984. I was also invited to wrestle in Puerto Rico from June 3-19, 1983, where I wrestled Pedro Morales.

Meanwhile, back in Florida, I was managing "Gorgeous" Jimmy Garvin. One gimmick that really took off in the territory was when the people would chant "weasel" at him. Jimmy would go berserk and would cover his ears with the palms of his hands.

I spent $150 to have "Weasel" printed on 1,000 bumper stickers. I took them to the arena and gave one to somebody who was shilling for us. When Garvin saw the guy walking around with the bumper sticker, he had to hold *me* back, and keep me from tearing the guy apart.

We sold the bumper stickers for $1.00 apiece. The fans would run down to ringside, buy a bumper sticker, and wave them all over the arena.

When we got into the ring for our match, we would have whoever was selling them walk by one of the babyfaces. While I held my pre-match conference with Jimmy, on the other side of the ring and with my back turned, the babyface would peel the paper backing from the bumper sticker, tip-toe up to me, and put one on my ass. When the people started to roar with laughter, I would suddenly notice the commotion and look around. *"What are you people pointing at? What are you laughing about?"*

I would walk around in a big circle and let everyone see the bumper sticker. Jimmy would finally see it, tell me about it, and I would pull it off.

Wearing the weasel suit

We did that same scenario all around the territory. When I walked out of the arena, my car would be plastered with "weasel" bumper stickers. Eddie finally said, *"Let's not overdo it."* Jimmy and I had some very lucrative weeks selling those bumper stickers.

I did a few entertaining videos with Wayne Daniels, a one-man cameraman and TV producer/editor. I first met Wayne in Charlotte back in the early '70s. He was very talented and worked long hours for Crockett Promotions. One of our collaborations in Florida was reincarnating Black Jack Mulligan and Dusty Rhodes as outlaws from the wild west. I don't know how many of you are old enough to remember the TV show called *Death Valley Days*. It was sponsored by The Borax Company (now known as Rio Tinto Borax), makers of 20 Mule Team Borax laundry detergent and Boraxo hand soap. The episodes revolved around western stories and legends based, and filmed, in and around Death Valley, California. The original host [1952-1963] was an old prospector character known as "The Old Ranger," who would do a lead-in to each weekly episode. From 1963 to 1965, the host was then-actor, and future-president, Ronald Reagan.

*The Saga of the Family* was a separate segment in our TV wrestling show. We developed a scenario similar to that used by *Death Valley Days*. We arranged a simple set. I sat in a chair with a saddle on a table beside me. I checked an old book out of the library and claimed that Mulligan was the reincarnation of one of the people profiled in the book. We opened with a title on the screen and background music.

Initially, it was intended as a one-shot deal, but it took on a life of its own and continued for four or five weeks. Each episode was budgeted for two minutes, but they sometimes ran twice that long. Similar to *Piper's Pit,* it was a creative way to further a storyline, without resorting to the same old trash-talk that fans were accustomed to hearing from the heels.

As a follow-up to *The Sagas*, we did a one-camera shoot in a limo, with me going to confront Mulligan and Rhodes at Dusty's ranch in Dade City, Florida. Wayne sat in the front seat, while I did the running dialogue.

Wayne got out and filmed the limo pulling up. I wore a tuxedo and ruffled shirt, and held my head high, acting very arrogant. As I stepped outside the limo, Dusty and Mulligan were seen on horseback, carrying rifles. When they saw me, they started shooting. It turned into a Three Stooges act as I jumped high into the air and started running. I fell over a sage bush, getting covered with dust in the process. We cut away and, in the next scene, I was standing in front of the camera, looking dirty and disheveled. I talked about running for my life, and how I had been attacked by armadillos.

One of the few times that Eddie Graham went crazy on me was over the series of *The Sagas*. He thought it was wasted television time. Eddie finally admitted that *The Sagas* accomplished what they were intended to do, and had created interest. However, Eddie much preferred the production at Dusty's ranch. The segment was entertaining and involved interaction with Mulligan and Dusty. To this day, I'm amazed that so many people tell me that they still remember those interviews and the scene at Dusty's ranch.

I met a lot of wonderful people during my career, and not all of them were in the business. When I was in Florida, there was a couple named Rob and Linda, who would pick me up at the Miami airport every week, transport me to the arena, and then take me back to the airport.

It was a treat to be able to fly now and then. A lot of the guys have died on the road. There were times when I would be coming home on a long trip, fighting to stay awake during those last few miles. There were times when I would almost hallucinate. And yet, during all my years on the road as an active wrestler, I only had one accident. I was driving home from Tallahassee on a Friday night when somebody ran a red light and sideswiped me. I wasn't injured, and no one with me was injured, either. I was very fortunate all around. Years later, my vehicle spun out on black ice, but that's a story for another chapter.

Since we didn't have to travel after the matches in Tampa at Fort Homer Hesterly Armory, Tuesday night was a night to unwind. The Imperial Room was the watering hole of choice for the boys. The lounge featured a live band every Tuesday night, and virtually every country and western musician played the Imperial Room on their way up the ladder of success. The fans all knew that the wrestlers hung out there, and the place was always packed. There were very few incidents and, by and large, the fans respected the wrestlers' privacy. Earlier, I talked about protecting the business in Amarillo. We did the same thing at the Imperial Room. The babyfaces congregated in one corner of the room, while the heels gathered in another.

Dusty went on a regular basis and usually brought his wife. Dusty has always been a wonderful family man and was very protective of his family. One night, when a guy made a pass at Dusty's wife, Dusty and the guy got nose-to-nose. Dusty didn't hit the guy, but he bit off the tip of his nose. If I remember correctly, it resulted in a lawsuit and cost Dusty some money. Contrary to what a lot of people think, the "Dream" is a very good athlete and not inclined to take sh— from anybody.

Two girls named Sherrie and Lynn were regulars at the lounge. They were great fans and fun to be around. I knew Sherrie better than Lynn. She had gorgeous, long, red hair. I lost track of her when she moved to Houston, got married, and had a family.

I never worked for Bill Watts directly, but I made a couple of shots in Louisiana with Dusty when he went to work for Watts on a weekend. Louisiana was a tough territory to work. The trips were long and many of them were down two-lane roads. Fortunately, we were only there for a weekend, so we didn't have to make any of those brutal road trips, but I heard enough about them to make me thankful that I never worked that territory full-time. That was a whole different environment for me. Dusty was brought in as the featured attraction and I was going along with him. We were treated royally while we were there. My impression of Bill Watts was that he was a disciple of Eddie Graham, just like I was, and much like Dusty was. Bill, however, had been very successful in his own right, and did very well in his own territory. He was very savvy and smart about the wrestling business. I heard horror stories about Bill Watts, and how he fined the wrestlers for infractions of his rules, but I never experienced that. I base my judgment of people on my own personal experience, not from what I've heard from somebody else. Based on the limited number of times I worked for Bill, I have nothing but respect and high regard for him

When I went to Florida in 1981, I was looking for a new idea. I wanted to do something different from what everybody else was doing, much like when I went to Canada ten years earlier. In the early 70's, all the wrestlers were wearing sequined jackets, and if you recall, I wore corduroy pants, a leather hat, and I chomped on a cigar. I wanted to do something unique in Florida, as well.

Jerry Prater, a talented guy who wrote the copy for *The Grapevine,* the wrestling program sold in the Florida arenas, was instrumental in giving me my new persona in Florida. Jerry enjoyed my interviews, and in each issue of *The Grapevine*, he ghost wrote a column for me. I never wrote a thing. I don't know what triggered the idea, but he introduced the name "King James" into one of my columns. From then on, I called myself "King James." I had somebody embroider "King James" on the breast pocket of a robe that I had worn before, and I carried a crown.

There have been many wrestlers who have used the "King" gimmick in wrestling, but the man most synonymous with the "King" moniker is Jerry "The King" Lawler. I didn't want to infringe on his gimmick, so I called him and said, *"Jerry, I'm not trying to steal your gimmick. It's just one of those things that happened as a result of something that Jerry Prater wrote. I'm not James 'The King' Dillon. I'm just 'King James.' At best, it's going to be a short-term deal."* Lawler didn't have any problem with it and gave me his blessing.

King James

Years later, Harley Race started to call himself "The King" when he was with the WWF. That caused a little bit of friction because Harley was using Jerry's gimmick in a much higher profile situation. Jerry was a big drawing card as "The King" in Memphis and Nashville, Tennessee. When Vince McMahon booked shows in Memphis and Nashville, he advertised the matches as featuring "The King," without mentioning Harley's name. The people would naturally assume that Lawler was going to be on the show. At the time, Lawler had his own promotion and wasn't even working for Vince, so he filed a lawsuit against the WWF. "The King" disappeared from all future WWF publicity.

Jerry Prater also called me Julius Caesar, for the second "J" in J.J. Dillon. I got tired of people asking what the second "J" stood for in "J.J. Dillon." I didn't want to get into the story of it being a professional name, and the second "J" really didn't mean anything, so I began telling everyone that my name was James Julius Dillon.

I had another "first" while I was in Florida. I got a perm. Don't ask me why I did it. My hair was darker at the time and it was just one of those crazy things that I decided to do on the spur of the moment.

Kevin Sullivan came up with a devil worshiping angle. Joining Kevin in the angle was Mark Lewin, who wrestled as The Purple Haze. If you had to pick two people to do that gimmick, Kevin and Mark would be the mix to do it. We introduced the Purple Haze by shooting footage of him walking out of the ocean under a full moon at Daytona Beach. It was freezing cold. Kevin talked and rambled about bones in the sand, whatever that was.

Since then, I have gotten to know Kevin much better, but at the time, I wasn't crazy about Kevin's gimmick. I didn't like the idea. Kevin comes from a Catholic background. In fact, he was an altar boy from Boston. A devil worshiper just doesn't seem consistent with the Kevin Sullivan character who got his start in Florida as the clean-cut, All-American boy. I was not a big fan of going in that direction. I think religion, or anything that creates an impression of religious overtones, is something you should stay away from.

In my opinion, Gordon Solie was the greatest wrestling announcer I ever knew. I might be prejudiced because I worked with him so much, but he was a credit to the business. When Mike Graham was a kid, his father, Eddie Graham, took him to the dirt track auto races one night. That was during the time when Eddie had just bought into the Florida territory. Mike told me that when the races were over, Eddie walked to the top of the bleachers and knocked on the door of the announcer's box. When the door opened, Eddie said, *"Are you the man who's been doing the announcing tonight?"*

*"Yes."*

*"What's your name?"*

*"Gordon Solie."*

*"Do you know anything about wrestling?"*

*"Nope. Never watched it."*

And Eddie said, *"That's okay."*

I've heard other stories of how Gordon got into the business, but that's the story that Mike told me. For the TV tapings, Gordon Solie would sit at his desk, and you would sit down with him. It didn't matter if you were accomplished at doing promos, or a nervous greenie. All you had to do was follow Gordon's lead. He would ask intelligent questions and lead you right down the path. Gordon was probably the best there ever was.

Eddie's son, Mike Graham, was a buzz saw. He and Dick Slater both went to Robinson High School in Tampa, where they were weight lifters and amateur wrestlers. Mike certainly paid his dues and was well respected. In a sense, though, he was in a thankless position because of the size that God gave him and for simply being Eddie's son. I've seen Shane McMahon, and I've seen Mike Graham, and they're like day and night. I think Mike handled it as well as one could have under those circumstances. Mike was a good guy, but no matter what he did, he was in a no-win situation. If somebody put him over, it was because he was the promoter's son. That was unfortunate because Mike sure had the credentials. Unfortunately, he just wasn't blessed with the size. If Mike had been blessed with six inches more height, God only knows where he could have gone in this business.

Angelo Mosca was a fun guy to be around. I managed the tag team of Angelo and "Cowboy" Bobby Duncum. One time in the dressing room, Kevin Sullivan was already dressed for his match, so he decided to take a short nap. Angelo saw it as an opportunity to give Kevin a hotfoot, so he tucked some lit matches into the sole of Kevin's boots. The boots went up in flames. Kevin jumped straight up out of a sound sleep, while "Big Nasty" roared with laughter.

The next week at the Tampa armory, Angelo got undressed after his match and went to take his shower, leaving behind a very expensive pair of dress shoes. Kevin took the shoes and set them on the floor in the middle of the bathroom. He poured lighter fluid over the shoes and lit them on fire! When Angelo walked out, the flames were shooting four feet into the air. He started screaming, *"Those are my shoes! Put that out!"* By the time Angelo put the fire out, the shoes had melted.

For the most part, pranks like that were all in fun, but paybacks were expected. The locker room fights I witnessed were far and few between. Generally, wrestlers were a fraternity of people who got along with each other. At the very least, they tolerated each other, if only for the sake of business.

I had a map on which I would blacken out each state when I wrestled there. In order to wrestle in some states, I had to wrestle in other territories, so in the spring of 1982, I took a week's vacation and got booked into the WWF. From June 6-13, I wrestled talent like Chief Jay Strongbow, S.D. Jones, and Pat Patterson.

Also during this time, Kevin Sullivan made contact with a promoter who wanted to book a wrestling tour in the Netherlands and St. Thomas Islands. Ric Flair and I went down and we stayed in the promoter's timeshare condo that the promoter *gave* him!

# Chapter 17
# The Garden

I was in Japan from February 11 through March 3, 1983, and got four bookings in Oregon and Washington for Don Owens on the way back. Rip Oliver, who I had known in Florida, was the top name in the Oregon territory. Stan Stasiak, who had been a big name in the business for many years, lived in Oregon. I got the opportunity to work with him twice. Stan's finisher was the heart punch. When he hit you with that punch, you went down like you were hit by a bazooka. On the night that I worked with him, he set me up, held his one hand in the air, measured me off, and hit me with his heart punch. Instead of going down, I started to walk around him. All of a sudden, I grabbed my heart and collapsed. I had a lot of fun with it because my reaction was something different that the people hadn't seen before.

By 1984, I had been to Japan several times. I had also wrestled in Germany, Australia, and the Maritimes. But I had not accomplished my third and final goal.

To wrestle in Madison Square Garden.

When I was working on top in Amarillo, I remember thinking that if there was ever a time in my career when I thought it would be possible for me to wrestle in Madison Square Garden in New York City, it was then. Now it was 1984, and it was much, much later in my career. I was managing, and I wasn't wrestling with any great regularity, so I wasn't in the kind of athletic shape I should be in if I wanted to have the match in the Garden that I wanted to have. The possibility of me wrestling in the Garden did not look too good at that point. My worst fear was to embarrass myself, but I so wanted to go.

Eddie and I talked about a lot of things. We would sit around and I would pick his brain. I just enjoyed being around him and listening to his stories about the old days. One day, I told him that I saw him team up with Dr. Jerry Graham in the Garden, and how it had always been my dream to wrestle there. We moved on to other topics, but suddenly, out of the blue, Eddie Graham said, *"That's a big thing to you, isn't it? You'd like to work in the Garden."*

*"Yes, but I don't think it'll ever happen."*

*"Then I'd like to call Vince for you. Would that be alright?"*

*"Oh, that would be wonderful, but I can't ask you to do that."*

*"Don't worry about it,"* he said. *"Vince and I have a great relationship."*

I was shocked that he made the offer, but it was as simple as that. When I walked into the office the next morning, Eddie said, *"You're booked!"*

*"Booked where?"*

*"The Garden,"* he said. *"You don't have to call anybody. You fly out on the morning of April 23rd. Pick up your ticket at Tampa International and you'll be wrestling that night."*

Later that day, I called Vince Sr. at his vacation home in Florida and thanked him for booking me. When I told him how much it meant to me, he said, *"Then I'm happy to do it for you."*

The Garden's physical presence has changed two or three times over the years from where the original building stood, but the name and the fact that it's synonymous with New York City—the greatest city in the world—made it irresistible to me. I was there to live a dream and I was thrilled to death to be there.

Early 1984 was a historic time in WWF history. Vince Jr. had recently bought the company and he was making huge changes. On January 23 of that year, Hulk Hogan won the WWF title from the Iron Sheik in Madison Square Garden. The following month, on February 11, Tito Santana won the Intercontinental title from Don Muraco in Boston, and on April 17, one week before my Garden shot, my old friend Dick Murdoch teamed with Adrian Adonis to defeat Tony Atlas and Rocky Johnson for the WWF tag team titles in Pennsylvania. Back then, title changes were extremely rare, so for Vince to have made that many changes in just three months was a big deal. It was a new era for the WWF. Hulkamania was in full swing, and the other promoters were noticing.

I worked on the card that night with Tito Santana, challenging him for the Intercontinental title. I knew Tito from when he wrestled in Amarillo as Merced Solis. Tito's scheduled opponent for that night was Afa the Wild Samoan. That match had been scheduled for some time, but for some reason, Afa couldn't make it, so I was bumped up on the card. The match went about eight minutes, which was just about right. I didn't want to wrestle too long and do something to embarrass myself.

I still have the tape of the match that aired on the Madison Square Garden Network. Gorilla Monsoon and Pat Patterson (in his broken English) did the commentary. I had known Monsoon for years, but neither one of them knew anything about my career, so they talked about everything but the match. That was fine, though. I had lived my dream of wrestling in the Garden.

Vince Sr. wasn't going to the shows because his health was bad, so I didn't get to see him. He was fighting the onslaught of cancer. Vince Jr. was in the building, but we didn't even say hello to each other. Jim Barnett, who worked in the office, was also there.

I saw a lot of the guys that I had known and worked with over the years. Roddy Piper, Bob Backlund, and Rocky Johnson were there. I even stayed at the Ramada Inn on 8th Avenue, where all the boys stayed. I had stayed there as a kid, and now I was staying there as a wrestler.

If my memory serves me correctly, someone booked me for the balance of that week, but it was an error on their part. I had to be back in Florida the following day, so they had someone fill in for me. The next morning, I upgraded my airline ticket to

128 • "Wrestlers Are Like Seagulls"

first class and flew back to Tampa. The only people in the first class section were me, Hulk Hogan, and his new wife. He wasn't on the card at the Garden, but he was in New York for some other business. When I got home, I checked off the last item on my list of career goals. A few days later, I got a check in the mail for $400.

Vincent J. McMahon, who we all knew as Vince Sr., died on May 27, 1984, just one month after my match in the Garden. I'll never forget him and Eddie Graham for making my dream come true.

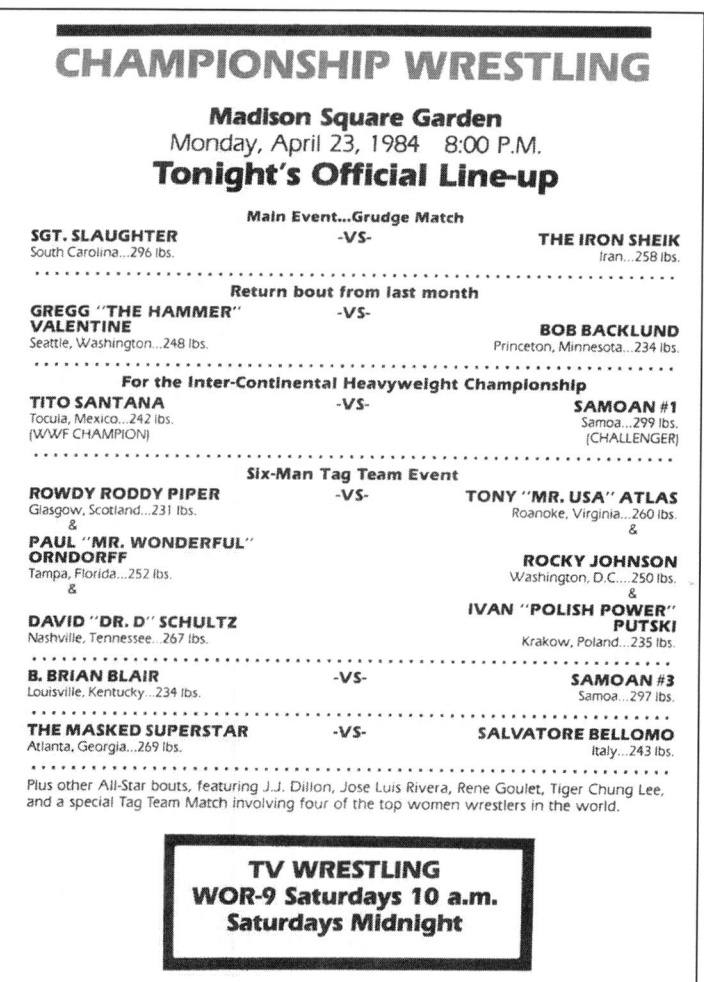

# Chapter 18
# Back to the Maritimes

On May 7, 1984, I left Florida for the Maritimes. I had been contacted by Al Zinck and Clary Flemming, who wanted to make an attempt to run the territory again. They wanted me to take the book and manage the promotion.

For several years, Emil Dupree promoted wrestling in the Maritimes. Even when I was there in 1973, he had his own promotion and television, and John Studd worked for him that summer. He used talent that came out of Montreal and ran a much smaller-scale promotion than that run by the Cormiers.

Al Zinck, Clary Flemming, Rudy Kay

In the Cormier promotion, Rudy Kay (Rudy Cormier) and Al Zinck were equal partners. Al Zinck had the television contracts in his name, but Rudy had the lease on the Halifax Forum. Zinck was a character. If I had to describe him, I would say he was almost a mark that you couldn't smarten up even if you tried. You might also describe Zinck as a nerd. If he wanted to use a chainsaw to cut down some brush, he would spill gasoline on himself and set himself on fire. He was that kind of a person.

Somewhere along the line, Rudy Kay and Al Zinck had a falling out. Al was a partner on paper, so he was tolerated by Rudy and the rest of the Cormiers, but they had no respect for him. Even when he was smart, he was still a mark. That was very frustrating for them. And yet, in his mind, Al Zinck thought he was the reason why they had been successful in the first place.

When they finally split apart, neither Al nor Rudy could make it on their own because of what they jointly brought in terms of finances, television rights, leases, etc. As a result, they both went out of business.

Emil Dupree continued to promote, but Emil was very frugal. For instance, he never ran the Halifax Forum because the rent was high, and he didn't want to take the risk. He did eventually run the building, but only took a half-step, and never attempted to run at the level that the Cormiers and Zinck did with their promotion. He was also very careful about the talent he brought in, and only ran small towns. He didn't make a lot of money in those towns, but he minimized the possibility of losing money. Financially, Emil did very well in his life. He owned a lot of real estate in New Brunswick, but was very fearful of losing everything he had, so he took no risks.

Once again, Eddie Graham came through for me. Not only did he give me his blessings to go, but he helped me in other areas. As the booker, I had to scrounge up enough talent to build the territory. Eddie loaned me his complete library of old tapes. I looked through the run sheets to see who was on them, looking for talent that had worked in Florida who might be available to work in Canada. My plan was to start airing the tapes on television in the Maritimes a full six weeks before we opened up. I was going to develop an entertaining television show, but the tapes would be a foundation on which to build upon to launch the territory.

Before I left to go to Nova Scotia, I told Dusty Rhodes that I had an opportunity to have ownership in a promotion. I was going to be a 50% owner in the company with no money upfront. All I was giving was my expertise and the availability of the tapes that Eddie had given me. Dusty hugged me, wished me well, and handed me a check for $500. I filled a suitcase with tapes, got on an airplane, and flew to Halifax.

I started with the promotion on May 12, 1984. Clary Flemming and I went to the studio in Halifax to tape an introduction to the show. We spliced in matches from the *Championship Wrestling from Florida* show that featured people I had contacted about coming into the territory. We recorded openings, ins and outs, and formatted six hours of television.

1984: International Title

When the season started, I was running the whole operation. Clary Flemming knew absolutely nothing about running a wrestling business. Clary, who handled the television commentary, owned an advertising agency that did all the advertising for a major grocery chain. He had done very well for himself with the agency, but wrestling made him a household name.

I not only booked the matches, but I would prepare the television promos, take the prints ads to the newspaper office, run the shows, and make the payoffs. I did everything. It was a real eye opener for me, not only of how much work there is to do, or how much risk is involved, but of all the problems that creep into every facet of the operation. I can't remember the number of times I relived that conversation I had with Terry Funk, about why he and Dory got out of Amarillo. I often thought about the modest rewards they received in return for their financial risk and hard work.

Originally, I was only going to manage Kendo Nagasaki, but we were so sparse for talent that I started working. At that stage in my life, I had no business trying to work on top again, but I did so for financial reasons—to justify what I was getting paid, and to keep the promotion going. It had been ten years since I had been in the Maritimes, and a few people remembered me, but most of them didn't. It was like starting my career all over again.

I brought in guys like Kendo Nagasaki and Mark Lewin. After three weeks, Mark wanted more money. When we told him we couldn't pay it, he left to promote in Singapore. I brought talent like Mike Graham in for a week as a special attraction. Dusty said he'd come up, but we never got to that point. I contacted Leo Burke and the Cormier's. They lived there, so I said, *"You're not working for Al Zinck. You're working for Clary Flemming. You will have no dealings with Al, and you'll never have to see him."* It was an opportunity for them to get back into the game. But as big as they were at one time, and New Brunswick was their home, their return just didn't make an impact on our ratings and drawing power.

One of our problems was due to a new cable network being launched. We had been promised that our show would air on the television network, not the cable network that only had 20% of the viewership. Your home had to be wired for cable to receive the signal, and at the time, if the broadcast station had a viewing audience of 100,000, the cable had an audience of 20,000.

Emil Dupree, meanwhile, had gotten his show on network television in a good timeslot. He also had contacts higher up in the network, so he was able to block our show from getting on. As a compromise, our show was placed on the new cable network.

We produced a quality television show, but unfortunately, it just didn't have enough viewers, and that's what we really needed to launch the promotion. If we had started two years later, when that cable station had grown and more homes were wired, we probably would have been able to make it. At the time, though, we took what we could get.

Week after week, we struggled to make payroll. There were times when we didn't know if the checks would clear. I could see that the company was going to fail, and it eventually did. After I left, I heard that Clary Flemming had put his house up as collateral and lost everything as a result. I felt very bad about that. I didn't have any money to invest, so personally, I didn't leave any poorer for the experience.

When I walked away after 13 weeks, though, I walked away knowing that I had given it everything I had. If I had not brought what I did to the table, the tapes and what knowledge I had, they wouldn't have been able to launch the promotion.

Once again, I was done in by a lack of talent and a television situation. Both factors were critical to success, and both were lacking.

I was looking for a life raft, so I called Dusty and said, *"Dust, I gave it everything I have, but it isn't gonna go. I have to get out of here because I'm worried about taking care of my family."*

That was when Dusty dropped the bomb. *"I left Eddie last week. I'm working for Jimmy Crockett in Charlotte."*

While I was in the Maritimes, Dusty had cut a deal with Jimmy Crockett to book the Carolinas. He put me on hold for a minute, then came back and said, *"You've got a job. I need you here with me. Be here next Monday. You'll be my assistant here in the office."*

"Do I need to call Jimmy?" I asked.

"Nope," he replied. *"Just be here. I'll work you out a deal."*

My last day in Canada was August 1, 1984. I packed my belongings and moved my family to Charlotte. It was going to be the beginning of a 5-year run.

# Chapter 19
# Death of the Master

I thought so much of Eddie Graham. He was like an invincible figure. I heard that he had gotten involved in a deal where the county had done road improvement on some land that he owned. It was one of those shady deals where word leaked out and an investigation was held. They then discovered that one of Eddie's partners had done prison time for something similar, years earlier. This time, Eddie's name was mentioned in connection with the deal. I never heard the exact details of what it was all about, but even with all that Eddie had done for the state of Florida—the Florida Sheriff's Boys Ranch and amateur wrestling—the problem was significant enough that he might end up doing prison time over it. At the very least, his reputation would have been irreparably tarnished.

Eddie was also guilty of FUI—flying under the influence. It was not uncommon for him to drink a considerable amount of alcohol, then climb into his airplane to fly somewhere. There are classic stories about him landing on the runway in Tampa with every one of the airplane's lights turned off. By the time the authorities reached the point where he had landed, he would already be gone.

Eddie Graham

Irregardless of what personal problems drove him to despair, on January 21, 1985, Eddie put a gun in his mouth and pulled the trigger. I was told that the shot blew out one side of his face, but it didn't kill him. He loaded and cocked the gun a second time, and finished what he had started.

Years later, I got to know Eddie's son, Mike, really well. Mike worked for *World Championship Wrestling* during the promotion's final days. During the last year of WCW, Mike worked in the Power Plant, WCW's training gym, as a trainer. He would fly from Tampa to Atlanta and work at the gym for a couple of days each week. He always took time to stop by my office and spend some time talking. I always enjoyed being around Mike. I have a tremendous amount of respect for him, not only because of his dad, but just because Mike is a likeable person. Mike often talked to me about his mother, and how they fell on hard times due to problems with taxes and the IRS. Somehow, they weathered it all.

During one of our conversations, Mike told me that his father had been very hurt by something that Dusty Rhodes had done. Basically, Dusty walked out on him on very short notice, and took many of the promotion's key players. I wasn't one of them. I had left Florida and was in the Maritimes when it all went down.

It was during the time I was gone that Jimmy Crockett made the overture to Dusty. Dusty took him up on his offer and left Florida. After being so good to Dusty for more than ten years, Eddie was left high and dry. Dusty even had points in the Florida territory that were given to him by Eddie. Yes, he had drawn a lot of money in Florida, but it was a mutual thing. In fact, it wasn't unlike the relationship between Vince McMahon and Hulk Hogan. They helped make each other. When Dusty left, Eddie was very hurt.

Leaving with little notice was bad enough, but Dusty also siphoned off a lot of Eddie's talent to give him a base to work with in Charlotte, and that really crippled the Florida territory. That action may have hurt Eddie more than Dusty leaving. I never really knew of the strained relationship between Dusty and Eddie, and the circumstances behind the Florida situation, until well after the fact.

When I was around Eddie, I was like a sponge, trying to understand where he was going, and why he was doing what he was doing. To me, Eddie was the best finish man in the business that I was ever around. He would lay out a finish in which each person had something logical to do. I might even go so far to say that he was the smartest guy I ever knew. I heard he only had a seventh grade education, but he was a street-wise guy who made his own way in life. He was a master of psychology and manipulation, and physically, he was a tough man.

I remember watching matches in other promotions where the manager would jump up onto the ring apron to distract the referee's attention. When the referee went over to make him get down, the manager would put a bearhug on him and hold him for an embarrassingly long period of time. Or, the referee would argue with the manager for a long time, to a point where the fans were screaming, *"Turn around, ref! Turn around!"* The heat was on the referee, not the heels who were doing the dirty work.

Eddie, on the other hand, made sure that something happened to make the referee look away momentarily. Whatever it was, it didn't take more than a second, but it was long enough for the heels to do whatever it was they were going to do without getting caught. The referee would turn around and count, *"1-2-3."*

In that case, the heat would go with the heels because the people saw that the referee was trying to do his job, and there was no way in the world he could have seen what happened.

It was a regular thing on television for a babyface or two to run in and save a poor job guy who was taking a severe beating from the heels. However, if Jack Brisco was at the studio, and they were going to shoot an angle like that, ten minutes before they shot the angle, Eddie would instruct Gordon Solie to interview Jack and say something like, *"Jack, I know you have to get going, that you have an appointment to see some underprivileged children at the local hospital who are looking forward to your visit. We appreciate that you've given us this time because I know you've got to rush over there."*

And Jack would leave. That little statement would seem unimportant, but later in the taping, when the heels did their dastardly deed, it would explain why Jack Brisco wasn't there to save the babyface. If not for that statement, the people would think that Jack was still in the back. And if he was, why didn't he come out to help? If Jack had been there, and came out to help, it would have diminished the heat and cast Jack in a bad light for not arriving *before* the damage was done.

Eddie was a master of those kinds of things, subtle things that most promoters never thought about. They were more worried about getting the heat, where Eddie was thinking of every individual who was there, and protecting his key people. That's just one of the reasons why I always thought of him as my mentor.

Bill Watts, Dusty Rhodes, and I were all products of Eddie Graham. I think a lot of the success that Bill Watts had came from being around Eddie. Bill probably took more time and effort to follow Eddie's logic than anyone else. As a result, he followed more closely in Eddie's creative footsteps. On the other hand, Dusty never focused on the nuts and bolts of the business. Dusty was too busy being Dusty, and he listened enough to learn Eddie's logic, but he did not do it with the attention to detail that Eddie did.

I got to know Eddie pretty well that first time around in 1975. I started my career late, so I wanted to concentrate on learning logic, and the creative side of the business. Eddie liked people who were interested in the business from that perspective. He didn't just want to hear people tell him what he wanted to hear. He wanted to hear from those who were genuinely interested.

It's funny, but after all the years of being around Eddie, my most vivid memories of him are of the time when he came into New York with his wrestling brother, Dr. Jerry Graham. Eddie was the silent one who stayed in the background, while Jerry was outrageously flamboyant and did all the talking.

As I learned more about the business, I realized that Eddie *was* the silent one, but he was also the businessman and the brains behind the success of the team.

1982 • JJ vs. Dusty Rhodes in a bullrope match

# Chapter 20
# Cadillacs, Mercedes and BMWs

Black Bart, JJ & Ron Bass

I returned to the Carolinas on August 6, 1984 as the manager of Ron Bass and Black Bart— The Long Riders. They wore long duster coats and big cowboy hats. I had managed them in Florida, as well, so we had a successful history together. They were two of the wrestlers that Dusty took with him when he left Florida.

Black Bart is just a dippin' country boy. He would dip constantly. He always had that dip in his lip. He never made big money in the business, so it was a big thrill for him to work at that level. Of course, that meant that he had to put a little money into his ring gear. He was worried sick every night that his gear wouldn't get back to the dressing room safely. And if it did, he was afraid that someone would rip it off, because the person who took it back would just lay it on a chair.

His hat was his prized possession. A Stetson hat is not cheap. At the time, Bart paid $125. One night, I got back to the dressing room before he did, so I put my hand on the top of his hat and squashed it. When he came back and saw it, he pitched a fit and blamed the ring guys not taking care of his gear. *"Look what they did to my hat!"*

*"That's terrible,"* I sympathized. *"I'm sure it was an accident. I'll make sure and talk to them."*

I did that on an ongoing basis. I didn't do it every day because I didn't want it to become too obvious, but it was so easy. I could squash the hat as I walked by without even slowing down. When he came out of the shower, he'd curse and threaten to fight everybody in the dressing room. That went on for months and months, and the last person he suspected was me because I didn't have the reputation for doing things like that. Nobody else in the dressing room knew who did it, either. I always picked my spot and I never got caught. There were times when the dressing room would be full of people, but when no one was looking at his hat, I seized the opportunity to smash it down.

One time, I had Jeanette go out and buy a queen-size garter belt that the Long Riders and I would use in an angle on Asheville TV. It was one of those things where I came into the ring for a schmoz [interference] at the end. The two heels (Long

Riders) pulled out, and all of a sudden, I was the last person in the ring and the babyfaces had me surrounded. I had nowhere to go, so I made a desperation dive for the ropes. They tried to stop me by grabbing my pants, but my pants came off. When I stood up, the audience saw that I was wearing women's stockings and a garter belt.

Of course, I didn't tell anyone about it beforehand. Ron Bass' eyes lit up. He did one of those double-takes that you used to see in slapstick films. I rolled out of the ring and Ron handed me his long coat. I whipped the coat around me, and it covered my shoulders, but the long end whipped all the way around and got wedged, leaving my butt exposed. I couldn't have done that if I had planned it. I proceeded to walk up the aisle, acting indignant and outraged.

The following week, I talked about how I was wearing the gear for medical purposes, as prescribed by a doctor, because I was suffering from varicose veins. I chastised the fans for laughing at me and showing little compassion.

Those were the types of things I did for pure entertainment. I did things like that because I wanted to entertain the people. I wanted to make them laugh. If you keep a straight face and don't crack, it's unbelievable what you can get the people to buy into.

Too often today, the boys do things with a wink and a nod to the people. *"I did this because I'm in on it."* When you do that, all the entertainment is gone because you've taken the true pop away from the people. To do it with a straight face and have timing is a lost art. Once you walk through the curtains to the back, then you can roll on the floor and laugh about it, but don't ever let the fans see you break character. That's like slapping them in the face. They laughed, but suddenly realize that you were playing them all along. That takes most of the fun out of it.

In addition to managing, I also wrestled on a regular basis in Charlotte. In fact, in August 1984, I had five matches with a young wrestler named Bret Hart.

I only worked under a mask one time in my career. In October 1986, Baba sent Hiroshi Wajima, the retired sumo Yokozuna, to Charlotte to train with Nelson Royal. Towards the end of Wajima's training, Baba flew in to work on the November 8 show at the Charlotte Coliseum. He would team up with Wajima against two guys, with the idea being to showcase Wajima, and the match would be taped for airing in Japan.

I was in the office when Dusty was trying to decide who to put against them. I said, *"Dusty, you just need a body to work with them. I worked with Baba many times in Japan. Let me put on a mask. The people won't know me."*

JJ & Hiroshi Wajima • 1986

Dusty thought it was a good idea and penciled me in. I wore a red, white, and blue stars-and-stripes mask that I bought years before when I was in Mexico. It had long tights and a top that went with it and I had never worn it. I wrestled as the American Eagle and teamed up with Gary Royal.

It was an honor to work with Baba again, but I was particularly excited about working with Wajima, who I had seen wrestle as a sumo Grand Champion. I was a big fan of his when he was a sumo champion, and now I had an opportunity to work with him. When Wajima retired, he gave me an autographed poster, which I have framed and hanging in my home. He also signed and gave me a copy of the retirement program that includes his history. That match in Charlotte probably meant nothing to everyone else, but it was a match of particular significance to me, personally.

After the match, I took a shower, put on my suit, and managed the Four Horsemen later that night. As far as I know, nobody ever knew that it was me.

There were so many great workers in the business during that time. I worked with Ronnie Garvin, who I thought was very believable, and his style was very credible. When I hear people disparage Ronnie's run as the NWA world heavyweight champion, I think of Vince McMahon Sr.'s philosophy concerning Bob Backlund. A lot of people say, *"Bob Backlund? Give me a break!"* What they don't consider is that Bob had legitimate credentials as an amateur, he was physically fit, he always conducted himself in a professional manner, and he gave credibility to the role of the world champion. Did that mean the titleholder had to be the person solely responsible for putting asses in the seats? No, because Vince had Andre the Giant, Dusty Rhodes, Superstar Graham, and a whole array of people. It was a package deal, and Bob Backlund gave "credibility" to that package. When I look at Ronnie Garvin, I look at him the same way. He was not always flamboyant, but what he did was very believable. I never would have second guessed Dusty's decision to have Ronnie as world champion.

I had a few matches with Paul Ellering. It was fun to work with Paul. We were booked on the card to entertain, not to show two classic wrestlers. Paul was always the more accomplished in terms of how the match unfolded, especially with his position with the Road Warriors, and compared to me, Paul was always in superb physical condition.

On October 14, 1986, our top babyface, Magnum T.A. (Terry Allen), was involved in a terrible car accident. After wrestling earlier that night in Greenville, South Carolina, he dropped Dick Murdoch off and lost control of his car while driving home. The entire territory went into shock. For awhile, we weren't even sure if he was going to live. The doctors operated on him for several hours, trying to repair the damage to his vertebra and nervous system. I believe the fact that he was in such tremendous physical condition was the only reason that he was able to pull through it.

Magnum TA

We were all concerned about Magnum. Doug Dellinger, who later went to WCW as their head of security, was still on the police force in Charlotte, but he handled Jimmy Crockett's security. It was through Doug Dellinger that Tully Blanchard, Ric Flair, Arn Anderson, and I, were able to go to the hospital and enter through a private entrance with no fanfare. Nobody knew we were there. Nobody but Magnum's immediate family was allowed in at the time because it was a touch and go thing. When we did get to see him, he was in such bad shape that we weren't able to talk to him. I remember walking into the room. Magnum was face down on an apparatus that had his head locked into a specific position, and he couldn't move. The table slowly rotated to about a 30-degree angle on one side. It would stop, then move back to a 30-degree angle on the other side. We were told that it was to keep his bodily fluids moving. To this day, it's a subject that I have a hard time talking about. As many times as we've been up and down the highway as wrestlers, when you see somebody in a situation like that, and know that their life is hanging in the balance, you can't help but think, *"That could just as easily have been me."*

There was a weekly television show produced in Toronto called *Learning The Ropes*. It starred Lyle Alzado as a schoolteacher who moonlighted under a mask as a professional wrestler. He had a daughter and a son who knew about his alter persona,

but at school, they could never let on that he had a dual life. And, of course, the principal was always suspicious and curious. Jimmy Crockett had a deal to supply guest talent, and I was fortunate enough to be sent to do an episode. I played a wrestler who enjoyed painting. In my case, I was in character, but also out of character. I was J.J. Dillon, the wrestler, not J.J. Dillon, the manager. They flew me up to Toronto, put me up in a hotel, and I stayed there from January 6-8, 1988, while we shot a 30-minute episode.

After Crockett's television show was being aired worldwide, he made a deal to promote a wrestling tour in Kuwait and the Middle East that ran from March 27 until April 4, 1985. Of course, I always wanted to go to new places, and working in the office made it easy for me to make sure that I was included on that tour. We took a great crew with us: David Crockett, Dory Funk, Crusher Blackwell, Dick Slater, Superstar Billy Graham, Bill Eadie, Lex Luger, the Great Kabuki, and Sgt. Slaughter. The star headliner for the tour was Adnan Al Kaissie He had wrestled as Billy White Wolf, but Adnan Al-Kaissie was popular over there because he's Iraqi. We tried to give the tour an international flavor, so I became an Australian and teamed up with Dory Funk.

There are so many things that I remember about our time in Iraq. We all stayed in a hotel. We were told that we couldn't go out and wander the streets at night, but it was safe during the day. We wrestled in an outdoor soccer stadium. There was a constant swirl of sand in the air. Five minutes after I brushed my teeth, I would have a gritty feeling in my mouth. I also remember seeing three water towers in the center of town.

The tour was an interesting, but uneasy, experience. I was happy to have had the opportunity to make the trip, but I was also happy to leave. It wasn't a place where you took a chance and did something that you weren't supposed to do. For instance, drinking alcohol was forbidden by the government. On an earlier tour, Jimmy Snuka got busted for bringing in marijuana. It was a big deal and they put him in jail for a short time.

We had visited several gold shops in Kuwait. The law in Kuwait stipulates that gold has to be 18 karats or higher. When we arrived back at Kennedy Airport in New York, everybody had all this gold on them. Luger bought a lobster claw chain that he still wears to this day. I remember thinking, *"We're gonna get killed in customs,"* but the customs people recognized Sgt. Slaughter and whisked us through.

I can't say anything bad about Jimmy Crockett. He was a very gracious, generous person. In June 1988, he flew everybody to St. Martin for an NWA meeting and paid our expenses. Giant Baba was there. Victor Jovica and Carlos Colon were there from Puerto Rico. Jimmy even allowed us to take our families. He also bought Dusty a Mercedes Coupe convertible. The car was so small that Dusty had to squeeze himself into it, like meat in a sausage casing.

I don't think anybody has ever written about what I call *The Myth*. When I was a fan, and even when I was in the business as a referee, I didn't know what kind of money the boys made. The guys didn't talk about their money. I just assumed, like most wrestling fans, that if you were on television, you were famous. And if you were famous, you made a lot of money. Putting two and two together, that meant that wrestlers were rich.

That was *The Myth*.

Of course, the wrestlers perpetuated *The Myth*. They wanted to live up to the image of how they were perceived by the public. Many times, I heard guys say, *"I can't drive a Ford or a Chevy. The fans think I'm a star, so I have to drive a Cadillac, Mercedes, or BMW."* From there, it moved to, *"I have to wear the Rolex watch,"* and then, *"I can't wear just any Rolex watch. It has to be a Rolex with the diamond bezel, like Flair's."* Dusty and Magnum T.A. ordered custom-made, coyote fur coats. They were all trapped in the *"I have to maintain an image"* mindset.

Jimmy's office was in an old convenience store that had been converted into offices. Dusty had a big office to the right of Jimmy's, while Gene Anderson and I shared the smallest office in the building. Every now and then, a local radio station would feature a story on wrestling. Their reporters would talk about the abundance of BMWs and Mercedes parked behind the building.

It was the exact opposite way of thinking from that of Jim Crockett Sr., but at that point, Jimmy and the other promoters not only allowed it to happen, but kind of encouraged it. I don't know if encouraged is the right word, but they were happy to see the boys spending their money and going into debt. They were easier to control when they had to have that paycheck every week in order to maintain the lifestyle they were living. Many times, the boys would get a cash advance on their pay. That was all part of the myth, and because of it, when their careers ended, a lot of the guys had nothing saved for their retirement.

I didn't know it at the time, but when I was a referee, the boys would often get a cash advance, or draw, from the office. That advance would be deducted from their earnings when they were paid off on Thursday in Washington, D.C. I don't know if the boys working for Jimmy Crockett did the same thing, but I would assume their lifestyles had them living paycheck to paycheck.

Dusty enjoyed being Dusty Rhodes. He kept his notes in a Louis Vuitton bag that he took pride in carrying around. Dusty liked that image. He would walk into the office and jot down his TV show on a piece of paper. Dusty could not spell for anything. He was constantly asking me, *"How do you spell —?"* He would write his notes down, drop them on my desk, throw his bag over his shoulder, and leave. Gene Anderson and I would then go through the notes and try to decipher what he wanted. Many times, he would have guys booked in two different towns on the same night.

Basically, I made a good living during those years by analyzing the shows that Dusty scribbled on pieces of paper, fine-tuning them and making corrections. I suppose you could say that I made a good living out of making Dusty Rhodes look good. That was fine with me. I never had an ego problem of wanting to take the credit for what I contributed to the end product. I'm not claiming the credit now, either, by saying that it was me, and not him, but I was an attention-to-detail person. Dusty knew how to entertain. He knew how to get himself over. He had the ability to develop a big picture. I fine-tuned that picture and made sure the end result was acceptable.

On Saturday mornings, we would tape the TV show for airing that night on TBS. I would use Dusty's notes to determine where to insert the commercials. I then designated a specific amount of time for each interview. The time alloted depended on who the interview subject was, what they had to cover, and their ability to do a good interview. Finally, I allocated a certain amount of time for each match.

During the actual taping of the show, I was constantly reworking the format. Many times, if I had a squash match scheduled to go six minutes, and we were three minutes into it, Dusty would look at me and ask, *"How much longer do I have to look at this sh—?"*

That was my cue to give the signal to go home [end the match]. I had to lengthen another match later in the program to fill the remaining time. On occasion, we would get a few minutes behind schedule, but I always had the ability to look ahead and know where I was going to regain that time.

There were many advantages to working in the office. Since I was part of the planning and execution, I always had the security of never having to worry about how many dates I was going to work the following week, where my position was on the card, or how I'd be paid. There is a certain amount of job security that goes with those things, especially when times are good, and those years were definitely good.

I was having a tremendous amount of fun during those years with Jimmy Crockett. I was also working very hard. I was going to the towns every night. There were nights when I could have said, *"I'm going to stay home tonight and not go to that town,"* but after working seven nights a week for the previous thirteen years, I wasn't geared to taking time off. The trips weren't as grueling, either. We made most of the trips in Jimmy's private jet. I would get home at a decent hour, get some sleep, and be back in the office the next morning. I didn't have a scheduled time that I had to be in the office, but I knew what had to be done, and I knew how much time it would take me to accomplish those tasks. Nobody ever said, *"Hey, you're expected to be here at so-and-so time,"* or, *"Where are you going?"* I went to the office, got my work done, and left. I would rush home, grab a quick bite to eat, pack my bag, and do a photo finish at the airport.

Dusty only worked a few nights a week. He eventually decided that he was no longer going to work the smaller towns. On the other hand, the Horsemen [who I managed; more on them soon] worked *every* night, and went to every town, regardless of size, and I went with them.

There was one unusual night when I came down with the flu. Dusty was going to the town that night, so I thought, *"I really feel bad. I'm not going to the town tonight. I'm going to stay home. Dusty is going to be there, so he'll take care of everything."*

I called Dusty to tell him that I had the flu and wasn't going to make the town. He got very indignant. *"If I'm there, YOU'RE there!"* He made it a point to let me know that I had to be there, to the point of threatening my job if I didn't go. It was something he was not joking about. That was my first real feeling of disappointment regarding Dusty. After all I had given of myself to the company, I didn't understand how he could cop that kind of an attitude on me.

That was also the era when the sheets [wrestling newsletters] and smart fans started to talk about something called the *Dusty Finish*. An example of the *Dusty Finish* would be if the referee gets knocked down during a match between Dusty Rhodes and NWA champion Ric Flair (or any two wrestlers). When Dusty makes his comeback and rolls up Flair for the pin, a second referee gets into the ring, counts 1-2-3, raises Dusty's hand, and gives him the title belt. As the crowd is celebrating Dusty's victory, the first referee, the designated official in charge, determines that the match should have been stopped some time back on a disqualification. And, of course, everybody knows that a title can't change hands by disqualification.

Finishes like that have been around forever. However, you can only use a finish like that occasionally. If you go back to that well too many times, the fans begin to feel screwed. Dusty went back to it far too many times, and that's why it became known as the *Dusty Finish*.

It was also during this time that I became part-owner in the Florida promotion. Buddy Colt owned 5% of the Florida office. When Jimmy Crockett contemplated going to Florida to revive *Championship Wrestling from Florida*, I bought Buddy Colt's 5% for $3,000. I bought my points just in time to see the territory fold and go under.

But I was an owner!

# Chapter 21
# The Four Horsemen

The Four Horsemen were formed spontaneously during the fall of 1985. It was not an idea that was planned in any great detail. At the time, Ric Flair was the world heavyweight champion, Tully Blanchard held the U.S. title, and Ole and Arn Anderson were the National tag team champions. We all walked out onto the studio set and did an interview, en masse. At the time, I only managed Tully, so I went out with him. There we were, all of the heels with all of the titles, and with all of the bragging rights.

As I said, the Horsemen concept was something that happened, but if anyone should be given credit for the idea, it should be Arn Anderson. As we did the interview, Arn grabbed the microphone and told the audience that they were witnessing history. *"Only once has so much damage been caused by so few,"* Arn shouted, *"and to find that source, you need to go all the way back to the Four Horsemen of the Apocalypse."*

When Arn held up his four fingers, the fans picked up on it. From that day on, the fans gave us the four finger sign—the symbol of the Four Horsemen—whenever they saw us. It was a sign that held a different meaning from the one-finger salute that the fans used to give us.

The origin of the Horsemen was just that simple. It was nothing that we put together by design. The gimmick simply took on a life of its own.

When I managed the Horsemen, there would be times when one of the members would be in a singles match. I wouldn't go to the ring with the Andersons, then with Tully, and then with Flair. I was smart enough to realize that by the third time out, there was no spark left to my appearance. I might go out with Arn, but not with Tully, or vice versa. I might go out with both of them, but go back to the dressing room when the bell rang to start the match. I would always go out and stay with Flair during his match, but I knew that being at ringside for all three matches was not a good business decision.

We had a lot of fun together. It was a time when we enjoyed each others' company. There were no selfish egos. If one of us got on a roll during an interview, and the others didn't get an equal amount of air time, it didn't create any tension within the group. I never heard anyone say, *"Hey, man! I didn't get my mic time!"* We were a unit—dedicated to doing what was right for business.

Many of the things we did were impromptu, like the first time Ric took his clothes off on television, and danced in his underwear. When something like that happened, we just went with it. It was a great time in the business.

Wayne Daniels, the cameraman I worked with in the Florida office, was back in Charlotte. He did a memorable one-camera shoot with all the Horsemen in the parking lot of Crockett's offices. It was the angle in a gas station parking lot where we were waiting for Dusty. When we saw Dusty driving up in his Mercedes, we said, *"That's

Tully Blanchard, James J. Dillon, Arn Anderson, and Ole Anderson

him!"

We switched our attention to the cameraman and said, *"You just keep shooting. You may not like what you see, but you're not a part of this. We're paying you good money, so don't stop shooting no matter what happens!"* That explained why the cameraman was there. I wanted people to understand that we paid the cameraman to record it.

When Dusty got out of his car, we pulled up behind him, got out of our car, and whacked him with a baseball bat. We pushed him up against a wall and beat the daylights out of him. It looked pretty brutal. It was an intense angle and we got a lot of mileage out of it.

We also came up with a reason to explain why Crockett aired the angle. The Horsemen had bought and paid for the TV air time as a way to send a message to our opponents. *"If you mess with one of the Horsemen, you mess with all of us, and we'll make an example out of you!"*

After the angle aired, people called in and said we should be arrested for assault. The segment had that kind of impact. In fact, it became such a legendary angle that there is even a myth associated with it. Many of Dusty's critics like to point out that just as we were about to pummel him, he yelled out, *"Make it good!"* Their interpretation is that he was speaking to us as a director, telling us how to hit him. I am officially dispelling that myth.

Dusty was ambushed by the Horsemen. Once he was hog-tied to the truck, he was defenseless, and he could see what was about to take place. "Make it good" was more of a challenge to us, kind of like the tough guy who says, "I'll give you the first punch, and you better make it good."

The segment was post-produced. Some language was bleeped out, and a spot was superimposed over Dusty's hand after the blow, lending the viewer to think that it was too gruesome to show on TV. Had Dusty's comment been an actual expose of the business, it too would have been bleeped out. We actually intended for him to say that. It was entirely on purpose!

Unfortunately, drugs and alcohol were a big problem in the business during that period of time. It was scary to see what drugs and alcohol could do. I saw grown men get so drunk that they wet themselves in bed while they were sleeping.

The drug of choice for many of the guys was cocaine. I'm not making a blanket statement by saying that everyone did cocaine because there were many who didn't. I'm sure there were lots of guys who wouldn't touch drugs, each having their own reason for making that personal decision. I could also name specific names of the people who did use cocaine, but that would be wrong. There is a code of silence in wrestling, just like in professional baseball, football, and basketball. Whatever happens outside the squared circle in our private lives is not discussed publicly, unless someone chooses to talk about their own personal situation without mentioning other names. I will go out on a limb and mention two specific people.

Did Ric Flair use cocaine?

Never!

Ric would have absolutely nothing to do with smoke or cocaine. The other boys used to make light of the fact that it was a good thing that Flair never wanted to touch cocaine, because with his nose being as big as it is, there wouldn't have been any left for anyone else.

And what about J.J. Dillon?

Well, I'm not saying that I never indulged. In fact, I'm somewhat ashamed that I wasn't strong enough to refuse it, but if somebody had it, I did a line. I never bought it or carried it, but it was readily available, and it was something I did occasionally. As I stated earlier, I never got involved with steroids, or the uppers and downers, because I was fearful of putting anything into my body that would take away my control. I never did enough to get hooked, but I saw what cocaine did to many of the guys, some of whom were good friends. It ruined their lives.

I'd like to take a moment to step away from my story for a moment. My primary motivation to write this book is to create an accurate and honest account of my life and career that I could leave to my children and grandchildren. In doing so, I have to be honest and open in my feelings and professional opinions about others. If I am going to do that, I have to be honest about all facets of my own life, as well.

I did a lot of soul-searching about whether to even bring up the subject of drugs and alcohol. I didn't feel like it was appropriate for me to name others who indulged, but to sidestep the subject altogether would have been wrong, too. As Scott Teal and I worked through the details, I spoke freely about my own experiences with drugs and alcohol. When Scott sent me a draft of the chapter, he suggested that I read it carefully and consider all possible repercussions my statements might have. I wasn't quite sure what he meant, but when he planted that thought into my head, he knew exactly what I would discover: *"What will my children and grandchildren think of me?"*

It is one thing to speak of things privately, and quite another to record them on a printed page to be read by the public. While the spoken word might be forgotten over time, the words in a book are almost impossible to remove, erase, or wash away. I am ashamed that I even have to write about drugs and alcohol in my life, but if I am going to be honest with both myself and my readers, I cannot in good conscience sweep this under the carpet and pretend that it never happened. When we first started this project, I promised Scott that I would talk about the good and the bad, the highs and the lows. This aspect of my life is definitely one of the "lows."

As hard as I tried to live my life in a manner where my children would be able to look up to me with pride, there were times when I failed miserably. Every parent tells their children to say "NO" to drugs and alcohol, and yet here is a parent who admits that he did it himself. I never got arrested. I never had an accident under the influence. My use was sporadic and casual. My use never developed into an addiction. And yet, somehow, I still have to acknowledge that it was wrong.

When the time comes, I will sit down with each of my children, and my grandchildren, and explain how wrong I was. The worst thing about it is, I can't use the excuse that

I was a reckless, irresponsible kid. At the time, I was in my forties. Hopefully, though, I will be able to help them understand how terribly wrong I was. Maybe my honesty and candor might help someone else who finds themselves in a similar situation.

On a positive note, when I retired from the ring and made plans to marry and have another family of my own, I put it all aside and never touched anything again. At the worst, I was a social drinker.

On a typical weekend, we would wake up on Saturday morning suffering from terrible hangovers. We would grab an extra hour sleep during the flight to Atlanta from Richmond, Virginia, and we would go directly to Wendy's for some "nutritious" food. When we arrived at the TV studio, we were still hung over. Many of those 12-minute interviews were done when we were not at our best physically or mentally, but it never showed when the camera light went on.

When we worked the Horsemen matches with Dusty, and it was time for Dusty to make the big comeback and clean house, Dusty would do the bionic elbow and the guys would feed him [run directly up to Dusty]. Dusty would drop them one at a time, then they would scramble to their feet, only to get dropped again. After each guy had taken the elbow twice, I would climb up on the ring apron and lean over the ropes, like I was trying to grab Dusty. Of course, he would see me with the eyes in the back of his head, and he would turn around. Bang! He would hit me with the bionic elbow.

The first time it happened, it was by accident, but it became my stock-in-trade spot. As I leaned into the ring, I put my foot on the bottom rope. As Dusty hit me, my body would pivot so that I was parallel to the ropes. Instead of just falling onto the apron, I would slide between the top and middle ropes, with the middle rope running from the crack of my butt to the top of my head. Once I got into that position, I could take my hands off the top rope and, for a few seconds, balance myself on the rope, almost like a turtle on his back, trying to struggle upright. I would flail my arms, moving side to side, until finally, I would turn towards the ring apron and do a flip-flop between the ropes. I would crash onto the ring apron and flop down onto the arena floor, sitting up with a goofy look on my face.

Arn called it the Hully Gully. Tully always felt that, in a real contest, you don't fall so smoothly. You don't take nice, neat bumps. You trip, stumble, fumble, or fall. That was Tully's style and he was very good at it. So instead of falling directly to the mat, I did the Hully Gully.

The Hully Gully was actually a takeoff on what Sky Low Low, the midget wrestler, used to do. When Sky (the heel) worked against Little Beaver in tag matches, Little Beaver and his partner would take the first fall. In the second fall, while Sky's partner distracted the referee's attention, Sky would scamper to the top rope and leap off, landing on his opponent. The referee would turn around and count, 1-2-3.

In the third fall, the heels would spend an inordinate amount of time trying to draw the referee's attention, and Sky Low Low would try to climb back up to the top rope to do it again. Invariably, the fans in the audience would yell at the referee, forcing Sky to scamper back down to avoid getting caught. It was fantastic to watch. Sky would climb a little bit higher each time. When he finally did reach the top, the people would scream, and he would slowly lose his balance.

When Sky fell, he had a way of falling through the ropes—over and under, over and under. It made me think of a Slinky: from the top rope, through and over the middle rope, through and over the bottom rope, finally crashing to the apron, and then to the floor.

Basically, the Hully Gully was a takeoff on that.

As I said, there were no internal problems between the Horsemen, but Ric Flair was battling some very real conflicts with the way Dusty Rhodes was handling our programs.

Dusty had an ego. He seemed to think that the Horsemen were to be used as his personal cannon fodder. We were there for one reason, and one reason only—to make Dusty Rhodes look good. That was true, but Ric would worry that we were giving away too much. We would take nightly beatings from Dusty, and Ric worried about losing our momentum. *"Can't Dusty see that he's killing us? We get beat every night. He leaves us laying in the ring, bloody and beaten, and he never puts anything back into us. He's killing our heat."*

At times like that, the tension in the dressing room was thick. I was caught in the middle because I was Dusty's assistant, and yet I spent most of my time in the dressing room with the Horsemen. The guys would get so frustrated. When we were on the road, and when we stayed over after the matches, they would say things like, *"You work with Dusty every day. Why the hell don'cha say something to him? It's all one direction. You can see the problem, can't you? We're gonna kill ourselves off and then it'll all be over."*

That was the closest our little group ever came to tension. They never put a tremendous amount of pressure on me, but I could feel their frustration. I balanced that line, stayed friends with them, and let them vent their frustrations. When it finally reached a point where the attitudes might cause problems and affect the product, I would take Jimmy Crockett off to the side and tell him that I needed to speak with him privately. I would tell him, *"There's something brewing and Flair is about to snap. Flair feels like he's being abused and I can see where he's coming from. Dusty's beating all four Horsemen every night and doing nothing to put heat back on them. Dusty's ego is running unchecked and you're the only one who can do something about it. If you don't, it's going to blow up in your face."*

Jimmy knew how to massage Ric's ego. He would call Ric, as if on the spur of the moment, and say, *"Hey, Ric. Why don't you come to the house and have dinner with us tonight?"*

That gave Ric his opportunity to vent to Jimmy, and Jimmy's attention would appease Ric. The next day, Ric would walk in with a whole new attitude. *"You'll never guess who called me last night. Jimmy called me. Man, it was like old times. We had dinner together and what a great talk we had. He's going to talk to Dusty, and he can see that they need to do a little bit for us."*

Jimmy also knew how to talk to Dusty without making it seem like he was telling Dusty how to do his job. He would say, *"Dusty, I'd like to do this, and do that,"* without letting on that anything had precipitated his suggestions.

When Ric would come back to the dressing room after a meeting with Jimmy, I would just sit there. I wouldn't say anything. Nobody knew the part I played during those years to "fix" those situations. At the beginning, I had to do that every six months or so. By the end of our run, I was running interference every three months. I was in a tough position because I was on the road with the heels at night. I was a part of the group. They were my friends, and we all enjoyed spending time together. But during the day, I was in the office with the guy on the other side of the ring, who had a huge ego and wanted people to do what *he* wanted them to do.

The Horsemen gimmick was a tremendous success. I remember one night, in particular, when the Horsemen were hot. On January 10, 1987, the NWA and the WWF both ran in Philadelphia on the same night. Representing the Horsemen that night were myself, Ric, Tully, and Arn. The babyface side had Dusty Rhodes, Dick Murdoch, and Barry Windham. Meanwhile, the WWF sent stars such as Randy Savage, Bret Hart, and Jake "The Snake" Roberts. We were at the Philadelphia Civic Center, they were at the Spectrum—and we outgrossed them! That was a real high. That was a barometer of how we were competing against each other—whether it was a genuine competition, or a subtle competition—but we made a statement that night. We drew a sellout of almost 11,000 fans paying $192,500, while the WWF did NOT have a sellout, and grossed $160,537. That gave us a tremendous feeling of satisfaction. It was a night I will never forget.

The Horsemen got a lot of coverage in the national wrestling magazines. Bill Apter published most of those magazines and put words in everybody's mouth. For the most part, everybody was happy with his work. In those days, it was a big deal to have a relationship with Bill and get a feature article written. It was an even bigger deal to get your picture on the cover. The annual awards were a political thing. Each year, Bill would decide who he would give it to and why. I'm sure it went to whoever he had an alliance with. I was awarded the *Manager of the Year* award in 1982, 1983, and 1988—and I'm still not sure if anybody really voted! I still have those plaques, though. George Napolitano headed a competing group of wrestling magazines, and in a similar way, he was a good friend to many wrestlers.

The Horsemen era was the first time I had an "opportunity to make money" through merchandising. Prior to that, there wasn't any real system set up to promote products like t-shirts, videotapes, or photos. The only thing I can think of that came close to that was in Tennessee, where the babyface wrestlers made extra money selling their pictures. However, even though we had the "opportunity to make money," the Horsemen themselves made very little on merchandise. The Crocketts eventually sued the guy in charge of the merchandising, claiming that he was ripping them off.

Ole Anderson

I have a lot of respect for Ole Anderson. I know a lot of guys don't understand Ole, and have trouble getting along with him, but I like him. If I had to pick one version of the Horsemen as my favorite, I'd pick the original quartet, for that reason. Ole is the kind of guy who always speaks his mind. You never have to guess where you stand with Ole. He lets you know without any hesitation. I think it's unfortunate that Ole didn't have more success with WCW when he was with them in the early '90s. The people at TBS should have listened to him and incorporated his ideas. Unfortunately, they didn't understand the wrestling business. They believed that any Joe off the street could run the company. Ole understood the business, and WCW might be alive today if they had given him the power he needed to do what should have been done.

Ole was the only member of the Horsemen who didn't fit Ric Flair's "Kiss stealin', limousine ridin', jet flyin' sonofagun" image. Arn did, and Tully certainly did. I could stand there and grin like a Cheshire cat, acting like I was having fun with it, but it really didn't fit Ole's persona. He was regarded as a grumpy old man who beat people up.

We had a lot of heat on us, but we needed more people to work with because the company was light on the babyface side. In early 1987, Ric was still the NWA world champion and Tully held the TV title, but the Andersons had lost the tag titles. We blamed Ole for that and fired him (in the storyline) on February 28 in Atlanta. That immediately gave us a new opponent for the Horsemen—Ole Anderson. Ole had worked long enough that he could work as a babyface without changing his style.

When Ole Anderson left, his spot became a revolving door. Our first recruit to replace Ole was Lex Luger, who was looking for work in a safe haven where he didn't have to watch his back. In December 1986, Lex was working in Lakeland, Florida, in a cage match with Bruiser Brody. In the middle of the match, Brody just stopped working and started no-selling [not reacting to] everything that Lex tried to do. Lex literally climbed out of the cage and ran for the relative safety of the dressing room. The altercation scared Lex badly and he wanted nothing else to do with either Brody or the Florida territory.

Lex had been working on top in Florida, so we brought him in. Unlike Ole, who was one of the best promo guys the business has ever known, Lex didn't have the gift of gab, so we told him to stand in the background and pose. Lex made an incredible living off of his look, or at least, the potential that came with that look. I don't know that he ever deserved legitimate credit for drawing a house. In January 1987, Luger became an "apprentice" of the Horsemen. Two months later, when we booted Ole out, Luger became an "official" member of the group.

Lex Luger

Eventually, Lex left the Four Horsemen. On December 2, 1987, he turned on me during a *Bunkhouse Stampede* in Miami Beach and solidified his face turn, giving us yet another fresh opponent. Lex worked against Flair at the Great American Bash in Baltimore, Maryland, on July 10, 1988. We were trying to figure out how to end the match without having to pin Luger. At the time, the Maryland commission had issued a ruling that there was to be no blood, and even sent a representative to the show that night. He said, *"If I see blood in a match tonight, I'll immediately stop the match."*

That gave us the "out" that we needed. It was a natural way to end the match. All I had to do was gig Luger. But that was easier said than done.

Lex was very egotistical about his body and his looks, even though he was no Rick "The Model" Martel, but in his own mind, he thought he was very good-looking. On that night, he was absolutely petrified about getting juice [blood]. I told him that I would gig him.

*"Look at my face,"* I reasoned. *"You really have to look closely to see any scars on my head. I'm not all scarred up like a lot of the guys who were bleeders over the years. I always took care of myself and I'll do the same for you. I'll take care of you. I'll cut sideways, in the direction of the wrinkles in your forehead, and I won't leave a scar. I won't cut that deep, but once I'm there, don't move. And when I say don't move, don't move, and I won't hurt you. Just take an aspirin or something to thin your blood down a little bit. When I gig you, the first thing you have to do is put your head down, hold your breath, and strain as hard as you can, because that will make the blood come out before it coagulates."*

I had to walk him through the scenario several times, but the actual event went smoothly. At the designated time in the match, I grabbed Lex, gigged him, and bit his forehead. One happened just moments before the other. Then I took my shoe and whacked him in the forehead. It had the desired effect.

That one spot in the Horsemen was always a revolving door. On April 20, 1988, Barry Windham joined the group during a match in Jacksonville, Florida. He turned on his partner, Lex Luger, allowing Tully and Arn to beat them and win the NWA tag team titles. I was very excited to get Barry as a member of the Four Horsemen. I knew him from Amarillo, and by the time he joined the Horsemen, he was a seasoned worker and a great looking kid—handsome, young, and appealing to the girls. In terms of his work rate, he was perfect for us.

That incarnation of the Horsemen only lasted until September 10, 1988, the last night Tully and Arn had with the NWA. They lost the tag team titles to the Midnight Express in Philadelphia and immediately left for the WWF. Years later, when the Horsemen team was revived, and I was no longer affiliated with them, other members included Chris Benoit, Sting, Dean Malenko, Sid Vicious, Paul Roma, Steve McMichael, Jeff Jarrett, Curt Hennig, and Brian Pillman.

Of the rotating members of the group, Ole was with us the longest—1½ years. Technically, though, the Four Horsemen were really Ric Flair, Tully Blanchard, Arn Anderson, and myself. We were the constant for those three magical years.

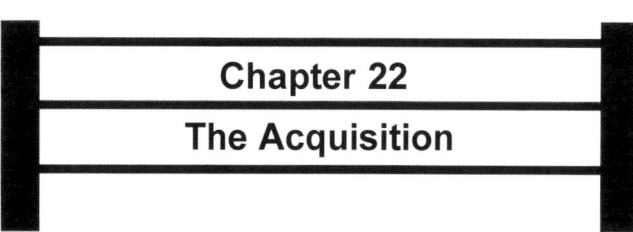

# Chapter 22
## The Acquisition

I was in the office every day with Jimmy Crockett, but he gave no indication that things were deteriorating. In fact, I don't think he knew the company was in trouble.

One week, my check was short because I didn't get paid for one of the towns. That was a red flag, because that just never happened. Eventually, Dave Johnson, Jimmy's accountant, told Jimmy, *"We need a million dollars cash flow."*

*"No problem."*

A week later Dave came back and said, *"We need another million dollars."*

Jimmy said, *"What's going on here? What's happening?"*

By that point, the financial trouble was deep enough, and serious enough, that Jimmy didn't have the financial reserves to fix it.

Things got so bad that David Crockett had to put fuel purchases on his personal credit cards for both of the private planes. One of the pilots had put some fuel on one of his own credit cards. He had done that in the past and had always been reimbursed, but that didn't happen at this point. The company was in serious trouble. Jimmy had moved the company to Dallas, and Dusty, Jimmy, and I all moved our families with it. We had huge overhead and business was bad.

I had huge overhead myself. I had a home in Charlotte, and I had bought a second home in Plano, Texas, a year earlier in anticipation of the move. Initially, prior to me actually making the move to Dallas, my Texas home had been leased back to the builder as his model home.

Jimmy had some serious discussions with Ted Turner. We were still getting good TV ratings. Turner had always wanted to get into the business as a promoter since he banged heads with Vince back when Vince was providing programming for TBS. With Ted Turner, it was a personal issue, and buying the NWA was Ted's way of being able to call Vince and say, *"I'm in the rasslin' business!"*

Jim Barnett helped bring the parties together when Turner purchased Crockett Promotions, but the person in charge of the acquisition was Jack Petrik. He had been with Turner a long time, and was held in high regard. The deal was signed on November 21, 1988.

Prior to the closing of the deal, and the contracts being signed, Petrik and a group of people from TBS interviewed the talent and everybody who worked in the office. Their mantra was, *"You people know what you're doing. You're wrestling people and you know the wrestling product, so we have no intention of interfering with that. Our job is to provide you with strong financial backing and further expertise in the television industry. We have connections all over the world that we will be able to bring you into."*

The reality was quite different. I quickly realized that the assurance they gave us in our initial interviews was not how it was going to be. Before the ink was even dry on the contracts, there were people who openly talked about the business as an exciting new venture that they would now have an opportunity to dabble in. Those same people were wrestling fans who had watched the product, and now that Turner owned the company, they were going to have an opportunity to have a say in that product.

Jeff Carr, who at the time was involved in programming on a lower level, said, *"I know how we can fix the ratings. Next week, we'll feature Ric Flair versus Sting!"*

*"Sure, it would."* I agreed. *"I can see where you're coming from, and you're right. Flair versus Sting on free TV would spike ratings. But what will you do the following week? In wrestling, you have to constantly balance what you give them on the TV. Yes, you want to whet their appetite, hook them and draw them in. But ultimately, your payoff comes from live arena revenue, or pay-per-view. If you give away your marquee matches too many times, you do it at the expense of your revenue streams."*

They pooh-poohed it. *"Yeah, yeah, yeah."* Their first priority was TV ratings. The logic, even to the end was, *"Well, if we get the TV ratings up, all the other problems will take care of themselves."*

Unfortunately, that logic in the wrestling business doesn't usually hold true.

We didn't know who the booker was going to be, either. Dusty was holding the reins when Turner took over, but it was made clear that he would not remain in that position. People dumped heat on Dusty as being the primary reason why the company got into the position it did. The first rumor I heard was that George Scott was coming in to run the company. I never worked for George, but he had a track record of success, so I didn't have a problem with it.

The higher-ups finally made a decision to bring someone in to run the wrestling division. Jim Herd, who was an executive with Pizza Hut, had been a station manager at Channel 11 in St. Louis, where Sam Muchnik had taped his show for many years. Logic with the television people at Turner was, *"Oh, we found the perfect person to run the company! We have one of our own—a television guy—who knows wrestling."*

So they brought in Jim Herd to be the head of the company. The NWA's big show of the year, Starrcade '88, was held on December 26, 1988, at the Norfolk Scope in Norfolk, Virginia. About five minutes before the show started, Jim Herd walked in with his wife. At their side was his good friend from his days in St. Louis, Lou Thesz, and Lou's wife, Charlie. Lou lived in Newport News, Virginia, at the time. They all sat front row ringside during the show. Jim Herd was displaying a cocky, arrogant attitude. *"I'm with Lou Thesz, and I've got all the answers."*

Things on the homefront were shaky as well. Jeanette and I were married for seventeen years and she traveled all over the world with me. We never had any children of our own. She always thought that I didn't like children. The truth is, she was five years older than me, and she already had three boys, so having a family of our own was never a topic of our conversation. I eventually had a vasectomy when I was in Amarillo in 1977, so having children after that was out of the question.

Although Jeanette traveled all over the world with me, was I a faithful husband during the times when we were apart? No. I was not the type of person who was with somebody different every night, but at the same time, it would paint the wrong picture to say that I was a faithful husband, because I wasn't. I'm not proud of that fact. It's just how it was. Being on the road, especially in the environment we were in, was very tough.

Unfortunately, Jeanette and I drifted apart and we went through a divorce during the time when Crockett was selling. In reviewing my time with Jeanette, I was a good provider and I helped raise her three sons. Jeanette received a social security benefit after her first husband died in an industrial accident, and again when we took in the two girls after her sister passed away. Jeanette personally received that money. I never saw it and don't even know how much it was. I used my earnings to provide a roof over our heads, food for the table, and the basic needs for everyday living. She used her money for other things for her sons and nieces.

I hold no ill feelings towards Jeanette, and as far as I know, she holds none towards me. As I look back, there are many things that I don't feel proud of, but I do feel good about helping her raise her three boys and two nieces. I don't stay in touch with the boys, but I heard from the younger of the two nieces when she took a job in real estate and moved to the Seattle, Washington, area. I followed up on her message and have had a few telephone conversations with her.

In 1988, I fell in love with a woman who was thirteen years younger than I was—Lindsey Townsend Barbee. Lindsey had been a model and a flight attendant with Pan Am. After going to school to be a travel agent, she went to work for American Express Corporate Travel and began handling Ric Flair's travel arrangements. When Jimmy (Crockett Promotions) went national, Lindsey was in the right place at the right time, and she worked in and out of the wrestling office, handling the travel arrangements for the company. That's where I first met Lindsey. One of my responsibilities was travel arrangements, so Lindsey and I worked together on it.

During that difficult time following the divorce, Lindsey and I both moved in with Tully Blanchard, along with everything I owned. He had a big house all to himself, and he had a housekeeper come in and clean. I had boxes scattered everywhere, but Tully never complained. He actually laughed about it. We stayed with Tully for close to two months and he refused to take any money. Tully knew that I was having a difficult time. I remember that Tully had a suit custom-made during that time, and it was expensive (maybe $750, I don't remember exactly). When the tailor was finished with the final alterations, I picked up his suit and paid for it as a small token of my appreciation.

To all the other wrestler's wives in Charlotte, I was the big villain in the divorce. I don't think anyone even knew where I was living, but Tully was a friend and he didn't care what anybody else thought. That is what friends are for, and Tully Blanchard will always be my friend. I will never forget his kindness and generosity. I have to say the same about Chip Burnham (the local promoter for the Georgia TV tapings and house shows), who was there for me when my last divorce went down.

On occasion, Lindsey would go to a show with me. Lindsey flew in one night after a show in Atlanta. The next night, January 6, 1989, I rented a car and we drove up to Philly for a house show. On the way, we ran into an ice storm. We were on a 5-lane highway when I hit black ice. With traffic in every lane around me, our car started to slide sideways and we went into a spin. I sensed another vehicle spinning beside me, as well. Our car slid towards the guard rail and we came to a stop. As we did, we heard a sickening, crunching sound, and we were sprayed with tiny chunks of glass. It all happened so fast. My first reaction was that we might be upside down, but I quickly realized that the car was still upright. Luckily, we both had our seatbelts on. The front doors of the car were jammed shut, so to get out, we had to climb over the front seat and into the back of the car.

I didn't realize the full extent of the accident until we got out of the car. The other vehicle was a pickup truck. It had rammed the guardrail nose first prior to us. When it hit, the back of the truck shot up into the air and became airborne. In that brief moment, I hit the same guardrail. As Lindsey and I climbed out of our car, we realized with a shock that the pickup truck was perpendicular to our vehicle and balanced on our roof. The driver's door opened and a man stepped out. He walked down the trunk of my car and jumped down to the ground.

All three of us walked away from the accident without a scratch. I remember another driver, who had somehow managed to avoid getting involved in the accident, saying,

*"If a TV truck was here, this would be on the eleven o'clock news."* A state trooper gave us a ride to the nearest police station and we waited two hours to get a replacement vehicle. The next day, Lindsey and I were so sore that I can't accurately describe how we felt. And yet, I still participated in a battle royal in Baltimore on the following night!

JJ Dillon, Lex Luger, Ric Flair & Arn Anderson

The original Four Horsemen: Ole, Tully, JJ, Arn & Ric

# Chapter 23
## Courted by the
## World Wrestling Federation

The WWF's overture came to me. I didn't call them. In September, 1988, two months before the Crockett's buyout, Tully Blanchard and Arn Anderson left Jim Crockett and went to work for the WWF. During the time when Jimmy's deal with Turner was taking place, Tully called me and said, *"I don't know what your situation is, or how things are going for you, but your name has been mentioned several times. Terry Garvin has spoken very highly of you, and, of course, Arn and I both had positive things to say about you. Vince and Pat do all the booking and write all the TVs. Their business has grown so quickly that it has really stretched them thin. They need help here creatively, and there's interest in you. If you're interested in coming to work for the WWF, give Terry Garvin a call."*

Terry Garvin was now working in the office for the WWF. He and I had worked together well in both Amarillo and Kansas City, and he thought my personality and ideas would be a good fit in the company (WWF). When I called Terry, he said, *"Oh, God. You'd do great up here. You and Pat Patterson would get along perfect. I told Pat that you're the man! You've gotta come up here and meet Vince. He's a wonderful guy to work for. This is the greatest place!"*

Terry went on and on about how much he enjoyed working for Vince and the WWF. Terry had always been very close friends with Pat Patterson, and he now had a position managing the WWF ring crew.

Jim Barnett was an intrical player in the sale of Jim Crockett Promotions and during the subsequent formation of Turner's WCW. Jim Barnett kept telling me, *"You don't have a contract with Turner. We need to get you locked up."* I avoided further discussion because I knew I had the meeting coming up with Vince, and I wanted to keep my options open. I also didn't like what I saw and I was concerned about the future of the company.

Lindsey and I had already arranged to take a 3-day vacation in New York to do some shopping and see some shows during the holidays, so I didn't have to shuffle my schedule around to get the time off. When we arrived, Vince sent a car to the Marriott in Times Square and the driver took me to Vince's house in Greenwich.

Pat Patterson was waiting for me at the house. He said, *"Vince is tied up at the studio so he's going to be late. Let's go into town and have a few drinks."* We went to a small bar and had a drink or two, then went back to the house. After a few minutes, Vince and Linda McMahon walked in. Vince had been doing on-camera work, so he was still wearing his makeup. We sat down in his living room and talked about what I was doing with the NWA. I was still managing and wrestling at that point.

Vince said, *"I envision you coming here to help us write the shows. Right now, Pat* and I are doing it all. We're booking three towns a night and producing two television shows—*Superstars* and *Challenge*. It's a monumental task. Pat and I realize that we need help. I've heard good things about you. If you come to work for us, I wouldn't expect you to be an on-air personality. I'll bring you in as a company employee with full benefits.

"You can do what you want. You can play it one of two ways. I'm hoping that you'll make a decision based on what we've discussed, but if you want to use me as leverage to get a better deal with Turner, I understand, and I have no problem with that. But, I would like to know what you want to do as soon as possible."

Vince McMahon, Jr.

I thanked him and said that I wanted to speak with my fiancée about it, since it impacted her future, too.

Lindsey thought it was a tremendous opportunity. I had reservations about the buyout with Turner. I was 46 years old, and the days of me being involved in the novelty matches were numbered. I was getting too old to get into the ring against people like Paul Ellering, or to be the fifth man in the ring with the Horsemen in matches like War Games.

Until I had my actual meeting with Vince, I didn't know why he wanted me on his team, but when I heard him say, *"I need help creatively. I'm looking at you strictly as an employee, not as an independent contractor or as a talent,"* I knew it was an opportunity that I couldn't pass up.

I always had a liking for Jim Barnett. A lot of people made fun of him, but he was one of the treasures of our business. He was one of the power brokers in our business for a long time. I always found him to be a fascinating person to talk with, with his history in the business and the many people he had known.

Jim and I were both living in Dallas at the time, so when I returned home, I decided to tell Jim about Vince's offer. Lindsey and I invited him to our home for dinner. Jim had worked for the WWF for several years, so not only would Lindsey and I have an enjoyable evening with him, but I could also pick his brain about what I might be getting myself into as an employee of the WWF. Who were the people who would help me, and who did I need to look out for? When I laid my cards on the table, Jim was genuinely happy for me. He didn't try to dissuade me from going. He simply told me that I would be very successful with the WWF.

When I called Vince to negotiate my salary, he said, *"Name your price."* I didn't want to price myself out of the market, or take a big step backwards. I had made $194,000 in 1988, so I asked him for $180,000. He didn't argue. He simply said, *"No problem."* He also offered to pay my moving expenses and gave me benefits. Lindsey said, *"I don't know how you can NOT say yes!"*

A few days later, I called Vince and accepted the position.

As I related earlier, I had started working as a referee for Vince's father when I was in college, and his father had been so kind to me. And now, 25 years later, I was being recruited by his son to work for the biggest wrestling promotion in the world. *From McMahon to McMahon.* To me, I was looking at the pinnacle of my wrestling career.

Everything was a positive. I was happy with the terms of employment. I was ready for a change of scenery. I was very excited and anxious to go, and had nothing but a positive outlook. I began to work on getting my personal life in order, which included getting married and starting a family of my own. In all, it was a good time in my life.

I wanted to give the NWA reasonable notice, so I gave my notice at the beginning of January. My last official match before retiring from the ring was a Battle Royal in

Kansas City, Missouri, on January 21, 1989. After taking two weeks off, Lindsey and I left Plano, Texas, on February 2 and flew to Connecticut. Even after so many good years with Jimmy Crockett and the National Wrestling Alliance, it was easy for me to move on. I saw no future for myself there. And once I arrived in Connecticut, I never once thought of looking back.

When I started working for Vince, one of my responsibilities was to do the same job that I did for the NWA. I timed the pay-per-views. The timing of the NWA's *Clash of the Champions* on TBS was critical because they were live shows, so I really had to stay on top of things. I had to know where we were in the show at all times so that I could time each segment for the remainder of the show. I handled it by myself and nobody looked over my shoulder to see what I was doing. In fact, nobody seemed to care enough to want to learn my job.

When I didn't receive my final paycheck from the NWA for Starrcade 1988, I called Jim Herd to ask about it. These aren't his exact words, but it was something along the lines of, *"Screw you. You bailed out on us and left us in a jam. I'm not paying you anything."*

When I mentioned it to Vince, he said, *"Why don't I give John Taylor a call and let him light a fire under their ass. He'll get your money."*

John Taylor, a big-time Atlanta attorney, was Jim Barnett's personal lawyer. He was also a big wrestling fan. Vince called John, who then called Jim Herd and threatened him with legal action. I received a $7,500 check in the mail on September 15, 1989.

On April 2, 1989, the NWA held a *Clash of the Champions* live from the Superdome in New Orleans. Since the higher-ups never had the foresight to make sure someone else could do my job, they had quite a few problems with the timing of the show. The show ran too long. In fact, the show was mistimed so badly that the last two matches—Sting defending his TV title and Lex Luger defending his U.S. title—never even aired. They ran out of time! They always took me for granted, but perhaps they appreciated my contribution when they realized how difficult it was to keep the show on schedule.

Somehow, I doubt it.

# Chapter 24
## The Big Time

My first day on the job as an in-house agent with the WWF was February 13, 1989. I really didn't know what to expect. For the first time in my life, I was going to be a full-time salaried employee, with benefits and profit sharing. I was no longer a wrestler on the road. I was strictly an employee. I had worked in several wrestling offices, so it wasn't a radical departure from my normal lifestyle, but I did have to deal with making the transition from being a talent on the road, to being an employee with benefits. I was going to wear a shirt and tie every day and work in an office.

This took place before Vince moved his offices into Titan Tower, which is located on East Main Street in Stamford, Connecticut. We were originally housed in a small, downtown building which had four floors. The offices were very small and cramped. Vince and Linda McMahon were on the 4th floor, while Pat Patterson and I were on the 3rd floor. I reported directly to Pat.

Compared to the NWA, the WWF was a bigger company, and there were a lot of people who worked there who weren't wrestling fans. Vince required all of his employees to be aware of what was going on with the WWF storylines. The company seemed to have an unwritten code. *"You are expected to watch all the TV shows, and know the talent and storylines."* In other words, in order to do your job effectively, you must know the product and the players. I don't know if everyone did, but I think there's a greater likelihood that WWF employees were more in tune with the product than the people were at the NWA.

Many of the employees knew me. Some, like Ed Cohen and Howard Finkel, had followed my career and were excited to have me onboard. Ed Cohen, who was a big wrestling fan, booked the towns and did the routing for WWF. When I walked in that first day, he told me it was a pleasure to meet me because of my hard work and dedication to the business. I have a lot of respect for Ed because of his work and dedication to the business, as well.

On the other hand, there were a *lot* of people who didn't know that I had been in the wrestling business, or that I had wrestled before I managed. Some people had a preconceived notion of what a wrestler looked like, and had a stereotyped image of a wrestler. Apparently, I didn't have that "image" when I walked in. Even after I had worked there for a long time, people would come up to me and say, *"YOU were a wrestler?"*

Other than on my checkbook or drivers license, when I worked for Vince McMahon, I was always referred to as J.J. Dillon, even though I was retired and had no intention of being a character in their storylines. Everybody in the business knew me as J.J. Dillon, so when I first got there, Vince asked me, *"What do you want me to call you?"*

"It doesn't really matter to me."

*"Well, everybody knows you as JJ, and you've already worked with most of the talent, so we'll keep it that way."*

Even my company ID had J.J. Dillon on it. Of course, my paycheck was made out to my legal name. There were a lot of people who didn't know my legal name. Years later, when people first heard about it, they would walk up and say, *"Oh! You have a famous name!"* My vanity led me to believe that they were referring to the "famous" James J. Dillon, but more often than not, they had just learned my real name. The famous name they referred to was Jim Morrison—of The Doors fame.

Shortly after I got there, Vince told me that Andre the Giant had come up to him and said, *"Hey, boss. What's Dillon doing here? We don't need him. He's from the other side."*

Having been associated with the NWA for most of my career, to many in the WWF, it was heresy to bring me into the fold, even to somebody like Andre. When we were in territories together, I had driven Andre around in my van, took him to my house, and fed him. And yet, when I showed up in the WWF, his first reaction was, *"Why do we need him? He's from the other side."*

When Vince told me about Andre's comment, he made it clear that Andre didn't say that to be vindictive. *"I'm not telling you this to make you feel bad, or to hurt your feelings, or to create any friction between you and Andre. I just want you to know that the statement was made. I told him that I want you here because I think your experience will help us."*

I never discussed it with Andre. I'm sure there were others who felt the same way, and Vince knew exactly what to do to counter the situation. *"I'm going to bring you in slowly. I'm not going to put you into a high profile situation, like at our TV's, where you're immediately barking orders."* He wasn't going to put me in a position where I would be supervising the guys who were suspicious of me. He wanted to give me the opportunity to make the transition—to allow the guys to see what I was there for, what I was doing, and what I was contributing. He wanted them to accept my presence there before giving me more responsibilities. That was a smart way to do it.

My first impression was how the WWF had so much more staff to handle the day-to-day, mundane tasks than the NWA did. I was used to working on a skeleton crew. When I worked on the creative side in an office, I wore ten hats, doing many different jobs. The WWF was much more organized, with people whose full-time responsibility was to do things I used to do in passing. There was a lot more attention paid to details.

For example, we created a poster of Hulk Hogan. The photo used on the poster was of Hogan, posing in the ring, with the crowd behind him. When the picture was taken, people had left their seat to go to the bathroom, or the concession stand, so a few empty seats could be seen in the background. Vince wanted to give the impression that every seat in the arena was filled, so he had an artist insert people into the photo. If Hulk's hair wasn't perfectly groomed, it would be touched up. Those were examples of the little things that the WWF paid attention to. Instead of flying by the seat of his pants, Vince insisted that his people pay attention to detail. The other promotions never noticed those things. If they did, they didn't think they were important, so they didn't take time to correct them.

Vince always had control over every aspect of his business. There were countless in-depth production meetings, where we discussed details and did walk-throughs. If a wrestler did a pre-taped interview, somebody would snap a photo with a Polaroid camera, so they could make a continuity check. Later on, if the wrestler went out into a live setting after that insert in the program aired, somebody made sure that he was wearing the same clothes. They didn't want the astute viewer at home to notice that he had changed his shirt, and possibly realize that the entire program wasn't live. Attention to small details like that showed Vince's commitment to presenting a professional product. Although they didn't seem too important at the time, in the big scheme of things, and over a long period of time, they were important to the quality of programming.

When I first walked out into the arenas, people would scream, *"JJ Dillon! What are YOU doing here!"* I thought to myself, *"I wonder if the WWF staff notices how many people up here still remember me from my days with the NWA?"*

For some of the boys, there was a perception that you were never really a player in the business unless you had been a star with the WWF at one time or another. If you were a star in another territory, but never made it as a star in New York, then you weren't perceived as a star at all. There was no validity to that, but there were a lot of people who did think that way.

For the most part, though, I had very limited exposure. They used me on-camera for occasional cameo appearances. I might have been at a table for a contract signing, but it was not brought to the viewer's attention as to who I was. I never had a role as a talent, and surprisingly enough, I wasn't bothered by that. At that stage of my career, being recognized as a talent was not important to me. It would have been nice if they had put me with Tully Blanchard and Arn Anderson, but Vince is the kind of guy who, if it wasn't his original idea, he had no interest in it. That may sound crazy because we had been successful in the NWA, and logic would say that he would reunite us, especially when Flair came in, but Vince didn't see it that way. He would rather put his heart and soul into his own ideas. He would rather bring someone in and repackage them as a new character, so that he owned the rights to their persona. Whether you agree with him or not, as a businessman, decisions like that made a lot of sense, and in fairness to Vince, our understanding from the beginning was that I would only be an office employee.

Even if Vince had seen fit to put me into a storyline with Tully and Arn, it wouldn't have lasted long. Just eight months after I arrived, Tully fell victim to the WWF's drug testing policy, but the repercussions also had a disastrous effect on Arn. In the summer of 1989, Tully and Arn held the WWF tag team title. At the same time, the other two original Horsemen, Ric Flair and Ole Anderson, were booking for the NWA. They decided that the time was right for a reunion of the original Four Horsemen, so they made a deal with Tully and Arn to get them to jump to the NWA. The deal was that Tully and Arn would each get $250,000 a year for three years.

Now I don't want it to seem as if I am spreading gossip about my former colleagues. Tully, just like all the Horsemen, is a good friend of mine, but Tully has candidly discussed this story in interviews, both in print and on video. Ric Flair also detailed this in his book, so I am not speaking out of turn when I say that Tully tested positive for cocaine.

According to Tully, they gave their notice to Vince in September, and agreed to work through the *Survivor Series* in Rosemont, Illinois on Thanksgiving night, November 23, 1989. As expected, Tully and Arn dropped the tag team titles to Demolition [Bill Eadie and Barry Darsow] in Wheeling, West Virginia on October 2. Everything was going smoothly until later in the month—when the WWF held a random drug test at the Philadelphia Spectrum on October 14.

At the time, the WWF's policy for a first time offender was a 6-week suspension. However, Tully says that by the time the results from the test came back, he only had 21 days left with the company, so Vince fired him on November 2. Somehow—and to this day, we still don't know who was responsible—NWA management were given details of the test. Fearful of a public relations backlash, they reneged on their deal with Tully. Flair, who was the head booker, had to call Tully on November 13th to tell him the deal was off. He also had to call Arn to let him know that he wouldn't be coming in as a tag team. He was also being "devalued" and would only get paid $150,000 a year. It was an unfortunate situation and a very tough time for both of them, but they have moved ahead with their lives. Tully is now healthy, happy, and sober. He is an evangelist and travels around the country teaching people about Jesus Christ. As a successful agent with WWE, Arn still keeps a foothold in the business.

Regardless of what might have happened if I had been used as a talent, I don't think my schedule would have allowed it. The office work was so complex that it required my full attention. I couldn't have done justice to both. I haven't mentioned it before, but that's one of the reasons why I admire Jim Ross. Not only did Jim handle the bookings and the payoffs, but he did the color commentary for the television shows. The commentary by itself requires a great deal of preparation. I couldn't do what Jim Ross has done. When you add the problems he was facing with Bells Palsy, and the fact that Vince fired him twice, he was facing more than his share of stress. Jim has done an outstanding job with the WWF.

# J.J. Dillon comes home

by Gwen Guerke

MILFORD - For fans of professional wrestling Saturday was a red-letter day. J.J. Dillon, once a heavy-weight in the ring, stopped by Carlisle Fire Hall to be greeted by his fans.

About 30 local firefighters and their children were on hand for autographs and friendly handshakes.

J.J. Dillon quietly entered about 3 p.m., escorted by his parents Blanche and J. Mitchell Morrison of Milford.

The soft-spoken, white haired gentleman lacked the flamboyance that some expect from the rough and tumble world of wrestling. Wearing blue jeans and a leather jacket, Dillon was relaxed as he signed autographs and responded to wrestling questions.

Now retired, Dillon, who introduced himself as Jim, serves on the World Federation Advisory Board. In the process of changing careers from wrestling manager to administrator, Dillon, 46, stopped home to be with his parents.

Growing up in the Trenton, N.J. area, Dillon was introduced to the

(continued to Page 5A)

J.J. Dillon

# Chapter 25
## He Did It His Way

Vince changed the wrestling business forever. Cable television worked against me throughout my career, but Vince was smart enough to turn the new medium to his own advantage. That changed the business dramatically. For many years, the little fiefdoms that made up the NWA were an entity unto themselves. *"If you don't step on my turf, I won't step on yours."* They presented a front of support for one another.

In reality, the National Wrestling Alliance promoters operated like a band of thieves. Each promoter had only one thought on their mind: To protect their own territory. It was a constant battle for self-preservation. In fact, each of the promoters knew that the others were all cut from a similar mold, but they supported each other in what could be termed a loose alliance. The only reason they lasted as long as they did was because St. Louis promoter Sam Muchnick was a diplomat who was good at holding them together.

When Vince was providing programming on Turner's network in 1984, Ted called him and said, *"I want to buy into your operation."*

Vince's answer was, *"No way. I own the company and I'm not going to sell any part of it."*

That caused a personal rift between Vince and Ted. The division was made worse when, subsequently, Vince sold the rights to provide the programming for TBS to Jimmy Crockett for a reported one million dollars. Vince used that money to bankroll the publicity for the first Wrestlemania on March 31, 1985 at Madison Square Garden. That was the event that really moved Vince out of *professional rasslin'* and into mainstream sports entertainment. Jimmy, on the other hand, used the exposure on TBS to launch his own national promotion. Later, when Turner bought the operation from Jimmy, and the deal was final, Ted's first order of business was to call Vince and say, *"Vince! I'm in the rasslin' business."*

Vince's comeback was something along the lines of, *"Well, I'm gonna kick your ass every week because you don't know anything about the business and you never will."*

A lot of people were mad at Vince for changing the face of the industry, but if Vince didn't do it, somebody else would have. Most likely, it would have been Jimmy Crockett, Verne Gagne, or Bill Watts. I have often wondered where Vince's business would be today if he hadn't gone in the direction he had. Vince took a lot of risks to take the business mainstream. He put his money where his mouth was. Did he make mistakes along the way? Absolutely. He declared bankruptcy twice before he finally made it. He was truly an entrepreneur.

Vince is an odd character. He would wear very expensive, tailor-made pastel suits.

Pat used to tease him about them, but that was what Vince wanted. They drew attention to him. Vince also had a carefree attitude. If he wanted to drive 100 miles per hour in a 40 mile per hour zone, he would do just that. One day, he got a ticket for driving 100 miles per hour when he was going to Boston. As soon as he got back on the highway, he went right back to the same speed — and got *another* ticket. A normal person would worry about their insurance rates, but not Vince. He had so much money that he did whatever he wanted to do. Another time, we drove up to a construction site where the cars were stopped. Vince simply drove down the shoulder of the road and went around everybody.

When Vince's son, Shane, started working in the business and traveling on the road, he would pass us in his own car with his own group of friends — and Vince and Shane would compete with each other. Vince was Shane's role model. If Vince did something crazy, Shane wanted to one-up him and do something crazier.

Shane was still in high school when I started working for the company. He had three or four friends that he hung around with. They got caught by the police one night when they were cruising around town, smashing mailboxes with a baseball bat. I don't know what the outcome was, but Shane was just a typical teenager who always wanted to be a rebel like his father.

Shane's future wife, Marissa, lived in a house in the community where the McMahon's lived. The homes in that area are huge mansions on large tracts of land. They were so far apart that you couldn't see one home from the window of another. Marissa's mother, who was best friends with Vince's wife, Linda, had been through a divorce, so she and Marissa lived together in their house. At that point, there was no chemistry between Shane and Marissa. As pretty as she was, I don't think he knew she existed until they were several years older.

I also saw Stephanie, Vince's daughter, grow up and mature right in front of my eyes. When she was out of school, she would hang around the pool at home with one of her playmates. She was just a very pretty, polite, young lady.

In my opinion, Vince and Linda had a very normal husband-wife relationship. He was always very attentive to her and I never saw them argue. They used to workout together. If he was busy, she would workout by herself, then she would come out and give him a big hug. They had a very loving relationship the whole time that I worked for them. I think Linda was very good for Vince. I think she balanced him. He was the P.T. Barnum and she was the behind-the-scenes businesswoman.

Vince Jr. once admitted to me that he (Vince) had been a handful to raise. He and his father had a rocky relationship. Vince Sr. had remarried, and Juanita, his second wife, was not young Vince's mother.

Vince Jr. told me about a time when he attended one of his father's wrestling events. His father also went to the town that night. From the story, I got the impression that Vince Sr. hadn't known that his son even knew any of the wrestlers. Vince Sr. was in for a big surprise. Driving in front of Vince Sr., in a convertible with the top down, were three blonde guys smoking cigars. It was Dr. Jerry Graham, Eddie Graham ... and Vince Jr. Vince Jr. had bleached his hair blonde. It horrified Vince Sr.

Shortly after that, Vince Jr. got shipped off to military school. Vince Jr. used to brag that he was the only student who was ever court-marshaled out of military school.

When I first went to work for Vince Jr., we didn't talk about his father all that often. When we did, we would talk about how Vince Sr. was so respected by the other promoters and the talent. One day, Vince told me that shortly before he died, his father started to see the other side of wrestlers — the negative side that wrestling management had to deal with every day. Vince Sr. said to his son, *"Wrestlers are like seagulls. All they do is eat, sh—, and squawk all day."* Hence, the title of this book.

# Chapter 26
## The Creative Process

When I worked for Vince, I had no other life. Ninety percent of the creative ideas were formulated at Vince's house on the weekends. In the summer months, Vince, Patterson, and I would work outdoors on the patio by his pool. In the winter months, we would work in his formal dining room. We would have open discussions and throw ideas out for consideration.

We would start working at eight o'clock in the morning. For lunch, we would go to the Little Red Barn, a deli in his town, for sandwiches. We would go back to his house and continue working while we ate. Later that night, Linda McMahon, or the housekeeper, would cook dinner, and we'd stop and have dinner together in their kitchen. We would then go back to work and work to the point where my brain was fried crisp.

On the one hand, it was very gracious of Linda to cook dinner for everybody. I'm not saying the food wasn't good, but Vince had very particular tastes, and Linda cooked what he enjoyed. On the other hand, even though I enjoyed the meals I shared with the McMahons, I had worked all day long. I was willing to work the long hours, both during the week and on weekends, but when we were finished working, I wanted to go home and enjoy time with my wife. Instead, I was sitting at Vince's dinner table with his wife and Pat.

Vince is a workaholic. He thinks about the business 24/7. Yes, he sleeps, but I think he dreams about the business even then. He used to talk about power naps. When we were working during the day, it would not be uncommon for him to say, *"I need a power nap,"* and go into his office for twenty minutes. I have a hard time doing that, but it worked for him.

Most of the time, we would work seven days a week. I was even expected to work when I was sick. Vince would say, *"Well, you won't be any sicker at the office than you are at home!"* That was how he felt. Vince set the pace and the tone, and never took time off for a vacation. He doesn't seem to understand the need for taking time off. Whenever I took a vacation, I was on pins and needles the whole time I was gone. It was not beyond Vince to call me about something when I was on vacation, either.

I was dedicated to the business, but it isn't a question of how much passion you have. You can only eat so much caviar or ice cream before you need a break from it. Then, when you eat it again, you appreciate it more. I felt the same way about work. I committed myself to doing my job to the best of my ability. But after a period of time, I needed to distance myself from work. I would recharge, then come back, not only with renewed energy, but with a different perspective on the things I did every day.

Vince couldn't relate to that logic. He pushed himself hard—24/7—and he expected every one of his employees to adopt the same work ethic. There was no time for myself or my family on weekends. My wife enjoyed going to Carnegie Hall, and to plays. And yet, on Friday afternoons, Vince would ask, *"So, what are you doing this weekend?"*

I quickly realized that he wasn't expecting an answer. In fact, before I *could* answer, he'd say, *"I'll give you a call in the morning."*

The implication was that I should be available whenever Vince called, so I would sit around the house on Saturday, waiting for the phone to ring. Sometimes, Pat would call and say, *"I just got off the phone with Vince. I'll meet you over there in thirty minutes."* It was never, *"Do you have anything planned later today?"* He would simply drive to the house, or tell me to meet him somewhere, and off we'd go on whatever errand Vince had in mind for us. At other times, Pat would call and ask, *"Have you heard anything from Vince?"* If I said no, he would say, *"I haven't heard anything either. Lemme give him a call."* When Pat reached him, Vince would say, *"Well, if you guys aren't doing anything, come on over."* For the first few months, I didn't mind it too badly, but after a while, it became frustrating.

I would sit around my house all day long, waiting for Vince to call, then think, *"I need to go to the supermarket and get some groceries."*

A few minutes after I left, Murphy's Law kicked in. Vince would call the house. When I returned home, my wife would say, *"Vince called."*

"Aw-ww, geez!"

I'd call him back and he'd say, *"JJ! I called you a half hour ago! Where have you been?"*

That's exactly how Vince was.

Vince's expectations made me paranoid, too. I would sit around the house all weekend long, afraid to leave because, as I told my wife a thousand times, *"Vince might call."* He wouldn't call, but on Monday, I would find out that Pat had gone over to Vince's house, just to look things over. They weren't really doing anything noteworthy, so they wouldn't call me. Of course, I immediately began to wonder, *"Well, gee. Why didn't they call me?"* That's the kind of paranoia that comes from working in the wrestling business.

On some days, after working long hours, I just couldn't wait to get home to see my wife. The next day, somebody would tell me that Pat went home, took a shower, went *back* to Vince's house, and they went out to dinner. After working with Vince all day long, that was the *last* thing I wanted to do. It wasn't anything personal. I just wanted to get away. But my situation and Pat's was different. Pat is someone that I have tremendous respect for, but Pat had no other life, either—no family, no children. His life was wrestling.

Talent would call Vince's house when we were working. He would put them on the speaker phone so we could all take part in the conversation. Hulk Hogan would call frequently, and often, Vince would take a break in order to talk to Hogan privately. He would talk to Hogan for as long as two hours at a stretch. That left Pat and I sitting there with nothing to do for hours on end. We couldn't be productive until Vince came back, because we were always working ahead. We had to wait for Vince to give us the material for where he wanted to go. My day was already shot and I had to sit there while Vince talked to Hogan. I went through the whole gamut of emotions. My experience working for Vince was enriching in many respects, and yet, in situations like that, it was very frustrating.

Vince has a knack for casually sitting down and putting people at ease. If Vince wanted to meet secretly with a talent who was working with another promotion, or if he wanted to make them feel comfortable by meeting in a personal atmosphere, he would invite them to his home. One of the things Vince would ask new talent was, *"If*

*I gave you a magic wand, what would you do?"* It was an effective way to get someone to open up and tell you what was in their head. Their answer would give Vince a direction to follow. He wanted to know what their interests, hobbies, and former occupations were. That's how he learned that Ray Traylor was a prison guard in Georgia. Vince took that small slice of Ray's life and created the Bossman. Vince was very effective in that aspect. I remember when Mark Callaway came in from WCW. He had been wrestling as "Mean" Mark Calloway and we discussed the possibility of using him as a Viking, complete with a helmet with horns. We eventually settled on a character called The Undertaker. When he debuted on November 22, 1990 at the *Survivor Series* in Hartford, Connecticut, we never dreamed that Mark's Undertaker character would be such a major success.

Vince's style was different from that of his father, but it was a different era. In the earlier days, the talent created their own characters, then came looking for an opportunity to get exposure on television. Vince Jr. would start by talking to a new talent, then he would have his art department make sketches, suggest costumes, and feed him ideas for characters.

I started working with Vince Sr. when the Northeast was a regional territory and wrestling was sold to the public as a shoot [real; legitimate]. That was the approach taken in every territory, and I worked hard to protect the business. Now, since I was working closely with Pat and Vince, I was privy to information that, historically, was only shared between the bookers, office staff, and the promoters. The wrestlers weren't even cued in on future plans too far in advance.

And yet, I was amazed at how open Vince was when discussing the creative direction of the company at meetings with the various departments. He would tell them about the programs he had planned, the angles they would use to enhance those programs, and even the outcome of those angles with specific talent. In my experience, it had always been emphasized that booking plans and information were not to leave the room. Kayfabe had been entrenched in me for so many years that it felt strange, and vaguely uncomfortable, to sit in a roomful of corporate employees, discussing things that had formerly been shared with only a select few people.

By that point, however, it probably didn't really matter. When I arrived in the WWF in February 1989, Vince shocked the wrestling world by publicly admitting that professional wrestling was predetermined, and was merely entertainment.

At that time, Vince ran three towns a night, and there were two TV shows—*WWF Superstars* and *WWF Wrestling Challenge*. We also had *Saturday Night's Main Event* on NBC (which later moved to the FOX Network), but that ended on November 8, 1992. On January 11, 1993, the show that would become our flagship show, *Monday Night Raw*, was launched on the USA Network. The shows featured non-competitive matches, except in ratings periods, such as the November sweeps, when we would put a competitive match in each hour of each show to boost ratings. It was hard to produce entertaining shows twice a week. We had to pay close attention to details. We kept a chart that listed when the guys worked, so we could be sure that everybody got air time, and so the people who were more important, or those who were featured on upcoming pay-per-views, were featured more.

Vince had the best TV people. Kevin Dunn was, and still is, the executive producer. He builds the show and puts it together. You won't find anyone who could do a better job. The director, who sits in the production truck as the show is taped, is Kerwin Silfies. He's also at the top of his field. My only negative observation is that because they're human, and because they're so good at what they do, there is a certain "sameness" to the television product. In some ways, that's a positive in terms of quality control, but it can also be a negative because there's a certain way it's done, shot, and put together in post-production.

When I first started working for the WWF, we only produced four major pay-per-views each year: *Royal Rumble* in January, *Wrestlemania* in March, *Summer Slam* in August, and *Survivor Series* in November. On December 3, 1991, we added a fifth pay-per-view called *Tuesday in Texas*, one week after *Survivor Series*. It was a one-shot, special pay-per-view event, designed to settle a controversial finish used at *Survivor Series* between Hulk Hogan and the Undertaker. Normally, the payoff to a series of matches comes on the pay-per-view itself, in that case, *Survivor Series,* but we decided to carry the grudge over to *Tuesday in Texas*. It was an experimental deal because we had to be careful about asking fans to pay twice for the blowoff.

In June 1993, we added *King of the Ring* to the pay-per-view lineup. In 1995, after *Wrestlemania*, we went to monthly pay-per-views called *In Your House*. They were run when the "Big 5" weren't being held. The first one was in May 1995.

On top of monthly pay-per-views and weekly television, we had to book our house shows to follow the TV. It was very tedious and detail oriented, but that was one of my strong suits, and probably the reason why Vince hired me. Vince approved the main event and supporting matches, while Pat and I would get together and fill out the remainder of the cards.

One of my job assignments was to produce the promos. Jim Myers, Jack Lanza, and I worked on that together. We produced the promos, which would then get edited into the local shows to promote the local events. Some of the guys were very gifted. They came prepared with notes, knew what they were going to say, and were very good at their craft. Others would walk in with no idea of what they were doing. Jimmy Snuka, for example, would have no idea about what he was going to say. We had a certain amount of time that we had to fill, and Jimmy was a big card, so we had to produce interviews with Jimmy. His interviews would take four times longer than the others. Some guys would walk in thinking they were prepared, but they weren't. When we made suggestions, they would get very upset. Jim "Ultimate Warrior" Helwig often didn't want to do interviews at all. When I would ask him about doing interviews, he would say, *"Later,"* or, *"Catch me tomorrow."* One time, he had a series of matches coming up that were very important, so we had to have his promos. One night, while the Warrior was showering after his match, Vince told me, *"You stay here. Wait for him while he finishes his shower. When he comes out, don't back down. Wait and have him reapply his face paint. You cannot leave the building without his promos."* I stayed there until 2:30 a.m. We had a clash of wills, but it had to be done. Does that mean I have a problem with Jim? No. We put a lot of pressure on the top guys, and sometimes, they couldn't see the importance of the small details—but taking care of those details was my job.

I was also in charge of the travel arrangements, or what we called "routing." In terms of cost to a promotion, the cost of talent is one thing, but the cost of travel is quite another. The range of travel costs could be substantial, so it paid to do a lot of homework. I made the final decision on routing, so once a month, I had a meeting with my secretary and a girl in the travel department. I had ideas on where we could go, so we would explore based on where those towns were.

Routing was something I had worked on with Jimmy Crockett's NWA, but much more so at Titan [parent company of the WWF]. It was easy when the NWA only ran one town a night. We'd leave Atlanta, fly to whatever town we were performing in, and fly back home. The system at Titan was more complex because we had talent based all over the country. When I first got there, they were running three towns a night. The coordination and logistics was a monumental task. When we had a TV scheduled, our three tour groups would funnel into one town. After the taping, they would realign and disperse to whichever of the three towns they were booked.

I think I handled the routing well for a couple of reasons. One, because of my position in the office, I looked for inexpensive travel costs. On the other hand, I had been on the road myself, so I understood the talent perspective. When cost became a non-issue, I would think, *"What would be the easiest for the talent?"*

Talent travel is really an aspect of talent management where Talent Relations and Arena Bookings have to work in really close harmony. Once Arena Bookings set a date and tickets go on sale, you don't want to scramble and hope that travel arrangements can be made for that specific date. We had to address travel arrangements long before we announced the cards and put tickets on sale.

Arena Bookings had an extra set of problems because we usually had commitments to run so many dates a year in a specific building. Even with that understanding, the availability of dates in those buildings could become a problem. Take, for example, The Palace in Auburn Hills, Michigan. They host sporting events and concerts. Yes, we agreed to run ten dates a year, but it's not ten dates at OUR discretion. It's ten dates that work into THEIR schedule.

Ed Cohen, who did the arena bookings when I arrived at the WWF, was the absolute best at that job. His goal, in order to protect the WWF, was to establish prime tenant status in the major markets. He would seek an understanding with the manager of a specific building by saying, *"When we run a date, you must agree to not run another wrestling event in that building for 45 days before or after we come in."* Depending on how he scheduled the dates, he had prime tenant status in the building, and would lay the dates out so there weren't any windows of opportunity for another wrestling promotion to come in. The building managers would work with Ed because they were getting their ten dates a year and doing big business. When the other promoters couldn't get a date in the building, they would scream foul and claim it was a monopoly. Of course, it wasn't a monopoly. It was simply a business arrangement.

I would work closely with Ed and his Arena Booking department to know what the routing was before tickets ever went on sale. If there were issues from a talent management side for travel, I could address them well in advance and the dates could be moved around.

The first thing I would do was get with Ed and look at his calendar. At times, there would be an open date on the calendar, and he would be looking for a building to fit into that spot. If we had an open date between shows in Philadelphia and Pittsburgh, Ed would look at someplace in-between, like Harrisburg, Johnstown, or even Youngstown, Ohio.

We had talent coming in from all over the country: Randy Savage, Florida; Kevin Nash, Phoenix; Bret Hart, Calgary. In those days, the most cost-effective travel was a 14- or 21-day advance fare. In the beginning, they used F for First Class and Y for Coach. Later, they added K fares and Q fares. We could get good fares and save the company money by purchasing the K and Q fares, but the boys had gotten spoiled by being able to upgrade from Coach to First Class. The K and Q fares were restricted—they weren't upgradable. From a Talent Relations standpoint, it was a nightmare, but coming from the perspective of a former talent, I understood the problem. Here's a guy who is away from his home and family for ten days. He's tired and wants to go home. When he tries to upgrade his ticket, they tell him he has to sit coach. When you weigh 275 pounds and you have to squeeze into one of those middle seats between two other people, it's wrong. As the liaison in Talent Relations, I had to take their phone calls and hear them vent their frustrations.

We always tried to book round-trip, too, because they were cheaper than single leg flights. If the first arena on the tour was The Meadowlands in New Jersey, I tried to get Bret Hart to travel from Calgary to Newark. At the end of the tour, he would fly back to Calgary from Newark on the return leg of the round-trip ticket. Randy would fly from Tampa to Newark, make the tour, then fly home to Tampa from Newark. If somebody flew into Newark, but went home at the end of the tour from Chicago, we had to pay several one-leg fares, and that got expensive. The one exception was Florida, where the airlines had a policy that allowed you to fly from and to any Florida city, and have it considered round-trip. In other words, you could fly into Miami, finish the tour, and fly out of Tampa or Jacksonville.

When I booked a flight, I never booked the last flight into a town. I always wanted a backup flight available in case something happened to our scheduled flight. Most of the time, I would book the first flight out in the morning to give the boys plenty of leeway in case of delays. Travel plans were well organized and well thought out, but it took a lot of work to anticipate problems.

When I worked with Arena Bookings, there were things that I constantly had to be aware of when I determined the routings. The frustrating thing was that in the 7½ years I worked for the WWF, no two tours were ever the same. For instance, on the night after we worked the Meadowlands, we might run Hartford, Connecticut. The next month, when we returned to the Meadowlands, we probably weren't scheduled to work in Hartford. Hartford only ran three or four times a year, while the Meadowlands was a monthly show, so we had to develop a new routing plan to take into account a show in a different town on the night after the Meadowlands. Planning each tour was like reinventing the wheel.

We tried to get as many venues as possible out of each round-trip ticket. For accounting purposes, if the tour consisted of four shows, that ticket would be divided by four as we were allocating transportation costs to each event. As an example, if a ticket for Bret Hart cost $1,000 for the tour, we would charge $250 against each town, and so on for everyone booked on that card. If we only got two shows out of the ticket price, we would allocate $500 to each show for Bret. If we had to buy another one-way ticket to the next venue because the distance wasn't drivable, the entire cost of that one ticket would be accounted in full against that town's travel costs to run. That method was the only fair way of allocating the travel costs, and it became a tool for setting up an advance budget to help determine if it made business sense to consider booking certain towns. However, it was sometimes better to run a town in the middle of a tour where you may break even, or possibly lose some money, rather than have the wrestlers with a day off on the road, with no income, but personal expenses. The office paid for the commercial airline tickets, but because wrestlers are self-employed, independent contractors, they paid for their own lodging and rental cars. That's where we come back to The Myth. Some of the guys wanted to be seen driving a Cadillac, or Lincoln Town Car, while others were happy in a Chevy or a Ford. Some guys wanted to be seen staying at the Marriott, Sheraton, or Hilton, while other guys were just as comfortable in a Super 8, Motel 6, or Red Roof Inn. The guys had the right to choose wherever they wanted to stay.

The rental cars were another situation. Since some of the guys were traveling great distances, we didn't want them to face a 200-mile drive when they landed at a major airport, so we flew them into the city where the tour was starting. If Detroit was the first stop on the tour, we flew them into Detroit. The talent picked up the rental car, which they paid for themselves, and on the next day, they would drive 90 miles to Cleveland. On the third day, they would drive 215 miles to Cincinnati, then travel on to Toledo for the final day of the tour. From Toledo, they would drive 55 miles to the Detroit airport and get the first flight out the following morning. That's the perfect routing because it's a round trip in and out of Detroit. Not only that, but the talent wouldn't have to pay extra fees for the rental car because they were able to return them to the point of origin. The rental companies would usually allow you to drop Chevys and Fords off at another location for a small fee, but they didn't allow that with the luxury cars. They only had a certain number of luxury cars allocated at each location, so they didn't want them moving around.

Quite often, the talent would rent a luxury car and tell the rental car staff that they would bring it back to that location. When they filled out the rental agreement forms, they would list the WWF as their place of employment (even though they were actually self-employed) and write down the phone number of the office, rather than give out their home phone numbers. At the end of the tour, they would park the rental car at another location, drop the keys on the desk, get on their plane, and go home. We would then get calls from the rental agencies, telling us they were going to send us the bills for the drop-off fees. When the bills for the extra fees were sent out, they came in the name of the talent in care of the office travel agency.

The company wasn't legally responsible for the bills because the talent rented and paid for the cars themselves. However, since we did a lot of business with the rental companies, we wanted to stay in good-standing with them, so we would pay the bills. When we tried to deduct the charges from the talent paychecks, the boys would complain to Vince, and he would tell me to reimburse the talent and eat the added expense. It was a no-win situation.

One thing the WWF was adamant about, however, was that we were not going to start paying for the rental cars. There were two reasons for that rule. The first was the substantial cost in actual dollars. Second, there is a fine line when you make the case that wrestlers are independent contractors and not employees. Titan didn't want to cloud that issue by taking care of rental car expenses for talent. That was quite a contrast to WCW, who didn't seem to care about those expenses, and thanks to Eric Bischoff, WCW spent a lot of money on rental cars.

A typical plan for routing would go something like this: The first thing I would do was meet with Arena Booking to find out what their tentative schedule was. From there, I would meet with somebody from Travel and say, *"This is where Arena Booking is planning to go. How much is the fare?"* Since it was very expensive to fly into certain cities, I would get an idea of where my red flags would be. If I had serious red flags, I might go back to Ed Cohen and ask him to flip-flop some dates, because travel-wise, it would really help the company. Every three weeks or so, we would set a day aside to actually book the travel. My two assistants, who worked under me in Talent Management, would meet with three representatives from Travel who actually booked the tickets. We had to keep constant tabs on the computer to be sure there were enough seats available to accommodate the huge number of people we had traveling. It was a logistics nightmare, but Travel was very adept at their job. They would know if there was a special fare going into Cleveland on a certain date. I would also ask a representative from Arena Booking to sit in on our meeting while we booked flights so they knew specifics about the ramifications of the towns they booked.

I had a great relationship with Ed Cohen and his staff. We worked together very well and I think we had a very smooth-running operation, especially when you take into consideration the number of people we had to move. I also had Dave Hebner, who was an agent on the road, call me with valuable feedback. He would call and say, *"We flew into Cincinnati. They're having a major renovation of their airport that will last for the next nine months. It took us forever to get rental cars."* I would factor his input into my database and avoid Cincinnati. The whole process required a lot of cooperation from many different people.

Before we moved to Titan Tower, Linda McMahon bought a travel company that was housed across the street from our office. There's a federal law that states that if a company does a tremendous volume of travel, they can't buy their own travel company to get the commission on that business. Their business could not exceed 25% of the business of the travel agency, so Linda's travel company took on other major clients, like the Jehovah's Witnesses. All of Titan's travel business went through Linda's agency. That's why the travel agents bent over backwards to work with me—because Linda owned their company!

Vince McMahon and the people who ran the NWA were at two opposite ends of the spectrum. Ted Turner's people ran their company on a day-to-day basis, and even then, they were usually behind schedule. Vince, on the other hand, booked almost too far ahead, but that's what Vince liked to do. He always wanted to be one step ahead of the game, and know the direction in which the company was headed.

In June, Vince would plan ahead to *Wrestlemania*, which didn't take place until March or April of the following year. I'm all for planning ahead, but Vince would go so far as to plan the feature match—for a show which was more than nine months down the road. Once he came up with an idea for the *Wrestlemania* main event, Vince would back up and program the January *Royal Rumble* and the August *Summerslam* pay-per-views in such a way that they led the company into *Wrestlemania*. From there, he would shift gears back to the present and begin working on everything leading up to those three events. Of course, planning that far ahead resulted in a lot of extra work and frustration for the employees. We would plan, expand, and implement his ideas, but by the time those ideas were scheduled to go into production, several things had changed. Talent figured into the mix would no longer be working for the company, or someone would get injured and be unable to fill their role in the program. Whenever a piece of the equation was taken out, it had a domino effect on all the other pieces. All of a sudden, Vince's long-range plan was impossible to carry out, and we had to start all over.

The *Wrestlemania* that I was very instrumental in booking was *Wrestlemania VIII* at the Hoosier Dome in Indianapolis on April 5, 1992. Pat was away on hiatus, so Vince and I did the writing of that show with no other outside help. We also wrote the TVs leading up to the show. When we finished, Vince gave his seal of approval to the package. Once production of the *Wrestlemania* was underway, I was placed in charge of the format, which I dictated to my secretary so she could type it up for distribution at the production meeting. When the actual show began, I controlled the flow of the show, picking up the pace, or slowing it down, depending on how things were going. Due to the amount of work involved with the formats, I was totally exhausted when the show was over. Riding in the limo with Vince after the show, I was quite pleased when Vince complimented me and told me how much he appreciated my talent and hard work. I never forgot that.

I also received a letter from Linda McMahon, who was the President of the WWF, complimenting me on the Fan Festival for *Wrestlemania*. The special fan events were organized in an attempt to generate extra revenue, and they involved a tremendous amount of work as I had to assign talent and oversee the event. I started with nothing and figured out ways to supply talent to the event, without tiring them out just prior to a big event like *Wrestlemania*.

Most of the ideas and programs came about as a result of brainstorming. I can't think of any particular gimmick or angle where full credit could be attributed to any one person. The bookers were Vince, Pat, and me, but we were always looking for fresh ideas. Bruce Prichard joined us at some point in time. When Randy Savage sent some ideas in, Vince said, *"Wow! He has some great ideas! Let's bring him in, too!"* At the end of the day, though, Vince took credit for everything and none of the blame for anything.

When we held production meetings for TV, Pat and I would sit in the back of the room. Vince would open his book and conduct the meeting as if the ideas were all coming from his mind alone. That was okay with Pat and I. We didn't care. We were never bothered by it. I had been in a similar situation when I worked with Dusty. Vince was very open to discussion and we discussed a lot of things, but the ultimate decision was his. Many times, we would change things three or four times. By the time we got to the production meeting, Vince would be confused, or he wouldn't be sure what our final idea was because he forgot to erase something. Either Pat or I would raise our hand and say, *"Vince, I have a note here that says you decided you wanted to do this, instead."*

He'd say, *"That's right! That's correct."*

We always deferred to Vince, as if we were note takers, or stenographers. In reality, however, the creative process was a collaboration between the three of us.

## The Creative Process • 169

Many of the ideas for characters were formulated when Vince, Pat, and I were sitting by the pool. For instance, speaking was not a strong point for Rick Martel, so we decided to find his strong point and capitalize on that.

*"Rick Martel is a polished worker, but how can we give him substance?"*

*"He looks like a male model."*

That was one of those moments when, at the instant the comment was made, we each immediately knew that it would work. That persona seemed to be a perfect fit for Rick. Models weren't expected to talk, so we billed him as Rick "The Model" Martel. It was a character that made sense for Rick.

In 1990, Vince wanted to do something with Tony Atlas. His idea was to portray Tony as an African warrior. I had gone to Africa on safari in the late 80's, and I had learned a smattering of the Swahili language, so I came up with the name Saba Simba, which means "seven lions." It didn't really mean anything in regards to Tony's character, but the words Saba Simba seemed to roll off the tongue.

Because of my love for sumo wrestling, I came up with the name Yokozuna for Rodney Anoai when Vince wanted him to be a sumo character. Yokozuna means *great sumo champion*. It is not somebody's name. I'm sure the Japanese people were snickering because it would be like someone in Japan calling themselves Stanley Cup, or Heisman Trophy.

I was also responsible for [and will take the blame for] Papa Shango. I made the suggestion that he should stare at his opponent when he gets into the ring, during which time the arena lights would go down for a few seconds. When the lights came back on, his opponent would be lying on the mat with his feet on fire. I thought it would be different and unique, which it was, but a lot of people thought the idea was horrible, so I'll take the heat for that one.

When Dustin Runnels came to work for us, Vince wanted to do something related to Dustin's father, Dusty Rhodes. Jimmy Crockett had "Stardust" painted on the side of his airplane, just to stroke Dusty's ego, so we came up with the name, Goldust. I told Vince about the James Bond movie, *Goldfinger*, and how the villain painted his victims gold.

I will NOT take the blame for the Gobbley Gooker. That was ALL Vince McMahon, so he can take the responsibility for that one. That was one of the biggest disasters of all time. The Gobbley Gooker made his debut at *Survivor Series* in Hartford, Connecticut, on November 22, 1990. I really think the fans thought that Ric Flair or Sting would come out of that giant egg. When Hector Guerrero came out as the Gobbley Gooker, dressed in a turkey suit, poor Gene Okerlund had to act thrilled—as he was getting booed out of the place. Vince can take ALL the credit for that one because it was all his idea.

And then we come to Terry Taylor and the Red Rooster. For a period of time, it made a star out of Terry, and he may have reached his highest level of fame during his run with that gimmick. He probably made more money than he had at any other time, too.

That was Vince's approach to the business. He was always trying to develop new characters. Doink the Clown. The Blue Blazer. Friar Ferguson. I don't think he spent money frivolously, introducing a character that he knew was going to fail, or doing it to humiliate someone, or to poke fun at someone else's expense. From my time spent with Vince, I don't think those factors ever entered the equation. Vince tried a lot of ideas, but above all else, Vince was a businessman.

You could see Vince's sense of humor and his [low] moral values come to the surface with certain characters, and he did many things that I thought were distasteful. Take Bastion Booger, for example. Vince had him eat food off the floor and pick his nose.

170 • "Wrestlers Are Like Seagulls"

Those were the kinds of things that entertained Vince. He had a sense of humor, but it was toilet humor, and the makeup of the characters came from his warped sense of humor. I firmly believe, however, that Vince never developed character traits as a plan to have someone fail by design. I believe he honestly thought that everyone would enjoy the things that he thought were humorous.

JJ & Willie Nelson at *WrestleMania* 7 • March 24, 1991

# Chapter 27
## Twins and a Miracle Baby

Lindsey and I got married in November 1989 in a church in New Canaan, Connecticut. I invited Vince and Linda to our wedding and they gave us a beautiful, cut-glass bowl as a wedding present. Dick Glover, Howard Finkel, Pat Patterson, and Pat's significant other, Louis Dondero, were also there.

A lot of thought went into getting married and having children. I already had a daughter, Pamela, from my first marriage. She was born in 1966. Lindsey and I discussed two options, donor sperm and adoption, but I wanted to reverse my vasectomy.

During my time off between my last night in Kansas City with the NWA, and the time I flew to Connecticut to start working for the WWF, I flew from Dallas to Amarillo to have vasectomy reversal surgery. I returned to the same doctor who did the original operation twelve years earlier, and had out-patient surgery. It was quite a harrowing experience. While the doctors were trying to bring me out from the under the anesthesia, I had a bad reaction to the drugs and went into cardiac arrest. They managed to stabilize my condition and I only spent one night in the hospital.

After more than two years of seeing several fertility doctors, our children came along in September 1992. I was 50 years old and I was the proud father of twins—a girl and a boy. Lindsey had a difficult time because she's a small girl and she developed gestational diabetes during the pregnancy. At the time of birth, the diabetes goes away as suddenly as it comes on. However, my twins were born seven weeks early. The girl spent 2½ weeks in intensive care because she had apnea. My son had greater problems. He was in intensive care for 3½ weeks and came home on medication to control seizures. He has cerebral palsy. He's been in therapy since he was six months old. It was a changing point in my life. I wasn't any less a fan of wrestling, and I didn't lose my passion for the business, but it was a time in my life when I had incredible responsibilities and I had a need to have a balance in my life to handle them. That eventually created tension between Vince and me.

As fate would have it, two years after that, the WWF wanted me to go to Japan ... and my wife got pregnant again! I found out on the day I was to fly to Tokyo. At age 52, I had another baby girl. Because of the effort we put into having the twins, we look at our youngest daughter as our miracle baby. We're blessed to have her. She's a wonderful girl.

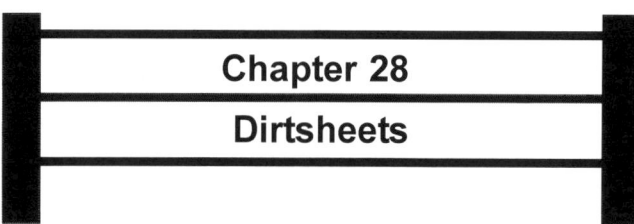

# Chapter 28
# Dirtsheets

Since 1983, there has been a lot of frustration over what we called the "dirtsheets," or insider newsletters. Jimmy Crockett once made an edict: *"Anybody who is found with a dirtsheet will be fired immediately."* Telling the boys that they couldn't do something was tantamount to taking out a subscription in their name. It stoked their curiosity. Many of the guys hated the fact that the dirtsheets exposed the inner workings of the business, and wouldn't have anything to do with them, but a lot of the guys were interested in reading about what was going on with other promotions. The boys used to hide them, and pass them around in the dressing room, because they were a source of information as to what was going on in all the other territories.

At WCW, there were people in the North Tower at the CNN Center who religiously read *Wrestling Observer Newsletter* and took everything it said as gospel—whether the facts were right or wrong.

The reporting in the sheets was frustrating to Vince and myself because of the kayfabe aspect, even though "kayfabe" wasn't adhered to as strictly as it once was. But we had to produce our TV shows in a specific manner in order to turn the shows around. We would tape three episodes of *WWF Superstars* and three episodes of *WWF Wrestling Challenge*. Two episodes would air before the pay-per-view, and one would air afterwards. Most of the title changes and important angles took place at the pay-per-views, so at the last taping, it was always a challenge to avoid revealing anything that we were doing at the pay-per-view. For example, if a tag team title was going to change hands at the pay-per-view, we would have the champions wear the belts to the ring during the first episode. During their match, somebody would steal their belts, so they had to work without them on the third episode. We went to a lot of extra trouble, and put in a lot of extra time and effort, to camouflage our plans. Very often, we taped multiple versions, just to throw a curveball. At times, the sheets would pick up on our subterfuge, and report our intentions to their readers. When that happened, Vince would get very frustrated, and as his sounding board, I echoed his sentiments.

Around that time, the 900 lines were a hot item. Howard Finkel's first responsibility in the morning was, at the company's expense, to dial the dirtsheets' hotlines and transcribe their report. Howard would fax the transcript to Vince's house so it was available for Vince to read when he got up for his morning coffee. Howard would also get hard copies of the actual newsletters and, depending on where Vince was at the time, fax them to Vince, or read them to him over the telephone.

To this day, people still marvel at the fact that the company held closed door meetings with talent or staff, and the information was reported within hours. When I was in a meeting in the board room at Titan Tower, I would look around, thinking that everyone in the room was a close-knit group of people who would not divulge any information from the meeting. And yet, something would be published about that meeting that could only have come from someone in that room. That was the greatest mystery. Who was talking to the sheet publishers about confidential information? The only thing I can say for sure is, it definitely wasn't me.

I don't know why the guys felt compelled to give information to Dave Meltzer, the publisher of *Wrestling Observer Newsletter*, over the years, but it's amazing that Meltzer has the sources that he does, even to this day. In my opinion, the talent subscribed to the "quid pro quo" theory. Perhaps they felt that if they talked with Meltzer, then he would write favorably about them. I always had the impression that Meltzer spoke highly of certain people who had dialogue and communication with him, like Terry Taylor. Terry talked to Meltzer all the time. When Meltzer wrote something negative about me, such as when he erroneously reported that I quit the NWA with no notice and merely left a telegram in my wake, I didn't pick up the telephone and tell him that I gave my two weeks notice. I had better things to do with my time.

Years ago, sportswriters used to travel with athletes. They knew their darkest secrets and saw the side of them that the public never did. Out of respect, because they traveled with them, and were accepted as part of that fraternity, they never wrote about those secrets. By the '80s, nothing was sacred. They wrote about anything and everything, and could care less about the long-term effects. To stay in business, they have to write about something, and if they can't, they'll create something to write about, because that's their job.

What sheet writers can't possibly relate to is what it's like to be in a room and have the responsibility of producing three hours of television on Monday, and within 48 hours, having to produce two more hours for Thursday. And while I was doing that, in the back of my mind, I was thinking, *What about the following Monday, and what about the next pay-per-view?*

You have to walk a mile in somebody's shoes before you can really put that into perspective, but that won't ever happen, because they don't have to. All they have to do is sit back and second guess our decisions. *Why did they do this? So-and-so is a lousy worker. They had a terrible match.*

That's another issue: The business really has nothing to do with who's a great worker and who's not a great worker. Some of the worst workers in the world drew a lot of money in the business. If you put Hulk Hogan on a sliding scale of workers, at the very best, he would be somewhere in the middle of the list. Working, however, isn't what Hulk brought to the table. I remember taping three hours of TV, with production problems and glitches, with Hulk advertised for the dark match [not aired on television]. The audience sat for 4½ hours before Hulk's music cranked up and he came out for the first time that night. His appearance absolutely electrified the people. I just stood in the wings and shook my head, thinking, *My God. He has something that may never be duplicated again.* He got into the ring, did his posing routine, and worked a short match. The people went home happy because they got to see what they came to see.

There are very few people in the business who have Hulk's capability. There were people in the business who were great mechanical workers, but never drew big money. Terry Taylor, Tim Horner, and Brad Armstrong—they could do anything. They were very gifted, but there was something missing.

Tex McKenzie is a classic example of a guy on the other side. He was clumsy and would trip over the ropes just getting into the ring. And yet, the people loved him! And he drew nothing but money.

So I would just chuckle when the dirt sheet writers talked about how somebody who was a great worker didn't get a chance, and why a lousy worker got a push that he "didn't deserve."

I used to get upset with the attitudes of the dirtsheet writers. I don't know if it comes with the wisdom of age, but I've learned that it's easy to be a Monday morning quarterback. It's easy to make calls when you're not on the firing line, and have to make a decision on the spur of the moment. It's easy to second guess the people who are actually doing it. And if the review of a movie gives the ending away, why would anyone want to see that movie? That's what the dirtsheets were doing, and I had a problem, especially in the beginning, with Meltzer giving out the conclusion to our movie before people saw it.

The other side of it is: Somebody has to fill that role.

Over the years, I came to terms with the situation and began to understand that dirtsheets were a part of our business, and as our business evolved, they were something that would not go away. From a creative standpoint, it made my job a lot tougher, but I learned to deal with it. I understood that they were a necessary evil.

Vince realized it, too. *"They're getting the information somehow, so why don't we be the ones to give them the information they're looking for. At least we can control what's being given to them."* That was Vince's logic in trying to control the information. I think it was a naïve approach to think that the other sources would quit giving Meltzer information, and that he would only publish what we told him. On the other hand, there were many things being reported that were totally inaccurate and totally incorrect. We hoped that by working with Meltzer, we could eliminate those inaccuracies, and possibly control what was getting out.

Vince designated me to be the point person with Meltzer. At first, Terry Garvin held that responsibility, but eventually, I became the official spokesman for the WWF. I was the only person given the authority to talk to Meltzer, but Vince would decide what I could tell him, and what I couldn't. In my first conversation with Dave, I told him, *"I'm going to share information with you so that you can confirm things that you may be contemplating writing, or I can officially tell you "yes" or "no" to things you may wonder about. But there are certain things that I'm not at liberty to disclose, such as the finish for the main event at the next pay-per-view."* I made it clear that I was speaking for the WWF, but could not be quoted, and that our relationship had to be kept confidential.

Over time, we discussed my thoughts on the ramifications of publishing the ending of a movie. The explanation he gave me was that the WWF was presenting a live performance when we did our TV tapings, or when we did an angle at an arena. Meltzer used to tell me, *"I understand where you're coming from, but the minute you tape a live show, it's available for public scrutiny. If I don't report on it, somebody else will, and I have a responsibility to my readers."* His responsibility was to be as out front and timely as he could be. The information was a part of history.

Our conversations were always on the telephone and I only met Meltzer one time. He came into a bar in San Francisco and someone said, *"There's Dave Meltzer."* If he walked up to me now, I wouldn't recognize him. At the time, though, I spoke with him on a regular basis, but it was kind of like a game. There was a lot of, *"I'm not at liberty to tell you that."*

I spoke with him for about a year, but it never worked the way Vince thought it would. I tried, as best I could under those circumstances, to have a rapport with Meltzer, but there were still other sources divulging inside information. If you think about it, what was I really giving him that he couldn't get on his own? The information that he really wanted from me were the things that Vince said I couldn't share with him. I was mandated by Vince to tell Meltzer *only* what he wanted Meltzer to know. I even told Meltzer, *"You know, if Vince finds out that anybody else is talking to you, they're going to get fired. I'm only able to do this because Vince has approved it, and I have to be selective about what I tell you."*

One of the subjects on which I agree with Meltzer wholeheartedly is that the Hulk

Hogan-Sgt. Slaughter feud was distasteful. I have made that point on several interview forums. The Hogan-Slaughter feud was a big event during the time when Meltzer and I were talking, and it was an example of Vince McMahon's personal lack of good taste. He used the war as a storyline while Americans were being killed in action, and even had them headline at *Wrestlemania VII*. I even expressed my opinion to Vince at the time, but he was adamant and set on moving ahead with the angle, so it was not a topic for further discussion.

That topic leads directly to an incident involving a letter from Dick Glover, Titan's Vice President of Business Affairs. At the time, in addition to publishing the Observer, Meltzer was writing a column for a magazine called *The National*. Meltzer had written an article criticizing the WWF for the Hogan-Slaughter angle, and how the company was trying to capitalize on the Gulf War of 1991. Vince blew his top when he saw the article. He asked me if Meltzer had checked his facts with me. When I told him that, to my knowledge, Meltzer had not called, Vince instructed Dick Glover to write a letter to Frank Deford, the publisher of *The National*. I had no prior knowledge that the letter was going out. In Dick's defense, like everyone else who worked at Titan, he was just following orders. In the letter, Dick wrote that Dave Meltzer was incorrect about certain assertions, and should have cleared them with me. Glover actually named me in the letter. It was wrong for Glover to go public about the relationship between Dave Meltzer and me, because Dave and I had the understanding that I was not to be quoted, and our relationship was to be kept confidential. The Glover letter violated that understanding, and it was Titan, not Meltzer, who was guilty of going public with that fact. I was shocked and unhappy that it was handled the way that it was. Vince couldn't have cared less about me. He was angry at Meltzer and he was venting.

The next thing I knew, Meltzer uncharacteristically devoted a large portion of the February 4, 1991 issue of his newsletter to attack me personally. He accused me of not being up-front regarding our relationship, writing that he thought we were "friends," and how he was surprised that I had been speaking to him all along as an employee of the WWF. He also defended himself by writing that he had tried to call me to verify the article, but I didn't call him back in time for the article to go to press.

If I had been told that Meltzer called, I most certainly would have returned his call, but I had no record of receiving it. I am not saying that Dave didn't make the call. I'm saying that I never received the message, and I did not, and would not, deliberately refuse to return a call if I knew for a fact that it came in.

If I had a reputation for not returning calls, that would be one thing, but Dave never made that accusation. His gripe with me came down to one call that he says was never returned. Why, all of a sudden, would I not return that one call? I always returned his calls. I was a professional, and calling him back to clarify facts was part of my job, even if only to say that I had "no comment."

I also don't understand Dave's claim that we were "friends." Dave had been covering the business for almost ten years before I ever called him, and when I did, it was to correct something he wrote about the WWF. It wasn't a personal call. Why would he assume that I wanted to be his friend when all I was doing was clarifying facts regarding a company I worked for? I was very clear with him about why I was calling him.

If we were "friends," why would I call Dave, and accept calls and messages from him at the Titan office, if it was anything but a professional business relationship? Why weren't we speaking from my home phone in the evening and on weekends? My calls to Dave were a matter of record in Titan's phone records, and the calls were made from my office extension, not some obscure phone booth somewhere deep in the Titan basement where I nervously whispered to him in code. I know I'm going over the top, but just think about it for a minute.

Meltzer is an intelligent guy, and he knew that we were working within the system.

In a moment of frustration, Vince himself picked up the phone and personally called Meltzer. Of course, once he did that, my relationship with Meltzer ended. Once he had that one-on-one dialogue with Vince, Meltzer would no longer call me for clarification. After Vince called him personally, Meltzer felt that he was able to call Vince directly to ask for information, so there was no reason for me to stay in the middle of the situation.

Dave has yet to justify why his frustration with Titan precipitated a personal attack on me. Since I did not write that letter, and I was up-front with him in regards to our relationship, it really came down to his perception that I never returned his call. What did Meltzer have to hang his hat on to be sure that I even received his message? If I never got the message, how could I be to blame? As a reporter, he should have asked himself those questions before printing his attack on me. Sure, Meltzer can read this and feign shock that I'm rehashing something that happened fourteen years ago, but then again, isn't the whole point of writing ones memoirs to examine the past? After reading this book, you be the judge if Meltzer's portrayal of me sounds fair and accurate.

Since then, I have felt that Meltzer was not a J.J. Dillon fan. I don't know whether it was my style, or just the aftermath of the relationship that was forced upon us by Vince McMahon. Meltzer got his fair share of cheap shots in at me over the years. In 2002, when Jerry Jarrett was putting together the TNA management team, Meltzer likened putting me in charge to the Peter Principle being alive and well. I also know that he reported other falsehoods about me, with one report claiming that I had negotiated with WCW before I left the WWF. That is flat-out not true.

What *is* true is that Dave Meltzer has withstood the test of time, and is still a part of the business—unlike me—and I respect him for that. What is also true is that I, to this day, have no trouble looking in the mirror every morning.

WWF TV, Amarillo • January 28, 1992
(l to r) JJ, Akio Sato, Dick Murdoch, Dory Funk Jr.

# Chapter 29
# The Players

There's an old saying about not being able to know the players without a program, so I thought I'd talk about a few of the people I worked with during my time with the WWF.

Vince Jr. is proud of the fact that he bought the business from his father, rather than have it handed to him. As I mentioned earlier, his father had several partners at the time, one of whom was Phil Zacko, who used to promote Baltimore. The other partners were Gorilla Monsoon and Arnold Skaaland. Vince Jr. bought each of them out in 1982, but part of deal was that they would always have a job with the company. Monsoon got a ten-year contract as television commentator, plus 1.5 times preliminary money on every WWF house show. Arnold still works in the office.

Many of the people who worked in the WWF office were people like Jerry Brisco and Sgt. Slaughter, who had made a living in wrestling during the era when I was active as a full-time wrestler. The road agents were George "The Animal" Steele, Jay Strongbow, Black Jack Lanza, Dave Hebner, Tony Garea, and Rene Goulet. I had never worked with Jack [Black Jack] Lanza, but he was also a veteran of the ring. I had a lot of respect for Jack, and still do.

The only agent who lived near Connecticut was Garea, so I would see him frequently. He would be the agent for the towns in close proximity to the office. Lanza lived in Minneapolis, Strongbow lived in Georgia, and Goulet lived in Charlotte, so I would see them every three weeks at our TV or pay-per-view tapings. I was also at every Madison Square Garden show, so I would see whatever agent was there. The agents had a very busy job. They were the first ones to get to the building and the last ones to leave. Most of the time, there were two agents at each event. One handled the box office and got money for advances for any of the guys who needed it. The other agent stayed in the dressing room, handled the lineup for the night, met with building security to make sure they understood how to accompany the guys to and from the ring, and worked with the sound system crew. When the show was over, they had to file reports by calling an 800 number. They reported the gross, the net, the attendance, the weather, who got advances, the order of the matches, what the finishes were, and any problems that might have come up.

Classy Freddie Blassie, a true legend of wrestling, had been working for Vince for more than 30 years. Every Christmas, Fred would put on a Santa Claus suit and play Santa for the veterans at the Veterans Home in Manhattan. He would also surprise the WWF employees' young children when he showed up at the home office for their Christmas party. I have a picture of my twins sitting on Fred's lap at one of those parties.

Lou Albano was a manager in the WWF at the time. I first met Lou when he and Tony Altimore [real name Anthony Altomare] wrestled as the Sicilians. I was still a young fan then, and to this day, Lou calls me Jimmy whenever we meet. Lou is one of the characters of our business, both in and out of the ring. I always enjoyed spending time with him.

In my opinion, Strongbow, Lanza, Myers, Goulet, and Garea all had a strong sense of loyalty—not to Vincent K. McMahon, but to the memory of Vincent J. McMahon. It's unbelievable how well thought of and respected Vince Sr. was. Most of them looked back at the good years they had, and the money they made, and they attributed it to Vince's father. Their loyalty was to those memories, rather than to Jr. and the company, so when you heard them talking about loyalty, they were talking about loyalty to the father, and all that he did for them.

Vince McMahon, Sr.

In the '60s and '70s, when Vince Sr. was promoting, the old-timers, many of them former key players whom had long since retired, would show up at Madison Square Garden and hang around backstage. In the early days of my career, George Bollas' partner was a guy named Jim Austeri. He also wrestled as the Zebra Kid, but his identity wasn't too much of a secret because one of his fingers was missing. Long retired, Austeri would visit backstage during the monthly shows. Before he left the Garden, Vince Sr. would give him $100. That was Vince's way of paying tribute to the old-timers because they didn't make big money in their era. Vince Sr. would also fly his top talent to Florida when he wanted to conduct business. If Vince Sr. booked Baron Scicluna into the territory to challenge Bruno, Vince would fly him to Florida and they would discuss their plan. *"You'll get three shots in the Garden, then we'll take the match to all the different arenas."* That's an example of the relationship and camaraderie that Vince Sr. had with talent.

Vincent K. (Jr.) and Vincent J. (Sr.) were as different as day and night. Vince Sr. was quiet, reserved, and very respected. He used to carry several half-dollar coins in his pocket. He had a habit of taking them out of his pocket, holding them in one hand, and repeatedly rolling the top coin to the bottom of the stack. I also remember that he was a heavy smoker. You seldom saw him without a cigarette in his hand.

Once a month, the WWWF would tape TV in Pennsylvania at the Allentown Fairgrounds and then at the Hamburg Fieldhouse. Vince and his staff would stay overnight in the area at the Abraham Lincoln Hotel in Reading, an old, exquisite place. After the TV's, Vince would host a dinner at the Crystal Restaurant on the square in Reading near the hotel. I recently saw Joyce Grable at the Gulf Coast Reunion in Mobile, and she told me that when the girls wrestled and appeared on TV in the New York territory, Vince would include them, too. It was an honor to attend and everyone was on their best behavior, or should have been. I have heard that there were some, like Lou Albano, who would drink their share of alcohol and become boisterous, but apparently, that was the exception.

At the time, I was still a young referee in college, but I was never invited to one of the dinners. However, when Lynda and I were married at the Albright College chapel in Reading in 1964, my father hosted a dinner for the wedding party at the same Crystal Restaurant.

By the time Vince Jr. bought and renamed the company, it had grown and changed, and young Vince never hosted a meal in the same fashion that his father had. However, Vince, Jr. often went out for drinks with the boys after the shows at Madison Square Garden. I was invited, or at least had an open invitation to join, but I always took the first train available back to Stamford in order to get home as soon as possible to be with my family. I was told about one occasion when Vince and the boys stayed out pretty late. Before the night ended, several of the boys were demonstrating their signature moves on Vince in the bar. One of the Road Warriors jumped off the top of the bar itself and clotheslined Vince. Pat Patterson rescued Vince and assisted him out to his limo before Vince was seriously injured. The next day, Vince woke up sporting a black eye and suffering from an injured neck.

For the most part, however, Vince Jr. didn't share the same feelings about talent that his father did. Jim Barnett was one person who learned that the hard way.

Jim was another player who worked for Vince. Jim, who had promoted *Championship Wrestling from Georgia* in Atlanta, brokered the deal where Vince took control of that company in a hostile takeover. Jim was also well-connected with television people all over the world. He wined and dined a lot of people. Jim was gone by the time I got to the WWF, but I used to hear stories about how he decorated his office with antiques. He was very particular about how everything was placed. Of course, that just made him a target of Pat Patterson and Terry Garvin, who would sneak into his office and move everything around—just to torment him.

In May 1987, Jim made a statement about how much he liked living in Atlanta. Pat Patterson passed the statement along to Vince at a time when Vince was in one of his moods. He confronted Jim with something like, *"I was told that you'd rather be in Atlanta than here, so I don't want to stand in your way. You want to go, so as of today, you're free to go."*

Jim, whose life *was* intricately tied to the wrestling business, was devastated by the news. He went home and took an overdose of sleeping pills. When Terry Garvin went to Jim's apartment to check on him, he saw that Jim was unconscious, and called 911. Terry and Pat both had a good laugh at how pitiful Jim looked as he was being carted out to the ambulance.

Having said that, I have to add that I have tremendous respect for Pat. Vince gets a lot of credit for things that Pat did. He is an extremely gifted individual. Of all the bookers I ever worked with, I would have to say that he was the best. Much of the credit for the success of the WWF should go to Pat Patterson, and he doesn't get the credit he deserves for what he contributed. I always felt that Pat knew Vince's likes and dislikes, and gave Vince the things he liked by the shovelful. Pat also knew how to effectively communicate with Vince, and few others ever mastered that ability. On the other hand, I know of people, Jerry Jarrett to name one, who presented ideas that were never given an opportunity to be tried because Pat would cut them off and say, *"Oh, no. Vince would never go for that."* The idea would never even make it Vince's ears for his consideration because Pat would cut it off before it ever got there.

In August 1995, when Pat and I were at Vince's house, Vince said, *"I've hired Bill Watts. I don't know what he's going to do, but I want him to come in and get familiar with our system."* Bill was a take-charge guy. That was how he ran his own wrestling business in Oklahoma, and that's how he was when he came in. Pat and I both got along very well with Bill. When Bill came in, he really wanted to get involved as a positive force. Vince liked to hire people and tap into their knowledge, but he also wanted to change and make the final call on every idea they submitted. That worked fine with somebody like me, or Pat Patterson, but Bill Watts wasn't the type of person to allow someone to mess with his ideas. When it came to his job, he wanted to be given free rein. Vince would never have allowed that. Bill didn't last long in the WWF. He quit on October 13, 1995. I don't know what went on behind closed doors when Bill and Vince met, but years later, Bill made a comment along the lines of, *"There was only room for one Titan at Titan Sports."* There didn't seem to be any problems between Bill and Vince, so I think it was an amicable parting of the ways. Except for a few shots, I had never worked for Bill on a regular basis, but I always respected him from afar. In my opinion, Bill was one of the really smart people in the business.

When Lex Luger debuted in the WWF at the *Royal Rumble* in Sacramento, California on January 23, 1993, Vince thought he was the second coming. After

Luger's heel run as the Narcissist, Vince promptly turned him babyface and sent him on a publicity tour called the Lex Express. Vince bought a bus, customized it, and had Lex travel across the country. It was almost like a politician on the campaign trail, except for the fact that Lex was very uncomfortable when it came to mingling with the fans. He has no personality, and that immediately shows when he has to mingle in a group of people. He feels uncomfortable, out-of-place, and acts stand-offish. As a result, that idea quickly died. Vince admits that the Lex Express was one of his big mistakes.

I can use another story about Lex to give insight on how thankless the talent relations job can be. Vince came up with a last-minute idea to do a photo shoot with the talent. It was going to be shot in Malibu at Surfers Paradise. It was one of these situations where the guys had a few days off, and my job was to call everybody on the list. I told them that I was making arrangements to fly them to California, where they would stay at a nice hotel. When I called Lex, he said, *"James, I'm not going. I have more important things to do. It's my daughter's birthday and I have plans. I'm just not going."*

He was right. His daughter's birthday *was* more important, but I couldn't tell him that I agreed with him. I was just the messenger, so that's what I told him. I said, *"Well, I'm just the messenger. All I can do is tell Vince."*

When I called Vince, I said, *"Lex says that he has more important things to do. It's his daughter's birthday, and on this short notice, he says he's not going."*

*"Call him back and tell him that I said to stay home,"* Vince replied.

Vince then told me to call Randy Savage. Randy is the kind of guy who doesn't like to give his free days up, but if you call him and tell him that it's business, he'll get on the next available plane. I called the hotel, cancelled the reservation I made for Lex, and made one for Randy. I did the same thing with the airline reservations.

I called Lex and told him exactly what Vince told me. *"Vince said to stay home."*

*"All right, James."*

Two days later, on the day of the photo shoot, I got a call from Vince. *"I've got Luger on the other line. He's calling from Malibu. He says you canceled his plane and hotel reservations. He had to make his own arrangements to get to California."*

If Luger had called Vince from Atlanta, then Vince may have remembered my conversation with him regarding Lex. However, by waiting until he got to California, Luger positioned himself as the babyface, and I was the heel, because he had to make his own arrangements.

I said, *"Vince, don't you remember when I called you the other day, and told you that Lex had more important things to do? You told me to call him and tell him to stay home? In fact, that's why Savage is out there!"*

*"Lex told me that he never said he wasn't coming, and that you canceled his plane and hotel reservation."*

That's a classic example of the deviousness of Lex Luger—and he's a guy who was on the road with me as a Horseman! It made me look like the bad guy, and Vince seemed willing to take Luger's word over mine. There was no upside for Vince to blame Luger and get into an argument, so he let the heat stay on me. That's the thing that sticks in my craw: that Vince would even question how it could have happened. That was the frustrating part of working for Vince. Even if he said, *"Oh, yeah. I remember you telling me that."* He could then say whatever he wanted to smooth it over with Lex. At least we both know the truth of the situation. That's just part of what you do to manage talent. But Vince wasn't that way. He could be very hard to work for.

Another good example of taking heat as the head of Talent Relations was brought to mind when I saw Abdullah the Butcher in Tampa in January 2005. We hadn't seen each other for years, and the first thing he said to me was that I made a big mistake by not bringing him into the WWF when I worked for Vince. After all those years, Abby still doesn't get it. Vince hired the talent—not Pat and not me.

When Dusty Rhodes came to the WWF in May 1989, Vince put him in a polka dot outfit, and gave him a black female named Sapphire as his manager. Vince never said that he did it to belittle or demean Dusty. As I said earlier, in all the years I was there, even in the private moments, it was never, *"Ha-ha-ha! I've put him in his place. I showed him."* He didn't say anything like that even one time. If that was Vince's reasoning behind the idea, he never expressed it. Dusty never acknowledged that Vince might be having fun at his expense, either. Dusty always looked at the gimmick as something only HE could pull off.

We immediately set him up in a program with the Bossman, starting their feud with an angle at a TV taping on June 27 in Rochester, New York. We figured that since they had previously worked together in the NWA, they would have natural chemistry. Their feud stretched throughout the remainder of the year, but it wasn't strong enough for us to feature them at *Summerslam*. They had ball-and-chain matches and matches in a steel cage, but for whatever reason, their feud just couldn't get off the ground. We put an end to it on January 20, 1990 in Baton Rouge, Louisiana.

Following that, we immediately programmed Dusty with Randy Savage. Their feud began in Orlando, Florida, on January 21, 1990 at the *Royal Rumble* when their managers, Sapphire and Sherri Martel, were guests on *The Brother Love Show* and got into a fight. We put a lot of thought into that angle and had big hopes for their feud. On January 29, Dusty and Randy had their first match at the Nassau Coliseum in New York. From there, they worked their storyline and matches in all the towns—and did absolutely horrible business. At *Wrestlemania VI* from Toronto on April 1, we put Dusty and Sapphire in a mixed tag team match against Randy Savage and Sherri Martel, hoping that would help. We even had Randy Savage's ex-wife Elizabeth manage Dusty's team, and Brother Love manage Randy's team. After *Wrestlemania*, we sent that match out on the road, hoping it would increase business, but it didn't.

We didn't want to give up too soon because we had invested a lot of time into their feud, so we sent Dusty and Randy on the road in singles matches, and tried as many gimmick matches as we could—bullrope matches, cage matches, and lumberjack matches. For some reason, the gimmick matches didn't spike attendance or heighten the interest of the fans, either.

Vince finally walked in one morning, said it wasn't working, and put an end to their program. Several dates that had been pencilled in were cancelled. Just as their program was being pulled, we went to one town, with Dusty and Savage on top, that did a little bit more business than everybody thought that particular town was going to do that night. Of course, Dusty used that one house as his opportunity to make a case. *"I can't believe you're cutting us off! This thing is just starting to get over. Look what we drew!"* We put the feud to rest on August 27, 1990 by having Savage pin Dusty in two minutes flat at *Summerslam*.

For our next attempt to program Dusty, we decided to match him against Ted DiBiase, the "Million Dollar Man." On September 13, 1990 in West Palm Beach, Florida, Dusty and Ted began a series of matches that didn't draw well at all, either. In November, we teamed Dusty with his son Dustin, who had been wrestling in the WWF since April of that year, against Ted and his servant, Virgil. Ironically, when Vince created the Virgil character in 1987, the wrestling rumor mill circulated the story that Vince intentionally selected the name as a direct insult to Dusty. Dusty had been booking for the NWA at the time and his real name is Virgil Riley Runnells. Since I didn't work for the WWF until 1989, and was not there when Virgil was created, I can't confirm or deny Vince's intentions. Once there, I never did question Vince directly. Mike Jones (Virgil) is a very nice guy from Pittsburgh, Pennsylvania.

When Mike later found his way to WCW, it appeared to be more than coincidence when his character name was changed to Vincent. No one would ever be quoted as to intent on the subject because this is the kind of thing from which lawyers make their living. What I do know is that Mike Jones made a decent living working for both the WWF and WCW for a number of years.

We tried as hard as we could to get the Dusty-DiBiase feud going in high gear, but after two months, it was obvious that the storyline wasn't getting over. In December 1990, just to end the feud, Vince booked Dusty against Virgil in a series of matches that would put it to rest. Night after night, Dusty put Virgil over in the middle of the ring, and Vince did it in a way that humiliated Dusty—having Dusty get pinned in a very short amount of time: 38 seconds (Columbus, 12/7), 45 seconds (San Antonio, 12/8), 35 seconds (Montreal, 12/15), 35 seconds (Springfield, Mass. 12/26), 30 seconds (Cincinnati, 12/29), and 45 seconds (Toledo, 12/30). Vince jobbed him out in the most humiliating way possible.

In my opinion, the humiliation was unnecessary. To Dusty's credit, in the ring, he did everything that was ever asked of him. As a booker himself, Dusty had been in a position where, as part of his job, he had to tell people that he was going over [winning], and they were going to do the job. He did not, however, ask anyone to do anything on any given night that he was not willing to do himself.

Vince was not going to renew Dusty's contract, and he met with Dusty at one of the TV tapings to tell him that. Vince did most of his personal business with the wrestlers every third week when the TV tapings were held. Later on, it was weekly when we started to tape the RAW show live every Monday night. At each taping, there was a line of chairs outside Vince's personal office, and they were usually full of guys waiting their turn to see Vince. Whenever Vince met with talent, he always wanted someone else there as a witness to whatever was said in the conversation. On this particular occasion, it was Vince, Dusty and me. I was completely taken aback when Dusty said, *"I can't believe you won't renew MY contract, and you're letting ME go. And yet, you're keeping HIM!"* He emphasized his point by pointing at me. He continued on to say, *"HE wouldn't have a job in this business if it weren't for ME!"*

Dusty then asked to talk to Vince privately, and I was excused from the room. Afterwards, Vince told me that Dusty made it seem as if he was the only person in the business who was on Vince's level, in terms of what he had accomplished creatively in the business. And I give Vince credit, because he, in turn, told Dusty that he was a legend in his own mind. I was not party to that discussion so I only know what Vince told me. Both Dusty and Dustin's final appearance with the WWF was at the *Royal Rumble* in Miami, Florida on January 19, 1991. After that, they went to WCW, which was the new name for the NWA. Dustin would later return to the WWF in 1995 as Goldust.

I suppose Dusty might have thought that I was responsible for him losing his job, but I didn't have anything to do with it. Vince made those decisions based on his own rationale. If he thought that Dusty could make him a buck, he would have kept him on the payroll.

There were times when my job required me to do unpopular things. For example, Sean Waltman called me from Green Bay, Wisconsin, and asked if he could leave the tour to go see Larry Simon—The Great Malenko—in Florida. Sean had been trained by the Malenkos, so there was a special bond between them. Larry was very sick from cancer at the time. I had recently spoken to Larry myself and, throughout the course of our conversation, he was very upbeat about his medical prognosis. In my conversation with Sean, I told him that I had recently talked with Larry, and that I was under the impression that his condition seemed to be improving. There was only one day left on the tour, so I told Sean that he had to finish it out, and offered to help him with his ticket if he wanted to go to Florida after the tour.

The sad part is, Larry Simon passed away the next day—on September 1, 1994. I can't count the times that I have, in private moments, thought about that, and wondered if I did the right thing or not. One part of me says, *"If there is any way I could do that over again, knowing that he was that sick and not likely to pull through, I would have told Sean to get on a plane and go see him."* But of course, I had no way of knowing that information. I was trying to do my job, and at times, I had to make tough decisions. With all the flak we were hearing from people regarding no-shows, and not giving what we advertised, I felt that he needed to stay on the tour. Irregardless, it's a moment that I have reflected on many times.

On August 11, 1992, we had a TV taping scheduled in Nashville. Before we left Connecticut, I got a phone call from Jerry Jarrett, who I had not seen or talked to in eight years. Jerry said, *"We had a hell of a run when you worked for me. I know you have some degree of influence with Vince regarding new talent coming in. I have a son, Jeff, who has been working on top in my territory. He learned the business the right way. We've done everything with him here that can possibly be done. He's reached a point in his career where he needs to spread his wings and move on. I'd like to introduce you to him and have you talk to him. My hope would be that Vince would be open to giving him an opportunity to see what he can do up there."*

At the time, Jerry was running a promotion in Memphis called the USWA. His two top stars were Jerry Lawler and Jeff Jarrett. The two of them even showed up at the August 9 WWF house show in Memphis, sitting in the front row and challenging the WWF wrestlers.

Jerry and Jeff met with me on the 11th at the Municipal Auditorium in Nashville, where we were holding our TV taping. The WWF catered lunch for the talent, so we spent a long time talking. Later that night, I introduced Jeff to Vince. The following morning, I met the Jarretts for breakfast at a Waffle House restaurant and we talked some more.

Based on that introduction, Jeff got booked on a few WWF house shows in October 1992. Jerry Lawler later signed with the WWF and debuted at the *Royal Rumble* on January 24, 1993, and in February 1993, the WWF began a loose association with the USWA that lasted until September 1996. Jeff Jarrett began appearing as an official WWF wrestler in October 1993.

Ultimately, Vince made the decision to hire Jeff Jarrett. I have a lot of respect for Jerry Jarrett and the way Jeff was raised in this business. I also admire the respect that Jeff has for the business. I would like to think that his attitude towards the business was a contributing factor in Vince's final decision to bring Jeff to work in the WWF. My point is that Jeff made it on his own in the WWF—as a result of his talent and what he contributed—not as a result of my influence with Vince McMahon, or me putting him in positions that he was not justified to get. He earned every bit of the success he had. All I did was pave the way for him to get the opportunity. I'm also pleased that my efforts resulted in Jerry Lawler securing a job with the WWF. To this day, Jerry has done a great job with the company and is a tremendous asset to their announcing team.

I also put together the very first all-WWF tour of Japan. At one point, Vince wanted the WWF to have a presence in Japan. Giant Baba was promoting All-Japan Pro Wrestling, so our first show was in conjunction with Baba at the Tokyo Dome on April 13, 1990. Andre the Giant teamed with Giant Baba for the very first time, and a 20-year-old Shane McMahon made his in-ring debut as a referee that evening. Vince became irate when Hulk Hogan's scheduled opponent, All-Japan regular Terry Gordy, backed out at the last minute. Fortunately, Stan (The Lariat) Hansen, another All-Japan regular who was a wrestling legend in Japan, stepped in at the last minute as a replacement. Stan was wonderful, and even agreed to do a job for the Hulk.

Vince enjoyed promoting the WWF in Japan, but he didn't like promoting with

Baba. Vince wanted to do things on his own terms, so I talked to Akio Sato, who is a good friend of mine. I had known Akio Sato since my first trip to Japan in 1974. When Americans toured Japan, we were pampered. We didn't speak their language, so every detail was handled for us by someone from the office. Arrangements for us to stay in the best hotels were made in advance, and as soon as we arrived, we were handed a room key. Joe Higuchi, who I mentioned earlier, traveled with us to make sure there were no problems when we ordered food. If we got ill, the Japanese office arranged for medication. By contrast, when the Japanese wrestlers came to the United States, they were virtually on their own. They had to learn to read a road map, and to get to the towns without much assistance. If more than one Japanese wrestler was booked in a territory at the same time, they would try to help each other. Most of them eventually learned our language, mainly from watching a lot of television. I mention all of this because I admire what the Japanese boys did to overcome the obstacles they faced here.

Sato and I went to Japan in October 1990 and set up an agreement with Genichiro Tenryu and the SWS [Super World of Sports] promotion. Tenryu left All-Japan Pro Wrestling on April 26, 1990 to help form the SWS. They held their first card on October 18 and we announced the working relationship on November 20, 1990. The arrangement turned out to be a good deal for both promotions and it lasted into 1992. Our biggest inter-promotional card was held on March 30, 1991 at the Tokyo Dome. Hulk Hogan, Shawn Michaels, Bret Hart, and other big stars from the WWF worked on the show, as well as SWS regulars such as Tenryu, the Great Kabuki, and my old friend Kendo Nagasaki. The most noteworthy event that stemmed from that card happened before a match between former sumo wrestlers John Tenta from the WWF and Koji Kitao from SWS. Before the match could begin, Kitao, apparently mad because he was asked to lose that night, grabbed the microphone and announced that wrestling was fake and that he refused to lose to a phony like Tenta. It was huge news in the Japanese wrestling world, and Kitao was promptly fired by SWS.

JJ & Genichiro Tenryu

SWS held their final card on June 18, 1992, after which time Tenryu immediately formed WAR, which stands for either *Wrestling And Romance* or *Wrestling Association R*, depending on who you ask. We continued to promote with WAR through September 15, 1992, until Vince said, *"I want to go to Japan, but I want to do it on my own. I don't want a partner."* Vince looked at me and said, *"You do it. You put the deal together. I want the first all-WWF event in Japan."*

With Vince's blessing, I again called on Akio Sato for assistance. I trusted Sato and had confidence in him. If there was a prayer of successfully promoting wrestling in Japan as an outsider, I knew that I needed his help. He did the research and set up our contacts.

At that time, Sato was working for the WWF, teaming with Pat Tanaka as the Orient Express. The two of us went back to Japan and Sato set up a meeting with his country's top concert promoter. After we struck a deal for a guaranteed minimum fee, plus a percentage of our gross revenue, the promoter flew to the U.S. where he, Vince, Linda, and myself, had dinner at the Helmsley Palace in New York City. While we ate, Vince and the promoter talked and we solidified the deal.

After the promoter checked on the availability of venues and we selected the sites, the promoter contracted for the building for the dates that we scheduled for May

1994. Once again, Sato's understanding of the buildings and their history was essential to our selection of the venues.

Vince let me book the cards and Sato offered his input. The Undertaker, Bret Hart, and Randy Savage all went over. Jack Lanza and Dave Hebner were the WWF agents for the tour, while Sato acted as mediator with the Japanese media.

I was quite pleased to have overcome the obstacles of setting up a business and running an event in Japan, where the established promoters don't like outsiders. Our biggest obstacle was a means to distribute and sell the tickets for the events. In 1994, Japan did not have anything like Ticketmaster or Tickettron. Japan had small independent outlets spread all over the country. Each outlet had their regular customers who would pick up tickets locally and pay on a cash basis. Many of those regulars were accustomed to getting a discount. The problem with having so many outlets was that you had no accounting of how many tickets had been sold, or what the gross revenue was, even on the day of the show. After the show was over, it took weeks to get a report and an accurate count. To make matters worse, they got "first count," which had its own set of problems. It was a nightmare.

Baba had a travel agent in Los Angeles who took care of securing work visas for the Americans who worked in Japan, as well as for the Japanese who came to the States, but Sato and I had to meet with the Japanese consulate staff in New York to get that done. Another difficult task was getting clearance to import WWF merchandise into Japan.

We didn't run in the Tokyo Dome, but we grossed more than $1.5 million for five shows. A lot of the WWF merchandise we shipped over was outdated domestically, so overall, after expenses and payoffs for the talent, we made a nice profit of about $150,000 on the tour. I was thrilled that we made any money at all because everybody had their own small piece of the pie—the promoters who also ran the ads, the ticket outlets, the arena settlement, etc. I don't know how the landscape has changed since 1994, but Sato and I re-invented the wheel for an "outside promoter" in Japan.

I take great pride in the fact that it was successful, but I have to give a lot of the credit to my friend, Akio Sato. Vince chose me for the tour because he knew that I had been to Japan several times and I had a working knowledge of the people and the culture. Fortunately, I had enough sense to call upon Akio to help me make it happen. If he hadn't been there to help, I couldn't have pulled it off.

Some time later, Vince decided against renewing Sato's talent contract, and once again, I had to be the messenger of bad news to a very dear friend. Akio was the one talent who understood the game. He knew my role and he was very professional when I told him about his notice. Sato continued to wrestle in both the United States and Japan. Two years later, after I had left the WWF and was working for WCW, I got a call from him. He had decided to retire from wrestling and was learning how to drive an "eighteen-wheeler." He had lined up a job, but he needed references. I was happy to write a glowing letter of recommendation for my old friend. He called to thank me for the letter on his behalf and to tell me that he got the job. After that, he disappeared from sight. I tried to contact him, but apparently, he and his wife, former lady wrestler Betty Niccoli, had moved. I often wonder where he is and how well he is doing. Akio Sato is one of the good people in wrestling.

During the summer of 1991, Ric Flair became available after almost twenty years of wrestling exclusively for the NWA. Because of my position with Titan, I was one of the first people to know that he was coming in before it was public knowledge, but I was not able to sit in on the meetings between Ric and Vince. Their business negotiations were held in private. It was a very big deal when he signed with the WWF, but I did not broker the deal or have anything to do with it. The obvious dream match that everybody wanted to see was Ric Flair versus Hulk Hogan. However, instead of waiting and presenting the big match on pay-per-view, Vince immediately booked Flair and Hulk in a series of house show matches.

That was not totally unusual for Vince to do, though. If he was going to have two wrestlers face each other on a big show in a main event match, and they had never worked together before, he would match them up at house shows so they could work together and feel each other out in front of a live crowd. By doing that on house shows, and not on TV, Vince wouldn't lose the bang of the big pay-per-view show.

We booked them around at several house shows, with their first historic meeting taking place in Dayton, Ohio on October 22, 1991. Vince found out fairly soon that the match just didn't have any luster. I would have thought that a first-time meeting between the greatest NWA champion of all time and the Incredible Hulk Hogan would have been a match that everybody wanted to see, but for whatever the reason was, it just didn't draw. On February 17, 1992, they had a match in the Sun Dome in Tampa. The house drew 10,000 fans and $32,000, but Vince thought such a main event matchup should have sold out the Sun Dome.

When that number came in, even though they were just 1,500 people shy of a sellout, Vince said, *"Cancel all the other dates. That match is five years too late."* That last line said it all because so many years had passed since Hogan and Flair became famous. Vince no longer thought that Hulk versus Flair was a marquee match. The idea of Flair versus Hogan at Wrestlemania in 1992 may have been entertained at one time, but once it became obvious from the house shows that there was no interest in the match, it was pointless to continue in that direction.

After Mick Foley (aka Mankind, aka Cactus Jack) released his first book, *Have a Nice Day,* he sent me an autographed copy. Below is a reproduction of what he wrote on the inside cover.

A personal note to Mick Foley: *"Hey, Mick! If you skip THIS page and the next one, I think you'll enjoy my book, as well."*

In the actual text of the book, Mick wrote about his efforts to get a job with the WWF. In his eyes, I was the roadblock. According to Mick, he would call my office once a year to see if there was any interest in hiring him. I would tell him that we weren't looking for talent at the moment, but to hang in there and call me back at a later date. Mick felt it was preposterous that we weren't constantly hiring talent, and thought I was giving him the runaround.

What a lot of people don't understand is that wrestling promotions have budgets, just like any other company. During that particular period of time, the WWF's talent budget wasn't exactly "the sky is the limit." Just as there are only so many employees a company can hire, there are only so many wrestlers that can be employed on a roster at one time. But aside from expense limitations, there are also "look" reasons.

Promoters have certain spots on their roster, and there are times, legitimately, when there are no spots open for a certain "look." There are the muscle man types, pretty boy types, big hairy types, fat types, and so on. A promoter must be careful not to have too many with the same look on the roster at one time—it devalues the appeal of that "look." At one point or another during their career, all wrestlers have heard, *"Sorry, we have no openings right now."* If you recall, I heard it plenty when I was looking for work after I returned from Germany, so believe me ... Mick is not unique to have been in that position.

Vince was certainly aware of Mick through videotapes, but Mick is heavy and, as I explained, has a certain look. Unfortunately for Mick at that time, we already had enough guys with that look, and Vince was not interested in hiring any more of that type.

In his book, after bitterly accusing me of personally blocking him from coming into the WWF, Mick speculated that perhaps it wasn't me after all. Maybe "Vince McMahon himself wasn't a big Cactus Jack fan" and felt Mick "didn't look like a star." Mick would be correct with those assumptions. The bottom line is, Vince had no interest in hiring Mick at that time.

Vince would often ridicule Pat and myself, to our faces, for being fat and out of shape. *"You guys don't take care of yourselves. You should be training more."*

While Vince understood the importance of hiring fat, out-of-shape wrestlers to balance out his roster, he didn't respect them. Vince was a mark for a certain look. Pat didn't have that look at that time in his life. I didn't have that look, and neither did Mick. Hulk Hogan had that look. Lex Luger had that look. Hey, even Vince McMahon had that look!

I told Mick flat-out that we weren't looking for talent and I was very kind about the way I said it. I was always on the side of the talent. Even though I had moved into management, I was still sensitive to what talent was going through. I looked at Mick as a guy—much like me—who loved the business and was pursuing his dream. He came to the WWF with the hopes of getting his foot in the door. I would get no satisfaction out of going on a power trip to crush his feelings.

Somewhere down the line, a spot opened up on the roster and Vince needed somebody with Mick's "look" for a character that eventually became Mankind. Suddenly, the idea of hiring Mick Foley was palatable to him. Vince hired Mick and he had a fantastic run. I'm proud to say that I was the VP of Talent Relations when he was eventually hired in 1995, so based on that fact alone, he should know that it was never personal. Besides, had Vince brought him in during the early 90's, when, according to Mick's book, the WWF was full of a "parade of stiffs" who "stunk up" the rings for "years," Mick's character could easily have gone the route of the Gobbley Gooker, Mantaur (two examples Mick used in his book), or some other gimmicky wrestler from that era.

In hindsight, I would have hoped that instead of still feeling the sting of rejection all those years later, Mick realized how fortunate he was that timing worked out the way it did, and that fate was clearly on his side. Vince became interested in Mick long after the so-called "parade of stiffs" were gone, and Foley came in just in time to enjoy the incredible success of the WWF's boom period alongside Stone Cold and The Rock.

As VP of Talent Relations, 1995-96 was an exciting time for me in regards to signing up talent. In the span of just one year, we signed Foley, Steve Austin, The Rock, Hunter Hearst Helmsley, and John "Bradshaw" Layfield, all of whom went on to become superstars and very important in the legacy of the WWF. I'm very proud of the incredible amount of talent that we signed during my tenure there.

I finally saw Mick again at an August 2004 convention in Fayetteville, North Carolina. Regardless of the way he wrote about me in his book, we spent about 45 minutes together and had a very nice talk. Mick said there was no heat between us and I would like to take him at his word.

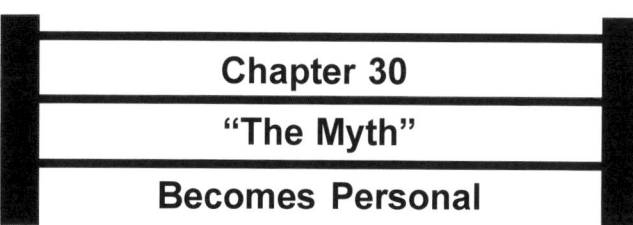

# Chapter 30
## "The Myth"
## Becomes Personal

My divorce from Jeanette cost me dearly. My alimony payments were based on my income from the previous year in the business, and I had some big years. I made $210,000 in 1987 and $194,000 in 1988. The courts don't look at you as an independent contractor. They simply look at what you gross, so I was mandated to pay $3,600 a month in temporary alimony. I even went to court in North Carolina to have the amount amended to reflect my current salary, but to no avail. It wiped me out and I got behind on taxes, at one point, owing $50,000 to the federal government. On top of that, I was hit with an IRS compliance audit that drained another $12,000 from my account. I was constantly juggling my finances. The one thing that helped my situation was the sizeable check I finally received from my final NWA pay-per-view appearance. Over the years, a lot of wrestlers became accustomed to using the fat pay-per-view checks to pay for major purchases, or more often, to cover those quarterly IRS estimated tax payments.

This brings us right back to *"The Myth."* If you're a wrestler, and a recognizable personality from television, then you are famous, and therefore, you are rich. You live in a big mansion on the rich side of town and have money to burn.

Everybody handles their life in their own way. Don't hold me to these numbers, but historically, before Vince began handing out fat contracts, a full-time wrestler could expect to make, on the average, anywhere from $250 to $800 a week. In later years, $500 to $1,000 was probably the norm. Some of the top guys might make more, but wrestling wasn't the lucrative profession that the public thought it was. By the late '80s, when Vince started handing out contracts that paid in excess of $100,000 a year, the boys were making more money than they had ever made in their lives.

Sad to say, many, if not most, spent the money as fast as they made it. The guys bought big houses, cars, motorcycles, boats, and every new toy that caught their fancy. To some degree, I fell into that lifestyle, too. It never crossed our mind that the cash cow might not last forever. The momentum and pace we were performing under, especially during the good times, didn't allow us time to reflect on important things — like what the future might hold. If somebody were to say, *"You should really downsize and buy a smaller house. You're making so much money that you could pay it off in a short time. There may be a time when that money isn't there,"* we would just shrug it off.

*"Yeah, yeah, yeah."*

And we just kept going. It was a never ending cycle. Make money, spend money. Make money, spend money.

I have to add that there were exceptions to the rule. Raymond Rougeau lived frugally. Lanny Poffo lived frugally. Ole Anderson lived frugally. There were others who just never got caught up in the lifestyle, and many of those guys are probably set for life. They didn't worry about what kind of car they were driving. They didn't party on the road. They weren't into drugs. They didn't go out drinking every night, throwing money around in the bars and playing the big shot. They probably saved their money, and have something to show for it today.

The only time I ever really got caught up in *The Myth* was in Atlanta. Ric used to go to a certain shoe store in Atlanta to buy these really nice Italian-made shoes. One time, Tully and I went with him to the shoe store, and I paid $400 for a pair of shoes. I can't tell you how many times I anguished over how I could have been so stupid to pay $400 for a pair of shoes. Not only was I stupid to pay an exorbitant amount of money for shoes, but I didn't even need them. I simply got caught up into *The Myth*. I eventually sold the shoes to a fan at a wrestling convention for $100—after autographing the soles!

The financial strain I was under must have been evident to others. One day, Pat Patterson and I were at Vince's house, waiting around while Vince finished a phone call. Out of the blue, Pat said, *"You look like something's really bothering you."*

*"I just keep getting kicked in the teeth,"* I answered. *"The IRS is after me. I just wish it would all end."*

At that point, Vince walked out and we went back to work. The following day, Pat said, *"Why don't you talk to Vince? If you explained it to him, I'm sure he would be happy to help you."*

I took Pat's advice and went to see Vince. Vince sat patiently and listened to my story, then said, *"Here's what I'd like to do ..."*

He gave me a salary advance of $30,000 so that I could pay the IRS and get them off my back. He also took a 5% interest-bearing unsecured personal note from me, and deducted an agreed-upon sum from my paycheck. Later that year, he gave me another advance. When I look back in judgment of everything that Vince did, I have to factor that in, too. On the other hand, the advance was interest bearing and it came out of my paycheck.

This is probably a good place to talk about my experiences with homes. I've had more than my share of problems with homes. I never made big money, but as you make more money, you tend to spend more money. That's human nature. I can remember wondering, when I was a kid, how I would ever be able to afford to buy my own home. When I was in Amarillo in the early 70's, Ted Heath had some luck acquiring properties. He found a great deal on a house and we each kicked in $3,000 to become equal partners in the house. He owned about a dozen homes at that time. He held on to that house and just sold it within the last five years. It was in a ghetto neighborhood and he had trouble collecting the rent. When it sold, he sent me a check for $9,000. My $3,000 investment paid off after thirty years.

That was my first investment. When I moved to Tampa in the early '80s, I bought my first home. I paid $59,000 for a small house in a tiny subdivision. When I moved to the Carolinas, I rented it out, and bought another home in Charlotte from Greg "The Hammer" Valentine for $112,000. A few years later, when Jimmy moved his operation to Dallas, I took out a 2$^{nd}$ mortgage for $20,000 and bought a house in Plano, Texas, which is a suburb of Dallas. That was a $220,000 house. It was really nice.

The bottom fell out when my marriage to Jeanette fell apart. Jeanette got the house in Charlotte, and I kept the houses in Plano and Tampa. I sold the house in Tampa for $57,000, but that money went to the IRS. Lindsey and I lived in the house in Plano for about six months. After we moved to Connecticut, a torrential rainstorm swept through Dallas. Water backed up into our house in Plano and ruined it. I did not have any flood insurance, and there was $15,000 worth of damage to the house. I had to walk away from it and negotiated a buyout with the mortgage company.

When it was all said and done, I had to reach into my pocket and pay them $10,000.

In the fall of 1993, when I had been with the WWF for four years, the people who I was leasing my home from wanted to put their home on the market, so I had to find another place to live. In a discussion with Vince and Pat, I mentioned a beautiful house that Lindsey and I had seen. Vince was very encouraging. *"Well, why don't you buy it?"*

*"What are you talking about? I'm looking to rent! Out in Wilton, because of the school district, houses aren't cheap. You know what I've been through with my credit problems and the I.R.S."*

*"I want you to have roots here,"* he encouraged. *"We'll make it happen. This is your home! You're here to stay. I want you to buy this home. You can go through my bank. We'll work through my bank and get it done!"*

I still wasn't convinced. *"Vince! Where am I going to get $450,000 to buy that house?"*

That sounds like a lot of money, and it is, but given the prices of real estate in that area, it wasn't out of the norm. Vince assured me of my job security and future with the company, then told Doug Sages, Titan's CFO, to do whatever he had to do to make things happen for me. Doug, who had come from NBC, was a heavyweight in the business finance world. He told me to go ahead and apply for a mortgage with the mortgage company. Because of my credit problems and the foreclosure in Plano, I was very pessimistic about my chances of being approved for the loan. Sure enough, Lindsey called me on afternoon and said, *"They declined our loan."* When I called Doug to give him the bad news, he said, *"Just disregard that letter."* Doug met with Vince and they came up with a plan.

To get the $450,000 loan, I had to put down 20% ($90,000) plus closing costs. To pay that, I liquidated the entire $80,000 in my Titan Sports profit sharing plan and paid the penalty for early withdrawal. The bank also wanted me to have a clean credit report, so I had to get a $60,000 loan from Titan to pay off my outside debts. The financial finagling only put me into a position to be able to "qualify" to buy the house. When it was all said and done, I had a mortgage and a $160,000 non-secured, interest-bearing note owed to Titan, with payments deducted from my salary.

The three-bedroom house in Connecticut was very unique and we loved it. It was a beautiful home with an open air atrium in the center of the

JJ with Japanese baseball legend Shigeo Nagashima

house. It had been owned by an artist, who painted a beautiful mural inside. When you opened the front door, you were looking into a large, open foyer, and a staircase against the back wall. The mural covered the wall of the staircase, as well as the wall in the back. From a distance, it camouflaged the staircase. There was a vase on a table and ivy hanging down. It was so unique that it's difficult to describe.

When I finally sold that house, I took a loss of $50,000.

## Chapter 31
## The Young and the Wrestlers

In 1991, one of the biggest scandals the WWF ever faced broke out when a recently-fired, young member of the ring crew, Tom Cole, made allegations of sexual harassment by company employees. The two employees he accused were ring announcer Mel Phillips and Terry Garvin. The allegations were reported by Phil Mushnick in the *New York Post*. Cole later appeared on television to do interviews with people like Geraldo Rivera, Maury Povich, and Tom Brokaw, and filed a sensational lawsuit against the WWF.

Prior to the scandal breaking out, there had been talk about young boys hanging around and helping the ring crew, but that had always been a part of the business. When I was a kid, I used to hang around selling programs, and I was never made to feel uncomfortable, although I'm sure there were unsavory and creepy characters around the business even in the '50s and '60s.

The wrestling business can be very vicious. Snide comments would be made at the production meetings. Bobby Heenan used to joke about Mel Phillips having a foot fetish for young boys, and sniffing their shoes. Until the sex scandal went public, I never knew what the comments were based on. Bobby would rib everybody, so I wasn't sure if there was any truth to the comments. Mel would never react, or deny the charges, so I didn't know what to think. Based on my personal observations, Mel Phillips was always very businesslike and straitlaced. Shortly after Mel was fired, we made a trip to Germany, and we traveled by chartered bus to Vienna. When the bus pulled up to the hotel, two young boys were jumping up and down, trying to see who was on the bus. As we filed off the bus, I could hear them asking, *"Where's Mel Phillips? He told us to meet him here!"* Everybody just looked at each other and rolled their eyes. Those are the only things I observed.

Vince eventually settled out of court, returning Cole to his position on the ring crew, and giving him two years back pay. The fallout resulted in Mel Phillips, Terry Garvin, and Pat Patterson, being let go from the company on March 2, 1992.

One Saturday morning, I went to Vince's house to work. When I walked in, I noticed that Pat's car wasn't parked outside. It was just Vince, Linda, and me. Vince told me that he had to ask Pat to let Terry go, because Terry reported to Pat. Knowing how close their friendship was, I know how tough it was for Pat to give Terry the news.

There are all kinds of people in the world, and I always judged people by my own personal dealings with them, regardless of what anybody else might say. I've always taken that approach. I had known Terry Garvin for a long time, and he never did or said anything inappropriate in my presence, so I regarded him as a friend. Terry worked in the office and was instrumental in me getting a job with the WWF. I met Terry's wife and children on numerous occasions. They invited Lindsey and I to have dinner with them in their home shortly after we moved to Connecticut. We had a new puppy, Boomer, so we brought him along to play with their puppy. I remember that vividly because Boomer crapped on their carpet. The Garvins just laughed about it. They were good people.

The only side I saw of Terry was the professional, business side. Terry worked hard in the business, and in his day, he was a very good worker who could work a gimmick as well as anybody. As a promoter, he was an asset to every promotion he ever worked for. I have to admit that he also had a reputation, like many other people in the business, as one of wrestling's bizarre characters.

Sadly, Terry and his wife eventually divorced. He passed away on August 17, 1998.

Vince also told me that he was getting ready to do the hardest thing he ever had to do. A few minutes later, when Pat arrived, Vince told him that he had to go, too. Vince and Linda were both crying. It was the only time in 7½ years that I ever saw Vince shed a tear. He thought that much of Pat. It was genuine emotion.

One could say that Pat was accountable because Terry worked for him. Either he knew about the harassment, or he should have known. I personally believe that Pat was never really let go, and that he continued to get a paycheck, although I don't know that for a fact. Maybe that was the right way for Vince to handle the situation— for Pat to go on hiatus for a period of time and stay out of sight. It was a tough, sad situation, because Pat meant so much to the business.

There were other incidents that took place during the months that followed. At the December 14, 1992 TV taping in Green Bay, Wisconsin, Kevin Wacholz jumped up, screamed at Vince, and shoved him down. He claimed that Vince had reached over and grabbed him on the upper thigh. Vince had him escorted out of the building. Wacholz called the police and filed a report, claiming that Vince had sexually harassed him. He also claimed that Vince had done it before in Madison Square Garden. To my knowledge, no charges had ever been filed on the Garden incident. I was in Green Bay that night and nobody was in the room with Wacholz (who was wrestling as *Nailz* at the time) and Vince, but the door was slightly ajar and you could hear voices prior to the sounds of the scuffle. Jerry Brisco and Jack Lanza were the first to reach the room, but they both arrived too late to witness anything. Both Wacholz and the WWF sued each other in cases that went nowhere.

Around that same time, the WWF's first female referee, Rita Chatterton, came forward with a story about being raped by Vince in the back seat of his limousine. That case was either dismissed for lack of evidence or settled out of court.

Everybody was trying to sort through all of the allegations, the comments, and the rumors. What was the truth? What wasn't the truth? They all seemed to be pieces of a pie. When you put the pieces together as a whole, the pie gave off a pretty bad stench. After awhile, there were so many stories that you began to think, *"There has to be some degree of substance to these stories."*

Shortly after we got married, Lindsey told me that she didn't like the wrestling business. She even went so far as to say that she was embarrassed to acknowledge that I was involved in the wrestling business, let alone that I had wrestled myself. If anybody ever asked her where I worked, she would say, *"Titan Sports," "In sports promotion,"* or later in my career, *"Turner Broadcasting."*

The sex scandal wasn't the catalyst for Lindsey's opinion. That's the way it has always been. Many people look down on wrestling as low-brow entertainment. That attitude carries over to their perception of the people involved in the business. I hate to admit it, but there's a degree of justification in people feeling that way because of situations that I've outlined in this chapter.

I had my own challenges in the realm of sexual harassment when I was with the WWF. There was a woman who was hired as the Vice President of Marketing. Even though she is not famous, and is not someone you would have heard of, I don't want to mention her name, so we'll call her *Sandra*. During her time there, Sandra was promoted to Senior Vice President. I don't know how she got the job because she had no connection to wrestling before coming to work for the WWF. She was a heavy-set woman, younger than I was, and wore a lot of makeup. When it came to business, Sandra was very hands-on, in more ways than one.

At that time, there was a change in procedure in the office. Up to that point, there was a direct line where everybody reported to Vince. The idea was to break that up, so people reported to other people up the food chain, and only one person would report to Vince. As a result, as Vice President of Talent Relations, I reported to Sandra, who was a Senior Vice President. Sandra, in turn, was the person who reported directly to Vince.

Before the *King of the Ring* pay-per-view in Baltimore on June 19, 1994, she called and said, *"I want you to pick me up at my apartment in the company car and drive me to Baltimore."* To do that, I had to detour through downtown Manhattan, drive her to the pay-per-view in Baltimore, and take her home when the show was over. After I left my house, Sandra called and left a message on the answering machine. *"I don't know if you've left yet or not, but I'm about to jump in the shower. Just come on up. The doorman will let you in."*

My wife called me on my mobile phone as I was en route to Manhattan to tell me about the message from Sandra. The message was totally inappropriate. When I arrived at Sandra's apartment building, I waited downstairs. I *did not* go up to her apartment. When Sandra finally walked downstairs, she had two bags in her hands. She plopped them in the middle of the car seat and said, *"These are for you!"*

In the TV production office, the crew kept a huge bowl filled with candy. Everybody backstage was in and out of that room. One of the first orders of business each day was for a runner to get different brands of bite-sized candy and fill the bowl. The days were long, and before the end of the day, the bowl would be empty. I have to admit that I have a sweet tooth. I like *Mounds*, *Peanut M&Ms*, and *Hershey's with Almonds*. Obviously, Sandra took notice, because the bags were filled with my favorite candies.

After the TV tapings, we would all stay at a hotel in the town, where the company provided rooms for the staff. Usually, it was Vince, Pat, Bruce Prichard, Sandra, and myself. When we checked in, Sandra would make comments to Vince, like, *"I want a room next to him,"* while pointing at me.

Vince liked to go to the hotel bar after the tapings. One night, I decided to stop by the bar for a few minutes, just to say hello. As I walked in, Sandra walked up behind me, grabbed my arm, and announced, *"We're here!"*

At first, it was like a series of little jokes, but when I started to report to her, I became bothered by the constant sexual overtones. I never acted rude to her. I just ignored her overtures and pretended like they never happened. It's career suicide to make an issue out of something like that. I was in a no-win situation, so I just ignored it.

At one of the TV tapings, I went to the hotel restaurant late one morning for breakfast. Moments later, Vince came in, and I invited him to join me at my table. Except for the two of us, the restaurant was empty. When Vince asked me, *"How are things going?"* I saw it as the opportune time to address the situation with Sandra. I told him about the ceaseless barrage of things she said and did. *"And to make matters worse,"* I said, *"you had me report to her. There were times when I thought you had set me up. Perhaps you didn't intend to put me in a bad situation, but you put me through hell."*

*"I wasn't aware of that,"* he said. *"I never realized what was going on. I'll look into it."*

Not too long after that, I was reassigned to another person up the line in management.

When Pat left, I was assigned to his office on the executive floor—the top level—in Titan Tower. Vince had a huge office with a window that wrapped around the end of the building, giving him a spectacular view of the harbor. Linda's office was at the other end of the building, overlooking downtown Stamford, although she had more of a view of traffic on I-95 than of the city itself. My office was situated between Vince and Linda's offices. I had a secretary and an assistant who sat outside in an adjacent office. I continued to work one-on-one with Vince for several months, with just the two of us doing what three were doing before. I also assumed all of Pat's duties. Pat used to calculate the payoffs for the talent, and Vince would approve them.

The one thing the talent knew about my job was that I was in charge of payoffs. The truth of it is, I didn't have the authority to make a hard-and-fast decision about a payoff. I was simply the messenger. When the time came to make the payoffs, I would write down my opinion of what we should pay the boys, basing it on what I thought each wrestler contributed to the success of the card. Of course, everything had to be looked over and approved by Vince. He would look at the payoff sheets, see something he didn't agree with, and make changes. After the wrestlers were paid, one of them would go to Vince and say, *"Hey, why did I get paid so little? I thought I meant more to the card than that!"* Vince would tell them that he would look into it. He would ask me for the sheets, look them over again, cut another check for the guy, and invariably say, *"You were right. I don't know what JJ was thinking."* The implication was clear to the talent that somehow I was responsible for any "mistakes." Vince always took credit for everything that was positive, but never took any heat for anything that wasn't.

But that was my job. As smart and street-wise as the wrestlers are supposed to be about the business, did they understand that? Very few of them did. And when I would explain it to them, they still didn't understand.

Six months after Pat left the company, while I was at Vince's house, Vince said, *"I have a surprise for you today."* As I stood there with Vince, Pat came walking around the outside of the house to the pool area where Vince and I were working. We hugged, he sat down, opened up his book, and the three of us started working as if nothing had ever happened. It was like old times.

I always thought a lot of Pat. I respected him. I had no reservations whatsoever about Pat coming back. He was such an important part of the success of the company. In fact, when he resumed his duties, he had so much more to offer. When he returned, Pat insisted that I remain in what used to be his old office, and he moved into my old, smaller office next to me. Pat, however, didn't spend as much time in the office as he had before his hiatus.

I continued to handle the payoffs, but I would show them to Pat to get his thoughts. Because of the time involved with the payoffs, travel, and other talent administration, I phased out of the day-to-day creative planning. Periodically, I would still sit in on creative meetings, but most of the time, I would have to leave after a brief time to take care of another responsibility. Creative was a lot of hard work, and it was tough during the time when Pat was gone.

After Pat came back, the steroid trial hit us with full force. A four-count indictment accused Vince of conspiring with Dr. George Zahorian, of Harrisburg, Pennsylvania, to dispense steroids to wrestlers between 1985 and 1991. Zahorian had already been convicted in an earlier high-profile trial of illegally distributing steroids. The federal government traced packages of steroids sent from Dr. Zahorian to Vince in Connecticut, and tried to link our top star, Hulk Hogan, with those steroid purchases. If somebody had taken those steroids to the Nassau Coliseum, in Uniondale, New York, they would have been charged with illegal distribution of a controlled substance across state lines—a federal offense.

Vince was convinced that the federal government would nail him. He knew how tough it was to fight the feds, with whatever flimsy evidence they had, and he was seriously concerned that he might do some jail time. Since the federal government was spending so much money investigating a high-profile figure such as Vince McMahon, it was obvious that they really wanted to make a statement by convicting him. With that in mind, he prepared Pat and I for that possibility. He would even joke, *"You two will have to come up on visitation days. Bring your paper and pencil. We can work over the visitors' telephone."*

He said it in a joking manner, but I think he realized that it could very well happen. That doesn't mean he was admitting guilt. It just meant that he was preparing himself for what he thought could possibly happen.

With Vince preparing for the worst case scenario—possible prison time—I brought him and Jerry Jarrett together. I saw Jerry as a mirror of what Titan was all about, and I thought Jerry would work well as a consultant for the company. Jerry promoted the Memphis, Tennessee, territory successfully for almost two decades. When the other regional promotions all went out of business, his territory survived. He understood how the business worked. He was an innovator of music entrances and video vignettes. To put it simply, in the '70s and early '80s, Jerry was doing the things that put Vince on the map in the late '80s and early '90s, although on a much smaller scale.

Jerry and Vince started talking on the phone for an hour each Sunday. Those calls turned into sessions that would last up to three hours. When Vince finally made the decision to hire him, Jerry was brought in to familiarize himself with the Titan Sports setup. I made arrangements for Jerry to move from Hendersonville, Tennessee, to Connecticut, where he lived in Vince's house for two months.

It was evident from his first day there that Jerry Jarrett was the best candidate for that position. Jerry was given carte blanche over every aspect of WWF business. Because of his overall experience, his view of the wrestling business was so much broader than that held by Pat or myself. Jerry should get the credit for expanding Vince's perception of what a successful wrestler can look like. Jerry, who isn't a big, muscular man, had been successful as a wrestler in his own territory, and he made a lot of money using smaller guys like Tojo Yamamoto and Jackie Fargo. Based on his experience in Memphis, Jerry suggested giving a push to guys like Bret Hart and Shawn Michaels, who also weren't huge monsters. Traditionally, Vince favored using wrestlers who looked like Hulk Hogan and Lex Luger, so using the lighter weight wrestlers was something that hadn't been done in the past. Jerry convinced him that he could draw money with the smaller guys. Ultimately, when Vince had success with Bret and Shawn, that opened the doors for people like Chris Benoit, who might not have had the opportunity had Jerry Jarrett not come along to expand Vince's horizons.

Jerry made many other positive contributions to the company. For instance, Jerry was used to running a small operation with a low overhead. After staying at Vince's house for two months, he moved to a hotel that the company had a deal with. One day, Jerry noticed the amount of money that we were paying for the room. Granted, in the northeast, prices are much higher than what Jerry was used to in the south, but he wasn't happy with the deal. What did he do? He drove to another hotel, just a few blocks away, met with the manager, gave a presentation, and said, *"I have a group of people who will be staying here on a regular basis. What is your normal rate and what would you charge me?"*

The manager gave Jerry a quote of $65 a night. The rate for the hotel he was currently staying in was $100 a night. Jerry thought, *Why is the company spending $100 a night when there's no difference between the hotels?* Jerry went back to the hotel where he was living, sat down with the manager, and gave him the same pitch. The manager gave him a quote of $70.

Jerry said, *"Well, I've been staying here with the WWF and paying $100 a night!"*

*"That's our deal with the WWF,"* the manager replied.

*"But why is that the deal? If you can afford to do it for me at $70, why does the WWF have to pay $100?"*

*"Because that's our deal, and I'm not going to budge."*

Jerry went to Vince and said, *"If we move our business to the other hotel, it will save the company money."*

Later that day, the manager called Jerry and said, *"I've changed my mind."*

*"No, thanks,"* Jerry countered. *"We've made other arrangements."*

Was the extra $35 a night going to make or break the WWF? No, but why should they pay more when they could pay less. Vince's business had grown so much that he lost sight of some of the smaller details, things that Jerry had to deal with every day in his own company's operation. Jerry *had* to do those things just to stay in business.

Jerry had a very positive effect on the WWF during the time he was there. We went from a year of losing money to a year where the company made money. But even with his track record of success, Jerry often talked about being frustrated over certain ideas not getting presented to Vince. Pat Patterson would cut the idea off at the pass by simply saying, *"No, Vince wouldn't like that."*

Jerry was also instrumental in getting Vince Russo the opportunity to become a TV writer. When Jerry was with the WWF, Russo was strictly a hack, writing for the company wrestling magazine. Jerry got involved in all aspects of the business, and he thought Vince Russo's ideas could put a spark into the television product. In hindsight, perhaps that might have been one of Jerry's ideas that would have been best if it had been halted by Pat.

The grand jury trial was a media circus, even though the feds didn't have that strong of a case. The prosecutors were banking on the hope that Hulk would hang Vince out to dry, but that never happened. I was subpoenaed to appear before the grand jury, but was excused when I told them, *"The foundation of this case took place before I started working for the WWF, so I can't testify to anything that may or may not have happened."*

When the acquittal was handed down on July 22, 1994, the whole experience of the trial, and the fact that Vince could have done hard time, could have affected him in one of two ways: He could have viewed it as a lesson in humility, and viewed life differently, or, it could have bolstered his *"me against the world"* mentality. If anything, it was the latter, as Vince became even more arrogant.

*"I kicked the federal government's butt! If I can beat them, nobody had better mess with me!"*

Vince even had a poster in his office that said, *"We won! We kicked their ass! Ya-aay!"*

After the trial, the results for the fiscal year came in. Vince held a meeting in a conference room with the front office employees and said, *"Attorneys' fees for the trial cost the company $5 million."* As he talked about the company losses, he continually gloated about winning the trial. *"The $5 million loss has put the company in dire straits,"* he continued, *"so we need to find ways to cut expenses. We have to make some adjustments until we can turn the business around."*

Up to that point, we had a security force at Titan Tower. In addition to inserting your I.D. card into a card reader, there were security guards in the building, and a guard stationed at the gate that gave us access to the parking level. The security force was let go that same day. Shortly after that, the coffee service and water coolers were gone. They cut everything they could.

Regardless of what my feelings are towards Vince, Vince understands the makeup of his business, and he maintains control over his company. After the trial, Vince did what he had to do. I can't fault him for that. As a cost-cutting measure, he cut salaries from about 25 to 40 percent for certain people in management. Unfortunately, I was one of those people.

This is my criticism over how Vince McMahon handled the situation. I understand that Vince went through a personal hell with the trial, but when it was all over, he showed his true colors. Vince wanted it both ways. He had people with a wrestling background who worked within his corporate structure. He would always say, *"You're not a wrestler anymore. You're an employee working for a company."* He would say that he wanted us to be professional, and not have a wrestler's mentality—whatever that meant—and yet, when he cut salaries, instead of cutting 5% across the board of all management, he cherry picked only those people in management who were veteran wrestling people — Jim Ross, Howard Finkel, Jerry Brisco, Pat Patterson, Alfred Hayes, and myself. Other corporate people were not affected, and that was what I took extreme issue with. If Vince had said, *"Okay, until we get over this hurdle, everybody in management has to take a 5% pay cut until we can rebound and recover,"* I would not have had a problem with that. But instead, the disdain that Vince held towards wrestlers finally showed itself. He isolated a small group of people—the former wrestlers—and our salaries were cut from about 25% to 40%. We were no longer supposed to be wrestlers, and yet, when push came to shove, his mindset was to look at us as wrestlers. *"In the old days, when the business was down, wrestlers took a pay cut, so they're used to it."*

When I received the letter about my salary reduction, I received it in person at a meeting in Vince's office. Sandra had instructed each of the old wrestling clan to meet with her and Vince in Vince's office, one immediately after the other. Even though I was no longer reporting to her, she still held a powerful position with the company. Sandra made it clear at the beginning that we had to agree to the terms, or our job was on the line. At least, that's what I was told. Sandra instructed me in advance to keep my mouth shut and she would take care of me—whatever that meant.

Alfred Hayes is a quality guy. He said, *"Well, that's it. I'm walking away."* He quit on the spot and walked out. Alfred relocated to Dallas and moved in with his daughter.

Jerry Brisco, who had worked for Vince for ten years, was flown up from Florida. Jerry had a history with Vince going back to Vince's hostile takeover of *Georgia Championship Wrestling*. Whenever Jerry would come to Titan Tower, he would get into the elevator and go wherever he wanted to go. He had free run of the building. However, on this occasion, when Jerry arrived, he was told to sit and wait until Vince was ready to see him. He sat in the lobby for an hour before somebody came down to get him. He was taken to Vince's office, where Vince read him the letter telling him that his salary was being cut. And yet, Jerry still works there. I don't fault him for that. Everybody has to make their own decisions based on their own situation.

As for Howard Finkel, well ... Howard is Howard. He was just happy to be there. He stayed there and weathered the storm.

I was at the higher end of the pay scale, so the reduction to my salary was huge. My salary dropped from about $200,000 to $120,000. When you're a salaried employee, you don't expect that to happen. It's not like being a self-employed, independent contractor wrestler. Salaried employees assume mortgages and buy cars based on whatever our income is, and we budget. The cut was a bitter pill for me to swallow.

That was when my relationship with Vince began to deteriorate. At that time, I had a young family. My twins were 2½ years old, one of whom is physically challenged, and our youngest child was just six months old. Through Vince's encouragement, I had entrenched myself in Connecticut. When our salaries were reduced, I still owed about $120,000 on my note to Titan Sports, and I was making interest-bearing payments out of my check. This was in addition to my mortgage payment and substantial alimony payments to my ex-wife. When my pay was cut 40% with no advance warning, it was devastating. When I told Doug Sages, the Chief Financial Officer for the WWF, that I would be unable to continue making the payments I was obligated to make, he told me the loan would be frozen for an unspecified period of time, and that interest would not be added.

Vince put me into a Catch-22 situation. He wanted me to establish roots in Connecticut, helped me buy the home, and then cut my salary. Yes, I was the one who ultimately made the decisions. Vince didn't sign the mortgage. I did. I bought the expensive house, but whenever I talked about renting, Vince kept pushing me, *"We want you to have roots here. I want you to have that house. Here's what we can do to make that happen."*

My decision was also based on the fact that I had been there for four years, had maintained a certain income level, and had no reason to anticipate that my income would drop that dramatically. And yet, between a Friday and a Monday, my income was cut by 40%. The only course of action left to me was to immediately put my house on the market, and Vince's actions led me to eventually declare bankruptcy.

I held a tremendous amount of animosity towards Vince. If I had no responsibility other than to myself, I could live in a phone booth and survive, but everything in my life had taken on a different perspective. I was an adult, and I could take whatever Vince did to me, but Vince's actions put my children in jeopardy.

In my opinion, Vince has a sick sense of humor. I think he gets a perverse pleasure out of taking someone under his wing, lifting them up to heights they never dreamed of, and then, when they least expect it, knocking the pegs out from under them and watching them tumble down. In my heart, I truly believe that. I saw that happen many, many times with different people. Every few years, he talks to Bruno Sammartino, but it's always when he's desperate and thinks Bruno has something he needs. Once Vince is back in control, and has gotten what he wants, he would be just as devious with Bruno as he ever was.

During their lifetime, Vince and his family could never begin to spend all the money they've accumulated. If the business failed tomorrow, the only people who would be poorer for it would be the wrestlers who would no longer have a means of making a living. And yet, if Vince and his family never worked another day in their lives, they will never have to worry about where their next meal is going to come from. Even during those times after the trial, when the company was in such *dire straits,* Vince got his full salary.

For what he did to my family, and the jeopardy he put them in by his actions—I will never forgive him.

# Chapter 32
## Resigned to Resign

When the acquittal came down, and Vince was found not guilty, Vince refocused his attention to once again spearhead the operation with renewed enthusiasm. Jerry Jarrett could see that his role was not what it once was and it became difficult for him to stay there. I don't think there was any tension between Jerry and Vince. However, I do know that Jerry wasn't crazy about living in Connecticut. He had strong ties and other business interests back in Tennessee. He also had a son, Jason, who was a senior in high school and the captain of his football team. Vince would fly Jerry to Nashville every Friday so he could see his son's game. Jerry finally said, *"Vince, why are you paying me to be here? There's nothing more I can do to help you."* Jerry turned in his resignation and went home to Hendersonville, Tennessee. Vince continued to pay him for another year.

When the steroid trial was over, Titan Sports needed to do damage control and polish the image of the WWF, especially as it pertained to steroids. To reach that end, Titan Sports developed a written steroid policy. I am of the opinion that Titan Sports wanted to distance Vince from the procedure, so that is the likely reason why I was named the administrator of the program. The first thing that happened was that Linda's office mailed the written policy to every major sports organization—the NFL, the NHL, the NBA, MLB, and the IOC—challenging each to rise to the standards that the WWF had set. The only other name that I recollect being mentioned was Maro (not Mario, as most people assume) DiPasquale, a doctor from Canada. He was an *expert* who knew about masking techniques (attempts to hide any banned substance that may be in the athlete's system) and the effects of steroids. I believe that he was the person to oversee the actual testing procedure as stated in the written policy.

As the administrator, my name was mentioned in the policy itself, even though I had very little, if any, say in the drafting of the policy. The policy was supposed to be confidential, so I never made any comments or released any written statements. Once the written policy was made public, I was concerned that if the policy was not strictly adhered to as written, I would be set up as the potential scapegoat.

Since it is public knowledge that I was the administrator of the WWF's drug policy during a very high profile time, I can imagine that many of you expect me to discuss my role in that position. Unfortunately, due to legal ramifications, I am not at liberty to discuss any aspect of my role or give any details of specific incidents that occurred during that time. I was told in no uncertain terms that if I ever commented on those specific incidents, I would be sued. I say "unfortunately" because I know that many readers would like to hear about what went on behind the scenes. I can empathize with you if you are disappointed, but I sincerely hope that you don't feel cheated.

I will add, however, that even if I could write about those experiences, I wouldn't.

While it's easy (and honest) to use the fear of a lawsuit as the reason I will not "name names," the other reason is that I would never betray the confidence of a former employer, who trusted me in that role. I would not want to write anything that would hurt the talent that I worked with, either. This is not intended to be a "tell-all" book about my days as the administrator of the WWF drug program. I was in a position of power, and to use that knowledge to my advantage years later would violate my personal code of honor.

Many stories have already been published in the press about certain individuals during that time, so an argument could be made that the stories are already public information. Those stories were written and published by reporters. I am not a reporter. And if the stories have already been published, there's no reason for me to rehash them here.

Wrestling, like many other sports, is a very tough business. The stress of the business can force people to make bad choices. For me to tell you about the bad choices certain individuals made would be unfair and mean-spirited. First of all, as you've probably already discovered, I was no angel. In fact, I've been more than honest with you about all aspects of my life. If any of the wrestlers want to write a book and detail their own personal experiences, then that is their choice, but that choice should not be mine to make. It wouldn't be fair to them or their families for the former drug administrator to go public about their past behavior. Everybody deserves a second chance, and many people who have dabbled with drugs in the past (whether it be steroids, cocaine, or any other controlled substance), have cleaned up their life and no longer depend on chemicals. Unfortunately, there are too many who never stopped taking drugs, and many have lost their lives because of it.

Steroid testing is a huge issue today, especially in baseball, and it's a fascinating topic. Every time a new test comes out, somebody finds a way to "beat the system." I know first-hand what senior management in major league baseball is going through, and how frustrating it is to be on the receiving end of the press, who write about how things "should" be done.

During my tenure with the WWF, the wrestling press would write about specific incidents in regards to drug testing. In some instances, they would detail how certain wrestlers were suspended or fired for failing drug tests. On other occasions, they claimed that certain individuals on the roster had failed a drug test, or were found with drugs, but received no punishment. How they got that information is beyond me, but it put me in an incredibly stressful position. I cannot count the number of times that talent complained to me about an alleged double-standard taking place, using articles in the press to accuse me of playing favorites.

My initial fear of being the scapegoat was, unfortunately, coming true. I might have been the administrator of the program, but ultimately, the decisions were not mine to make. In talent administration, taking more than a fair share of heat from talent comes with the job, although the heat is quite often not justified.

I hope I've given you enough of an explanation, one that both the law and my conscience allows, to help you understand why my role in the drug administration policy played a very large part in my decision to leave the WWF.

As additional insight into the decision-making process that eventually led to me tendering my resignation from Titan, I need to elaborate on a meeting in Vince's office. When I received the letter about my salary reduction during the meeting with Vince and Sandra, the topic of the conversation broadened. Around that period of time, I had stopped traveling as part of Vince's entourage, and chose to travel with ring announcer Howard Finkel. We would stay at the same hotel and rent a car together. During my meeting with Vince, he said, *"What's the matter? You don't like Vince any more?"*

Vince would talk about himself in the third person.

"No," I said. "That's not the case at all."

"Well, you don't want to ride with me anymore?"

I decided to plunge in and tell him exactly how I felt. *"Vince, do you want me to tell you the truth?"*

"By all means."

"When I was in your car, you would drive 100 miles an hour, knocking over construction cones. I laughed as hard as everybody else, and never thought about, 'What if?' But when my children came into the world, I had to make a reality check. I started to look at life in a different light. I was no longer comfortable sitting in the car with you. I had to consider things like what would happen to my family if I died when the car wrapped itself around a telephone pole. Instead, I chose to travel with Howard Finkel. My decision in this matter isn't a question of my commitment to this company or to my job. I want my job and I need my job. I need to provide for my family. It doesn't take away from my passion for this business. It has nothing to do with that."

And that was true. I've done dangerous things in my life, like skydiving, but for the first time in my life, I began to make conscious decisions like, *I'm not going to ride with Vince. He drives like a maniac.* I didn't need to go out with Vince and his entourage at four o'clock in the morning, and watch him eat a dozen, scrambled egg whites. Getting a good nights' sleep was more important to me at that point in my life. Instead, I chose to ride with Howard Finkel, and I was ridiculed for that.

Vince sat there with his chest all puffed out. I finished by saying, *"You wanted the truth. Well, that's the truth."*

Shortly after my meeting with Vince, I received notification that I was on *"probation,"* and that my job performance was being monitored. I personally felt that it was more to create a paper trail with Human Resources (HR), in the event that Vince later decided to fire me for standing up to him. Some time later, I received a very complimentary letter from Linda McMahon, stating what an outstanding job I was doing. Maybe Vince had other fish to try, but in spite of the positive letter I received, my salary was not upgraded to the previous level prior to the reduction. I never asked the others about their situation, because I did not feel it appropriate to ask even a friend about his salary, but we had all been told at the original meetings that the salary reduction was "temporary," and would be reviewed at a future date.

Due to the salary reduction, I had to sell our house and get out from under the mortgage. There were several problems standing in the way of a quick sale, the primary reason being that I didn't buy the home with the idea of having to sell it three years later. First of all, it was in an area where homes are very expensive, but the biggest drawback was that the artist who had originally owned the home had converted one of the four bedrooms into an atrium. The atrium was the showpiece of the house, but when people buy a home at that price level, they expect four bedrooms, at the very least.

There were times when I thought we were going to lose the home before we could sell it. A few miracles were the only things that forestalled that eventuality. One day, we returned to the house to find that the hot water heater had ruptured and two inches of water flooded the basement. We had to inventory everything that could not be salvaged. We lost oriental carpets, a sofa bed, and a collection of over 100 VHS movies. We received an insurance settlement of just over $10,000. That money caught us up on past-due mortgage payments and helped us for another month or so. Had that not happened, we would not have made it. I call that a miracle in disguise. We were also helped over the hurdle when my wife's grandfather passed away and left her some money.

Eighteen months dragged by before we were able to sell the house. After showing the house over fifty times, we stopped counting. I have to laugh every time I see the current commercial for a realty company. The phone rings in the home of a woman who has young kids in the bathtub. She smiles when she is told that someone is interested in their house, until the doorbell rings and she realizes that the people are standing on her front doorstep. The woman's expression tells it all. We could relate to that. We had 2½-year-old twins and a 6-month-old in diapers. If you have ever sold a house while you were living in it, you know what is involved each and every time you have a showing, including the times when the people don't show up as scheduled. Our house sat at the end of an extended cul-de-sac, about 100 yards off the main road down a one-lane path. Every time a car would stop at the top of our lane and pause facing our house, our hearts skipped a beat.

The contract with the realtor, including an extension, expired before we sold the house. Lindsey actually sold it herself during a casual conversation. We took a loss of about $50,000, but we were happy to be out from under the debt. I ended up with about $20,000 in hand at the closing, which was far less than the down payment that was initially made at the time of closing on the original purchase.

On the day of the closing—September 13, 1996—I promised myself that I would not work one more day for Vince McMahon. If you have ever owned real estate, you know that the purchaser usually requests the closing date based on their needs and the loan process. The closing date had been set in advance for several weeks, but it was delayed for a few hours at the last minute, so I had to make a quick decision. Should I go ahead and resign from the WWF, or wait until the closing was finalized and I had a check in hand?

I chose the latter.

Once the deal was finalized, I just wanted to leave. I never gave one thought to changing my mind. I didn't have another job, but I was leaving. There was nothing to discuss with anyone — even with Vince. Gradually, during the week in which I resigned, and without being too obvious, I cleaned out my office a little each day, except for a few personal belongings I had on my desk. I left just a few things on the desk that I could scoop up when I left for good, along with the last few personal pictures on the wall.

Vince had meetings all morning on Friday, and he would often eat lunch in his office, so I waited until I knew his schedule was open. When I heard his voice in the hallway, I poked my head around the corner of my doorway and asked, *"Vince, can I see you for a minute?"*

*"Yeah. C'mon in!"*

I went directly to the point. *"Vince, I met with you on the day you offered me this job, and I feel that on the day I choose to leave the company, the right thing to do is to face you man to man, not by sending a letter to Human Resources."*

I put my resignation letter on his desk and slid it towards him. *"If you want to discuss my reasons for resigning, I'd be happy to. If you don't feel that it warrants a discussion, I'll understand that."*

*"I can't believe this! By all means, I want to discuss this!"*

*"You helped me out by giving me this job,"* I said, *"and I'm grateful for the help that you gave me, but you caught me off guard when you told me you wanted me to stay here and have roots, that this was my home, and that I should finish my career here. You insisted that I buy that house, and you helped make it happen for me. You also gave me a note that I could pay based on the salary I was earning. When you reduced my salary by almost 40%, I could no longer pay you that note. You've threatened the security of my children. More than one time, we thought we were going to lose everything. You're the one who put me into this position, and then you pulled the rug out from under me! I don't have to like you, and you don't have to like me, but to do my job at this level, we have to have respect for each other. I'm not*

*leaving because I have a job somewhere else. I'm leaving because you didn't respect me, and as a result, I've lost all respect for you."*

We talked for over an hour. Vince and I discussed everything in great detail, especially the philosophical differences regarding the handling of my job responsibilities. I pointed out inconsistencies of things that were happening in my department. There were decisions being made, and actions being taken, that I wasn't responsible for. And yet, because of my title, it looked like I was. I felt like I was being positioned to get buried as a scapegoat, and I didn't feel right about that. Again, you can't have it both ways. If you're going to have policies and programs, then do it with consistency. If you don't, then do away with those policies. It's like Vince used to tell Pat and me all the time, *"You can't be half-pregnant."*

My exact words at that point were, *"I wanted to quit a long time ago, but I had no choice until my house was sold. Now that it has, we have nothing more to talk about, except to thank you for taking the time to listen to me. I also thank you for the opportunity you gave me, and for the things that I learned while I was here."*

As I walked out of his office, Vince followed me through the vestibule, where his secretary sits, and through the glass doors. I went into my office, scooped my remaining personal items into my arms, and turned around to walk out. Vince, who was still standing in his doorway down the hall, said, *"Hey, pal. You need help with anything?"*

*"No, thanks, Vince. I can handle it."*

I took the elevator from the 4th floor to the 2nd floor, where the HR office was located, and handed in my access card, key pass, the key to my office, and a copy of my resignation letter. I left the building and drove away.

I later spoke on the telephone with my secretary, who told me that after I got on the elevator, Vince ran down the hallway, screaming, *"Stop him! Stop him! I want to talk with him!"* He ran down the stairwell to the second floor in an attempt to catch me in the HR office, but when he got there, I was already gone. My secretary said, *"Vince seems to be desperate to talk with you."*

At that point, feelings of paranoia began to creep in, because Vince has money and is connected in many different ways. I started to think about Vince's political clout, and the power and influence he held in that community.

In my heart, I believe that Vince did not immediately grasp what I had done. It didn't dawn on him right away that I had previously cleared out my office, and that I was making my final trip, with a stop at HR. That had been my plan all along. I assume that he must have walked into my office, and when he realized that I was gone for good, panic set in.

Later that day, Vince and I talked on the telephone. He said, *"Are you planning to go into Manhattan and call a press conference, to start an embarrassing scandal on me on the weekend of Shane's wedding, when all our out-of-town family and guests are here?"*

I was dumbfounded. *"What are you talking about? Press conference? Where did you ever get that idea? You never heard me say that. The thought never crossed my mind."*

I realized that *my* feelings of paranoia were *nothing* compared to the paranoia that Vince was dealing with. Vince's next words were, *"Well, you've restored my faith in humanity to hear you say those words."*

I said, *"Well, Vince. I guess we both feel very emotional about what's going on right now, with your son's wedding this weekend, and what my family's been through for the last year and a half."*

Somehow, from our conversation, Vince thought I was going to make a grandstand play by calling a press conference to sling mud on the company. The timing happened to coincide with that of his son's wedding, on the weekend when guests were coming into town. He thought I planned to parlay the attention on the wedding into a news conference. That was not the case. All I wanted to do was to leave and, hopefully, never see him again. My resignation that week had nothing to do with the timing of Shane's wedding. It just happened to be when we closed on the house. After what Vince put me through, I wasn't going to wait until Monday, when the wedding was over, to resign. When I said that I couldn't work for him one more day, I meant it.

*"I want to do right by you,"* Vince said. *"I know you've made up your mind, but will you call me back in an hour?"*

I agreed to do that. When I did, Vince told me to contact Human Resources the next day, on Saturday. *"I want to do right by you,"* he repeated, *"and when you speak with them, I think you'll be comfortable with what I have in mind."*

On Saturday morning, Lindsey and I packed our three kids into the rental car and drove to Boston. From the highway en route to Boston, I called HR on my mobile phone. Vince wanted to continue my salary for two years and forgive the outstanding note, but I had to sign a non-compete clause. I told Lindsey, *"Well, at least we'll have a clean slate. We'll have a little money in hand, and I can find a job. We could put our lives back together and get away from this nightmare."*

HR wanted me to come in immediately and sign the agreement. I said, *"There's no way that I can come back. I'm on my way to Boston."* We had purchased tickets to the Boston Red Sox–Chicago White Sox games for both Saturday and Sunday. They then asked me to come in on Sunday, which was also out of the question. *"Look,"* I said. *"I can live with what Vince wants to do for me, even after all we've been through, but I can't be there until Monday morning. I'll sign the agreement, but I want my lawyer to look at it before I do."*

One of the things I was concerned about was the fact that I owned, and still own, the rights to the name J.J. Dillon. I didn't want Vince to create a character with that name—which he might be inclined to do—to make fun of and ridicule me. I wanted it to be clear that I owned the rights to the name and that it was *my* professional name, and no one else had the right to use it.

The original agreement was faxed to my attorney for review, and my attorney handwrote some minor changes, adding a paragraph about the rights to my professional name. On Monday, I met my attorney and I signed the agreement, which included our changes. That night, when I called my attorney, he said that he hadn't heard anything from Titan. When I called the following morning, he said that he had received a faxed letter in the middle of the night from one of Titan's attorneys, stating that the offer had been withdrawn due to alleged conversations I had with people at Ted Turner's *World Championship Wrestling*. I stress the word *alleged*.

No doubt, the allegation stemmed from a trip I made shortly before my resignation when my family and I took a three-day vacation to *Walt Disney World*. As we were walking down Main Street, I ran into Scott Hall, who was wrestling for WCW at the time. We were both doing the family thing: He had his son with him, I was pushing a stroller. Scott was a big star at the time and was very recognizable. I was recognized, as well, but certainly not at the level of Scott Hall. Celebrities are often spotted at *Walt Disney World*, but as a rule, as long as you are with your family and keep moving, people would leave you alone.

We swapped stories about working for Vince and the WWF, as opposed to working for WCW. Scott made a comment about me being needed at WCW because nobody knew what they were doing. I made a flippant remark along the lines of, *"In this crazy business, you never know where I might show up."* I wasn't going to say more because it was too much of a risk. I had three young children and I was fearful of losing everything. The only risky thing I did was put my house up for sale. During those 18 months, if someone who worked for Titan, or who knew Vince, had looked at the house, I could have been in trouble. My only explanation would have been that I had to sell the house because of the salary reduction, at which point I would have to go back to renting. If it ever got back to Vince that I even entertained the thought of leaving, I believe he would have fired me without batting an eye. He did it to Jim Barnett. Even with all his power in the business, and the clout of his position in the WWF, Jim was let go by Vince after making a simple comment about how much he missed living in Atlanta. For those reasons, I couldn't afford to approach WCW, and I certainly would not have brought up the subject with Scott Hall before I closed on my house. It was too big of a risk.

WCW had a taping session scheduled for that afternoon at *Walt Disney World*. I was not previously aware of the taping and I did not go near it. I simply spent a few minutes talking to Scott. I didn't ask him for information regarding WCW and I didn't try to call him at a later date. Our conversation was cut short when people started to stop and gawk at us. As fate would have it, that chance meeting with Scott Hall may have been the reason why people assumed I had advance contact with WCW, which was absolutely not true.

Titan also made reference to, once again, using the word *alleged,* unauthorized charges that I had made on my American Express card. I told my attorney, *"You can respond by telling them that I will testify under oath that I have had no contact with WCW. Secondly, in regards to my American Express card, I turned it in because I was late in making payments a couple of times, so I didn't even HAVE a company card!"*

My attorney responded with my comments, but only received one other letter, which stated that Vince and Linda had discussed the situation, and were *"shocked at the magnitude of the offer"* made to me. When they saw the actual number, the offer was withdrawn.

After I left, Vince went to an agents' meeting at the next TV taping. His spin was that I was no longer with the company because I had tried to extort money from him. That is what people present at that meeting told me. The truth is that I never asked for anything. Vince tendered an offer, I accepted it, and he reneged on it.

That was in 1996. The pertinent specifics of the conversation I had with Vince on that Friday afternoon remain between him and me. We both know the truth. I have not spoken with, seen, or corresponded with Vince McMahon since that last phone conversation on the evening of my resignation—Friday the 13th.

I don't remember whether it was a matter of days or weeks, but after my resignation was final, I received a letter from Titan Sports, demanding payment—which included all interest from the time of my salary freeze, which wasn't supposed to accrue—of $123,000. I went to great lengths to avoid filing for bankruptcy, but when I consulted an attorney in Georgia for advice, I was told that bankruptcy was my only option. In May 1997, Lindsey and I filed Chapter 13.

When I left Connecticut, there were people who wondered, *"Who in their right mind would walk away from the WWF?"*

Well, you have to walk a mile in somebody's shoes before you can truly understand.

## Chapter 33
## The Obsession

I quit working for Vince with no other prospects at hand. Since I had over 25 years of experience in the business, some of which included working at an executive level, logic told me that WCW might have an interest in me. Had I talked to them? Nope. Had I given it any thought? Not really. It was a roll of the dice, and at times, you take chances in life. As scared as I was because of the responsibilities for my children, I couldn't remain with the WWF any longer.

When Lindsey and I decided to leave Connecticut, we circled three cities on the map. One was Atlanta, where WCW was based. The second possibility was Nashville, where Jerry Jarrett was located. Jerry knew that I was frustrated at Titan, but he had no idea that I would be leaving Connecticut. He owned a construction business, so I thought he might be able to find work for me in Nashville. When I called, however, he told me that his business was such that he didn't have anything at that time that could provide a good income for my family. The final circle was drawn around Orlando. There weren't any wrestling opportunities there, but with the abundance of entertainment and theme parks in the area, I felt certain that we could make a fresh start in a new industry. Orlando would have been our last choice, though, because I had no contacts there. I didn't know how much money I would be able to command, but Lindsey and I opted to roll the dice and move to Atlanta, in the hopes of pursuing an opportunity with WCW, which was the only other major wrestling organization still in existence.

The wrestling business had been whittled down to two major players: Titan Sports, which later went public and became World Wrestling Entertainment, and WCW, which was owned by Time Warner. My plan was to contact someone at WCW and try to get a job interview. In my heart, I knew there had to be someone who could do something for me.

When I arrived in Atlanta, I called Tony Schiavone at the WCW offices. Tony transferred the call to Eric Bischoff, who was the President of WCW at the time. I had never met Eric, and had never even talked to him, but he was willing to meet with me, so we set up a meeting for the next morning. I left early because I didn't want to be late, but as fate would have it, there was an accident on the expressway. I got caught in bumper-to-bumper traffic and arrived at the CNN Tower ten minutes past our appointed time. While stuck in traffic, I had called Eric's secretary to explain the situation and to confirm that I was on my way, but running a few minutes late. Eric was waiting in his office when I walked in, and he immediately commented on the fact that I was late. So much for first impressions.

Eric also made a comment about the way I was dressed. As always, I wore a suit and tie, as any professional would in my situation. Eric said, *"We're laid back around here. We don't dress up very often."* Even if that was the case, if I had interviewed somebody that I had never met, and they weren't dressed up, I would have been offended. That factored into my first impression of Eric Bischoff.

My interview with Eric took place in late September 1996, during a very hectic time for WCW's parent company, Turner Broadcasting System. On September 22, it was announced that Turner Broadcasting would be merging with Time Warner. That deal would become official on October 10, 1996. Bischoff said, *"Right now, there's a hiring freeze and I can't hire you as an employee. What I can do, though, is bring you on as a consultant for thirty days. I want you to come to the office, look over everything, and come to the TV. I want you to take note of what you see, then tell me where you think you can help make things better. If I like what I hear, we can talk about it. In the meantime, I'll try to find something for you. I have to sell Harvey Schiller on the fact that I want you here."* Harvey Schiller was the president of Turner Sports, and a member of the Olympic Committee. *"I don't often get somebody walking in my door with more than 25 years of experience in the wrestling business, especially at the level you worked with our competitor. We will talk again."*

*"I'll be right up front with you,"* I said. *"My situation is such that I'm not coming here in a position to make a lot of demands. I just want to work here and, hopefully, have a positive influence on this company. All I ask is, if I prove myself to be an asset, that you'll re-evaluate my situation in the future and reward me accordingly based on what I contribute to the company. I do need to make some decisions regarding my future, so I will need to know as soon as possible if you have interest in bringing me aboard full-time. If not, I understand."*

Once again, I called upon my friend, Jim Barnett, for his advice. *"You will be an immense help to Bischoff,"* he assured me, *"and I hope he taps into what you can bring to the company. If he does, you'll be a big help to him."*

Eric didn't want me showing up at TV on Monday unannounced, so he told me to wait and show up at the office on Tuesday. In the meantime, he would talk to his booking committee, which consisted of Kevin Sullivan, Terry Taylor, Arn Anderson, Paul Orndorff, Jimmy Hart, and Annette Yother. Annette was a young girl who worked as an assistant to one of the television producers. Kevin was the self-appointed leader of the group, but Eric had the final say on booking ideas.

The first time I walked into the booking room, the reception was kind of chilly. I had worked with everybody on the committee (except Yother), so it wasn't like we were strangers. When I sensed the tension, I took Kevin aside and said, *"I want to be up front with you. We've know each other for a long time. I'm not here to take your job or to replace you. I left the WWF because of some issues that I don't want to get into. I have a young family, I needed a job, and Eric hired me. I'm here to help in any way that I can, and I'm willing to contribute to the booking committee, but I want you to know that you're not being replaced. I'm not here in that role."* Kevin thanked me and said he appreciated me saying that. Word got around and it eventually put everybody at ease.

Basically, I just worked around the office, sat in on the booking meetings, and went to the TV tapings. As a consultant for the month of October, I was paid $10,000. After two weeks went by, I called Eric and asked him if he had given any more thought to our talk. He told me that he got approval from Harvey Schiller to skirt around the hiring freeze. As of November 1, I would be an official employee of WCW with a salary of $125,000. We made tentative plans to meet again, and two weeks later, we had a very general conversation. *"I do not have an empty executive-level office at the moment,"* he said. *"I don't know what position I'm going to place you in, either."*

At first, I was an agent—whatever that was. I talked about the agent position in an earlier chapter, but at WCW, the agent title seemed to be on everybody's job description, and the job responsibilities were very vague. Obviously, I didn't want to take a step back, which is what I was doing, but I also realized that I wouldn't be able to start at the level I had left. I told Eric, *"I left the WWF of my own volition, but I would hate to take a step backwards career-wise. I was a Vice-President there."*

*"Well, I can't do that for you here,"* he said, *"especially with the hiring freeze. Getting you hired is one thing, but titles are another. The best I can do is give you the title of agent."* I was able to live with that, especially when I was starting with the same money I was making at Titan with the salary reductions. They also compensated me for moving to Atlanta, covering all my out-of-pocket expense to move, which wasn't very much.

*"I really don't care what you call me,"* I said. *"I'm just here to work and help the company. That other stuff will all sort itself out."*

I didn't work as a talent when I was with the WWF, but when I returned to WCW, I had a small, on-air role as "The Commissioner." There was no continuity or organization to my role, but I did have some exposure. It started when Eric asked me to make a big announcement on TV. My return to television took place on the April 21, 1997, *Nitro* from Saginaw, Michigan. I did it live, after being off-camera for eight years, and everybody said, *"Wow! You're a natural in that role!"* After that, I was asked to do other things, but the problem was, in order for that role to work, I needed to be an authority figure with a lot of credibility. Before I knew it, they had me in the ring, taking bumps and getting spray-painted. I've always been a team player, so I didn't want to say "no" when they wanted me involved in a skit, but it diminished the role that I was supposed to play. I performed that role for about three years, until March 2000.

There were many differences between the WWF and WCW. The WWF had been around longer, was more structured, had proven themselves as a company, and had a sustained level of success to build on. WCW, on the other hand, was struggling, and had not made a profit since they started. I think they stayed in business as long as they did because they were primarily a television company that had the ability to minimize their losses by juggling figures around on paper.

Due to the lucrative advertising fees they commanded, the production of original TV programming seemed to be the primary motive of Time Warner, while the house shows became a by-product of the television. On September 4, 1995, when WCW began airing *Monday Nitro* head-to-head against the WWF's *Monday Night RAW*, the ratings began to climb. Sponsors lined up to promote their wares with both promotions. Except for 1997 and 1998, when WCW showed a profit, the advertising and house show revenue never offset the cost of running the company.

Initially, I didn't know what to make of Eric Bischoff. His attention span seemed to be very short, and my first impression was that people skills were not his strong point. He was a type-A personality, a salesman type, but not your friendly, smiling salesman-type who had good people skills.

Eric was one of a long line of people who tried unsuccessfully to run WCW. In my opinion, the people who didn't succeed were those who did not have a wrestling background. Ole Anderson had a wrestling background, but he never ran the company. He was there as the booker. The only person with a wrestling background who actually ran the company was Bill Watts. Unfortunately, somebody in the company wanted Bill out, so they painted Watts as a racist after he made some comments in one of the dirtsheets. Bill was the one guy in the business who, if given the chance, would have had a real chance to make the company profitable, because he understood how a wrestling company should be structured.

Eric didn't have a wrestling background. He got his job by submitting a creative resume, leading the company to believe that he had an elaborate background in professional wrestling, and that he was the driving force behind the success of Verne Gagne's Minnesota-based American Wrestling Alliance [AWA]. If a true resume was written, it would list him as an announcer for the AWA, and nothing more. Once he was entrenched in a power position with Turner, he manipulated the former AWA talent and executives (who were now with WCW) out the door, because they had the ability to expose him as a fraud. If somebody asked why they were no longer with the company, Eric put all kinds of spin on it. *"They weren't willing to work as hard as I was, and I couldn't count on them."* Eric got rid of anybody who might possibly pose a threat to his position.

I don't fault Eric for aggressively going after an opportunity. There were several people vying for the position with the company, including Tony Schiavone, another announcer who had no other experience in the wrestling business. Eric was able to sell himself and convince someone to give him the opportunity. I'll give him credit for one thing. He is a *great* salesman. The only problem is, once he makes the sale, he has to deliver, and that's where he gets lost. In one way, Eric was like Vince McMahon. When he saw an opportunity loom up in front of him, he took a chance and rolled the dice. The difference between them, however, is that Vince was gambling with his own money. Eric was spending somebody else's.

In 1997 and 1998, Eric did increase the revenue stream and take WCW to a level it had never been to before, but he did so without a business plan that made any sense, because he didn't know what it was that made him successful. At the height of Eric's perceived success, an Atlanta magazine ran a story about Eric and WCW. It featured a large picture of Eric with his name in bold print at the top of the page. As we sat in his office prior to a meeting, he was gloating about the feature story. Being the detail person that I am, I pointed out to Eric that they had misspelled his last name in the headline. Apparently, Eric had not noticed it. If he did, he probably hoped that nobody else would. All I got was a cold stare.

When Eric first got the job, he sought out the assistance of Jerry Jarrett. He went to Jerry's home and spent several days with him. What he was trying to do was to get a crash course in the workings of the wrestling business. Jerry wanted to remain in Nashville, so Eric hired him for a year as a consultant. Not surprisingly, in a matter of several days, Eric thought he knew it all and didn't need Jerry any longer. He never used Jerry's services. He paid him out for a year and did not renew the deal when it expired. Jerry offered to attend and critique some shows, and drive to Atlanta for important meetings, but Eric never took him up on his offer.

Eric was a very confident guy, but he was obsessed with putting Vince McMahon out of business. That was all he ever wanted to talk about. Even during my initial meeting with Eric, when I was being interviewed for the job, that obsession was very apparent. *"I don't see how much longer he can last. You know him. What's he like?"* I didn't give him a definitive answer, but in the back of my mind, I knew that Vince McMahon was not going to go out of business. At the time, though, it wasn't in my best interest to say, *"Eric, it's never going to happen."* Eric, however, was convinced that it was just a matter of time before he ran Vince out of business.

Eric never took into account the fact that even when WCW was doing good business, and was kicking Vince's tail in the ratings, our pay-per-view numbers were still abysmal because we were giving so much of our good material away on free TV. Again, we were working for a television company whose focus was strictly on the ratings, and not the financial health of the company. And yet, even with their low TV ratings, Vince was still doing respectable pay-per-view numbers. When his business was down, Vince concentrated on producing his product and controlling his costs. As a rule, Vince never panicked. He rode it out until the business pendulum swung back in his direction. When it did, his pay-per-view numbers rose dramatically and his ratings went up.

Whenever Vince and I went into a bar after a TV taping, the first toast he would offer up was, *"Here's to kicking Ted Turner's ass!"* That was the toast of every TV, and that's where Vince's focus was. In contrast to Eric Bischoff, though, Vince wasn't consumed with putting Turner out of business. He just wanted to give Ted a run for his money. While Eric was expending his energy on what he could do to put Vince out of business, Vince concentrated on running his business. He seemed to realize that Eric Bischoff was not a wrestling person, and he knew the smart thing to do was to do nothing. If he gave Eric enough rope, he would hang himself, and that is exactly what Eric eventually did. He self-destructed, and Vince's company continued to flourish.

Did I ever, in my wildest imagination, think that Eric could put Vince out of business? No. Would I ever tell Eric that? No, but I do know that Eric could have been a good leader. In fact, if he had spent his energy coordinating the company and bringing people together, instead of consuming himself with the destruction of Vince McMahon, there's no telling what he might have accomplished.

When the Monday night wars were going on, some viewers made a habit out of switching back and forth between the WWF's *Monday Night RAW* program on the USA Network, and *Monday Nitro* on TNT. *Nitro* aired live every Monday night. *RAW*, on the other hand, was taped every other week. Two episodes were taped—one airing live on the night of the taping, the other airing on the following week.

On the December 29, 1998 *RAW* taping held in Worcester, Massachusetts, Mick Foley beat the Rock for the WWF title during the "second" hour of the taping. When that hour aired on the January 4, 1999 *RAW*, we were airing the show live from the Georgia Dome. Eric Bischoff instructed *Nitro* announcer Tony Schiavone to actually tell the fans what the outcome of the Foley-Rock title match would be on *RAW*, thinking that if the fans knew who wins the match, they wouldn't bother changing the channel to watch. *"Fans! Don't even think about changing the channel, because we've learned that on our competition's show, Mick Foley, who used to wrestle here as Cactus Jack, is going to win their world title! Talk about putting asses in the seats."*

Eric's brilliant idea backfired. Instead of keeping their televisions tuned to the live WCW show, the fans turned the channel to watch Foley win the title on a taped *RAW*! Thanks to the efforts of Eric, *RAW* beat *Nitro* that night in the ratings. *RAW* posted a 5.76 rating, while *Nitro* got a 4.96. Even worse, in the time period immediately after Schiavone told fans NOT to turn the dial, *RAW* hit a 6.2 rating, while *Nitro* got a 4.1! That means that due to Schiavone giving away the ending of the WWF's title match, ½ million people turned the channel!

That great strategy steered a lot of fans *from* WCW to the WWF. Instead of taking care of WCW's business, Eric was promoting the WWF's product. Except for a two-week period in September, the *RAW* ratings for the remainder of 1999 never dipped below a 5.1, while *Nitro* struggled to reach a 4.0.

Eric never bothered to have anybody analyze the trends in the business, or the pattern of the ratings. I had a lot of experience doing analysis, comparing WWF's business to that of WCW, so I approached Eric with the idea of doing the same thing for WCW, only in reverse. *"Eric, I have a lot of knowledge right here in my head. If there are things you want to know about the WWF, or if you just need some direction before you make decisions, I'm here and available. Just tap into me, and I will be open and helpful in any way that I can. I think it's healthy for the business to have competition."*

*"I don't want a competitor!"* And he went right back to, *"How much longer do you think Vince will be able to stay in business?"*

Eric could have brought me on board and tapped into the wealth of knowledge and experience that I had of the WWF. I had handled the WWF's payroll and knew what their talent made. I knew how the WWF was structured. I understood their revenue streams. I wasn't talking about proprietary information and documents. I was talking about solid information that I gleaned from working at one of the top levels of the company. I could have been a significant asset to Eric.

That's not what happened. Deep down, Eric was very insecure, although on the surface, he was full of himself because he had some initial success. As soon as Eric realized that I had an understanding of the business that he could never grasp, he treated me not as an ally—which I was—but as a threat, as if he were afraid that I would expose his lack of knowledge to his superiors.

Eric didn't have any experience in wrestling, and he worked for a television company run by people who knew nothing about it, either, so they were unable to monitor and guide him. Harvey Schiller didn't even like wrestling, so he didn't want to be bothered with it. He just wanted it to prosper so he wouldn't have to get involved. So basically, Eric reported to Schiller, but worked without anyone looking over his shoulder.

The problems between Eric and I began early after my arrival. When a situation crops up that is detrimental to business, I want to address the situation by offering a solution. I understand that you can't always openly express how you feel, which is what got Ole Anderson into trouble a lot of times, but by the same token, I have never been a yes-man. I speak up, and try to come up with solutions to problems.

I never wanted Eric's job. I knew that where he was at his best, I was at my weakest. I was not flamboyant. I am not the type of person who lights up a room when I walk in. I was not comfortable schmoozing with the people in the North Tower, either. If you put both Eric Bischoff and me into a room together, and give us each five minutes of your time, when you leave the room, who are you more apt to be impressed by? The answer is Eric Bischoff. I knew the product and the industry, so my talents were best served as an advisor. If I were involved in politics, my role would be as a member of the Cabinet, and not as the President. I could be an asset simply by giving advice gained from my years of experience. Eric could have tapped into me as a resource to help him make decisions.

As time went by, I began to think that Eric hired me with one thought in mind. *"How can I not hire him? Everybody in the North Tower is reading the dirt sheets. They all know that JJ was one of Vince McMahon's two right-hand men, and that he walked out of the WWF. They know he's available. How can I explain why I didn't hire him?"*

And yet, I was a threat to him because I was one of those people who could expose him. That's what drove the tension between us from the very beginning.

For those of you who don't know what the North Tower is, here's an explanation: In CNN Center, the center of the building is open almost to the top floor, with shops and a food court on the street level. There were tables and chairs where people could eat lunch, snack, or chat. They even produced a live show for TBS each day at three in the afternoon, shooting it in the lobby area. There are banks of offices with windows that overlook the center, hence the North Tower and the South Tower. A catwalk connects the two towers. The top executive offices at CNN were in the North Tower. The slang for top management was always "North Tower" or "suits in the North Tower." After two years or so under the Time Warner banner, WCW moved from what they called the South Tower at CNN Center to a separate facility near the outside perimeter in Smyrna.

One of the questions I had asked Jim Barnett before going back to work for WCW was, *"Jim, are there any 'land mines' that I should be aware of and avoid?"* Jim had warned me in advance of a situation where one of the producers of the TV, who was married, was having an affair with his assistant. Barnett said, *"Everybody knows about it. He has such a pretty wife. I don't know what he sees in that girl. She's kind of chubby."* It created a very difficult environment. There was constant friction because the relationship gave her power, and she abused it by making everybody's life difficult. We had to work around her whenever we wanted to get something done. There was a story going around that another employee had also hit on her. I don't know the details, but she filed a sexual harassment complaint against the employee. Of course, she was the apparent avenue by which Dallas Page got his pet projects written into the shows without the wrestling people knowing any details. [I'll expound more on that later.] Eric definitely knew about the affair, tolerated it, and never addressed it, in spite of all the problems it caused. As most affairs go, for her, it had its moments, but when the producer and his wife had another child, she was crushed. At that point, I was of the impression that the affair was still going on. Everyone consoled her, trying to ease her grief. It was as if she had a death in the family.

After a few weeks, I began to realize just how big of a mess the company was in. Since WCW was now a television company, the most important thing to the executives was ratings. They wanted to produce original television, rather than use the medium as a means to make a profit. They didn't understand that you can't structure a wrestling company around ratings. You had to run your company in accordance with the revenue streams, which means putting your focus on promoting profitable house shows and pay-per-views.

Based on the Nielsen information, I knew what the WWF's TV ratings were in 1997 and the early part of 1998. The information showed that WCW was beating the WWF. However, there was never a proportionate correlation between WCW's TV ratings and the pay-per-view buy rates. When Scott Hall and Kevin Nash left the WWF and "invaded" WCW as the NWO [New World Order] in May 1996, it had a big, initial impact on ratings. When Hulk Hogan joined them two months later, throwing off his babyface persona and showing up in WCW as a heel, it also made an impact. But even though Vince was losing the Monday night ratings war, he never panicked. He came from a wrestling background and could see what was happening. The angles being shot by WCW were one-shot angles. When they formulated the idea of the NWO, they never stopped to think, *"Where are we going with the angle once we introduce it?"*

Eventually, when the ratings pendulum started swinging back in favor of the WWF, Eric panicked. He became obsessed with the quarter-hour splits. Eric walked into a booking meeting one day and said, *"I want an angle every quarter hour."*

Instead of inserting our commercial breaks where they best fit into the flow of our show, he dictated the content to accommodate the positioning of the WWF's breaks. One of the WCW crew would sit in front of a monitor, watching the WWF show. When the WWF went to a commercial break, Eric would order something big to hook the fans who switched over from RAW during their break. In the old days, that's what we called "hot shot booking." Once you go in that direction, it's hard to return to the slower-paced format.

That spontaneity caused us to take breaks at very inopportune times. You can't always break away at a moment's notice. If the action in the ring is hot, and the people are into the angle, you should be able to stay with it until a logical breaking point can be found. We had television production people, who knew nothing about wrestling, dictating what was happening with the in-ring product in order to meet deadlines. *"Get this match over! We've gotta get to a break!"* At times, there was open conflict between the "TV production people" and the "wrestling people." Eric almost always supported the TV people because he was a former announcer himself. As a TV person knowing so little about the wrestling business, he certainly could never be considered a wrestling person. I am of the opinion that Bischoff was fearful of empowering the wrestling people within the company.

Eric got involved in creative at that point, thinking he could turn things around. He would sit in the booking room with a blank legal pad on the table in front of him. He had no clue about how to write a TV show, so an hour later, the paper would still be blank. Eric would eventually get up and leave the room, at which point we would start to lay out some ideas, fine-tune them, and make plans. Eric would come back later in the day and give the script his blessing.

There was a running—but true—joke to see how much of that script would change between the time he approved it and the time we went to TV. Talent would always get to him and talk him into making several changes. He was so manipulated by the talent that it became comical after a while.

In an attempt to push up television ratings, Eric also fell into several other traps. He placed too much emphasis on violence. He began to present violence for the sake of violence. *Extreme Championship Wrestling* is a good example of a promotion that fell into that trap. Their product, which was based on violence, garnered them a lot of attention and a cult following of fans in a small area of the northeast. The idea took off for awhile, but when your premise is pure violence, you will eventually reach a point where your product becomes passé. The fans go crazy when you slam your opponent through a table. When the novelty of that wears off, you stack one table on top of another and slam your opponent through both of them. That leads to three tables. At that point, you have to stack up four tables and leap onto them from the balcony. Once the fans have seen that several times, you have to introduce something else, so you bring out barbed-wire baseball bats, chainsaws, and you set off explosions in the ring. Eventually, you reach a point where you can't surpass the violence you presented the night before.

Eric also spent hours trying to come up with a way to "fool" the Internet fans. Since he didn't understand the importance of pay-per-view and house shows in the revenue stream, he gave away important matches on free television—matches that should have been built up over a long period of time. When *Nitro* came on the air on September 28, 1998, the first thing the announcer said was, *"Tonight, we have Hulk Hogan versus Bret Hart!"* That match should have built up over six months for a huge payoff on pay-per-view. Instead, the challenge was made at nine o'clock, the match was over three minutes after it started, and we could never again recapture that special, first-time confrontation between the two. Eric did that time after time, and sacrificed the lucrative revenue we could have derived from pay-per-view and house shows by doing a long-range buildup between the two stars.

# Chapter 34
# ATM Eric

Eric was very generous with Time-Warner's money. He gave out huge, guaranteed contracts to talent. The problem was, when the gross revenue streams dropped, and they did so to a dramatic extent, the WCW budget remained at an all-time high level. Our pay structure was much like that of the Atlanta Braves. When business is good, and Turner Field is filled with paying customers, the baseball franchise makes money, so higher labor costs can be justified. But when the stadium is half-empty and business declines, those high labor costs become a huge drain on the company resources.

When talent began jumping to WCW for the guaranteed contracts, Vince was forced to offer guaranteed contracts to his talent, but he controlled his labor costs by structuring most contracts with a "minimum downside guarantee" that still included an unlimited upside. When business was down, the talent would get a minimum guarantee, which would usually allow them to make a comfortable living during those slow business times. When business was good, they would be compensated at a much higher level. The downside guarantee allowed Vince to adjust his labor costs to the company's income.

An unwritten law says that to be a successful wrestling promoter, you have to keep your labor cost at 25% of your gross revenue. That rule holds true for a huge wrestling promotion like the WWF, or a small, independent promotion. Vince's numbers might be larger than the independents, but the percentages are applicable.

The labor cost at WCW was closer to 60%.

One big advantage to working for the WWF was the income from the separate merchandising and licensing agreements for all talent. It was reported numerous times that some WWF wrestlers made more money from the ancillary sources than they did from wrestling. I can see where that could have been true in some cases.

Merchandising is where Vince really revolutionized the business. He promoted the extra, ancillary forms of revenue and shared the proceeds with his talent. Some of the talent made a lot of money from merchandising. In the WWF, I saw the contracts and the agreements. There was a detailed accounting process put into place that allowed the company to send printouts to each talent, showing them exactly how many of each item had sold, and the exact dollar amount they would get. It would even factor in returned items.

Unfortunately, WCW never had the structure in place to develop a workable merchandising program. The WWF was light years ahead of WCW in that area. WCW only scratched the surface in setting up licensing and merchandising deals. Even if they had made more deals, the company didn't have the infrastructure to track and manage those revenue sources. They had no way to track what was being sold. Of course, guys like Kevin Nash and Scott Hall, who came from the WWF, were accustomed to getting an accounting of what was sold, so they were very suspicious over their merchandise payoffs in WCW.

At that point, could the problems with the company have been fixed? I'd like to think so. Would it have been a lot of work? Absolutely. If someone is taken to the hospital after being involved in a horrible car accident, with cuts all over their body, the surgeons have to decide which wound to treat first. Any one of the injuries could get infected. Will their efforts work? There's no way to know for sure. You can't always know the outcome of your actions, but you have to start somewhere. The longer you sit around and talk about the patient, and argue about where to start, the worse the patient will get. WCW was in that kind of shape, and many of the contracts were guaranteed for two or three years, but we had to start somewhere.

When I went to my first TV taping, Kevin Nash and Scott Hall took me by the arm and said, *"Let's go to the lunchroom and have a little talk."* After steering me to a table in a remote corner of the lunchroom, Kevin said in a low voice, *"Whatever you do, do not tell Eric Bischoff what kind of money we were making in the WWF."*

I laughed, Scott and Kevin smiled, and that was the end of our conversation. They told me everything I needed to know about Eric in that one statement. They knew that I was familiar with the specifics of their WWF contracts, and that I knew their earnings while at the WWF. They had negotiated a much sweeter deal with Eric, a high-dollar guaranteed deal, and they didn't want anybody rocking their boat. At that point, I didn't know what my role was going to be, or what was going to be required of me, so I didn't say anything.

There was one particular talent who worked for the WWF when I was there. He was a top name in the business and had a minimum downside guarantee with the WWF that was consistent with most contracts at the time. After I left and went to WCW, the WWF failed to renew his contract and he spent one year working on the independent circuit. All of a sudden, I heard that he was being brought on board by Eric. His guaranteed contract was more than double what he had been making with the WWF.

That was a classic example of someone I could have helped Eric with. I knew the numbers. I knew about his situation. How could Eric justify offering the guy such a lucrative contract, especially without talking to me, who could provide him with the details he needed to *negotiate* the contract. Even if it was just 15 seconds over the water cooler: *"What do you think he's worth? What's your read on him? What do you think his expectations will be?"*

I relate a lot of things to baseball, so let's say there was a guy who plays baseball, and for whatever reason, he leaves the big leagues and moves down to the Mexican leagues. As a major league team owner, you hear that he can still hit and catch, so you recruit him back out of the Mexican leagues and guarantee him a contract making three times what he was previously making in the major leagues. How many baseball teams could stay in business making decisions like that? Worse than that, if you had somebody with information that could help you make an "informed" decision about the fair market value of that player, why wouldn't you call that person in and say, *"This is what I've come up with. What do you think he's worth?"*

None of that ever happened. My experience was in the management of talent, and he didn't take advantage of it until it was too late.

When I started working for WCW, the legal department sent me a printout of the talent, along with details of their money deal. On my copy, the numbers of key people were blacked out. I wasn't privy to the information of those key people until Eric walked in one day and said, *"I really need your help."* At that point, the information became more forthcoming.

Eric's biggest problem surfaced when the talent realized that they could manipulate him. They quickly learned that if they walked into his office and threw a temper tantrum, they would get whatever they asked for.

"I need you to pay for my hotel rooms."

"I won't fly coach. It's first-class or nothing."

"I want my own dressing room."

There was a time when just about everybody on the roster was traveling first-class because Eric bought into their song-and-dance act. I got calls all the time, *"Effective today, so-and-so flies first class."* The guys with contracts—contracts that were binding on both WCW and the talent—were even able to get their contracts rewritten in their favor. The hole just kept getting deeper and deeper. Behind his back, Eric Bischoff was referred to as *ATM Eric.* If you pushed the right buttons, he'd spit cash out at you.

The wrestling business had reached a point where the mentality of a wrestler was, *"Me, me, me!"* I know that everybody is interested in getting the best deal for themselves and their family, but it got to the point where the talent devoured the carcass of WCW, bones and all, until there was nothing left for anybody.

Diamond Dallas Page, a neighbor and friend of Eric Bischoff, was getting a big push with the company—a push that someone with his skills, look, timing, and age, wouldn't have gotten if someone like Eric hadn't been in his corner. I really didn't have a problem with that. There are a lot of success stories of somebody being in the right place at the right time. Breaks come in different forms, and people do what they can to help people. In fact, initially, I was happy for Page. I could relate to Page because he had the same kind of passion for the business that I did when I was young. He was finally getting the opportunity that he had dreamed about and worked so hard for all of his life. I was genuinely very happy for him. I remember my first Christmas there, when he and his wife, Kimberly, came to the office wearing Santa caps. They brought in a couple of cases of White Star champagne and gave a bottle to everybody in the office. I thought that was a classy thing to do and wrote him a thank you note to tell him so.

I also remember meeting Page when I was in the WWF. Page came to *Wrestlemania VI* in Toronto. He wasn't famous at that point, but he loaned us his pink Cadillac convertible for the event. Vince even allowed him to drive the car down the aisle for the entrance of Greg Valentine, Honky Tonk Man, and Jimmy Hart. Dallas was so excited to be a part of Wrestlemania. He was a big fan and seemed to be very passionate about the business.

As time went by, though, I saw the other side of the coin. The influence that Page had with Eric became detrimental to the company. Whenever he had a segment on TV, Page went into business for himself, and did things that hurt the continuity of the show.

I can recall one instance vividly. Kevin Sullivan and I were watching the matches from the back of the arena. The show was running smoothly, everything was on schedule, and we felt good about what we had planned for the main event later that evening. At that moment, however, Dallas Page was in the ring with his opponent. All of a sudden, Page and his opponent leave the ring and fight their way through the audience. Kevin and I just stood there, looking at each other, asking, *"Where did this come from? Who told them to leave the ring?"* They continued to fight as they worked their way up to a secluded corner of the building, where special lighting suddenly came on and lit the scene.

Special lighting doesn't just happen. Somebody had to know that the spot was coming.

When we laid out a show, we had specific plans for everybody. If the finish for the main event called for somebody to hit somebody else with a chair, we weren't going to allow anybody else to use a chair on the show. The chair was an integral part of what we were trying to sell in the most important match of the night, and we didn't want the effect watered down by using it twice. We didn't want any match to overshadow the main event, either. We had an agenda laid out that built the show from the first match to the main event.

And yet, Page surprised us constantly. He would *just happen* to find props under the ring—props that had no business being there. He would have a match that had no continuity to anything else in the program. Of course, when he came to the back, he was glowing about whatever his concept had been, and how well it had been executed, never realizing how detrimental it was to the overall program as a whole.

You can't put somebody like Kevin Sullivan in charge, and then have Diamond Dallas Page unexpectedly go into business for himself on television, or book his own matches for the upcoming pay-per-view. For the overall good of the company, and the hoped-for-success, Page should have worked together *with* Kevin. Instead, we wound up with two factions of talent working against each other. There was no harmony, no continuity to the product, and no strategy. Page didn't fit into the big picture because he was painting his own portrait.

I never questioned Dallas Page's work ethic. I don't question his passion and love for the business. I am just very critical of how he used his influence to the detriment of the company, even to the point of manipulating himself into winning the WCW world title on two separate occasions. Of course, maybe that wasn't a big deal. In 1999, the world title didn't mean what it did a decade or two earlier. A year later, the belt would be worn by David Arquette and Vince Russo. That being the case, being the world champion during those years could be looked at as somewhat of an embarrassment.

While we're on the subject of the world title, there has to be a prize, or a pot of gold at the end of the rainbow. Whether it's the green jacket presented to the winner of the Masters Golf Tournament in Augusta, the cup held aloft by the men's champion in tennis at Wimbledon, or the yellow shirt worn by Lance Armstrong for the last six years at the Tour de France in bicycling, the prize has to be perceived as having value. To trash it, or demean the value of it, takes away from the aura of winning it. When you make a Hollywood actor, David Arquette, the world heavyweight champion in his *first professional match,* where do you go from there? Even the fans begin to wonder, *"Why are those guys trying so hard to win something that has no value?"*

When you study the lineage of the WWF Intercontinental heavyweight title, you'll learn that Pat Patterson became the first person to hold the title when he won a tournament in Rio de Janeiro in 1979. There's no record of that match ever taking place (because it didn't), but at least it was a logical enough beginning of the story. In the days of the regional territories, the fans didn't get hung up questioning the validity of those claims, as long as there was continuity to everything else you did. The one problem the fans did have was that the promoters would have world title matches in the towns, and yet the title would almost never change hands. There was always a fear that the fans would realize that and would quit coming to the matches. The other side to the argument was that if you changed the title with too much frequency to alleviate that problem, you would diminish the validity of the title and the fact that it really *is* hard to become the champion.

It comes down to understanding what your product is by adopting an overall philosophy, then following whatever path it is you choose to take. If you look back at the history of the wrestling business, every territory was unique in its own right. Each promoter had their own style and adopted their personal, overall philosophy of presenting their product to the general public. However, above all else, they understood that they had to protect the credibility of their product. If you don't have a wrestling background, you can't understand that concept.

Bill Watts is a good example of someone who had a good philosophy of his product.

Bill required a logical explanation for *everything* that happened on TV and in the ring. The person watching television at home could adopt what we call a *temporary suspension of disbelief*. It was no different than going to a movie theater. You buy your ticket, a box of popcorn, and a soft drink. When the lights go down, the movie screen fills your world. If the movie is good, you forget where you are and put your troubles out of your mind. Eventually, you forget that you're watching a movie. You forget about the special effects. You become a part of what is taking place on the screen. When the shark leaps out of the water in *Jaws*, you jump. *Temporary suspension of disbelief*. When the movie ends, and the credits begin to roll, you come back to reality.

Wrestling is very much like that. Even today, when the promoters and wrestlers themselves admit that the wrestling matches are predetermined, the people who buy tickets want to believe that what they're seeing is real. In fact, some *do* believe. The rest of the people, who don't believe, still want us to make an attempt to convince them, because they want to be entertained. If the quality of the product is at its very best, it becomes real to those fans, and that's when wrestling is successful. That was always the philosophy of Bill Watts, Eddie Graham, Verne Gagne, and most other promoters.

One of the things that really griped me was something I saw happen with Bob Ryder. Ryder is currently working with the Jarrett's TNA promotion, but at the time, he was working as an announcer for WCW online. He also was the owner of the 1wrestling.com website and owned a travel agency in Louisiana.

WCW was trying to get Tank Abbott over, so on the April 24, 2000 taping of *Nitro* in Rochester, New York, an angle was set up where he would go out to the ring to pitch a fit about something. The camera crew went down to ringside for a web interview. When Tank got to ringside, he grabbed Ryder (who was there to do the announcing) and threw him into the ring. He proceeded to pull up Ryder's shirt, expose his belly, and slap him on his love handles, leaving pink handprints behind. Immediately afterwards, Ryder went back to his booth and said, *"I knew that was gonna happen. We rehearsed it this afternoon, and I said it was okay."*

Now, why on earth did Bob Ryder—an announcer—have to tell the people that he was in on it?

To me, the secret of the business was very simple: magic. I was always fascinated by magic. When FOX aired the special that exposed the secrets of magic, and showed how the stage illusions were done, magic lost its mystique. The methods used to present the illusion were simple ... almost too simple.

When I was a kid, I was smart without being smart. In other words, no one had to smarten me up. And when I was with a circle of wrestlers, I conducted myself in an appropriate manner. I never asked them questions. In time, they respected me because they knew I was smart without being smartened up. When the business got away from that, and everyone wanted to be smart and say they were smart, then the public as a whole lost respect for the business.

In many cases, when a father takes his son to see wrestling, it's because his son wants to see the action in a live venue. The father knows that wrestling is make-believe, but he wants to go with his kid. If the performances they watch are presented in a believable fashion, the father gets caught up in the emotion of the action in the ring. He starts cheering. He gets mad at the villain and wants to throw something at him. When the show is over, he goes home and goes to bed.

Now, did the show change his mind? Does he believe wrestling is real?

No, probably not. His opinion hasn't changed, but because the performance was presented so well, for a portion of the time he was at the arena, he got wrapped up in the emotion, and for a short time, actually believed.

Jerry Jarrett was quite an innovator. He was the first person to present scaffold matches, evening gown matches, and countless other matches that were based on some kind of a stipulation. At the time, he was criticized by the other promoters for being outlandish, but Jerry was very successful with what he did because he had educated his audience to that product. However, he never compromised the credibility of the titles that he featured in his promotion.

When Vince McMahon would bring in a celebrity, he would choreograph something to capitalize on the celebrity's name and reputation, but he would use them in a way that wouldn't overshadow his regular talent. For instance, Chuck Norris was involved in the 1994 *Survivor Series* match between Undertaker and Yokozuna. Jeff Jarrett ran down to ringside and shoved Chuck. Chuck gave Jeff a superkick, knocked him on his butt, stepped over him, and walked out. Chuck's involvement got a big pop from the fans, but it didn't kill Jeff Jarrett's career and it didn't overshadow the entire show. At *Wrestlemania XIV, XV,* and *XVI*, Vince talked Pete Rose into allowing Kane to drop him with a tombstone piledriver.

That was one end of the spectrum. WCW was at the other. As I said, they made David Arquette the world champion in the first professional match of his career, but another example of their insanity took place at the *Road Wild* pay-per-view in Sturgis, South Dakota, on August, 8, 1998. The main event featured Hulk Hogan and Eric Bischoff against Diamond Dallas Page and Jay Leno.

Jay Leno is a tremendous person and fun to be around. He was very friendly, approachable, and affable to everybody at the show, and I think he enjoyed the experience. I know he enjoyed being in Sturgis for the Sturgis Rally and Race. He even brought his own bike.

Near the end of the main event, with Hulk on his knees, Page tagged out and Jay came into the ring, wearing a pair of baggy pajamas. He proceeded to clamp an armbar on Hulk. Hulk Hogan—the greatest attraction our business has ever seen in my lifetime—was on his knees with a look of anguish on his face, selling Jay Leno's armbar.

When the matches were over, I left with Kevin Sullivan and Jimmy Hart. We had a long, 30-minute ride to our hotel. There was an uncomfortable silence for the first ten minutes or so. I finally said, *"I can see the picture in the newspapers tomorrow morning. Hulk Hogan on his knees, begging off from a Jay Leno armbar. My, God. Where have we taken our business?"*

Jimmy didn't think it was a big deal. Apparently, they had rehearsed the whole thing the day before in California. He pointed out that Hulk had endeared himself to Jay, and at some point, Jay Leno's door would be open for him. By contrast, Kevin and I saw it all as a very strong indicator that it was the beginning of the end. It had nothing to do with Jay Leno as a person. I don't blame him for anything, but it was a sad day—not only for WCW, but for the wrestling business.

On June 14, 1998, as we were preparing to go live with the *Great American Bash* pay-per-view in Baltimore, Maryland, somebody came to me and said, *"The production office got a phone call. Someone is trying to get a message to Bret Hart. Apparently, his father, Stu Hart, has died."*

Eric Bischoff told Bret about the call and offered to charter a flight to Calgary. Meanwhile, I took my phone book out of my briefcase and called Stu's house in Calgary. When Stu answered the phone, I said, *"Stu, we just got a phone call from someone who said you were dead. Thank God it's not true. This is somebody's horrible idea of a joke, and I apologize that I even had to make this call."*

I hurriedly found Bret and said, *"I just spoke with your father and everything is fine at home. This was a horrible, cruel hoax, and I have no idea who would do something like that."*

Even with my assurances, Bret was shaken, but like a true professional, he went on with the show, and teamed with Hulk Hogan to wrestle Randy Savage and Roddy Piper. That's the unfortunate side of being a celebrity.

Kevin Nash was different from other talent who came from the WWF. He knew the WWF would always be a force in the wrestling business, so he kept an ongoing communication with Vince. It paid off because he went back to work for Vince in 2002. Kevin wasn't a young kid when he was with WCW. He had bad knees and had been through multiple knee surgeries, and yet, he was a lot smarter than any of the others. He knew how to promote himself.

At the time, Eric Bischoff was more into being a big-time producer than a "wrestling" promoter. He (or should I say, WCW) was paying a small fortune each week to have a special effects expert at each TV. Talent would spend hours being decked out with putty, make-up, costumes, etc., in preparation for Eric's skits. Kevin Nash preferred to mirror the Hollywood gig, as opposed to being in the ring and having to expend physical energy.

At the September 1, 1997 *Nitro* in Pensacola, Florida, Eric featured a skit with Kevin, Marcus Bagwell, Sean Waltman, and Konnan mocking the Horsemen. I always tried to be objective. I didn't like the mocking of the Horsemen, but it wasn't just because they were mocking the Horsemen. I just didn't think it was good television. It wasn't the best use of Kevin's talents, either, but he had fun with it. Kevin was very smart. He was being rewarded very well financially, and he knew how to position himself politically, so he did what Eric wanted him to do. Kevin knew how to play Eric like a violin. He was very good at it.

But there was one fundamental difference between Kevin Nash and Dallas Page. Kevin wasn't pitching the ideas to Eric. He was doing what Eric wanted and keeping him happy, but at the same time, he was having fun.

Page, on the other hand, was brainstorming extravagant segments that featured himself, and he was selling Eric on the ideas. Page went into business for himself, and not the company, with Eric's full support behind him. He also enlisted the support and cooperation of the TV production (non-wrestling) people because they didn't know any better. A show would be written and the Dallas Page segment would be listed on the run-down sheet, but nobody had any idea about the content. All too often, it would be like having a TV drama build for an hour to a climax, only to have an unrelated segment (Page's) inserted to air before the final 15-minute payoff. That segment was a complete story unto itself, complete with its own beginning and ending, with the ending often being more dramatic than the ending to the main show.

More often than not, that extra segment would feature the disciples of Dallas Page, such as Chris Kanyon and Ernest "The Cat" Miller. They had their own little clique and cast of characters. To some degree, the influence of those inner-circle groups on people like Bischoff contributed to the ultimate demise of WCW.

Since 1997, Kanyon had been wrestling under a mask as Mortis, a mid-card level wrestler. At the April 9, 1998 *Thunder* taping in Tallahassee, Florida, Kanyon posed as a fan in the audience and jumped into the ring, attacking Raven. He repeated the angle on two Nitro shows in April, attacking Billy Kidman. The angle went completely over the fans' heads. They didn't know who Kanyon was, and as far as we could tell, the fans didn't realize that it was the same person each week. If anything, the angle seemed to encourage fans to jump into the ring. On the May 4 *Nitro* from Indianapolis, Indiana, Kanyon was walking through the audience, posing as a drink vendor. During Perry Saturn's match, Kanyon jumped over the barricade from the audience side, got into the ring, and clobbered Perry with the metal tray he had been using to vend drinks. The big blowoff came at *Slamboree* on May 17. In the middle of the match between Dallas Page and Raven, a man in a SWAT team uniform ran into the ring. He dramatically took off his SWAT mask to show that he was actually Mortis. He then ripped off his Mortis mask and posed in the ring as Chris Kanyon. He got no reaction from the audience because nobody knew who he was, or why he had done what he did. More than likely, the people simply didn't care. The wrestling writers would just stare at each other in disbelief, while the TV people would smile proudly, as if they had just witnessed *Gone With The Wind*.

Eric appointed Kevin Nash as the liaison between talent and the booking committee. Kevin didn't want the booking position because he knew what a thankless job it was, especially when you're talent. Everybody thinks booking is an easy, cushy job, but it requires hours of hard, tedious work. It's not easy to start with a blank piece of paper and create a television show. Ask Eric Bischoff about that. You never get credit when you're successful, but you always get the blame whenever there's a downturn, or a period perceived as failure. And in time, every booker burns out. On the other hand, talent liaison was an ideal situation for Kevin. It gave him the ability to sound off to Eric and protect his own position. I don't fault Kevin Nash for that. In fact, I think it was a good move on his part. At the time, Kevin Sullivan was the official leader on the booking side, and Nash wanted to keep it that way because he had a good relationship with Sullivan. They understood each other and saw things in a common light.

Eric treated Chris Jericho the same way he did Steve Austin and Cactus Jack. He didn't recognize their individual talent, or have any idea of their true value to the company. Eric disrespected Chris and made no effort to pay him at a level equal to his abilities. Eric made life so miserable for Chris that it led to a confrontation. When that happened, Chris had no option but to move on. I called Chris and told him I regretted the decision he made to leave. I looked at him as a great talent and was dismayed that Eric didn't make every effort to keep him. I meant every word of what I said to him. What took place after he left speaks for itself. Chris left WCW in June 1999 and went to work for Vince. It was a good move because he has had a phenomenal run in the WWF.

I worked closely with Diana Myers, an attorney for Turner Sports whose full-time job was to oversee contracts. I hate to keep repeating myself, but like most of her peers, she knew nothing about wrestling. Diana is the person who came to my office and told me, *"Jericho's gone. He's finished, but Eric has already hired somebody to replace him—somebody who's better than Jericho."*

Of course, my mind immediately started to race through the talent. *Who could the replacement be who is "better" than Chris Jericho?* I couldn't come up with an answer on my own, so I asked her, *"Who?"*

*"Shane Douglas,"* she replied.

Now this is not a knock on Shane Douglas. Shane is a good guy who works very hard, but I was around Shane when he wrestled as *Dean Douglas* in the WWF. He wasn't very happy there and felt that he was being held back—and that may have been the case—so he left. He had a good run prior to that with *Extreme Championship Wrestling*, where a lot of what went on was built around him, but I knew he wasn't going to fill the shoes of Chris Jericho. Shane came in, but he never reached the level of success that Jericho did.

I tell the story to once again underscore the fact that Eric Bischoff didn't know talent. While Diana Myers made the comment about Douglas being better than Jericho, it was Eric who sold her on the idea. Eric's attitude was that Chris didn't have any value to the company, so he didn't care if he left.

Bobby Eaton was also mishandled by Eric, although Bobby brought some of his problems on himself. Bobby lived in Charlotte at a time when Eric was becoming more cost conscious. Eric wanted people to move to Atlanta, so he made a rule: If you choose to live in another city, we will provide transportation to the shows from Atlanta, so you are responsible for your own transportation from where you live to the Atlanta airport. That was one of the cost-cutting measures Eric took when the high-guarantee money contracts became unwieldy. This rule didn't apply to the big names like Ric Flair, or agents like Arn Anderson. They were both from Charlotte, as well, but Bobby was strictly talent.

The transportation issue played right into a second cost-cutting measure. There was a list of contracts coming up on their 90-day cycle, so Eric began to ask, *"Who can we let go?"*

I don't want to say that I looked out for people just because they were my friends, but I always had a soft spot for Bobby Eaton. When I expressed my opinions on who was important to the company, Bobby was at the top of my list. He would go out, work hard, and give the fans a quality match every night. I went to bat for Bobby more than a couple of times to keep him from being cut. To protect Bobby, I suggested that we use him at the Power Plant—the WCW training gym—as a trainer, which made it easier to justify keeping him on board.

Bobby kept a low profile and didn't draw attention to himself, until he failed to turn in a rental car on schedule, which resulted in a huge amount of expenses for the company. Bobby stoked the fire even more when he didn't show up at the Power Plant for a couple of weeks. The fallout resulted in Eric letting Bobby go in April 2000.

Whenever one of the boys was released from their contract, they received a letter from the company. To most of the guys, who were struggling to make ends meet, that was devastating news, so I made it a practice to call and warn them before the FedEx package arrived. Whenever the guys heard my voice on the phone, they knew it must mean trouble. Most of them were appreciative that somebody cared enough to take the time to say, *"I don't want you to get this letter, open it up, and deal with a bad situation that you didn't know was coming. I would rather be a man and call to tell you about it. This isn't my decision. Legal drafted the letter and Eric signed it, then they called me to tell me the letter was going out."* I had been talent long enough to know that I would appreciate a call from somebody so that I could prepare my wife before the letter arrived.

When I called Bobby at his home, his son answered the phone. I could hear Bobby in the background, but he never got on the phone. Bobby holds some ill feelings towards me over being let go. I felt really bad when I heard that Bobby told people that I never gave him the courtesy of a phone call or a letter, and that we just stopped paying him. That is absolutely not true. I never responded to those comments because of the circumstances. I knew the loss of his job was devastating to him and his family. He said those things when he was going through a very tough time in his life, so I didn't take it personally, but we both knew the truth. The only person I told about the situation was Terry Taylor. Terry was very close to Bobby, so I asked him to call and set Bobby straight.

The next time I saw Bobby, it was at the 2004 *Mid-Atlantic Wrestling Legends Fanfest* in Charlotte. Bobby was very cordial and gave me a big hug. To this day, Bobby is one of my favorite people in the business. If there was a definition in the dictionary for "nice guys," it would read: *Bobby Eaton*.

There was a period of time after I had been with the company for two years when the bloom was off the rose. The company was struggling again. Vince was way out in front in both the TV ratings and attendance at the house shows.

Jamie Engle was Eric's executive assistant. I knew Janie from when she worked for Joe Blanchard, the wrestling promoter in San Antonio. She also worked for Jimmy Crockett after he moved to Dallas. One day at WCW, Janie told me that she had learned so much from me, and thanked me for teaching her most of what she knew about working for a wrestling company. I suspect that Janie may have finally gotten through to Eric in his hour of desperation. At a TV taping in Bangor, Maine, she reminded him that there was someone right under his nose who could help him ... someone who would be happy to help. I was surprised to get a call from Eric at my hotel room in Boston following the drive back from Maine. It was very late that night, and Eric never called me about anything. He asked me to meet him in his office when I got back to Atlanta.

When I arrived in Atlanta the next day, I went to Eric's office. You could have knocked me over with the proverbial feather when Eric said, *"I misread you. I should have tapped into everything you brought with you. I realize now that I need to find a more meaningful role for you, and get you more involved. I really do need your help."*

That admission was a gauge of the desperation that Eric was facing. I said, *"Great! That's been my intent from day one. All I've wanted to do is help."*

At that point, I launched into a subject that I thought needed to be addressed. Through a reliable third party, I had knowledge of a situation that took place at a TV taping. A third party, who was somebody I respected very much and had known for a long time, told me that they walked into a room while on location where drugs were being used openly during the TV taping. I didn't want to betray any confidences, so I spoke to Eric in general terms, without naming names. *"Eric, you really need to be in tune with what's going on around you. You have drugs being used openly on location. If there was a police raid, or if word leaked out that drugs were being used, with the ideals that our parent company has, they would shut us down in a heartbeat, and we'll all be looking for jobs."*

To say the least, Eric was dumbfounded. *"Going back to what I was talking about earlier,"* he said, *"I really do need your help. I want to help secure your family by putting you under contract."*

Only Eric knows his true motive for putting me under contract, but I always wondered if it had been a means of silencing me. As I look back, I think Eric thought I had witnessed the drug situation personally. He didn't ask any other questions about the drugs and the subject was never brought up again. Regardless of his motivation, he gave me a three-year contract: $165,000, $195,000, and $235,000. By my third year, I would be making slightly more than I was making at Titan before the salary reduction.

At first, Eric expanded my responsibilities. He had me book all the house show matches and take care of the finishes at those shows. That allowed creative more time to focus on the TV. I was even invited to travel with Eric and the "TV production" people on the private charter, but I opted to stay over and fly commercial with the other wrestling people. I may have been in management, but my feelings and loyalties never changed.

I was also given the task of overseeing the Power Plant. When the WCW offices were moved from CNN Center to Smyrna, the Power Plant remained in the original leased building that was part of an industrial strip mall. Part of the reasoning for moving WCW to the chosen location in Smyrna was the flexibility to incorporate the new Power Plant into the same structure with the new offices. It was even suggested that WCW could provide tours of the new Power Plant for a fee, similar to the public tours conducted for a fee at CNN Center, but WCW never went through with the plan. The building we moved into was chosen because of the cost, plus the potential to expand and grow. There was a section of the new building that was a huge, open warehouse with a large, interior, roll-down door that led to a second section of the warehouse. It was the perfect location for the new Power Plant. The wrestlers entered and exited from one of two doors that led to the side parking area. There was another door to the Power Plant in the main WCW office section, and a receptionist sat there to permit access. WCW employees were not permitted back there unless on official business. The main warehouse space had no showers or locker rooms, and no office space to speak of, so we met at least once a month with designers and engineers to remodel the warehouse and make it fit our requirements.

We had a progress chart on the wall that covered all phases of construction. The construction took longer than we expected, so the school went on hiatus for a couple of months when the lease on the old facility ran out. WCW couldn't move in until the county issued a Certificate of Occupancy after everything had been completed and inspected. We installed men's and women's lockers and showers, and added a second floor accessible by stairs at the end of the building. I don't remember the exact numbers, but I am certain that Turner spent well over $500,000 in renovations before the work was completed. The whole project probably took six to seven months to complete.

Eric put Paul Orndorff in charge of the new Power Plant and Paul reported to me. Mike Graham, who was a trainer at the school, also reported to me. Prior to that, Jody Hamilton had been in charge of training, but he was put in charge of ring assignments and transportation, maintenance of the rings, and construction of two new rings for use in the new Power Plant facility. I have remained friends with Jody over the years and I respect him greatly. I worked closely with Jody Hamilton and spent a lot of time observing the young kids who were being trained there.

Bill Goldberg was a product of the old Power Plant, and Jody deserves most of the credit for Bill's development. I know Jody was disappointed that he did not have direct involvement in the training aspect of the new school. He still stopped by on occasion, but being the professional that he is, he didn't want to interfere with Paul's new responsibilities.

There was also a wrestler named Bob Sapp who trained at the new Power Plant until the day the doors closed. Bob had played pro football and his nickname was "The Beast." Bob went on to become a pop-culture phenomenon in Japan. Japanese media reported Bob as having *"leveraged his success in a novelty sport into a level of superstardom rarely experienced by the country's top baseball players, rock musicians or actors."* He has appeared in thousands of interviews, appeared on hundreds of TV programs, been a pitchman for more than 20 products, and made in excess of $3 million in 2003. He recently appeared in the movie *Elektra,* the spin-off from the 2003 film *Daredevil.* I'd like to think that Paul Orndorff, Mike Graham, and I, in some small measure, helped prepare Bob for his success. He is a great guy. He paid his dues and I am proud and happy for him.

For some reason, once my contract was in place, my relationship with Eric Bischoff really began to go south. If Eric and I held any negative feelings toward each other, they really began to manifest themselves. At one point, he was looking for a way to fire me in spite of my contract. Eric actually called me into a meeting in his office with someone from HR. After the meeting, which was short and to the point, the HR rep came into my office and told me that as I walked out of Eric's office, Eric said, *"He's got a bull's-eye on his back."* The rep said, *"I just want you to know that you do not have to be worried about your job. He cannot and will not fire you. We will not allow that to happen."*

By spring 1999, Kevin Sullivan and I both knew the company was a freight train heading for a brick wall. On more than one occasion, I would sit with attorney Diana Myers and tell her, *"The company can't be managed like the Atlanta Braves, or any other entertainment venture the company has. We have to get a handle on our labor costs if we're going to survive. If not, we're the Titanic headed for the iceberg."* Diana would give me a puzzled look, like she was oblivious to what was going on around her.

WCW was running like a ship without a rudder, and the talent continued to go into business for themselves. One of the worst examples of that took place on the January 4, 1999 episode of *Nitro* from Atlanta, Georgia, when Hulk Hogan pushed Kevin Nash down with one finger and pinned him, winning the WCW world heavyweight title. *One finger!*

On July 5, 1999, we had a live Nitro from the Georgia Dome. The North Tower suits all made an appearance that night. When they saw 25,338 cheering, screaming fans in the building, they thought all was well. They were completely oblivious to the Goldberg blunders that took place behind-the-scenes.

First of all, we had spent a lot of money to get the Goldberg monster truck to the building, and then it was never shown on camera. It just sat in the back of the arena, parked in a dark corner. Secondly, Bill Goldberg was scheduled to make his big, return appearance that night. Heavy metal group Megadeth played for what seemed like forever and went on very late into the show. I don't know if any wrestling fans were still tuned in when they finished, as the rating for that segment hit 2.13—one of our lowest ever—but Megadeth finished their set as the stage filled with smoke. Goldberg was supposed to emerge from the smoke, making his triumphant return to WCW. For some reason, or perhaps for no reason, we went to a commercial break ... just as Bill walked out through the smoke. I don't think anybody had time to recognize him. It was a comedy of errors and a horrible, horrible night. I remember thinking, *"The iceberg is already on the Titanic's radar screen."*

What I didn't realize was that the iceberg had already ripped a hole in the side of our ship, and we were taking on water. Eric didn't realize how much trouble the company was in, either, until it was too late. He started running to cover his tracks, but it was much, much too late.

At that point, the company had lost $15 million and was losing $5 million a month. We were producing five hours of original programming every week—three hours on Monday and two hours on Thursday—and we didn't have the talent pool necessary to sustain that level of programming. My fear all along was that our shows were going to follow the *"Who Wants To Be A Millionaire"* route. In 1997, when we hit the number one spot, the executives started talking: *"Imagine how much advertising we could sell if we air a show every night!"* Nobody took into consideration the law of simple supply and demand.

The production budget for *Monday Nitro* was $600,000 an episode. Nobody was held accountable for their extravagance. If they wanted to blow up four cars, somebody went out, bought four cars, and set them on fire. When Sting was using the "crow" gimmick, they contracted an animal trainer to bring a crow, and paid him $5,000! They had to buy three plane tickets: one for the trainer, one for the crow, and one for the backup crow. All of that for a 5-second shot of the crow, then the camera switched over to Sting.

As if that wasn't bad enough, two weeks later, they brought the crow back ... and paid another $5,000 plus expenses.

Logic tells me that if they wanted to use the crow as a continuing part of the storyline with Sting, they should have shot video of the crow from every conceivable angle the first time they brought the crow in. Later, when they wanted a different shot of the crow for the new segment, all they had to do was edit a shot of the crow from the tape into the new segment. I'd like to think that I learned fiscal responsibility from my many years in the business, but that kind of thinking has nothing to do with experience. It's just good, old, common sense.

By late summer 1999, corporate people who had never been involved in WCW business before—numbers people—started to take a hard look at the books. They started asking questions, wanting to know things like why the company had lost so much money. Of course, Eric didn't have an answer. If he had an answer, he could have done something to prevent the loss. Somebody from accounting called me, asking me to participate in a breakfast meeting offsite, and for the first time since I started to work for the company, I was asked for details about how the company was being run. Based on those interviews with several key personnel, a meeting of WCW staff was called for the following week. The meeting was held in a conference room at CNN Center. Eric was the last person to arrive and he sat in the back of the room—on the floor. We had no idea what the purpose of the meeting was, but it was basically Harvey Schiller discussing how Eric had gotten us to where we were.

When the meeting was over, Eric bolted out of the room. The rest of us went to a place called *Jocks & Jills Sports Grill*, which was located in the atrium of the CNN Center. We were all looking at each other like, *"Well, what was that all about?"* The consensus was that Harvey Schiller's speech came across as a vote of confidence for Eric Bischoff! That made no sense! Eric was the reason the company was in the shape it was, and yet, Schiller had encouraged us to band together and stand behind Eric. It also seemed strange that Schiller never asked Eric to speak. Eric wasn't asked to throw a new light on things, give new direction, or do anything that might uplift and encourage us. Fifteen minutes after we sat down, we saw Eric walking by. Somebody yelled out, *"Eric, would you like to join us?"*

*"No,"* he huffed. *"I have to get back to the office. I have work to do."* He never looked in our direction, he didn't make eye contact, and his voice dripped with sarcasm, implying we were all being lazy because we were taking time to eat. He was *much* too busy to consort with the likes of us.

One day, I was talking about baseball with Ross Forman, the editor of *WCW Magazine*. Ross and I are both big baseball fans. While we were talking, Eric walked by and asked, *"What are you two talking about?"* He said it abruptly and in an angry tone of voice.

*"We're just talking about baseball,"* I answered.

*"Baseball? We're losing $5 million a month and you two are talking about BASEBALL?"*

He threw his hands up into the air and stormed walking down the hallway. It was obvious that he was in a panic. He didn't know what he could do to fix the situation. How could he? If you don't know how you got to where you are, how can you possibly know how to get back?

Eric Bischoff was fortunate enough to have had some initial success, and he definitely increased the gross revenues, but since he didn't have a wrestling background, he structured the company in such a way that the expenses were way out of line with the revenue. When business leveled off, and later took a dip, he was saddled by set costs that he couldn't adjust. That's what brought about his ultimate demise. I've said it several times before, but I'll say it again because it bears repeating. Nobody above him understood it, either, because they weren't wrestling people. They didn't understand the uniqueness of the wrestling business. When the people from AOL began to look at the books, Eric's superiors were thinking to themselves, *"How do we explain the fact that we thought everything was okay, but now we're losing $5 million a month with no indication that it will stop?"*

Bill Busch, who was the Vice President of Strategic Planning for WCW, had been with the company since 1990, originally as an accountant. He was also Eric's right-hand man. Like everyone else at WCW, in the beginning, Bill believed in Eric and his ideas.

Whenever Eric would get an idea, Bill would work up number projections and put the idea into presentation form. As an example, if Eric wanted to hire Bret Hart for "X" number of dollars, Bill would determine the impact of hiring Bret. Bill would project the financial gain or loss if the pay-per-view numbers increased to a certain level, or if house show business improved. After Bill determined the amount of money it would take to implement the idea, Eric would peruse the pitch to make sure it was presented as something positive for WCW. He simply crunched the numbers for Eric. He did confide to me that he personally questioned the potential rewards versus the financial risk, and that he would not have implemented many of the deals, but he was never asked for his opinion. His job was to crunch the numbers and provide Eric with ammunition to sell the idea to Harley Schiller. Eric would take the reports to the North Tower and meet privately with Schiller.

If anybody in the company knew Eric Bischoff's shortcomings and limitations, it was Bill Busch. Bill was the one guy who knew what had to be done to pull the company out of the financial hole it found itself in. He wasn't a wrestling person, either, but he was smart enough to ask questions. He was the first person to pull me aside and tap into what I knew from my years in the business.

On September 9, 1999, Bill Busch was told that Eric was being reassigned, and that he—Bill Busch—would be running the company and would be promoted to Executive Vice President. "Being reassigned" was a nice way of saying that Eric was being sent home. Eric didn't go hungry, though. He still had time on his contract, so WCW had to continue paying him.

After taking over, one of the first things Bill said was, *"ATM Eric is gone. There will be no more fat deals. We need to take a close look at each talent, determine what they have to offer the company, and offer them a fair contract with incentives for performance."* Many times, my opinion was asked about various talents. I didn't have any say on what they were offered. I was just a sounding board.

I quickly developed a rapport with Bill Busch when he took over. Gary Juster did, too. Gary was a Vice President, and he had been around the business for a long time, but he was limited to promoting in Baltimore and working with Zane Bresloff, who booked the towns. What Gary did have was a knowledgeable opinion on the direction of the company. Gary usually knew whether certain house shows, or pay-per-views, had cards strong enough to draw and be profitable. Unfortunately, Gary really wasn't connected on the inside. Bill liked him, but he valued my opinion more than Gary's because I had a much richer background in so many different areas of the business.

Bill wanted to run WCW like a business, so he involved me in the decision-making process, asking me for rationales about decisions he was making. The first thing he wanted to know was where we could cut expenses, and talent became his first target. Bill knew that if the company was going to survive, he had to drastically cut talent expense. At the time, Dusty Rhodes was doing commentary on the Saturday night TBS show, but management felt that it wasn't enough to justify his salary. Bill took a hard look at what we were paying Dusty and said, *"I don't know what to do with him."*

Dusty's forte was promos and projecting a persona, so I suggested he utilize Dusty at the Power Plant, teaching the young guys. All I wanted to do was help Dusty find some longevity with the company. I wasn't giving him something he didn't deserve, and I wasn't repaying him for anything. He had been a big part of the company for a long time and it just seemed like the right thing to do. When Bill approached Dusty with the idea, Dusty jumped in with both feet ... until his ego took over. Instead of laying low and staying off the radar screen, Dusty kept coming around and saying, *"Okay, what can I do next? I've taught the kids the promo stuff."* Had Dusty grasped how bad things were, he wouldn't have given Bill the impression that there was nothing else for him to do at the gym. He was in Bill's face so often that Bill finally said, *"Dusty says he's done everything he can at the gym. I don't really have anything else for him to do. I can't justify paying him."* Bill told me to call Dusty and ask him to meet with us.

I called Dusty and said, *"Bill wants to have a meeting with you."*

*"What's he want?"*

*"Dusty, I don't know. He didn't tell me."* Which he didn't.

The next morning, just before our meeting with Dusty, Bill told me, *"I'm not renewing Dusty. When he comes in, I'm telling him that I'm letting him go, but I want to do it the* right way. I don't want Dusty to leave with bitter feelings. I'm going to give him a severance check for $100,000. Do you think that's being fair?"

I said, *"You're giving him $100,000 because you don't have anything for him? I think you're being more than fair."*

When Dusty arrived at the office, I went out to get him. Now, in the few moments that I had with Dusty as I walked him to Bill's office, how could I have said, *"Dusty, he's going to let you go, but he'll do right by you."* If I gave him advance warning, and Dusty didn't handle it well, then it would come back to bite me. Bill would have said, *"Why did you say something to Dusty? That's MY job! That's why we set up this meeting!"* I decided that it would be inappropriate of me, even with all of the things I had been through with Dusty, to tell him what was about to happen. Bill Busch was my boss, and I was accountable to him.

When Bill gave Dusty his verdict, Dusty looked like he had been hit with a load of bricks. *"You're telling me that you're firing me?"*

*"Dusty, I don't have anything for you right now,"* Bill explained. *"I have a check that I want to give you because I want to do the right thing. If I can get the business turned around, and if I can find a role for you, I would love to have you come back to work for us."*

Dusty made the situation very difficult when he let his ego kick in. *"Well, when you want me back, my price tag will be astronomical!"*

He said something at that point that I couldn't understand. *"How do you justify giving jobs to HIM* (pointing at me) *and Mike Graham? They wouldn't be in the business if it wasn't for me—and yet, you're letting ME go?"*

The next thing I heard about Dusty was that he had opened up his own wrestling school—Turnbuckle Promotions—in Marietta, Georgia. One day, Bill Busch asked me to call Dusty and ask if he'd come back for an event. Bill thought it would be good to do something with Dusty and his son, Dustin, who had been hired by WCW, so he wanted me to find out how much money Dusty would want. When Dusty answered the phone, he was very cold to me. *"Tell Bill to call me,"* he said, *"but I don't think he has enough money in the bank to pay me what I'm worth."* Bill got the gist of the message, so I'm not sure if he even called Dusty. I do know that there was no negotiation, and Dusty did not come back for that particular show.

In his book, *Reflections of an American Dream,* Dusty wrote that I was responsible for him losing his job at WCW. His exact quote was: *"I found myself fucked over— first by my assistant for many years, James J. Dillon, and then by Bill Busch."* Dusty is giving me too much credit and far too much power if he thinks I made the decisions about who to fire.

## Chapter 35
## The Other Vince

About two weeks after Bill Busch took over, I got a call from someone I had known at Titan Sports. He worked under Ed Cohen, who handled arena booking. He said their head writer, Vince Russo, who was a friend of his, was very unhappy in the WWF. He didn't want to call personally because if there was no interest, word might get back to Vince McMahon and it would jeopardize his job. *"Would you ask around to see if there's any interest?"*

"All I can do is ask the question," I said. I went to Bill and told him what I knew. *"I don't know Russo on a personal level. I know he got started on the magazine and worked his way up to being one of the main writers. He wants to make a move from the WWF. I can relate to that because I went through something similar. Maybe this is the person we need to give us a new look, new ideas, and to help turn the company around."*

"Have him give me a call," said Bill.

I called my friend and told him to have Russo call Bill. Instead, Russo called me personally. *"I don't want to call Bill Busch. I want him to call me."* I went back to Bill and he said, *"Okay, set up a meeting. Fly him into Atlanta on Saturday and book him a room at the Marriott. Book us a separate suite and have it catered. We'll meet there."*

On Saturday, I spent the entire day at the Marriott with Bill and Russo. Russo wanted to be the lead writer for WCW and he did a great job of selling himself to Bill. Russo told Bill that *he* had been writing the shows for the WWF, and not Vince McMahon. He also claimed that McMahon would make a cursory glance of the scripts and sign off on them.

When I worked with Vince McMahon, he was very hands-on in all aspects of the business, but especially creative. While I thought it was odd when Russo said he did all the writing without McMahon, it had been three years since I had left the WWF, and a lot can change in that time. I also knew that McMahon was preparing to take the WWF public on October 19. That was just a few weeks away, and I thought he might have his hands full with executive matters, so what Russo said kind of made sense.

Russo also spoke on behalf of Ed Ferrara, saying that Ed was his right-hand man and that he couldn't do the job without him. We made another phone call and flew Ed in on Sunday morning. By then, Bill thought we could reach a financial agreement with the two of them. It was nowhere near the amount of money that Russo was looking for, but it was still a nice salary with incentives tied to the TV ratings and pay-per-view buy rates. Bill said that if business increased under Russo's tenure, his salary would increase proportionally. Harvey Schiller also showed up at the Sunday meeting because he had to meet them before giving his approval, as did Brad Siegel, since we would all soon be under Siegel's watch. (Harvey Schiller was leaving the company to work for George Steinbrenner at the YES Network. Siegel, who would be taking Schiller's place, lobbied to have WCW shifted from Turner Sports to Turner Entertainment.) Several calls were made between Bill Busch and TBS's lead attorney (not Diana Myers), who had put the contracts together, and a letter of agreement was signed on October 3, 1999. Vince Russo called Vince McMahon immediately after signing and said, *"I won't be at TV tomorrow."*

That's how Vince Russo got hired. I was the catalyst and go-between that brought the parties together. I was happy to help him and I supported the idea that he could help us.

Shortly after he started working, Russo told me that Jeff Jarrett also wanted to leave the WWF. Jeff had put Chyna over in the middle of the ring at the WWF's October 17, 1999, *No Mercy* pay-per-view. Jeff's contract expired the day before the event, so Russo told Bill Busch that Jeff was available. I said positive things about Jeff to Bill, just like I did when Vince McMahon asked about him. I respected how Jeff was raised, what he had done in the business, the price he had paid, his work ethic, and so on. I tried to structure a deal that would give Jeff a chance to make good money.

One afternoon, Jerry Jarrett called me and said, *"Jeff thinks you low-balled him."*

*"Jerry,"* I replied, *"trust me when I tell you: If there was a better deal to be had, I would have gotten it for him, but the timing is bad and the situation around here is not what it once was. If Russo does everything he says he's going to do and turns things around, and Jeff is in an important part of it, we can always sit down and reward Jeff by reworking his deal. But right now, Brad Siegel won't approve another fat contract."*

That prompted Jerry to bring up Bill Goldberg's high-dollar, guaranteed contract, and questioned how that had just been approved. Goldberg had been with the company since June 1997 and he was one of the company's biggest stars. I wasn't aware of the details of Goldberg's 1999 contract re-negotiations, so I got clarification from Bill Busch and passed the information on to Jerry. I explained that Goldberg's deal had been negotiated by Eric Bischoff, and had subsequently been approved by Harvey Schiller and/or Brad Siegel, *before* Bill Busch had passed the mandate of no fat salaries. For some reason, even though Goldberg had signed a letter of intent and all parties had agreed on a certain amount of money, Goldberg's contract wasn't signed and finalized until *after* Jeff had signed his contract. It would appear than an exception was being made for Goldberg, but the guidelines in place when Goldberg's contract was written had been changed by the time the company started to work on Jeff's deal. Unfortunately for Jeff, he came in precisely at a time when WCW had stopped offering high-dollar guarantees. This story may have been the ammunition that Russo used to convince Jeff that I had stood in the way of Jeff getting a Goldberg-like deal.

Ultimately, Jeff came on board. Shortly before he did, Russo called Bill Busch while I was sitting in Bill's office. Bill put the call on the speakerphone and said, *"I talked to Jeff, but I don't know if he's gonna come in or not. He's got high expectations and I've done the best I can do for him. I don't know if that's gonna be enough to get him to leave the WWF."*

Russo then said, *"Well, it doesn't matter to me. If you can get him, fine. He's a good talent that I can use, but if not, that's okay, too."*

That was the extent of it, but the story Russo told Jeff was that he pushed for a much bigger deal, but I blocked it and stood in the way.

Bill Busch did not have the authority to write high-dollar guarantees. Under Bischoff, the contracts were structured in such a way that a lot of the talent got paid even when they didn't work, so I advised Bill to structure new contracts in a manner that would create incentives for the talent to want to work more. If you worked more than a specified number of dates in a 12-month period of time, you made more money. If a talent earned good money, WCW management could justify the situation to North Tower accountants by showing a correlation between the earnings and the number of dates worked.

Jeff made a point that since we advertised our cards at least six weeks out, he would have to sit on the sidelines while the clock was ticking. I knew Jeff was a workhorse, so I added him onto cards—even though he wasn't advertised—to get him on the fast track and help him reach the threshold of days worked. By giving him a reasonable guaranteed base salary, based on performing a specific number of dates, and then adding bonus incentives for those dates worked over and above certain thresholds, Jeff would make good money. It also allowed Bill Busch to justify the money to the North Tower bean counters. Jeff was a good talent, and of value to the company, so I did everything I could to help him during a time when big contracts had become a thing of the past.

When Terry Taylor left WCW to work for Vince McMahon in January 1999, I gave him some advice. *"Vince will want you to sell your house and relocate to Connecticut. Keep your options open. I know you're excited, but he will let you fly back and forth. Just keep telling Vince you're trying to sell your home. That's all he wants to hear. But keep your options open, and see how you fit into their structure."*

After eight months or so, Terry got into some political situations with the WWF, so he called me, looking to get back into WCW. There was some resistance against Terry from certain corporate people because he had some issues with Human Resources (HR) when he left to work for the WWF, so I tried to help Terry get a job by lobbying Bill Busch. When Bill talked to Siegel about hiring Terry, Siegel said that HR preferred that Terry not be rehired, but he would allow Bill to make the final decision. When Bill asked me for my advice, I said, *"Bring him back. I'll be responsible for him. We need all the help we can get. Terry goes back to Bill Watts, so he has a good, strong foundation."* I got Terry his job back at the same salary he was making when he left the company.

The only problem I had with Terry was that he got wrapped up in the Vince Russo concept of having scantily-clad women in every segment. The show that once featured wrestling became nothing more than a vehicle for eye candy. I talked to Terry about it. *"Terry, the initial shock factor of the women is okay, but over the long term, they're not the solution."*

*"Times have changed, James."*

That disappointed me, because deep down, I thought he should have known better. In the long run, though, I thought Terry was a good talent and a likeable guy. I had known Terry since I was booking Kansas City. In 1998, my family and I had moved from a rental house in Norcross, Georgia, to a three-bedroom apartment in Marietta. I was trying to get back on my feet and the rent was significantly less expensive. However, after two years, our family of five felt somewhat confined in the small space.

When I say our family of five, I have to amend that to seven. Our pets were as much a part of our family as any of us. When I first met Lindsey, she had a cat named Stokley. Stokley and Boomer, our mixed breed Irish Setter-Golden Retriever, were pals. Stokley lived to be 19 years old (which seems like a long time for a cat to live) before we had him put to sleep while we were still living in Wilton, Connecticut. After Stokley was gone, we adopted Laddie, a purebred Sheltie, when his owner discovered that she was allergic to dog hair.

Boomer was also an integral part of our family. He had long red hair (more like an Irish Setter) and a beautiful disposition. We had adopted Boomer from PAWS in Westport, Connecticut. PAWS is an organization that finds homes for stray dogs.

While we lived in the apartment, Boomer became incontinent and contracted a form of cancer that causes a tumor to wrap around the back of the spine in the area of the bladder. I drove Boomer to the College of Veterinarian Medicine at Auburn University and he underwent surgery. I took him back several more times to have a series of chemotherapy treatments. When we returned home, we had to administer a pill while wearing gloves. He resisted taking the pills and it must have been horrible for him. Each trip to Auburn was a several hour drive, but my efforts bought him a year. When the cancer returned, we were told that there was nothing further that could be done. A vet came to our apartment while Lindsey and I held Boomer in our lap on the sofa as he died. We both cried and I am emotional as I relive the scene. It was one more reason to get out of that apartment, and one more thing to add to the list of things that Lindsey and I faced. Maybe that was just life, and perhaps everybody goes through what we went through, but it sure seemed like we had more than our fair share.

We really wanted to get out of the apartment, so I pulled our finances together and we bought a $390,000 house in Marietta. I used every resource available to scrape up the money, but didn't have anything left to pay for window treatments and closet organizers. Terry Taylor stepped up and said, *"I can lend you some money."* He did, and I agreed to pay him back over the next two or three months. The three months turned into two years, but I did pay back everything that I borrowed from him.

Vince Russo did some crazy, outrageous things. One of the questions originally asked of him was, *"Do you see yourself being a talent on camera?"*

*"Oh, no,"* he said. *"Absolutely not."*

Right out of the box, he created a persona for himself and had a camera shooting over the back of his head. Both Russo and Ed Ferrara were written into shows as "The Powers That Be." You would hear their voices and see their hands extend into camera view as they directed the wrestlers to do certain things. This created a curiosity to eventually see who they were and what they looked like. Russo was eventually seen and identified, while Ed started to appear on-air as Oklahoma, a Jim Ross rip-off. He even sank so low as to make fun of Jim's Bell's palsy. The two eventually become on-air talent, which is exactly what they said they would NOT do.

I always tried to give a person an opportunity to succeed, or fail, before I judged their worth. After six weeks passed by, Kevin Sullivan said to me, *"Have you really looked at the content of the shows lately, and the pattern we're developing?"*

*"No,"* I said. *"I think I've been looking the other way, giving him a chance to see what he can do. Let me take a look and we'll continue this conversation later."*

For the next three weeks, I reviewed every show that Russo wrote, including the ones he had already shot. I made notes on several things: the amount of actual wrestling time in a given hour, the number of times a referee got knocked down, the number of foreign objects or props being used, whether or not we had a winner and loser, and the number of times we used run-in interference. All of a sudden, I saw a pattern of actions that was hurting our credibility. The guys were using rubber baseball bats, rubber crowbars, and a myriad of props. When they gave Scott Steiner a rubber crowbar, he didn't just hit his opponent once. He hit him over and over ... until the crowbar bent and the audience could see that it was rubber! The referees were getting knocked down an embarrassing number of times. The credibility of the referees was being compromised because the guys, both babyface and heel, were breaking the rules ... right in front of the referee. How do you explain it when a referee counts 1-2-3 after somebody hits their opponent with a bat?

*"Ahh, this is sports entertainment. It doesn't really matter."*

Match after match, show after show, week after week ... each ensuing week saw more of the same thing. When I started to calculate the actual wrestling content on a three-hour show, I saw the number shrink every week. At first, we had forty minutes of in-ring wrestling action. At one point, we were down to a 27-minute low ... in a three-hour show!

The ratings had not risen dramatically, and to continue the course without some modification was to court disaster. I finally went to Bill and said, *"I'm all for giving Russo a chance to succeed, but over a ten-week period of time, he's taken our wrestling product and shrunk it down to nothing. We have no finishes (nobody wins), we're knocking the referees down, and we're hot-shotting the shows. If we don't redirect Russo, or reel him back in, we're in big trouble."*

Bill agreed with me and called a meeting of Russo and all the agents. He said, *"We're concerned about where we're going with the content of the program. Don't compromise the in-ring wrestling. Find a better balance. Do an occasional ref bump, or use outside interference, or use a prop, but not with reckless abandon. Maybe it's exuberance of wanting to succeed, but we have to watch where we're going and the pattern we're developing."*

In front of everybody at the meeting, Russo stood up and gave an ultimatum: *"You're either for me or against me. There's no compromise. I'm the head writer of this show. It's sports entertainment and I'm not going to change. I can't believe there's anyone in this room who would even QUESTION what I'm doing. You should be using that energy down in the CNN Center fighting against Standards & Practices!"*

In my opinion, Russo's ultimatum proved that he had his own idea of how things were going to be at WCW. I am convinced that Russo resented the fact that Vince McMahon had to manage him, and did NOT, as he alleged, give him final say in creative. I believe Russo saw WCW as an opportunity to prove to all of his naysayers, and especially to Vince McMahon, that he could be successful on his own.

On the January 10, 2000, episode of *Nitro*, Russo brought in three wrestling legends—George "The Animal" Steele, Tito Santana, and "Superfly" Jimmy Snuka—to wrestle Jeff Jarrett in three individual matches. The idea was to promote the Souled Out pay-per-view, which would be held six days later. Jeff would be wrestling Chris Benoit in three matches billed as "Triple Threat Theater." The first match was going to be a "Dungeon Match," the second would be a "Bunkhouse Brawl," and the third would take place inside a steel cage.

Common sense would have Jeff beating all three men on *Nitro*, making him seem unbeatable and a true threat to Benoit. Instead, Jeff got beat by all three of the legends ... wrestlers who had been retired so long that most of the people in the audience didn't even know who they were. To make matters worse, when Snuka came off the top ropes, he landed wrong and gave Jeff a concussion.

I went to Bill Busch and said, *"Do you realize that Jeff Jarrett just got beat on TV by three old legends? Why would anybody want to buy a pay-per-view to see him fight Chris Benoit? On top of that, he has a concussion and may not even be able to work the pay-per-view!"*

My fears came true. Jeff wrestled the next night in a tag match on *Thunder*, but was unable to work on the pay-per-view.

On the following night, I was at the production meeting for *Thunder* in Erie, Pennsylvania, along with Vince Russo, Ed Ferrara, David Crockett, Bill Busch, and others. When the subject came up of the possibility of Jeff not being able to work on Thunder, Russo said, *"We need to do something big!"*

At the time, Terry Funk was using his flaming branding iron gimmick in WCW, but we had already been told by the local fire marshall that we couldn't use the flaming branding iron in that particular building. Vince asked David Crockett, *"What would it take to get the fire marshall to leave the building early?"*

Russo wanted to wipe down the entire ring with a flammable gel, have Terry come to ringside with his branding iron, and set the whole ring ablaze. At that point, we would go off the air. As Russo talked about the ring going up in flames, Bill looked up from the run sheet and made eye contact with me. I just shook my head, but Bill gave no reaction. No explanation was necessary.

Bill decided that it was time to act. Shortly after the meeting adjourned, Bill took Gary Juster and me to meet with Brad Siegel. When we walked into Siegel's office, Bill said, *"Things are out of hand and Vince Russo is out of control."*

Gary and I had also tracked the ratings. If we had been able to show a huge spike in ratings, and if that ultimately affected our pay-per-view numbers, then you could argue to stay the course, but we never saw that spike. We were not seeing the benefits of a long-term booking philosophy. Siegel listened for a few minutes and finally yelled, *"Okay, okay, okay! I get it! I get it!"* That was Siegel's favorite response whenever you gave him the information he needed. He'd immediately cut you off and gruffly say, *"Alright! I got it!"* That was when Siegel gave Bill the okay to take Russo out of his position.

On January 14, 2000, that's exactly what Bill Busch did. Of course, once again, the blame was laid on me. Russo made it a personal thing between us. It never was personal. It was strictly business, but that course of action drew the battle lines.

When Harvey Schiller left Turner Sports, Brad Siegel lobbied to get his job with WCW. Brad, who had been very successful as president of general entertainment networks for Turner Broadcasting, came into the company thinking that since *"it's just wrestling,"* it would be an easy fix and another feather in his cap. He said he would separate creative from the business side and oversee both operations, as had been his modus operandi with the made-for-TV movies at Turner Entertainment. He intended to appoint Stu Schneider, an old college buddy, to run the company on a day-to-day basis, but ironically, Vince McMahon hired Stu as President of WWF before Brad could make him President of WCW.

One of the first things Brad did was call a meeting of the department heads. We were told that it would be the first of many such meetings to promote open communication between WCW and North Tower management. There were people with WCW who asked very pointed questions that Brad didn't have the answers for. His responses showed him to be ill-prepared and he became very defensive. After the first meeting, we never had another ... until eighteen months later when WCW closed the doors. Going in, Brad Siegel thought it would be easy to fix the company, but he soon learned that the company was really in a mess.

We spent a lot of money on a marketing survey regarding interests among viewers who followed wrestling. The report looked like a small phone book. The results pointed out that the fan base of WCW yearned for a certain style of product. They didn't care for the music and costumes. They wanted substance. They wanted to see the old, hard-hitting style of wrestling that the NWA was known for. However, it appeared that we ignored the survey because WCW tried to copy the WWF product, especially after Russo started writing the shows.

Scott Steiner was another talent who went into business for himself on TV, this time on Brad Siegel's watch. On February 7, 2000, at a live *Nitro* in Tulsa, Oklahoma, we asked Scott to go into the ring and talk about an upcoming match. His job was to promote the pay-per-view, which is an important revenue stream, by throwing out a 15-second line. Instead, Scott got sideways about something and went on a 3-minute personal tirade against Ric Flair.

*Flair should be riding in a cab instead of a limousine.*
*Flair should get his crooked yellow teeth fixed.*
*Flair's career was over and he's a joke.*
*Flair was the reason for all of the problems in WCW.*

Steiner even said WCW sucked! He then brought up Buddy Rogers, saying that even though Flair stole Rogers' gimmick, he couldn't steal his class. Steiner also said that when Flair was doing his interview on *Nitro* the previous week, he [Steiner] *"turned the channel to the WWF to watch Stone Cold,"* who Flair had fired because he was *"a jealous, old, ass-kissing, butt-sucking bastard."* By the time we got him off of the mic, the flow of the entire show was lost. Steiner had gone on for so long that several pre-taped segments scheduled to air that night had to be axed from the show, and the entire evening's format had to be re-arranged on the fly.

When Scott came back through the curtain, I said, *"Scott, what were you doing?"*

*"Well, Flair's a piece of shit!"*

*"But your personal feelings about someone don't mean anything! This is live television! You can't do that!"*

There was no angle between Steiner and Flair. Most of the boys in the back seemed to think the reason Steiner did that shoot was because Flair had just returned to WCW after a brief absence, and Steiner felt Flair's return would hurt his chance of becoming the lead heel, which he felt he was in line for.

Gary Juster wanted to fire Steiner immediately. My opinion was that firing him should be a last-resort measure only. I was in favor of a one-month suspension without pay. I am a businessman first. That's one thing I learned from Vince McMahon. Scott Steiner was a good card who meant something to our fans and WCW had invested a lot of effort and TV exposure to get him over. However, we wanted to send a strong message to the rest of the talent, some of whom might consider following Scott's lead. If we didn't draw a line in the sand, the inmates would be running the asylum. As it was, they already had keys to most of the doors. Bill Busch gathered everybody's input, and even brought Brad Siegel into the mix. Bill's eventual decision was to give Scott a two-week suspension without pay.

When Scott came to the office, I had to meet with him and explain the decision. He was irate about it, and made an excuse about Hulk Hogan cutting a promo on Flair six months earlier. His reasoning was like comparing apples to oranges. Hulk Hogan had been involved in a storyline with Flair. In Hogan's mind, there may have been a nugget of truth in what he said about Flair, but the promo was consistent to further the storyline, and not just a personal issue between the two. But in Scott Steiner's mind: *"Hulk did it! Why is everybody upset with me? I just told the truth!"*

Well, to Scott Steiner, our decision was unacceptable, so his lawyer, John Taylor, called Brad Siegel and had the decision overturned. When Brad intervened on Scott's behalf against Bill Busch and me, he destroyed our credibility. Not only that, but Bill got called on the carpet for making that decision. Before the day was over, Bill gave Scott Steiner a bonus equivalent to his fine. I said, *"Bill, I know you're under a tremendous amount of pressure, but do you realize what you've done?"* Bill did realize what he did, but he was consistently being second guessed by Brad Siegel and upper management. In fact, he expended a lot of his time and energy dealing with them, and he didn't have the time or energy to come up with a solid plan that would turn the company around.

The following week, Scott Steiner went on TV to do his promo, and said, *"They tried to fire me, but I showed them."*

That's just one of many examples of the disarray and chaos found behind-the-scenes of WCW.

My father passed away on March 10, 2000 at the age of 85. He had been ill for a year-and-a-half and my children had not seen him for awhile. I finally planned a trip for all of us to travel to Delaware to see my parents. We were scheduled to fly out on Friday morning. I talked to him on Wednesday and knew that he was weak, but he sounded excited that he was going to see us. At 5:00 a.m. on Friday morning, my mother called to tell me that my father had passed away in his sleep during the night. We all made the trip, anyway, and flew back home on Saturday night. I flew back to

Delaware on Sunday to attend the memorial service on Monday morning following the cremation. I then drove to Providence, Rhode Island, for the March 13 *Nitro*. I felt that I needed to be there for Bill Busch. Brad Siegel was there that night, and he was the only person who didn't say something to me about losing my father.

One Friday afternoon at about five o'clock, the entire creative staff and everyone directly involved with the actual wrestling product were called to a meeting in Brad Siegel's office in Smyrna (which was Eric's old office). It was the end of a long week and everybody was tired and ready to go home for the weekend. Kevin Sullivan was trying to catch a flight home to Miami. Brad held court over the meeting and said, *"I challenge you to find the next big idea!"*

Brad wanted to know what the plan was for "the next big idea." After some desultory discussion that went nowhere, I finally spoke up. *"Wrestling is totally different from the made-for-TV-movie business. We can't buy the rights to a book, or write a script, and cast for the movie. In wrestling, we have to establish the characters first. We have to give them personas, preferably based on their own persona, and make people like or dislike them. Once the audience is somewhat familiar with a character, and start to care about the individual, then—and only then—do we develop storylines based on their character. That's what wrestling is all about."*

I continued on to say, *"Imagine me coming to you two years ago and telling you about a football player from the University of Georgia who is at the Power Plant. He has a shaved head and he looks a lot like Steve Austin. He doesn't have any wrestling experience, he has a bad knee, and he isn't very articulate in terms of wrestling promos. But I think we should bring him in and let him beat everybody in a minute or less. We'll give him a finishing move called the jackhammer and push him to the moon.*

*"You'd look at me like I was nuts. But that is the story of Bill Goldberg. We didn't map out a complicated storyline. We weren't even sure if we should call him Bill Goldberg or just Goldberg. He couldn't work and he couldn't talk, but we used him because we needed somebody fresh on our roster. We put him on television and had him beat people in less than a minute because we were afraid he'd be exposed. We didn't want him hurting anybody, so we got it over quickly.*

*"After pushing Bill Goldberg for a period of several weeks, he became a huge superstar, but it wasn't something that we knew would happen. It just took on a life of its own. That's typical of the wrestling business. For every success, you might have two failures. Once you go down one path, you might run into an obstacle, so you have to change directions. That's the nature of the wrestling business ... trial and error. You introduce a character, allow the fans to watch his story unfold over a period of weeks, and make adjustments depending on how the fans react to each part of the story. So you can't ask for the next big idea. Our business isn't structured that way. It's a form of entertainment unlike any other."*

That wasn't what Brad Siegel wanted to hear, so Eric Bischoff, who had a contract and was being paid sitting on the sidelines, told Brad what he *did* want to hear. On March 22, 2000, Siegel told Bill Busch that he was bringing Eric back. Bill, knowing the history and understanding the skeletons in the closet said, *"You can't do that!"* Bill didn't waste any time reminding Siegel about the damage done to the company by Eric, and that he was the reason whey we were in such bad financial shape.

Bill had just signed a three-year contract for what I would imagine was more money than he had ever dreamed of making during his ten years with WCW. Bill told Siegel that if Eric came back, he—Bill Busch—would walk. I don't believe that Brad thought that would ever happen, but he didn't count on the fact that Bill Busch is a man of principal. Bill is a smart man who deserved an opportunity to run the company, but it was never given to him. Bill Busch held his head up high and walked. When I think of Bill, I think of a quality human being and a good family man.

Not only did Brad Siegel make the stunning announcement that he was bringing Eric Bischoff back, but he *also* declared that Vince Russo would be re-instated! When Bischoff and Russo came back to work, they looked at Kevin Sullivan and me as the enemy. Brad Siegel called me on the Sunday night before they returned to work [April 9, 2000] and said, *"You're supposed to fly to TV in Denver tomorrow, but I want you to stay home and come to the office as usual in the morning."* I went to the office on Monday as usual, but Siegel had flown to Denver himself and didn't return until late Tuesday. On Wednesday morning, he walked into my office and said, *"One of the conditions Eric and Vince demanded was that you, Gary Juster, and Kevin Sullivan be let go. You have a contract with the company, so you won't lose your job. I'll see to it that you stay here. I don't know what your role is going to be, but Eric and Vince need an opportunity to succeed without you getting in their way. Give me a little time and I'll get back with you."*

On the night of the *Nitro* following my father's death, I vividly remember Siegel and Hulk huddled together in a corner, and in hindsight, I figured that Brad was sharing his plans with Hulk. Hulk also played Eric Bischoff like a fiddle, so I'm sure that Hulk was happy to know that Eric was coming back.

I didn't hear from Siegel again after he left my office. In fact, he never spoke directly to me again after that day. For the next twelve months, whenever Brad left his office, he could either make a right turn, which meant he had to pass my door, or he could turn left and walk down a hallway, then turn right down a longer corridor. Nineteen out of twenty times he would take the long route so he didn't have to have any interaction with me. When he did walk by my door, he would scurry by. I used to refer to him as "The Ferret" because he would scurry by with his head down and his shoulders scrunched over.

Bischoff and Russo wanted Gary Juster out, but Gary was a Vice President, so he was better insulated than Kevin and I were. Gary had enough sense to stay in his office and keep his mouth shut. Kevin Sullivan got a phone call from Siegel, who told him to go home and stay home. Kevin appeared to be the sacrificial lamb, but in fact, he too was still under contract, so he got paid for at least another couple of years. The last show that Kevin Sullivan wrote was in South Padre Island, Texas, on March 27, 2000. I don't remember who gave him the instructions, but he was basically told to book the show without furthering any storylines or introducing anything new. I think it was announced that Eric Bischoff would be on the show the following week, and on the night of Kevin's last show in Texas, Russo was on the phone with Terry Taylor and the TV production people, giving input for the show.

Kevin Sullivan has been around the business for a long time. I have a tremendous amount of respect for Kevin, both personally and professionally. He is one of the smartest guys that I have ever worked with. To this day, I'm good friends with Kevin, so someone might say that I'm a bit prejudiced in my opinion, but he did get a raw deal, because he had the ability to understand the big picture. When things were at their worst, he could give direction, even though he constantly had people working against him. He never had the support of Eric Bischoff.

People claim that Kevin Sullivan booked his own divorce. I don't know what was going on between Kevin and his wife, Nancy, at that time. What I do know is that Kevin would not leave any stone unturned in terms of doing business. I'm not saying that he has no values. Kevin, at the time, was in a tough position. When he put Nancy together with Chris Benoit, it was for what he thought was the right reason at the time—to draw money. What happened after that is what happened. You'll have to go elsewhere to find out what that was. It's something that I've never really talked about with Kevin. I do know that he absolutely did not harbor personal vendettas against people. If anybody could have had personal issues with Benoit, it was Kevin, but he didn't, and he proved that when he put the WCW title on Benoit. Kevin and I both thought it was the right thing to do for business.

When Kevin was still the head booker, Chris Benoit, Eddie Guerrero, Dean Malenko, and Perry Saturn banded together and demanded that Sullivan be removed from WCW, or else they would quit. They charged that Kevin was holding them back in retaliation for Benoit getting together with Sullivan's former wife, Nancy. The ironic part of the situation is that they made the claims at a time when Kevin had chosen Benoit to win the WCW world title. Kevin does what is best for business, but they wanted him out anyway. It was nothing more than a power play on their part. If we had caved in to their demands, and fired Kevin, it would have been more of the same thing: The inmates are running the asylum, so Bill Busch had NO choice but to tell them, *"If you insist on giving me an ultimatum, then you can pack your bags and go."*

On January 19, 2000, we sent them their release forms, and they promptly signed contracts with the WWF. It was a regrettable situation, but you can't always control what other people want to do. Chris Benoit is a real commodity and Eddie Guerrero is a great talent. Dean Malenko is probably as good a mechanical wrestler as there has ever been. I like Dean, and I knew his father, so I was very sorry to see him go. As for Perry Saturn, he was trained by Killer Kowalski, so I had a soft spot in my heart for him. Originally, Shane Douglas was with them, but they turned on him at the last minute and left him out.

Bob Mould was also on the WCW booking committee. Bob was a musician/singer/songwriter whose band, Husker Du, was considered to be very influential in the music world. When Husker Du disbanded in 1987, Bob began a solo career, and later formed a band called Sugar.

Bob was a huge wrestling fan and a good friend of Gary Juster. Gary used to tell us about all the ideas and scenarios that Bob had shared with him. Everyone was so impressed with his knowledge and ideas that Bob was eventually hired as a consultant to the booking committee. He is a nice guy who was liked by everyone. Even though he didn't have a wrestling background, I believe he was a traditionalist in his thinking regarding wrestling. Over time, Bob began to notice the unscrupulous, back-room politics that stifled the creative process, and was particularly frustrated with Russo's shenanigans. He was also in the meeting when Russo gave his ultimatum. When word got out that Bischoff and Russo were headed back, Bob Mould turned in his resignation and left. He resumed his solo career and is doing very well for himself.

The show in Denver on April 10 was a live *Monday Nitro*. I watched the show at home as it aired. Vince Russo and Jeff Jarrett had done a pre-taped backstage segment that was rolled into the show as if it was live. In the skit, Russo wanted Jeff to wrestle Curt Hennig later that night. When Jeff questioned Russo as to his reasons for wanting him to do that, Vince shot back at him with, *"After all we've been through together, you don't trust me? Who do I look like ... J.J. Dillon?"*

They made it personal. I was told by a friend that Brad Siegel was in the back watching the monitor at the control position, and was seen laughing about the line. I feel that it was inappropriate and unprofessional for Russo and Jeff to make it personal regarding me. Jeff's attitude towards me has always been a mystery because I helped Jeff get a job with the WWF, and I got him the best deal I could with WCW. You can make a case that J.J. Dillon is a character, so anything and everything is fair game. However, their comment had nothing to do with business or drawing money. It was strictly an unwarranted cheap-shot. Along the same lines, Brad Siegel's behavior and attitude was even more inappropriate and unprofessional than that of Vince and Jeff.

I had another eighteen months left on my contract. I spent the first twelve months sitting at my desk, watching them destroy what was left of the company—right up to the day the doors closed. I came to work each day based on Siegel's open-ended comment: *"I'll get back with you."*

During the last twelve months that WCW remained in business, they didn't give me any responsibilities, but I would go into the office every day. I would talk to Jerry Jarrett quite often. I would tell him, *"Something has got to happen."* Jerry has been around. He's been a survivor in the business. Jerry told me many times: *"You need to be prepared, because one day, Brad Siegel will walk through that door and say, 'We're in trouble. You've got an extensive background. I need to hear what you would do to take care of our problem and how you would turn this ship around.' When that happens, you'd better be prepared."*

I took his advice and began following everything wrestling-related on the Internet. I drew my own charts and graphs of WCW ratings, WWF ratings, and pay-per-view buy rates. I made notes to pinpoint when key talent came in and out. As an example, Kevin Nash was out for a long time after he broke his leg. Nash's role was limited, and his absence had a negative impact on ratings. I reviewed taped copies of our shows, and made notes for myself.

Of course, Brad Siegel never asked me for advice, even though on several occasions, Jerry Jarrett even told him, *"You'd better tap into your people who have wrestling experience, or you're going to suffer the same fate as every one of your predecessors. They all failed, and ultimately, lost their jobs because of it."* Brad looked at Jerry with an arrogant smirk on his face, as if that would never apply to him.

While I was sitting in my office, people repeatedly walked in to tell me, *"Terry Taylor is lobbying for your job."* Terry saw the situation I was in as an opportunity. At first, when I heard that Terry had Siegel's ear, and was openly lobbying to take over everything I had done, it was disconcerting, but I didn't (and don't) harbor any ill feelings towards him over it. He was simply trying to provide for himself and his family. If anything, I was more disappointed that Terry appeared to buy into all the crap that Bischoff and Russo spewed out. Terry eventually got the job of booking and running the house shows, and handling the agents. I still regard Terry Taylor as a friend.

One day, I was in my office, with the door open, and on the phone with Kevin Sullivan. We were reviewing what we saw on *Nitro*, and how the pattern was very alarming. Vince Russo must have been outside and overheard me talking, because all of a sudden, he stepped into the doorway and yelled, *"You're nothing but a negative piece of sh—!"* I was really bothered by that, and my first instinct was to get up, walk across the room, and punch him. However, if I had done that, I would have lost my job, and I had a family to consider. Besides, I would not lower myself into the gutter with him. It took all of 15 seconds. He said his piece and he was gone. He said it loudly enough that my secretary overheard every word, and his unprofessional conduct got back to Brad Siegel and Human Resources. I don't think he had planned to do that. He was just so brazen and arrogant at that point that he thought he could say and do whatever he wanted.

Deep inside, I hoped that things would never get so bad that the company itself would be in jeopardy in terms of their very existence, but that's what happened. Two years before they closed the doors, Kevin Sullivan and I knew that WCW was in serious, serious trouble. We would talk about it privately, hoping that there would be a change in management. We couldn't understand why nobody opened their eyes wide enough to see the numbers and realize that something wasn't working.

HR did performance reviews four times a year. Once a year, one of the evaluations was more comprehensive and included a grading system. The system was something like: Highly exceeded expectations, Exceeded expectations, Meets expectations, Below expectations, Did not meet expectations. As management, you were encouraged to grade most people at the mid-level, or *Meets expectations.* Allegedly, Turner's standards were so high, that anyone marked as *Meets expectations* could still be doing an excellent job. There was a graph chart that gave recommended bonus levels and percentage increases for salaries based on the performance reviews.

Even though Brad had me sitting in my office with no specific responsibilities, I was still considered a department head, so I submitted reports for five or six people who reported to me directly. When I submitted my reports, I gave positive feedback, but I did not recommend bonuses or raises because WCW was losing so much money at the time. HR contacted me by phone and told me that I should be consistent with everyone else at WCW, and recommend bonuses and raises for my reports that would be in line with others at WCW. They used formulas involving percentages that corresponded to the performance evaluations I gave. I told HR that in good conscience, under the circumstances, I couldn't recommend any raises, and a bonus should be out of the question. The company was losing millions of dollars. Why should anyone get a bonus?

HR insisted that I make recommendations based on the reviews. If I felt like my reports didn't deserve a salary increase or bonus, I should go back and downgrade their performance evaluations. I didn't think that was fair because my reports had all done a great job, especially in light of the circumstances and atmosphere at WCW, so I told HR to make their own recommendations based on my performance reports. I said, *"You can revise my recommendations according to what you see as consistent with everyone else at WCW and Turner. I will go along with whatever you think is appropriate."*

As mind boggling as it may seem to you, most of my reports got a big raise and a bonus. Long term, the raises didn't mean much because the company went out of business, but the bonuses were real dollars that were immediately deposited into the bank.

For the record, I did not get a bonus or a raise.

This is not totally relevant to the story, but I thought it might be helpful to list the titles of the people I worked with as listed in the WCW directory (revised on August 16, 2000). Craig Leathers is listed as VP Executive Producer. I believe that when Bischoff became President, he was also named Senior Executive Producer, so that Craig could move up. I am listed as a department head with the title Director of Talent Management. I had an assistant. Jamie Engle was Talent Relations Manager and reported to me at one point, as did Terry Taylor (Live Event Coordinator), Vince Russo (Writer), Ed Ferrara (Writer), Bill Banks (Assistant Writer), and Alto Gary (Nitro Girl Manager). Along the way, Ferrara, Banks, and Gary either quit, or as in Russo's case, were reassigned. Elena Bowen is listed separately under Talent Travel as Talent Travel Coordinator, and she reported to me. Paul Orndorff was listed under Training / Power Plant and was called Training Center Staffing. Brenda Smith (who used to work for Jody Hamilton at the old Power Plant) was Training Center Coordinator, and she and Paul both reported to me.

In the end, Russo and Bischoff got caught in a trap of their own making. On the April 24, 2000, Nitro from Rochester, New York, they poured fake blood from the ceiling and splattered it on everybody in the front row. They also had the WCW world heavyweight title change hands nine times between April and May. Finally, at *Bash at the Beach* on July 9, 2000, Jeff Jarrett deliberately laid down in the middle of the ring and allowed Hulk Hogan to put his boot over him for the pin to win the WCW title.

At that point, the company losses jumped from $15 million to $80 million. Siegel was doing damage control, cutting everything he could find to cut. When he finished, they had reduced the debt to $60 million, but they couldn't reduce it any further. With all of the guaranteed contracts the company was obligated to honor, we were projected to lose another $60 million going forward, and that's when the decision was made to pull the plug.

What I never thought would happen, but feared *would* happen, finally happened. The financial losses were so big that AOL-Time Warner reached the end of their patience and pulled the plug. Maybe I was naive, and perhaps maybe I still am, but I think with the right team of people and proper support, WCW could have been fixed. Unfortunately, the TV executives didn't have the patience to listen to the people who would have been able to formulate a plan to fix it. They were in the television business, and their barometer was focused on ratings. One of the executives said, *"We don't want to risk losing any more money. If we shut it down now, we can write this off as one huge loss. At least that way, it won't continue to be a thorn in our side."*

I spent almost eight years working alongside Vince McMahon. I had information about his company that could have helped WCW immensely. And yet, right up to my last day with the company, nobody ever tapped into that data bank. I never had ambitions to run the company, but I can't understand why nobody ever asked questions like, *"How did Vince structure his company?"* Or, *"How does our production facility compare to the WWF's?"* Why would they put me in an office, pay me, and not even attempt to ask me? It would be like stealing one of Vince's computers—the one with all the company secrets—and leaving it on a desk in an unused office without ever turning it on.

I can only assume they didn't WANT the information. To me, that is arrogance and stupidity, which is what I saw time and time again ....

Most of the talent had the opinion that their success was going to last forever. They proved that when they insisted on having their own way at WCW, up to the point when the company finally closed its doors.

Several of the boys later told me, *"Maybe we should have done something differently. Maybe we could have made some accommodations."* That's what Kevin Sullivan, Bill Busch, and I tried to do, but we had a lot of opposition.

Some wrestlers can be like seagulls.

## Chapter 36
### Sold to the Lowest Bidder

The question a lot of people ask is, *"Why would anyone have wanted to buy WCW when they were, for all intents and purposes, a failed company?"*

My answer is: they weren't really buying a company. The heart of a company is the management team. If someone wanted to buy the WCW management team, I would be asking the same question. In reality, they would be buying three things: wrestling rings, talent contracts, and the most valuable product, the rights to the television programming, along with the rights to the library of tapes of shows and matches already aired.

As early as 2000, it became apparent that WCW could not stay in business under the conditions that existed after Bischoff and Russo were brought back. When Bischoff and Russo failed miserably in their attempt to turn the company around, rumors began to circulate about WCW being on the auction block. Who? Why? None of it made any sense.

Brad Siegel wouldn't confirm the rumors, until one morning, when a meeting was hastily called at the WCW offices in Smyrna. Most of the department heads were called individually and invited to attend the meeting. With no advance warning, Brad introduced everyone to a "new group of owners." I can't tell you exactly what was said because I wasn't included on the list of invitees, but someone who was present told me that Bischoff was there. The "new group of owners" referred to him as "our wrestling expert."

When he was running WCW, Eric Bischoff made frequent trips to Los Angeles. He was good friends with Jason Hervey, one of the young actors on the TV series *Wonder Years*. At times, I wondered if Eric was using WCW as a launching pad for a career in Hollywood. He didn't have a passion for wrestling, and wrestling seemed to be nothing more than a means to an end for him. Bischoff and Hervey, however, had something to do with bringing the new owners, a company called Fusient, into the negotiations. Apparently, the deal had been put together rather quickly, and the small group, along with Bischoff, had flown all night from California in a private jet in order to make the formal announcement.

To quote the great Yogi Berra, *"It's like djà vu all over again."* When Eric was first hired into WCW, he used a "creative resume" to sell himself to the executives in the North Tower. Now, he was trying to sell himself *and* a failed company that he had run into the ground to a group of investors who obviously knew nothing about wrestling.

I was told by others who attended the announcement meeting that Fusient representatives intended to meet with many people working at WCW as part of the due diligence process that was estimated to take four to six weeks. WCW employees were told there might be ongoing employment opportunities with the new company.

That may have been a strategy to keep the current people from taking shots at Bischoff, in the hope that they might keep a job with Fusient.

Fusient sent some of their people to our offices to investigate the company. One representative commandeered one of the WCW offices and was there every day for weeks. He never spoke to me and I never spoke to him, other than an occasional "hello" to each other as we passed in the hallway.

After a full month passed by, I received a phone call from a woman who identified herself as an attorney for Fusient. She told me that she had contacted Diana Myers for general information about how talent contracts were structured in wrestling. Diana was unable to answer her questions and redirected her to me. In my most sarcastic tone of voice, I started the conversation by saying, *"I'm surprised you didn't call Eric Bischoff about this because he's your wrestling expert. He wrote almost every one of the current contracts. However, you must have been referred to me because you already realize that he doesn't know any details of those contracts.*

*"In case you're interested in my background and my credentials, I can tell you that I have been involved in the wrestling business for over thirty years. Before WCW, I was with Titan Sports for 7½ years as Vice President of Talent Relations. I did the preliminary payoffs, subject to final approval by Vince McMahon, including the payoffs on all the pay-per-views. I know the formulas that are applicable so that you can keep your talent costs in line—which is the most essential piece of the puzzle to keep your company profitable.*

*"As you continue your due diligence process, you may want to inquire why someone with my background and experience in wrestling has been sitting here in an office for the last year ... with absolutely nothing to do. I will tell you up front that I can help you. However, if I were to give you the information you seek, it would be useless to you without someone like me. There aren't many people in the wrestling business, and none in this company, who have the knowledge and experience to administer the process. I have less than twelve months remaining on my contract. If you have an interest in my services, I would be delighted to sit down and talk with you. Otherwise, I am probably wasting your time."*

End of conversation.

I never heard from her again. In hindsight, I was rather flippant with her and probably came off as arrogant. Anybody who knows me knows that I am normally a somewhat humble person, and that conversation was very uncharacteristic of me. I suppose my frustration boiled over after sitting around for four years, staring at WCW's walls.

The Fusient deal was publicly announced on January 11, 2001. They sent out a press release and added the WCW logo and pictures of the talent to their website. On March 16, 2001, Siegel sent out an announcement stating that as of March 27, 2001, all WCW programs on Turner stations would be cancelled. With the television deal gone, Bischoff panicked and tried to negotiate deals with SFX, USA Network, and FOX, but to no avail. With no television programming, Fusient officially backed out of the deal on March 20, 2001. That was a good business decision for Fusient because the offer they made for the company was ridiculous—$60 or $70 million.

With the collapse of the Fusient deal, it was now apparent that WCW was up for grabs. Eighteen months earlier, I had introduced Jerry Jarrett to Brad Siegel, recommending that Jerry be brought in as a consultant to help oversee our operation. Jerry wasn't interested in moving to Atlanta, or in full-time employment, but he was willing to help us turn the company around. During the meeting with Siegel, Jerry was very candid. He told Brad that the company had to be run with an iron fist and that he had better be prepared to go that route, or he would likely fail and suffer the same fate as his predecessors. Jerry also pointed out that he had met each of the people who had preceded Brad, and that doing it his (Jerry's) way was the only way to achieve success and turn the company around.

Of course, since Brad Siegel already knew everything about everything, he already had things figured out. He didn't need Jerry Jarrett's help to rescue WCW. After more than a year had passed, and right after the Fusient deal fell through, Jerry came back to the offices to make Siegel an offer: He himself wanted to buy WCW.

I accompanied Jerry when he went to meet with Siegel. He made a genuine attempt to buy the company. I was included in that meeting because I was going to be a part of Jerry's management team. Jerry had the financial backing and wherewithal to purchase the company. He was convinced that if someone with a wrestling background—someone like himself—could take control and run the company in a manner in which a wrestling company should be run, they could make the company profitable. Brad Siegel listened to Jerry's pitch, but he never even considered his offer.

Instead, Siegel basically gave the company away ... to Vince McMahon. It was reported that Vince paid as little as $2 to $5 million for WCW. The figures in this deal pale in comparison to the money that Fusient had planned to pay WCW. Nobody knows how much Jerry Jarrett was willing to offer because, for some reason, Siegel made sure that conversation never took place. In the end, AOL-Time Warner was probably lucky to get what they did because as soon as Jamie Kellner (the Chairman and CEO of Turner Broadcasting Systems) made the decision to discontinue programming, they really had nothing to sell. At that point, the only thing Vince wanted was the rights to the backlog of tapes. He could use the matches and promos to produce career retrospectives on tape or DVD of people like Steve Austin. He already had the rights to footage of Steve's Stone Cold character. Now he could use the WCW footage to tell the whole story.

That was a mystery that goes unanswered to this day: If you have something to sell, and more than one person is interested, why wouldn't you sell to the person who is willing to pay the best price? And why wouldn't you entertain multiple offers in order to get the best price possible for what you're selling.

There was a cloud over the whole process of selling WCW, and many questioned the fact that Vince was the only person considered in what should have been a bidding war. We couldn't help but look at the fact that Brad Siegel's fraternity brother, Stu Schneider, was the President of the WWF.

On March 26, 2001, Vince McMahon was at the live *RAW* taping in Cleveland, Ohio. He was simulcast on both *RAW* and the final episode of *Monday Nitro*, which was shot in Panama City, and announced that he had bought WCW ... Ted Turner's wrestling company.

I had been pulled off the road for the previous twelve months, so I was not at the TV for the final *Monday Nitro*. I actually watched it at home like everybody else. When Vince appeared on both *Monday Nitro* and *Monday Night RAW* simultaneously, and made the announcement that he owned them both, it was a surprise to me ... and yet, it really wasn't a surprise. Vince boasted about buying WCW, and gloated about how he won the wrestling war against Ted Turner. He did that on TNT—Turner Network Television. Ted Turner didn't deserve that. From an ego standpoint, I understood how attractive that was to Vince, but Ted deserved a better sendoff than that. Vince's statements were a huge putdown to a man who had done so much for the wrestling business, starting in the '70s when the TBS SuperStation first became a reality. I thought it was a sad day for Ted Turner and a sad day for professional wrestling. The other sad thing is that 200 people lost their jobs and had to find something else to do. Many of them had spent their entire life in the wrestling business, and very few of them found lateral moves into the WWF.

On the day that WCW officially closed the doors, I was in the office. I believe that everyone received one month's basic severance pay, plus an additional month's salary for each full year of service. Since I still had about six months left on my contract, Turner honored my contract up to the expiration date in lieu of any severance, which would have been a lesser amount. In my opinion, we were all treated fairly by Turner. I had been with the company for 5½ years. If it had been five years later, I might have walked away from it and said, *"Well, it was time for me to go, anyway."* The truth is ... it wasn't time. It didn't have to be that way.

After the sale, I stayed in touch with Zane Bresloff, Gary Juster, Chip Burnham (the local promoter for the Georgia TV tapings and house shows), Don Edwards (WCW's Director of Strategic Planning), and of course, Kevin Sullivan.

I have very strong, negative feelings about Brad Siegel, Eric Bischoff and Vince Russo. It's hard to lay all the blame on Bischoff, even though he structured the company in such a way that it was doomed to fail from the start. Today, Eric is working for Vince McMahon as a storyline character, which quite frankly, is what he was suited to do from day one. It's almost poetic justice to see Eric working for the man he was consumed with putting out of business. I can picture Vince McMahon waking up each morning with a smirk on his face, knowing that he can get Eric to do just about anything he wants him to do. Mark my words: The day will come when Vince will get tired of having Eric around. When that happens, he will have his fun with Eric and will cast him aside.

Vince Russo? I don't have a lot of respect for him as a person. Do I hate him? No, I don't. He had a family to take care of, just like the rest of us, and in order of importance, he was down at the bottom. However, the financial numbers tell the story. Vince Russo helped speed the company to the brink of disaster.

I *am* angry with Brad Siegel because he allowed it to happen. He was the last link in the chain, and he acted arrogant and self-important, refusing to listen to people who could have helped him, and he let the company fall to ruin around him.

There are people who blame Jamie Kellner for the demise of the company, but they don't understand the big picture. Yes, Jamie made the decision to remove WCW from Turner programming, and by doing so, hammered the final nail into the coffin. However, if WCW upper management had been doing their job properly all along, the ratings and revenue would have been up and he would have had no justifiable reason to cancel the shows. In the end, Jamie Kellner did what was best for the future of Turner Broadcasting. Can Brad Siegel or Eric Bischoff say they did the same for WCW? Anyone who knew Vince and worked closely with him knew that he had spent his whole life promoting the WWF brand-name. He didn't promote professional wrestling. He promoted the WWF. He didn't promote the world heavyweight champion. He promoted the WWF title. He didn't promote wrestlers. He promoted superstars. The on-air talent was instilled to echo those sentiments, and they were taught that the organization was bigger than any individual.

When Vince bought WCW, he was smart enough to pick and choose the talent he wanted. Vince didn't want the entire cast of characters, because that would mean he had to pick up the high-dollar, guaranteed contracts of people like Bill Goldberg. Instead, he had the option of cherry-picking from the WCW talent roster. He took people like Booker T, a very good talent whose contract was more in line with what Booker T brought to the table.

I was surprised when Vince attempted to promote an invasion of WWF by the WCW talent he had picked up. He was doing so with a fraction of a roster that had already failed, and the talent he was bringing in were not the big stars who had the huge contracts. The invasion seemed to be a half-hearted attempt at recreating the success WCW had in 1996 with the "nWo" storyline. When Kevin Nash and Scott Hall entered the WCW as the New World Order, in the eyes of the fans, WCW was truly in jeopardy. When Vince copied that idea by having WCW invade the WWF, it had some initial impact, but after getting a buzz for a couple of weeks, business settled right back down and the fans lost interest.

# Chapter 37
# Total Nonstop Anxiety

The weeks following the sale of WCW to Vince McMahon were a stressful time for me. Once again, I found myself out of work, and I was worried about losing our house. Fortunately, Jerry Jarrett stepped in and said, *"Don't worry. I'll make sure you don't lose your house until you can get back on your feet again."*

Jerry did just that. If Jerry Jarrett had not been there, I would have lost everything. He's a friend that I will always be indebted to.

I was still getting a severance check from WCW when I went to work for Jerry in his construction business. He called me and said, *"I have a major contract that I need help with. I need somebody based in Atlanta that I can trust and don't have to worry about every day."* I agreed to work for him and we handled two major projects in the Atlanta area. The first project was to build a private school in Marietta. The second was to re-image Amoco gas stations into BP stations through a management firm.

At one time, Jerry talked about naming me President of Jarrett Construction, but he decided to give the title to his youngest son, Jason, who was very active in Jerry's construction business. Jerry said that I would be better received by the companies we dealt with if I held the title of Chief Financial Officer. As the CFO, I handled all of the invoicing and payroll. The time cards came to me every week and I combined the information into a form that went to Nashville. The payroll company cut the payroll checks, sent them to me, and I dispersed them. Since I didn't have an accounting background (and really didn't know anything about it), it was an interesting two years because I had to learn the job by the seat of my pants. I was also the liaison for the company. I would present estimates for approval before construction started. When the work was finished, I would present a final bill for payment. My primary job was to chase down and get our money. Once again, I was learning by doing.

At the same time, Jerry Jarrett and I were very interested in getting involved in professional wrestling again. It's like a variation on the old saying: You can take a wrestler out of the wrestling business, but you can't take the wrestling business out of the wrestler. We began to work on a business plan for a new promotion, and looked for an investor, or creative ways to get financial backing to do a start-up company. There was a lot of unemployed wrestling talent floating around, and many of them still had name value. If we could have signed new talent, and given them the rub of established stars like Sting, Scott Hall, Kevin Nash, Goldberg, and Scott Steiner, we would have had a nucleus to launch a new promotion. However, time was of the essence, because with every day that went by, the stars became farther removed from television exposure, and we couldn't start up a company with all-new talent.

Our plan was to find an investor who would be willing to bankroll our startup costs. As soon as we could make the company profitable, we would go public. That's where the big money is. In August 2001, Jerry Jarrett, Jeff Jarrett, Scott Steiner, and I met with a potential investor at his offices in lower Manhattan. The investor had been part of a group that had promoted boxing at several casinos, and the prospect of promoting wrestling intrigued him. He told us that he needed some time to contact his people and sell them on the idea, but he would do his best to get a commitment for the funding we would need. I would categorize his mood as one of cautious optimism.

One month later, the Twin Towers were destroyed by terrorists. Many of the people who were interested in investing in our start-up promotion lost their businesses in the tragedy, and several of them even lost their lives. As a result, the deal never came to fruition.

Jerry and Jeff eventually found another investor and put TNA (Total Nonstop Action) together. Jeff put everything on the line—his savings and the mortgage to his house—to start the promotion. Jeff also had contacts with people in Nashville's music industry who had financial resources and were willing to step up to the plate and help him. Jerry had an investment stake in the operation as well, but the lion's share of the financing came from Jeff. However, even though Jeff had the finances, he needed Jerry's name and financial reputation as a package to make the deal work.

Bob Ryder had the original idea of just offering a PPV product, without a broadcast or cable outlet to drive it. Ryder relocated to the Nashville area and began providing the talent management services that I would have been suited for. Even if he hadn't, I probably wouldn't have pursued a management position with the company because Jeff still had underlying feelings of resentment towards me. It didn't help when Jeff surrounded himself with Russo and his clique: Jeremy Borash, Bill Banks, and Disco Inferno. I would never have felt comfortable in that mix, in addition to knowing that Jeff had issues with me that to this day I do not feel were justified.

Jerry always said that Jeff made the final decisions on everything, including acquisitions of talent. I don't know what Jerry's feelings towards Russo were at the time, but Jerry did everything he could to help Jeff succeed. Jerry is a wonderful human being who loves his children. He didn't want to see Jeff lose everything he had, so he was willing to go along with Jeff's decisions and try to make things work.

I made two on-air appearances—both in Nashville—for TNA as their Commissioner. The first time was on February 12, 2003. Jerry wanted me to go out and do a compelling "reality" angle with Vince Russo. He tried to sell me on the raw emotions of having a "shoot conflict" on live TV with Russo. That sounded good, but in wrestling, there needs to be a trust factor between the two parties involved in a storyline. When Terry Funk does a back flip off of the top turnbuckle, he needs to rely on somebody—usually his opponent—to break his fall. All through my career, I had that same understanding with the people I worked with. Believe it or not, Vince Russo was the *only* person in my entire career that I had no trust in. Vince didn't have the same agenda that I had, and so it was doomed to failure.

When I voiced my concerns about the respect and trust factors, Jerry tried to convince me that it didn't matter. I should just go out and say what I wanted and how I felt.

Russo and I were given specific talking points that would allow each of us to make our case. When we got into the ring, I was quite shocked when he started his rant by calling me a "piece of sh—" because there were children in the audience. Russo then proceeded to veer so far off the script that he literally told lies.

Now, I can go toe-to-toe in a verbal shoot with anyone, because I have nothing to hide and I can answer for everything I've done, but when the person I'm "shooting" with is just making things up, then it's no longer a shoot. After that, he started to tell his lies. He claimed that when we both worked at the WWF, Vince McMahon kicked me "to the curb." This was coming from the man who resigned by calling Vince on the telephone. He couldn't do it man-to-man, face-to-face, the way that I did. After that, he accused me of "selling a bill of goods" to WCW, but bringing "nothing to the table." If THAT isn't the pot calling the kettle black, I don't know what is. He then said that I was the reason why WCW was "in the toilet." I would love to know how that was my fault.

Russo's revisionism continued as he claimed that he came in to "save" WCW, after which I "politicked and buried" him until he was kicked out. He ended by blaming me for taking his childrens' "food off the table" and for trying to force him out of the wrestling business. Russo went much longer than he was supposed to and ad-libbed to the point of being ridiculous.

The funny thing is, as he was raving like a lunatic at me, the audience was chanting *"Russo sucks!"* over and over.

I just stood there respectfully until Russo finished his harangue. When my time came to respond, Russo laid down on the mat and began to yawn, acting as if my speech was putting him to sleep. He then stood up and interrupted me, asking the audience, *"Is there anybody else in here bored? Does anybody want to hear this dribble?"* He did everything he could to draw the focus to himself and away from the exchange that was supposed to be *between* us. Before I could really rebut anything he said, or get my points across, he instructed the Harris Twins to storm up the aisle and chase me.

If you work for people who share a passion for what you do, and have trust enough to make themselves vulnerable, then you have a comfort level that allows you to put yourself into a position as one of the parties involved. Unfortunately, but not unexpectedly, Russo doesn't fall into that category. He has no respect for the wrestling business or anyone in it, especially me. Instead of doing what was right for business that night, he decided to push his own personal, selfish agenda.

At times, Russo and Jeff tried to work everyone else around them. Russo eventually got mad and quit. Jerry later went on record talking about Russo in a very negative manner, claiming something to the effect that he almost cost them the company.

My only criticism of the way Jeff runs the company stems from something I've heard a lot of people say: *"Jeff Jarrett is the owner, and yet, he makes himself the champion and keeps himself on top."* If I had been in his position, I would have gone to great lengths to keep the ownership aspect a secret.

On February 19, I made my second appearance with TNA. Dusty Rhodes was also booked on the show. For the first time since we had that meeting in Bill Busch's office, and the subsequent telephone conversation when Dusty was very cold to me, I was finally going to see Dusty face-to-face and talk to him. As I drove to the building, I was wondering, *"Oh, boy. How's THIS gonna go?"* With Dusty, you never knew.

I saw Dusty walk into the building with his big cowboy hat and bag over his shoulder. Nothing had changed. He was stopping every few feet, glad-handing and laughing with everybody. He was just being Dusty Rhodes. I walked straight up to him and held out my hand. He grabbed my hand, pulled me in, and gave me a great, big hug. It was somewhat superficial, but it was almost as if nothing bad had ever taken place.

Looking back on our time together, I've always felt that Dusty was good to me when we first started working together in Florida. I'm grateful for the things I learned from him. He wished me well when I left for Canada, and he paved the way for me to return to Charlotte. Those are the things I will always remember about Dusty. At the same time, I feel that I paid my own way in terms of what I contributed to the end product, and I always made Dusty look very good. Dusty always got all the credit. That didn't bother me. That wasn't my personality. I didn't need to get the accolades. Kevin Sullivan's relationship with Dusty was similar to mine. He worked with Dusty and made Dusty look good. Kevin is not as much of an attention-to-detail person as

I am, but Kevin never had that huge ego, either. Kevin and I have often laughed about "the ego." You can best sum Dusty up by simply saying, *"Dusty's Dusty."*

After two years with Jarrett Construction, which was actually a satellite company of Jarrett Builders, there was no new business coming in, and we were having trouble getting money to complete the unfinished projects. Eventually, Jerry told me that he couldn't afford to keep me, and Jarrett Construction ceased to exist. Jerry moved everything back to Nashville, including the construction equipment, and continued to operate as Jarrett Builders. My last day with Jerry was March 25, 2003.

Once again, I no longer had a job. For the second time in two years, I worked for a company that had ceased to exist.

TNA wasn't an option, either. If I was going to appear on the TNA shows, I would have to drive from Atlanta to Nashville. They didn't pay for my hotel, so when the show was over, I had to drive the 210 miles back home. Jerry said the best they could pay me was $300 a week. I knew that I could stay home and make $290 a week in unemployment benefits, so that wasn't even a choice to be considered.

For the first time in my life — I had to go on unemployment.

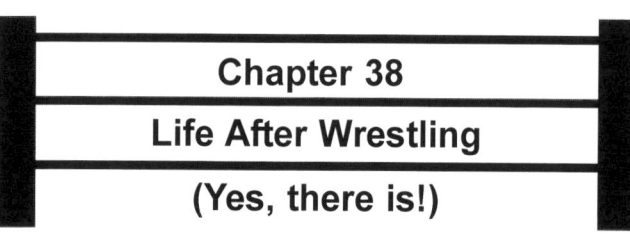

# Chapter 38
## Life After Wrestling
### (Yes, there is!)

Looking back to the fall of 2001: Three months after I went to work for Jarrett Construction, Lindsey applied to Kennesaw State University School of Nursing, was accepted, and started attending classes. In mid-December 2002, she graduated with honors with a Bachelor of Science degree in Nursing, and passed her boards in January. She immediately pursued graduate school and was accepted at Emory University with a full scholarship starting in fall 2003.

In fall 2002, while Lindsey was still in school, we sold our house and moved into a smaller, older rental home. On the day we closed the sale, our dog Laddie was laying on the carpet, while the movers worked around him. He had stopped eating, could no longer stand up, and along with all the other emotions of that day, Lindsey took Laddie to have him put to sleep.

As soon as Lindsey graduated from Kennesaw, I immediately applied for real estate school at Kennesaw State and took a course with 25 classroom sessions that ran until April 1, 2003. I completed the course and received my certificate. One month later, I took the state exam, got my real estate license, and was hired by Prudential. Unfortunately, there's no salary to draw from and there are minimal, ongoing expenses that you have to pay each month, as well as initial investments.

On June 3, I was served with divorce papers. It came as a total surprise. Not only was I a devoted father to my children, but I had been a faithful husband to Lindsey. After fourteen years, though, Lindsey had apparently reached a point in her life where she had become very unhappy. We went through a lot of heartache and trials

**Jim Morrison**
Sales Associate
www.Jimmorrison.prudentialgeorgia.com

**Georgia Realty**
3775 Roswell Rd, Ste 200
Marietta, GA 30062
Bus 770 973-▓▓▓▓ Fx 770 973-▓▓▓▓
Direct 678 594-▓▓▓▓ 1 800 231-▓▓▓▓

An independently owned and operated member of The Prudential Real Estate Affiliates, Inc.

together when I was working for both WCW and the WWF. Just like the aches and pains in my body remind me of the accumulative effect of all those years in the ring when I crawl out of bed each morning, the ups and downs of the previous fourteen years had an accumulative effect on our marriage, as well.

The divorce, which was final in mid-July, was devastating to me. It scuttled my career in real estate before it ever began because I needed a home to work out of and a computer at all times. Without those, I couldn't sell, and if I didn't sell, I didn't make any commission—Prudential doesn't pay a base salary.

In the days following the divorce, the lease on our rental home ran out, so I helped Lindsey move into another rental home in the same subdivision. I moved into an efficiency motel and lived there until I realized that I could not support myself or my kids by remaining in Georgia. The only income I had was unemployment. I couldn't afford to pay much towards child care. The $290 barely covered my own living expenses. It was a tough time for me—a time of soul-searching. My only alternative was to move back to my mother's house in Delaware and look for work in that area. It was a tough decision to leave my children, but at that point, I was starting over. I literally had nothing. I stayed in Atlanta until the kids were due to start the new school year. The day before I had to leave, I did the hardest thing I ever had to do in my life—break the news to my children. My son cried the hardest. I guess there is some validity to how special a father-son relationship is, just like that of a mother-daughter. We all hugged, and I wept along with them. It was a very sad day.

Was I angry and bitter over the divorce? Probably, but Lindsey and I now get along. Lindsey deserves to be happy in life, and if that means a divorce and separate lives, then so be it. As long as she is a loving mother who cares well for our children, which she is and does, I can live with what has happened. I can't undo what's been done, so for the good of my children, why would I harbor any resentment? The kids love their mother, and they love me, too. That's how it should be.

In the past few years, I have attended several wrestling legend reunions. When I was at FanFest in Fayetteville, North Carolina, I saw Ole Anderson for the first time in more than five years. I had always gotten along with Ole, and I like him personally. I first bumped into him in the hall of our hotel. He said, *"Come on into my room."*

We proceeded to talk for the next two hours, and then we went out to eat. Ole even picked up the dinner tab! We talked about our feelings, our beliefs, and our perceptions and frustrations on where the business has gone. Ole and I see things similarly. As our conversation turned personal, I told Ole that I couldn't understand why my third marriage failed, especially when I had become a faithful husband for the first time in my life. I thought that would be the key to a successful marriage. Ole is very outspoken, and he doesn't sugar coat his words. He bluntly said, *"Maybe you're paying the price for the first two times around."*

Wham! Thanks for the punch in the gut, Ole.

But as I reflect back, I remember that I walked away from my second wife after seventeen years of marriage. This time, I had been married fourteen years, and the same thing happened ... only this time, the shoe was on the other foot. I had never looked at my situation in that light.

On a lighter note, while I was living at the efficiency motel, I had some much needed dental work completed. The process involved a couple of crowns, one of which was to be fastened onto a large molar in the back of my mouth. During the final fitting, without realizing it, the dentist accidentally popped the crown off. At first, I thought I had a small particle in my throat. When I started to cough, I was offered a drink, which I accepted. A minute or two went by while the dentist worked on something else. When he looked for the crown, he couldn't find it. *"Is it possible that I could have swallowed it?"*

*"No, that couldn't happen."*

Several minutes later, following a thorough search, and by the process of elimination, they decided that I must have swallowed it. It was the only possibility. They sent me to have x-rays made, and sure enough, there it was. They followed the progress of the crown by taking another set of x-rays a few days later. It took nine days for the crown to finish the trip ... if you get my drift. Jay Leno would have had a field day with this one. It could only happen to me, but I still laugh about it.

When I returned to Delaware, I immediately began to look for a job. I was 61 years old, so I could have taken an early retirement and lived on social security retirement benefits, but there were two reasons why I wasn't ready for that. First of all, I've been blessed with good health, so I wasn't ready to leave the workforce, but the most important reason was that I had three small children to help support. Even though we were separated by 750 miles, I needed to do my financial part to help raise them.

I aggressively went out and searched the job market, and I was more than willing to adjust my lifestyle, but I went through a terrible time of not being able to find work. It's a terrible feeling to have a college education and over 30 years of experience in the wrestling business at all levels, including the executive level, and realize that at age 61, I don't have any unique skills, such as computer training or a business degree, that would make me a commodity to be hired. My age was also a factor. No prospective employer would ever say, *"We can't hire you because you're too old,"* but no matter how favorable of an impression I made, I couldn't get past the first or second interview. I eventually went to a job fair. While there, the Delaware Department of Correction and I found each other. I was hired as a Correctional Officer (we don't use the term "prison guard" anymore because it's considered to be a demeaning description) and I wear a uniform. Each morning, I walk through a metal detector and I'm patted down, while someone x-rays the contents of my lunch bag. I then go through a series of electronically-opened doors to get where I'm stationed that day.

This is the first time since college that I've had to work in a blue-collar environment. There are a lot of wonderful people who work with me at the institution who never had the opportunity to get a college education like I did. They work here because they have families to feed and bills to pay. I respect them for what they have to endure. They are dedicated people who often find themselves at risk because that is a part of the job. It's been a humbling experience.

Along with the position, I have medical insurance, which had previously expired the day I got divorced. I have liberal sick days and holidays, and I will be vested by the State of Delaware after five years. I will also qualify for a pension to supplement social security.

There are always things you can do to improve your situation, and I'm making an effort to do that. There are other opportunities with the Department of Correction, one of which is Correctional Counselor. The person in that position works personally with inmates and helps them cope with their personal problems. They help them through the rehabilitation process by making the inmates aware of the programs, educational opportunities, and treatments that are available to them. I submitted an application for that position, and it was accepted. I took the examination to qualify and passed that. Now I'm waiting for an opening in that line of work. If I get the job, I'll move a couple of pay grades up. I would have all my weekends free, I wouldn't have to work on holidays, and I wouldn't have to work double-shifts.

The number of people who recognize me at the institution where I work is unbelievable—not only the staff, but many of the inmates. A lot of those people have been there for a long time, and they've watched a lot of television. One of my responsibilities is to maintain security in one of the housing units. When you do that job, you interact with the inmates. One of them told me, *"I'm from Philadelphia, and my dad used to take me to the Civic Center to watch you. My dad loved the Horsemen and he loved you!"*

I said, *"I'll tell you what. Give me your dad's name and address and I'll be very happy to send a picture to him."*

When I arrived home at the end of the day, I autographed a photo and sent it to his father.

I worked death row one day. There are sixteen inmates on death row at the moment in Delaware, and they're all at my facility in Smyrna. After feeding them lunch, I was in the process of picking up the food trays, which we do through a drop-flap in the cell doors. One of the inmates spoke up and asked my name. I said, *"Morrison."*

He said, *"No, I know you by another name."*

When I confirmed his suspicions, he became like a little kid, and told me how he also used to watch the Horsemen on TV with his father. We spoke for several minutes and it was a pleasant surprise, but it left me lost for words. I simply said, *"Be strong!"* and I moved on.

Every now and then, with a smile on their face, one of the men will playfully say, *"I think maybe I could take you."*

I just say, *"Look at it this way. If you were to try me on for size and you get the best of me, you're just beating up an old man, so how tough are you? On the other hand, if you come up short and get your butt kicked by an old man, how would you justify that to your friends? Either way, it's a no-win situation for you, so the best thing is for you to go your own way, and I'll go mine."*

I smile, we both laugh, and that's the end of it. They call it IPC—interpersonal communication skills—and I use it a lot.

I meet a LOT of people who say, *"I know you from somewhere ...,"* but they just can't place their finger on it. I see other people in the institution who say, "What are YOU doing HERE?"

I say, *"Well, it's a simple story, really. I was married three times, divorced three times, went through a bankruptcy, and all of a sudden, the business that I spent my whole life in died before I died. That's why I'm here. Did I make some big money? Yes, I had some very good years. Now when you say big money, I'll bet you're thinking in terms of millions of dollars. Trust me. The number of people who made that kind of money in the wrestling business are in a very, very, very tiny circle. I was never in that circle."*

When people at the institution—either inmates or officers—ask me if I'm frustrated because of how my life turned out, I say, *"No, because it's almost like I am living my life in reverse. Some people work hard all their lives, sacrifice, and save their money, in the hopes of doing things that I've already done, and going places where I've already been."* I no longer feel compelled to chase "The American Dream," no pun intended. How many people have a dream of what they want to do in their life, and actually get to live that dream? I am so fortunate.

It seems that I'm best remembered for my years with the Horsemen, and that was almost twenty years ago! That's what people talk about the most, and that's the era they remember me from. Granted, my appearance has not changed radically, which contributes to the recognition, but I always believed that when you were no longer on television, you would no longer be remembered.

At one of the Mid-Atlantic Wrestling Legends FanFest reunions, I met Dick Bourne, a fan and wrestling historian from Mount Airy, North Carolina. Dick pulled video segments from various Mid-Atlantic wrestling shows from the mid-80's that featured me and created a DVD for my personal collection. Watching that DVD, I came to further appreciate the quality of the talent that surrounded me and just how special a time that was in my career.

I also met a girl named Vicki during my run with the Horsemen. She was a big fan of the Horsemen. When I walked into the FanFest reunion in Charlotte in 2004, she was standing there, waiting to see me. She lives in North Carolina with her mother, works hard, and still has all of her scrapbooks. She's a tremendous gal.

When I did the first FanFest reunion in January 2004, Jim Cornette was scheduled to do the Q&A late at night. The Fanfest promoter took me aside and said, *"I'm trying to over-deliver to these people by giving them something extra—not advertised—for their money. If you don't mind, would you come in unannounced and sit in the back. The fact that you took the time to be there yourself says to the fans that what's going on is something special."*

That night, Jimmy Cornette held court, and as usual, Jimmy was being Jimmy. I hadn't seen Jim Cornette in a long time. The nature of the wrestling business being what it was, a lot of times you think, *"I don't remember if I have heat with this guy or not ..."* and with someone like Cornette, there's a possibility that he might cut a promo on you when he sees you. There might have been some friction between us at one time, although if there was, it wasn't on my part. When we were both managing for Crockett, business got a little bit slow. Since I worked in the office, I would go to the towns with somebody I was managing, and we would ask Jim to stay home. Jim may have not been too happy with that, but if that was the case, it wasn't anything contrived on my part.

Jimmy had Tommy Young, the referee, on the stage. Jimmy was teasing Tommy about being light in the loafers. I mean, it was embarrassing. My old friend Les Thatcher was on stage, too. At one point, someone told Cornette that I was there. He said, *"What!? Where is he?"*

When Jimmy spotted me, he gave me one of the most flattering introductions that I have ever heard, or expected, in my life. One of the comments he made was. *"And what most of you people don't know is that J.J. Dillon was a better worker than most of the guys he ever managed."*

I don't know about anybody else, but that meant a lot to me, because Jimmy is on the inside, and he knows. That was a wonderful thing for him to say.

One of the things I respect about Jim Cornette is his work ethic. He works hard at everything he does. Jerry Jarrett used to say there was a fundamental difference between Jim and me as managers. I had to work to get people to dislike me, but Jim was so annoying that just the sight of him made the fans want to slap him. I have nothing but good things to say about Jim Cornette. Jim has a tremendous passion for this business. He put a lot of his own money, his heart, and his soul, into his own promotion—Smoky Mountain Wrestling.

I don't have what I would call close friends or contacts from my years in the wrestling business. The atmosphere of the wrestling business isn't one that lends itself to the development of genuine friendships. You have a lot of business "associates," and you become closer to some guys than to other, but in most cases, you won't find true friendship.

When I got out of the business, Jim Barnett was one of the few people I stayed in touch with. I would talk with him frequently. I talked to him on a regular basis until his passing on September 17, 2004, and I was very saddened by that. He was very sensitive in his retirement. Ole Anderson gave him a pounding in his book, *Inside Out,* and Jim felt badly that things had turned out between them as they had. Jim was very close to both Vince McMahon Jr. and Ted Turner, and was the middle man for business deals that took place between them. People joked about Jim Barnett because he was very prissy, and not someone you would think of as being a power figure in the world of professional wrestling, but he had a gift. We called it "smelling money." Who else would have smelled money in Tommy Rich? Tommy wasn't a great worker, and he didn't have a good body, but Jim Barnett saw something in him. As a result, Tommy became a huge star in the business. Jim started and gave breaks to a lot of the great, great names in wrestling, and he doesn't get the credit that he deserves. In my opinion, Jim Barnett was one of the true treasures of our business. Jim was also a great baseball fan, and would call me to ask about somebody in baseball — their stats, who they were playing for, or what happened to them. He had always been kind to me and his death was a real loss for wrestling.

I talk to Tully Blanchard every now and then. A lot of wrestlers have become "born again," and there's a natural skepticism from their associates because of the nature of the wrestling business. However, I look at people like Tully Blanchard and Ivan Koloff, who feel very strongly about their faith, and I believe they are sincere about the path they've chosen.

Ric Flair and I talk a few times each year. I usually call him. He doesn't call me, but he's on the road every day and he has a lot of demands on his schedule. He changed his phone number last year, but when we were at the FanFest in Fayetteville, North Carolina, Ric's son walked up and said, *"Here's dad's new phone number."* On the way home that weekend, I called, not having any idea of where he was. He was at a pay-per-view in Toronto. He must have checked his messages because thirty minutes later, he called me, and we talked for twenty minutes.

I talk to Mike Graham with some regularity because I have such fond memories of my time with his father, and I just enjoy talking to Mike. Every now and then, I'll bump into Dave or Earl Hebner. I always thought a lot of them. They are hard-working and very loyal. Gene Okerlund has a condominium in Sarasota, Florida, and he gave me an open invitation to go down and have the use of it. He's a great guy who I have always admired professionally. "Mean Gene" is somebody that I respect, and will always regard as a friend.

I did a show with Major League Wrestling on February 14, 2004, in Orlando, Florida, and I was very surprised to see Gary Hart there. It was good to see him. We only did one TV taping, but two old managers spent some time together, talking about the old days. We were both hopeful that MLW was an opportunity that would bear fruit, but unfortunately, that didn't happen and the promotion folded.

Les Thatcher has been a very close friend over the years. Les has had his ups and downs and he has been through some tough times. He remarried and seems to be very happy. Les is what southerners call "good people," and I regard him as a special friend. He bailed me out of jams more than once during those early years in Charlotte.

Anne and Bill Bowman have been wonderful friends through thick and thin for almost thirty-five years since we first met in Charlotte. I'll never forget the surprise 30th birthday party they threw for me when we were in Charlotte. My wife, Jeanette, baked a cake. Before the night was over, Jerry Brisco picked it up and threw it in my face.

It was Anne and Bill who introduced me to Scott Teal, and through Scott, I met Philip Varriale. Without the help of Scott and Philip, I would not have been able to tell my story. I would hope that this is just the beginning of a lifelong friendship with both Scott and Philip.

Bill Busch now lives in Pensacola, Florida. We still talk from time to time. He is currently the Chief Operating Officer of a large firm that manufactures and distributes clutch assemblies for automobile transmissions. If I was offered an opportunity to manage a wrestling operation, I would call Bill to ask him to join the team. That is how much I value, trust, and respect Bill Busch. A man of principle, people like Bill are few and far between.

I don't think any of you will recognize the name Mike Vettraino, but I met him at a baseball card show adjacent to the Cow Palace at a WCW event in San Francisco. Mike is a wrestling fan and has become a great friend.

The only other person that I talk to with any regularity is Kevin Sullivan. Kevin and his wife, Linda, own property in the Florida Keys. They built a gym and they have a nice business going. Kevin and I stuck by each other during some hard times. I was loyal to him and I refused to distance myself from him during our final year at WCW, and he did the same with me. I don't believe in being a fair weather friend. If I'm your friend, I'm your friends always. When it comes to remembering people who were good to me along the way, I don't get amnesia. I'm sure you've heard the old saying, *Be careful who you step on during the way up, because you may have to step over them on the way back down.* Just some food for thought.

I'm thankful for so many things in my life, such as being born to middle-class parents who worked hard. I was never aware of a day when they strained to meet the mortgage payment. I was a kid who was allowed to be a kid, without having to worry about whatever it was that grownups worried about. I never had a day that I didn't have a roof over my head, clean clothes, and food to eat. Thank goodness that my parents scrimped and saved to pay for my college education because I was too dumb to know that I should have applied myself, and gotten a scholarship so they didn't have to.

My mother turned 90 years old on December 29, 2004. She's amazing. She's in marvelous health and takes no medication. She's even in a bowling league! Her only downside is that her eyesight has suffered, and she can no longer drive.

I'm also blessed to have a wonderful sister, Joan, who is three years younger than I am. She is married and lives in Matthews, North Carolina (near Charlotte) with her family. I always knew how special she was, but my feeling of love for her has grown due to the love and support she has shown me during these last few years.

Out of financial necessity, I'm in Delaware and not with my kids in Marietta, Georgia. At the same time, this is a good place for me because I live with my mother. My father worked at General Motors, which provided benefits that few other companies provide, so my mother is taken care of. She doesn't live in the lap of luxury, but she lives in a comfortable home that is paid for. She has given me a place to stay. In return, I drive her around and I do all the cooking. In some ways, perhaps the hand that was dealt to me has been a blessing since I can be here to take care of her.

The bad thing about living in Delaware is that I miss being with my children. I'm amazed at how my outlook on life has changed since they were born. They are the number one priority in my life now. I talk to them on the telephone every night. I have a cell phone plan that allows me to do that. In addition to that and e-mails, I also see them every two to three months. I will fly to Atlanta, or bring them up here for two weeks in the summer. Last summer, I took my son, Geoff, fishing for the first time in his life. He caught four fish to my none. Geoff and Missy, the twins, are both all-A students. Niki is in the fourth grade and on the honor roll.

I've grown closer to my oldest daughter, Pam, who lives two hours away in Reading, Pennsylvania. She has three children, ages 10, 15, and 16. I am just now getting to know them after all these years. Pam and I are very much alike. She's a free spirit, which I'm sure caused angst for her mother. She understands me and I understand her. When she has problems, she picks up the phone and I try to be a source of strength to her. I feel fortunate that I'm able to do that. When I went to the FanFest in Charlotte in 2004, Pam and my youngest granddaughter, Meghan, flew together to Atlanta. We rented a van and picked up my youngest kids in Marietta. We all went to a photography studio, and for the first time in my life, I had a portrait made of me with all my children. (see page 9) I will treasure the photo until the day I die.

On January 28, 2005, I took Geoff to his first rock concert. We saw Joe Cocker at the Tabernacle in Atlanta. Two weeks later, on February 13, Pam and I went to see Joe Cocker on the same tour when he came to Wilkes-Barre, Pennsylvania, near where Pam lives. I love movies and music, and Joe Cocker has always been my favorite music artist. When I would go to Australia and Japan, I would make tapes of artists I like ... Willie Nelson, B.B. King, and Ray Charles. I've had the opportunity to meet Willie on a couple of occasions. I really do like his music. I also like the blues. I guess I just like music. I find it very comforting. But to this day, Joe Cocker is my favorite entertainer. I saw him twice in Dallas in a very small venue. He didn't draw very well, but he put on an unbelievable show. I also saw him when he was the opening act in Atlanta for Tina Turner's farewell tour.

That's the summary of my life today. I'm making the best of it. My life is my children and grandchildren. I savor the time that I have with them, and when we part, I look forward to our next meeting. I think the separation has been the hardest on my son, who just turned twelve. He has cerebral palsy and walks with a walker, but he's healthy and goes to public school with his sister. He is an inspiration to me.

I don't worry about myself because I'm a survivor. If I worry about anything at all, I worry about the world that my children have been brought into, and what the world will be like for their children. With the changes in our day-to-day lifestyle due to terrorist threats, and the difficult economy, the world is a much harsher place than it was when I came into it.

When I look back at my life, there are things that I could, and would, have done differently. However, I wouldn't change most of it because I was living a life that most people only dream about. I've traveled all over the world. I lived my dream of wrestling in Madison Square Garden. That in itself was a stroke of luck because I was the last non-WWF wrestler to get a deal like that. After Vince McMahon Sr. died in May, just one month after my shot in the Garden, Vince Jr. offered NO favors to other promoters. Wrestlers from other territories appearing as a special attraction in the WWF never happened again.

When I was 44 years old, I went skydiving because it was an experience that I wanted to feel. I relate that to my first commercial flight at the age of 22. I flew from Reading to Pittsburgh, and then to Dallas, for training with a life insurance company. I remember being horrified that even though the flight crew instructed us about using seat cushions as flotation devices, we were not issued parachutes. Talk about being naive.

In 1988, I went to Africa on a photo safari, and lived on a game reserve in Kenya for three days. The safari company does not guarantee that you will see all of the animals. It's unusual to see the rhino, and very rarely will you see a leopard. I have photos of both animals, including one of a leopard soon after it had made its kill, dragging the dead animal up into a tree. I've always been fascinated by mountain gorillas, so I spent two days among a family of gorillas before the civil war broke out in Rwanda. There are only a few hundred of those gorillas left in the world, and they are only found in that one region. I sat on the ground with my head lowered, while a 500-pound male silver-backed gorilla sat down—back to back with me—and chewed on some food for 30 seconds. My heart was pounding out of my chest! I also went on my one and only hot air balloon ride.

Facing a 500-lb. male, silverback gorilla

JJ with gorilla trackers in Rwanda • Dec. 10, 1987

I started collecting baseball memorabilia in 1989 when I was living in Connecticut. That was when I rekindled my love for baseball. I developed a sizable collection of autographed baseballs, bats and pictures, but later chose to auction off a big portion of it. The pieces I retained are displayed in my room like a mini-museum.

In 1991, I went to Japan one day before a WWF event in the Tokyo area, and attended a Japanese-American baseball clinic at Yokohama Stadium. I met Sadaharu Oh, the international home run king (868 career home runs) and almost all the other legendary Japanese counterparts to our MLB Hall of Famers. I also met several players from America who played in Japan. One was Charlie Manuel, a good ole' country boy from Virginia. To my surprise, he told me that he used to watch me wrestle at the old Roanoke Arena. I saw Charlie several years later in Cleveland. The WWF was next door to Jacobs Field and Jerry Lawler was scheduled to throw out the first pitch for the Indians game. Charlie was the Cleveland manager and he introduced me to many of the players, including Jim Thome. This season, Charlie is the new manager for the Philadelphia Phillies and has been reunited with slugging first-baseman Jim Thome. I hope that Charlie and Jim both have a great season this year.

As an old Brooklyn Dodgers fan, one of the highlights of my life was to attend a Dodgers' Baseball Fantasy Camp in 1995 and be in the locker room with the legendary Duke Snider, "The Duke of Flatbush," who played center field for the Dodgers during a time when two other legends played center for New York teams: Mickey Mantle for the Yankees and Willie Mays for the Giants. All three are in the Baseball Hall of Fame. I have had a lifelong love for baseball, and there I was, in a batting cage, with "The Duke" giving me batting tips. I have been SO fortunate!

The camp lasted a full week and about 75 people attended, including Spike Lee, the movie producer. We were divided into six teams and played against each other all week. On the final night before the camp ended, the team of instructors played a game against the campers under the lights at Holman Stadium. It was exciting to know that I was playing on the same field where Jackie Robinson stood over fifty years before, as well as the likes of Roy Campanella, Sandy Koufax, and of course, Duke Snider. The locals in Vero Beach bought tickets to see the game and the proceeds went to charity. The game was run exactly like they would run a professional game, right down to playing the National Anthem and introducing the players.

By lottery, our team played first against our instructors, and everybody got to bat at least one time. I came up to bat in the second inning. Catching was former Major Leaguer Steve Yeager with MLB umpire Bruce Froemming calling balls and strikes. On the mound was Hall of Famer Tommy Lasorda. Most people know Tommy as the former Dodgers manager, but what they don't know is that he also had a three-year stint as a left-handed pitcher for the Dodgers (1954-1955) and the Kansas City A's (1956). Lasorda struck every batter out before me. On the first pitch, I hit a line drive base hit to left field, our first hit of the game. If you ever saw the classic picture of Pete Rose standing on first base in 1985, when he passed Ty Cobb to become the all-time hit king, standing behind him, and the first to offer his congratulations, was first baseman Steve Garvey. On this night, playing first base was ... Steve Garvey, who was the first to congratulate me. The ball was taken out of the game and I still have it today. Who says dreams don't come true? Not me!

Over the years, I met Ted Williams, Joe DiMaggio, Hank Aaron, Willie Mays—the who's who of baseball from my era. Like a kid who would get excited about meeting Hulk Hogan, I was like that with the legends of baseball. On the other hand, I was surprised at the number of baseball players who were wrestling fans. When WCW would appear in Minneapolis, Kirby Puckett would show up with his family and come backstage. He was as excited to have his picture taken with us as we were with him! Roger Clemens brought his sons backstage, as well.

When I was with WCW, I got a call from an old friend: John Filippelli, one of the most respected people in baseball TV production. I first met "Flip" when he was the Executive Producer for the WWF. He was very good friends with Jeff Torborg, who recently managed the Expos and the Marlins. Jeff had a son named Dale who was trying to break into the wrestling business, and he wanted to know if Filippelli knew someone in wrestling that he could trust. Jeff had talked to somebody at the WWF, but nothing ever came of it. After a series of phone calls, Jeff and Dale Torborg both came to our next tapings at Universal Studios. During a break, Dale went into the ring with Bobby Eaton and I was impressed. I got him a developmental contract and he proved himself to be willing to do whatever was asked of him. He had good size and a lot of athletic talent, but he came into the business when opportunities were shrinking, and he never really got a chance to show what he could do. Jeff Torborg and I became good friends. When I took my son, Geoff, to Turner Field, we would go see Jeff in the managers' office, where John Holland, the Brave's visiting clubhouse manager (and a wrestling fan himself) always made us feel welcome.

I have a lot of respect for people who withstand the test of time—people like Kirby Puckett, Roger Clemens, and Tony Gwynn. Time is the greatest test of someone's true ability and their talent. Wade Boggs is a wonderful, personable guy who would sit in the front row with his kids at WCW events in Tampa. I was glad to see Wade voted into the Hall of Fame this year.

When I went to the fantasy camp in 1995, somebody recognized me and said there was someone who works in the Dodgers' clubhouse named Jerry Turner who was a huge wrestling fan. When I introduced myself to Jerry, all I wanted to talk about was baseball, and who he had crossed paths with. Jerry has been with the Dodgers for over twenty years. At the same time, all he wanted to do was talk about wrestling, and who I've crossed paths with! Jerry loved Dick "Destroyer" Beyer, so I asked Dick to autograph a mask and send it to him. I even made arrangements for them to go to a ballgame together. When Dory Funk wanted to meet Japanese pitcher Hideo Nomo at the height of "Nomomania," Jerry came through. Jerry has been a great friend.

I've become a Yankee fan over the years, and I met Alex Rodriguez when he came backstage at a WCW event in Miami. I subscribe to DirecTV's MLB Extra Innings Package and go into my depressed mode when the World Series comes to an end.

260 • "Wrestlers Are Like Seagulls"

JJ up to bat against Tommy Lasorda in the Instructor-Camper baseball

## Brooklyn Dodgers Baseball Fantasy Camp
## February 16, 1995

JJ and Duke Snyder

Base hit against Steve Garvey

I look forward to the announcement of the Hall of Fame, and then I begin to yearn for spring training.

As far as my health goes, I count myself as being very fortunate because I know a lot of wrestlers who have retired from the business and now use walkers and wheelchairs, or have trouble with arthritis. I haven't experienced that much discomfort, and considering the amount of abuse my body has taken during my career, I am blessed with good health.

The most I ever weighed was 255, and that was toward the end of my career when I was managing. My current weight is 240. I would like to lose more weight because it's hard on my knees and back. I do have some lower back discomfort now, especially when I'm on my feet for a long time.

JJ, Alex Rodriguez & Konnan • 2000

I only had two mishaps that I considered to be serious. Early in my career, I damaged the ACL on my left knee. That was before the doctors performed arthroscopic surgery. In those days, all they did was immobilize the injury until it stabilized, which often left you with an area of weakness surrounding the injury. I never did have the injury repaired. Instead, I wore a knee brace and a knee pad. Even today, I wear a brace to give it added support. My doctor told me that I need a knee replacement, but if I can hold off for a while, more than likely, it will be a one-time procedure and I will never have to have it done again.

On July 4, 1987, I received the most serious injury I ever had when I separated my shoulder during the War Games in the Atlanta Omni. Ric Flair, Arn Anderson, Tully Blanchard, Lex Luger, and I were against Dusty Rhodes, Nikita Koloff, Paul Ellering, and the Road Warriors, Animal and Hawk. We put two rings together and surrounded them with a cage.

I was the last member of the heel team remaining at the end of the match, and I would drop the deciding fall [get pinned]. Hawk wanted to beat me with a clothesline, but I was reluctant to take a clothesline while I was perched high on the shoulder of Animal. Basically, when Hawk hits you, you flip over backwards, pan-caking onto the mat, face-first, with your knees taking the shock of the landing. I didn't want to take that bump because my knees had been banged up over the years. My neck had also taken a beating over the years, so I wanted to avoid any possibility of serious injury. But it didn't matter what I wanted to do. Animal and Hawk were determined to use that finish. Animal picked me up and Hawk climbed to the top rope. As Hawk came off of the ropes, I shifted my body to try and get down. In the process, Animal lost his hold on me and I fell towards the mat, head first. At the last second, to keep from breaking my neck, I tucked my shoulder and landed on it.

I went backstage and put ice on my shoulder, but I knew that I needed to go to the hospital. After being up all night and having X-rays taken, the doctors told me that I had two choices. They could operate and I could have a pin inserted into my shoulder, or they could immobilize my shoulder in a sling for six weeks, and I would have a hump on my shoulder. I opted for the sling. The healing process was slow, but I returned to the ring three months later, on October 2, 1987, when I wrestled Kevin Sullivan in Daytona Beach, Florida. I even went on to participate in sixteen more War Games in 1988. The battle scar I have from that first War Game, though, is a small hump on my right clavicle.

Most of my aches and pains are the result of the accumulative effect of the bodyslams and pounding I took. Even if you are disciplined in how you take bumps, the ring in the St. Louis Kiel Auditorium wasn't much softer than the cement floor. The ring in the Dallas Sportatorium was about the same. There were places where the rings were much better, but the constant pounding takes its toll over time.

When I had my neck x-rayed one time, the doctor asked, *"When did you break your neck?"*

*"What?"*

He showed me the x-ray and explained about the tendons that attach to the tips of your vertebrae. When you have a whiplash effect, those vertebrae bend forward. The tendons are so strong that the tips of the bones, where the tendons are attached, will crack before the tendons snap. That leaves you with a hairline crack, but over time, the injury calcifies. My doctor told me that from the neck up (inside my body), I look like an 80-year-old man, but from the neck down, I look like a 25-year-old. I feel that now. At times, a tingling will spread down my arm and into my small fingers. In order to sleep in comfort, I sleep with my arms over my head. Somebody pointed out to me that when I sit in a chair to watch television, or when I'm in casual conversation, I raise my arm and bend it over the top of my head. It's a way of alleviating the pressure on my neck. I can't sit in a normal lounge chair for an extended period of time with my arms on the handle, because after a while, I get a tingling sensation in my fingers. Inadvertently, I'll raise one arm over my head, put it down, then raise the other one.

Over the years, even though I've held executive positions in professional wrestling, I've never been looked upon as a shaker in the wrestling business. I've always been a peripheral player. When I was a manager, nobody bought tickets to see me. I was simply the catalyst to get people into the arena because people like Kimala and Abdullah the Butcher didn't speak. Once I got the people into the arena, the focus was on what was in the ring. I became secondary.

Fame is fleeting, but I never thrived on that, and it didn't drive me. However, I have to admit that it is nice every now and then to have somebody recognize me. I get tremendous satisfaction out of the messages that are left on my website by people who I have touched.

For the most part, wrestling has far exceeded almost every other form of entertainment or professional sport. Television and technology has evolved, so there are a lot more individual "stars" and personalities in football and baseball than there were twenty years ago. Everything is so much more personal and in-depth. Yes, the public knew who Joe DiMaggio and Mickey Mantle were, but they knew little about the other players. They all wore the same uniform and looked alike from a distance.

Wrestlers, on the other hand, were well-known as individual personalities, and much more recognizable than so-called stars from other sports. As a wrestler, you appeared on television in nothing but a pair of tights, or whatever your gimmick was, and the focus of the television camera was on you alone. Your image and persona filled the screen.

Typically, if a wrestler would stand alongside a famous baseball player, the people wouldn't know who the baseball player was, even if he wore his uniform with his name on the back, but they would gravitate to the wrestler because they knew who he was. On some occasions, it was embarrassing to find myself in that situation. I went to an autograph signing in Philadelphia. I was sitting at a table with Tully Blanchard and Kent Tekulve, who was a very successful and respected relief pitcher. Nobody knew who Tekulve was, so there was nobody in his line.

It probably surprises some people to realize that James Morrison's persona is almost a direct opposite of J.J. Dillon, the manager. In real life, I'm an introverted, sensitive, and quiet person. I'm also a very private person. When I was away from the business, I was AWAY from the business. In some ways, that hampered me, but it was a personal decision. My wife used to kid me because when somebody would recognize me in public, she said she could see Jim Morrison make a transformation into J.J. Dillon. I would develop a smug, arrogant expression. I thought she was crazy, and when I told her so, she would point out that I didn't even realize that I was doing it.

If I am remembered at all, I hope I am remembered as someone who lived his life according to the Golden Rule. I tried to treat people as I would want to be treated. You'll always have people who feel you've done them wrong, but I never deliberately hurt anyone or used them to my advantage. As I reflect back, I feel good about that.

I don't look back with regrets. If my glass is half full, I'd rather be happy to have that to drink than to be angry about the glass being half empty. That's an overused cliché, but that best expresses how I feel. When you reach a crossroad in your life, you're there at that moment with the information that is available to you, and you have decisions to make. I've always been one to take whatever opportunity I had at that moment, play the hand that's dealt to me, and do the best with what I have. To me, life itself is a precious gift. I am very thankful for what I have and where I am, in a country where I could do what I wanted to do.

I have one of those inspirational/motivational picture frames on my desk at home. Previously, that same frame sat on my desk at WCW, and at the WWF before that. I don't know the origin of the message, but in big print it says, "PRIORITIES," followed by, "A hundred years from now, it will not matter what my bank account was, the sort of house I lived in, or the kind of car I drove ... but the world may be different because I was important in the life of a child." In the frame is a picture of my children. Given all I have been through, I look at this picture many times each day ... and it puts my life into perspective.

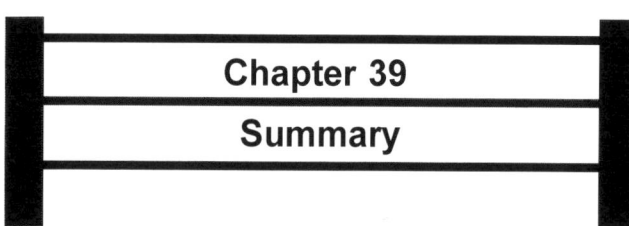

# Chapter 39
# Summary

Vincent K. McMahon (Jr.) will go down in history as the greatest wrestling promoter of all time. In terms of growth and mainstream acceptability, Vince took wrestling to levels that other promoters never thought possible. There are things he's done that I don't agree with. He's presented storylines that go against my beliefs, and my feelings of right and wrong, but that can happen anywhere. It's a matter of personal taste. Pat Patterson used the ice cream analogy: That's why we have so many flavors of ice cream. They all taste good, but everybody has their own favorite flavors. That carries over to the wrestling business. It would be impossible for anybody to always be in harmony with my tastes, beliefs, and feelings about things.

I worked with Vince for over 7½ years, longer than I have worked for any other promoter or wrestling company in my career. If I wanted to continue working in the wrestling industry after AOL sold WCW, my only option would have been to go to work for the WWF, or WWE (World Wrestling Entertainment), as it is now called. However, my feelings have not changed since I left the company in 1996. On several occasions, I have made the statement that I would rather flip hamburgers for minimum wage at McDonald's before I would ever pick up the phone and ask Vince for a job. It would be hypocritical of me to go back to work there, and for the rest of my life, I would wake up every morning and wonder, *"Is this the day that Vince will decide to have some fun with me?"* For that reason, I have never entertained the idea of contacting Vince McMahon. I chose, instead, to walk away from the business.

Regardless of how I may come across in this book, I don't have any hatred for Vince McMahon or anybody in his family. I've reached a time in my life where I hold no anger or ill will towards anybody. I don't hold ill will against Vince McMahon. I just don't want to work for him.

I DO have issues with things that happened while I was working for the WWF, and I don't feel any differently in regard to the reasons why I left.

Having said that, I would also like to go on record and say that I am thankful for the opportunity that Vince gave me. I went to the WWF with high expectations. I realized that it was a tremendous opportunity because it was a chance for me to learn and grow ... which I did. I look at the time I spent working for Vince as being my graduate school, and I learned a lot about television and how it should flow.

Don't put two wrestlers with a similar look on TV right after each other.

Don't put two tag team matches back to back.

If a manager is managing two guys, put those two guys on at different spots in the show.

If something of importance is going to happen, put something of less importance on right after it, so the announcers can reflect and elaborate on the importance of the angle.

I came from the NWA, where the shows would start with a solid wrestling match and crescendo to the main event. The WWF took a different approach. They would open their show with a good, action-packed match, and the main event matches would be sprinkled throughout. They might even give you the actual main event right after intermission. At the end of the show, they would give you a feel-good, send-home match.

Unfortunately, due to the way things played out, I could not stay there, but I am grateful for the experience and information I gained there, even though those new skills were never utilized in my subsequent job.

Many things have happened in the McMahon family since I left. Shane got married and had a child. Stephanie got married to Hunter Hearst Helmsley (Triple H). Vince has had a couple of health scares.

Vince is a fascinating individual. He is driven and has no life or interests outside of wrestling. As I mentioned earlier, Vince has no need for vacations, and he resented people who did. When I returned to work after a vacation, I always had the feeling that I'd somehow have to pay penance for taking off for that period of time. I suppose I was one of the lucky ones. There were people he brought back from vacation and fired! To me, vacations are important, because no matter how hard you push yourself, sometimes it's healthy to separate yourself from your work and recharge yourself mentally, physically, and intellectually. When you come back to work, you have a fresh slate on which you can begin to create. But that's Vince, and if he's happy with that lifestyle, I wish him the best.

Vince is now a grandfather. I don't know if he still drives at 100 mph, either, but maybe now that he had a grandson, perhaps it has changed him and given him a perspective that he never had before. I'm not suggesting that my name ever crosses his subconscious, but I wonder if he ever remembers our conversations and thinks, *"Now I know how JJ felt."*

People ask me all the time if I miss wrestling. My answer is always the same, *"No, I don't, because professional wrestling has changed so much. It is not like it used to be. The business that I was in no longer exists. If anything, I miss what wrestling once was, but I know it will never be that way again."* Most people seem to understand my answer to their question.

I don't watch much wrestling, either. Occasionally, I will catch a glimpse of the Nature Boy and pause to watch. I am amazed that he is still active at this time in his life, but I'm not surprised. Let's face it. There is nobody with enough talent to replace Ric Flair.

I do notice how post-production sweetens the product so well on TV today. Even on live shows, the production crew can insert canned sound, and the instant the theme music starts playing for a ring entrance, the audience breaks out into a thunderous roar. They associate the music with the persona being introduced. As soon as the wrestler gets into the ring and the bell sounds, though, you can hear a pin drop.

This is only my opinion, so you can take it or leave it, but professional wrestling is in big trouble. I have this fear that the business is dying, on life support ... and maybe already dead. Wrestling is still a talent-driven business. Sadly, wrestling is not currently set up to develop enough good talent to replace what we have already lost. When Vince put the other wrestling organizations out of business, his talent pool dried up. The same fate would face Major League Baseball if somebody got the bright idea to stop supporting and subsidizing their minor league system to save money. You wouldn't feel the impact for the first few seasons, but over time, the overall quality of MLB would suffer terribly from the lack of qualified new talent. The wrestling business will lose even more as "Father Time" takes his toll.

The Undertaker has been a big drawing card for Vince, but they've done everything they can with him. They changed him from a dead man who said nothing into a much more complex character. Steve Austin is a great character, but he's taken a lot of physical punishment, and due to a bad neck injury, he is finished. Shawn Michaels still has a lot of charisma, but he isn't in the best physical shape, either. The Rock has gotten a taste of Hollywood and the money that comes with it. It's not very likely that he'll ever be back in any major role. Triple H? How much more can he do?

When I first started working for Vince, he was running three towns a night, with each card limited to six matches and a total of twenty wrestlers, including referees and agents. As time went by, the number of towns run each night dropped to two, and then one. Now Vince has eleven matches on his shows because nobody knows how to tell stories, and he still has thirty guys to pay off. If he was selling out, he could afford to do that, but when the house show business is down (and it is), the payoffs decrease and morale drops.

Making regular tours of the Far East, South Pacific, and Europe will not be the answer. The lack of new talent will take its toll on the international market. There is also a lack of big venues sufficient to support an on-going global tour. When a promotion comes back too frequently with the same talent, people will be reluctant to pay the high ticket prices that make the tours viable for the company today. The costs of touring are so great that it takes sold out arenas with big grosses to cover the expenses.

In my opinion, WWE will eventually become primarily a television company. I'm sure WWE will always do tours in some fashion, but when they stop selling out Madison Square Garden, they will start to run less frequently. In time, WWE could conceivably become the Harlem Globetrotters of wrestling.

Sorry, Eric, but Vince will never go out of business. There will always be a WrestleMania. However, the number of wrestlers with licensing and merchandising appeal will become fewer and fewer, and there will be fewer exclusive, high-dollar contracts given out.

In my opinion, a second, successful major promotion could revive the industry. It would take somebody like Ted Turner, who has vast financial resources, or a TV network with a visionary in charge, who could foresee the potential of starting and owning a new company that would provide cost-effective original programming with ratings potential. There are still some recognizable wrestling names out there who could provide the "rub," while new stars are being created and developed.

I hope Jerry and Jeff Jarrett's promotion, TNA, makes it. They have a tough road ahead of them, but if anybody could pull it off, it would be Jerry Jarrett. Jerry is a good guy who has given his life to the business. If his promotion succeeds, it will afford talent an alternative place to work, and that will benefit Vince McMahon in the long run. The better workers will eventually gravitate to Vince because the financial rewards will be greater. For some reason, though, I don't think Vince's ego will allow him to see it that way.

If Vince asked me his question about what I would do if I had a magic wand, and if I had the desire to start a wrestling promotion, I would use the wand to develop a team of people like Bill Watts, Jerry Jarrett, Ole Anderson, Kevin Sullivan, Bill Busch, and Pat Patterson. That would only be the beginning. There are many more people that I would want on my team in some capacity.

Ironically, the one person who would benefit the most from my efforts would be Vince McMahon himself. There would be a new basis for comparison, and that would excite Vince and drive him to new heights.

There are countless numbers of independent promoters who want to promote wrestling. Let them run the live events to keep the talent busy. The work would keep their skills honed and allow them to make a decent living. There are literally thousands of small towns across America that would love to see wrestling again, and they would support it. Those are the same towns that Vince doesn't play, and probably never will again.

Unfortunately, under the present system, many of the wrestlers on independent shows weigh 170 pounds or less and look just like the people in the audience. They don't stand out from the crowd. They also know the mechanics of the crash-and-burn moves they do in the ring, but they don't have a reason for doing those moves.

If a prize could be established over time that is respected, prestigious, and worthy of obtaining and fighting for, then you have a foundation on which to build. You must be able to draw a comparison to the Stanley Cup of hockey, or the Lombardi Trophy in football. I have nothing against David Arquette, but I guarantee that he would never become champion. He might be lucky enough to be allowed to hold the championship belt in his hands. No photos, though.

Wouldn't it be great if Dave Meltzer and Wade Keller had something else to report about? If the level of performance and execution reaches that of bygone years, then once again, the product would look so real that to the fans, it would become real. The Internet "smart marks" will say I am crazy. Yes, maybe I am crazy all right ... crazy like a fox.

At some future date, maybe wrestling will become wrestling again. Just maybe there is another 14-year-old boy growing up in Trenton, New Jersey, or any number of towns like it. The youngster grows wide-eyed by what he sees in the ring. Perhaps he might even fantasize about being a part of it in the distant future. Dare to dream!

Remember, as I said in the beginning of my story, dreams can come true.

In Jim Morrison's case, his did.

# Photo Gallery

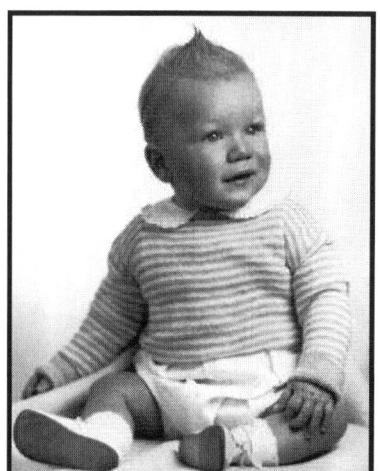

Clockwise from top left: 8 months old; 9 months old with mother Blanche; Childrens Choir, Bethany Presbyterian Church, 1955, age 13 years (Jim is to left of the director)

Photo Gallery • 269

Clockwise from top left:
June 1949, Jim with sister Joan
June 20, 1957, Jim with his father at 9th grade graduation
June 1969, Cowboy Jim Dillon
June 1960, High school graduation photo

# Japan
# January 1974

Clockwise from top left: Jim Dillon and Roger Kirby (9/19/75); Early promo photo (11/75); Relaxing in Colorado Springs; JJ and the Stomper with Gordon Solie on Georgia Championship Wrestling; (center) JJ being interviewed by Nick Roberts

Clockwise from top left: Dumping Haystack Calhoun over the top rope; JJ vs Cyclone Negro; A victorious Kendo Nagasaki and JJ Dillon; Ready for a Street Fight Match; (center) JJ in 1982

Clockwise from top left: JJ chokes Mike Davis; JJ in the steel cage; Relaxed pose (late '70s); Mike Davis holds their opponent as JJ comes off the ropes (Japan); (center, l to r) Dos Caras, unknown, Mr. Ito, Mr. Hayashi, JJ Dillon, Victor Jovica, Tiger Jeet Singh, Mike Davis

Promo for JJ's bathtub match against Paul Boesch (9/10/76)

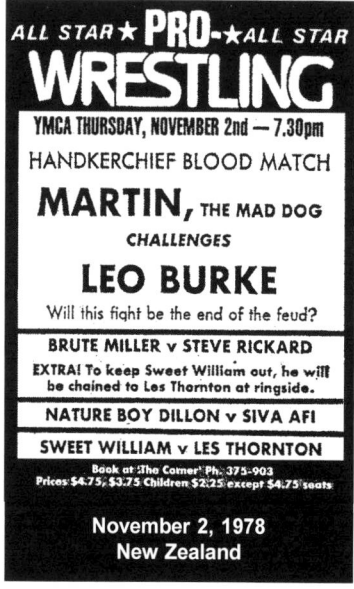

November 2, 1978
New Zealand

Don Fargo's artistic rendering of JJ Dillon

Baton Rouge • Feb. 7, 1979

Photo Gallery • 275

JAMES J. DILLON,
A VERY SUCCESSFUL MANAGER!!!

T'BOLT vs. ABDULLAH

THE STOMPER vs. JAMES J. DILLON

(top left clockwise)
Macon, Georgia: February 16, 1977
Amarillo, Texas: October 11, 1979
Atlanta, Georgia: March 11, 1977
Houston, Texas: September 16, 1977

Clockwise from top left: JJ and Barry Windham (1988); JJ and Big John Studd (1982); JJ and Adrian Street (1983); JJ and Ron Bass; JJ and Angelo Mosca (1983)

Photo Gallery • 277

Clockwise from top left: King James and Jim Garvin (1982); Buddy Landel and JJ; Kendo Nagasaki and JJ (1982); JJ and Bulldog Brower (1976); (center) JJ and Abdullah the Butcher in Atlanta, Georgia (1977).

Wade Boggs
Tampa, Florida, 1999

Charles Barkley
2000

Celebrating Kareem Abdul-Jabbar's son's birthday at the Los Angeles Forum (back row, l to r) Pez Whatley, Ric Flair, Kareem Abdul-Jabbar, JJ Dillon, Michael Cooper, Tiger Conway Jr.

Photo Gallery • 279

Arn Anderson, Dusty Rhodes, Kirby Puckett, and JJ
Minneapolis, Minnesota
2000

Jay Leno
Sturgis, South Dakota
August 8, 1988

Wayne Gretsky
WCW show in Los Angeles

Dinner during an NWA meeting at Caesar's Palace in Las Vegas.
(left to right) Arn Anderson and wife, Fred Ward,
Bobby Eaton and wife, J.J. Dillon, Elliott Murnick and wife (1980s)

JJ and Abdullah the Butcher in Japan with
the owner of the Suehiro Steak House (1977)

Opposite page: Dad with his children

(clockwise from top left)
Geoffrey (8/3/04), Missy (8/3/04), Pam (7/4/04), Nicole (8/3/04)

JJ and the Horsemen with his family, November 27, 2004
(front) Ole Anderson, Geoffrey, Arn Anderson
(center) Nicole, Missy
(back) Pam, JJ, Tully Blanchard

Photo Gallery • 281

JJ at the Carlisle Fire Hall in Milford, Delaware
with his cousins, Robert Roach (left) and Donald McIlvain (right)
February 8, 1989

## The last photo taken of the original Horsemen

Secaucus, New Jersey: August 29, 1999
(l to r) J.J. Dillon, Ole Anderson, Tully Blanchard, Ric Flair, Arn Anderson

# INDEX

Abdullah the Butcher, 86-89, 105, 181, 262
Adonis, Adrian, 127
Al Kaissey, Adnan, 138
Albano, Lou, 177-178
Albright College (Reading, PA), 19, 28
All Japan Pro Wrestling, 88
Allen, Terry (see Magnum, T.A.)
Altimore, Tony, 177
Alzado, Lyle, 137
Amarillo Fairgrounds, 90
*American Bandstand*, 23
American Wrestling Association (AWA), 84
Anderson, Arn, 137, 141, 145, 147, 153, 157, 207, 261
Anderson, Gene, 39, 43, 45, 47
Anderson, Ole, 41-42, 45, 86-87, 98, 118, 146-147, 157, 189, 251, 254
Andre the Giant, 56, 94, 156
Anoai, Rodney, 169
AOL-Time Warner, 241
Apollo, Argentina, 25
Apter, Bill, 146
Armstrong, Brad, 173
Arquette, David, 217, 219, 267
Atlas, Tony, 98, 127, 169
Austeri, Jim, 178
Austin, Steve, 187, 221, 235, 236, 244, 266
Austra-Asian title, 93
Australia, 92-96
Baba, Shohei (Giant), 63-64, 87-89, 136, 183-185
Backlund, Bob, 54, 69-70, 116, 127, 137
Bagwell, Marcus, 220
Baker, Ox, 95, 155
Banks, Bill, 240
Barnett, Jim, 84, 92-93 117, 127, 148, 153-154, 179, 207, 211, 254-255
Bart, Black, 135
*Bash at the Beach*, 240
Bass, Ron, 135-136
Bastien, Red, 74, 78, 93
Bayfront Center (St. Petersburg), 120
Beast, The, 46-47, 49, 51-54
Beaver, Little, 144
Becker, George, 38-40, 44-45
Benoit, Chris, 93, 147, 195, 233, 237-238
Bernard, Brute, 89, 92-95
Berry, Viktor, 11
Berry, Wild Red, 14, 21
Beyer, Dick, 63-64, 87
Big Heart, Chief, 14, 23

Bischoff, Eric, 167, 206-227, 230, 236-240, 242-243, 245, 266
Blackburn, Stanley, 91
Blackwell, Crusher, 138
blading, 118-119
Blanchard, Joe, 80
Blanchard, Tully, 11, 62, 80, 137, 141, 144-147, 150, 153, 157-158, 189, 255, 261-262
Blassie, Fred, 177
blood, 118-119
Blue Blazer, The, 169
Bockwinkel, Nick, 64
Boesch, Paul, 80-81, 84-85
Bollas, George, 17-18, 178
Booger, Bastion, 169
Bossman, The, 181
Bourne, Dick, 253
Bowman, Anne, 10, 255
Bowman, Bill, 10, 255
Brannigan, Butcher, 95
Braves, Boston, 14
Brazil, Bobo, 44, 98
Bresloff, Zane, 245
Brisco, Jack, 46, 55-56, 98, 116, 133
Brisco, Jerry, 46, 63, 98, 116, 197, 255
Brody, Bruiser, 62, 92, 146
Brokaw, Tom, 191
Brooklyn Dodgers, 258
Brother Love, 181
Brown, Big Boy (Luke), 45
Brown, Bulldog Bob, 69-70, 109, 114
Bruiser, Dick the, 109
Brumbaugh, Bruce, 22
Burke, Leo, 46, 49-50, 53, 81, 96, 131
Burnham, Chip, 245
Busch, Bill, 226-236, 241, 255
Bushwhackers, The, 96
Calhoun, Haystack, 44
Callaway, Mark, 163
Capitol Arena (Washington DC), 24
Carr, Johnny, 32
Championship Wrestling from Florida, 132, 140
Championship Wrestling from Georgia, 179
Charlotte Os, 47
Chatterton, Rita, 192
Cheslock, Eddie, 11
Cholak, Moose, 88-89
Civic Arena (Pittsburgh), 36-37
CJCH-TV (Halifax), 51
Clark, Dick, 23

*Clash of the Champions*, 154
CNN Center, 223
Cobo Hall (Detroit), 37, 88-89
Cohen, Ed, 155, 165, 167, 229
Cole, Tom, 191
Colon, Carlos, 138
Colt, Buddy, 44, 72-74, 140
Colt, Chris, 31
Cook, Charlie, 115-116
Cormier, Jean-Louis (see Kay, Rudy)
Cormier, Leonce (see Burke, Leo)
Cormier, Romeo (see Kay, Bobby)
Cormier, Yvon (see Burke, Yvon)
Cornette, Jim, 11
Cornette, Jim, 254
Costello, Al, 14, 20
Cow Palace (San Francisco), 255
Crockett Sr., Jim, 42-43, 46-48, 139
Crockett, David, 47, 138, 148, 233
Crockett, Francis, 47-48
Crockett, Jackie, 47
Crockett, Jimmy, 47, 131, 137-140, 145, 148, 153-154, 164, 169, 172, 189
Curry, Bull, 33-34
Curtis, Don, 44
Dallas Sportatorium, 91
Darsow, Barry, 157
Davis, Bobby, 14
Death Valley Days, 122
DeFazio, Johnny, 37
Deford, Frank, 175
Dellaserra, Bob, 77, 103
Dellinger, Doug, 137
Demolition, 157
DeNucci, Dominic, 20
Destroyer, Sensational Intelligent, 63
Detroit Wheels, 59
Dianabol, 42
DiBiase, Iron Mike, 90
DiBiase, Ted, 59, 62, 90-91, 181
Dillon, J.J. (origin of name), 78
Dillon, Jim (origin of name), 32
Dillon, Nature Boy (origin of name), 50
Dodgers, Brooklyn, 14
Doink the Clown, 169
Dondero, Louis, 171
Douglas, Barry, 103
Douglas, Shane, 221
Dubois, Mike, 46-47, 65
Duncum, Bobby, 62, 125
Dunn, Kevin, 163
Dupree, Emil, 129, 131
Dupree, Ron, 31
Durso, Frank, 37-38
Dwyer, Larry, 110-111
Eadie, Bill, 138, 158
Eaton, Bobby, 221-222, 259
Edwards, Don, 245
El Santo, 65
Ellering, Paul, 137, 153, 261
Embry, Eric, 115
Engle, Jamie, 222-223, 240
Fargo, Jackie, 195
Farhat, Eddie (see Sheik, The), 31
Farouk, Abdullah, 31
Fernandez, Manny, 62

Ferrara, Ed, 229, 232-233, 240
Filippeli, John, 259
Finkel, Howard, 155, 171-172, 197, 200-201
Finlay, Fit, 103
Finley, David (see Crockett, David)
Flair, Ric, 81-82, 111, 115-116, 125, 137, 140-141, 143-147, 149-150, 157, 169, 185-186, 189, 222, 234-235, 255, 261, 265
Flemmng, Clary, 129-130
Florida heavyweight title, 117
Florida TV title, 74, 87
Foley, Mick, 61, 186-187, 210
Forman, Ross, 226
Fort Homer Hesterly Armory, 123, 125
Freeman, Ace, 36-37
Friar Ferguson, 169
Friend, Percival A., 63
Froemming, Bruce, 259
Funk Jr., Dory, 45-46, 53, 55, 62-63, 65, 88, 90, 97-99, 102, 117, 138
Funk Sr., Dory, 46, 66-69, 91
Funk, Terry, 46, 58-59, 62-63, 68, 75, 88, 90, 97-98, 102, 117, 119, 233
Furr, Joe, 39
Fusient, 242-244
Gagne, Verne, 84, 159, 218
Galento, Two-Ton Tony, 25
Gallagher, Doc, 21
Gallagher, Mike, 21
Garea, Tony, 177
Garvey, Steve, 259
Garvin, Jimmy, 47, 121

Garvin, Ronnie, 47, 137
Garvin, Terry, 47, 95, 97, 99, 102, 108-110, 153, 174, 179, 191-192
Geesink, Anton, 69
Geigel, Bob, 105, 107-109, 112, 114
George, Gorgeous, 21
George, Mike, 110
Georgia Championship Wrestling, 86, 197
Georgia Dome, 210, 225
Georgia TV title, 86
Gilzenburg, Willie, 23
Glover, Dick, 171, 175
Gobbley Gooker, 169
Godoy, Pedro, 32-33
Goldberg, Bill, 224-225, 230, 236, 246
Goldust, 169
Gordienko, George, 106
Goto, Tarzan, 64
Gouldie, Archie (see Stomper, The)
Goulet, Rene, 177
Grable, Joyce, 178
Grabmire, Jim, 37-39
Graham, Billy (Superstar), 31, 138
Graham, Crazy Luke, 24
Graham, Dr. Jerry, 14, 72, 126, 134
Graham, Eddie, 44, 72, 77, 98, 107-108, 115-118, 121-128, 130-134, 218
Graham, Mike, 44, 77, 115-116, 124-125, 131-132, 224, 228, 255
*Grapevine, The*, 123-124
*Great American Bash*, 219
Greensboro Coliseum, 47
Griffin, Bob, 59, 63
Grobbe, Jacob (see Mortier, Hans)
Guerrero, Chavo, 66
Guerrero, Eddie, 66, 238
Guerrero, Gory, 66-67, 88
Guerrero, Hector, 169
Halifax Forum, 50-51, 129
Hall, Scott, 204, 212, 214-215, 245-246
Hamburg Fieldhouse, 178
Hamilton, Jody, 115, 224, 240
Hamilton, Larry, 54
Hansen, Stan, 59, 62, 183
Hanson, Swede, 41, 45, 77
Harris, George (Two-Ton), 41
Hart, Bobby, 59, 63
Hart, Bret, 136, 145, 165-166, 184-185, 195, 213, 219
Hart, Jimmy, 207, 216, 219
Hart, Playboy Gary, 45, 72-74, 99
Hart, Stu, 105-107, 219
*Have a Nice Day*, 186
Hawk, Rip, 41, 45
Hayes, Lord Alfred, 82, 197
Hebner, Dave, 177, 185, 255
Hebner, Earl, 255
Heffernan, Roy, 14
Heideman, Johnny, 47
Hell's Angels, 31-32
Helmsley, Hunter Hearst, 187, 265
Hennig, Curt, 147
Hennig, Larry, 76-77
Herd, Jim, 149
Hernandez, Gino, 80-81
Hervey, Jason, 242

Hester, Frank, 41
Hickey, Frank, 25
Higuchi, Joe, 70, 184
Hirai, Mitsu, 64
Hiroshi, Wajima, 87-88
Hogan, Hulk, 116, 156, 162, 164, 173, 175, 183, 185-187, 195, 212-213, 219-220, 235, 237
Honky Tonk Man, 216
Horner, Tim, 173
Horsemen, The Four, 140-147, 157, 220, 253
Iaukea, King Curtis, 93, 95
Igor, Mighty, 98
Imperial Room, 123
Iron Sheik, 127
Jack, Cactus, 221
Jacobs, Art, 41, 43
Jaggers, Bobby, 115
Jardine, Don, 115
Jarrett, Jeff, 147, 183, 230-231, 233, 238, 240, 247-248, 266
Jarrett, Jerry, 121, 176, 183, 195-196, 199, 206, 209, 219, 230, 239, 243-244, 246-247, 249, 254, 266
Jericho, Chris, 221
Joe, Yaqui, 102
Johnson, Rocky, 74, 78-79, 127
Jones, Rufus R., 109, 114
Jones, S.D., 125
Jovica, Victor, 138
Juster, Gary, 227, 234-235, 238, 245
Justice, Ben, 65-67
Kabuki, The Great, 138, 184
Kangaroos, Fabulous, 14
Kanyon, Chris, 220-221
Kay, Bobby, 46, 49, 53-54
Kay, Rudy, 46, 49-50, 52-53, 55, 129
Keller, Wade, 267
Kellner, Jamie, 244-245
Kelly, Mike, 112
Kelly, Pat, 1112
Kent, Don, 77
Kidman, Billy, 220
Kiel Auditorium (St. Louis), 262
Kimala, 121
King James (origin of name), 124
*King of the Ring*, 164, 193
Kirby, Roger, 74-75
Kitao, Koji, 184
Koloff, Ivan, 98, 261
Koma, Masio, 64
Konnan, 220, 261
Korakuen Baseball Stadium, 64
Kowalski, Killer, 24-25, 32, 44
Kox, Killer Karl, 32, 56, 59-61, 69, 93
Kozak, Jerry, 56, 88, 98
Kozak, Nick, 56
Krupp, Killer Karl, 53, 56
Kuma, Great, 55
Ladd, Ernie, 98
Lamont, Frenchie, 48
Lang, Cowboy, 79
Langhorne (PA) SPeedway, 14
Lanza, Jack, 164, 177-178, 185
Lasorda, Tommy, 259
Lawler, Jerry, 120-121, 124, 183

*Learning the Ropes* (TV show), 137
Leathers, Craig, 240
Lederberg, Peter, 11
Leno, Jay, 219, 252
Leone, Antone (Ripper), 105
Lewin, Mark, 93, 124, 131
Lindsay, Luther, 41, 43-44, 106
London, Mike, 57, 88
Long Riders, 135
Lothario, Jose, 82-83
Low Low, Sky, 27-28, 144
Lubbock Coliseum, 99
Lubich, Bronco, 21, 83
Luger, Lex, 138, 146-147, 154, 179-180, 187, 195, 261
Macias, Clifford, 41
Macon title, 87
Madison Square Garden, 15, 27, 63, 126-129, 159, 178, 192, 257, 266
Magnum T.A., 137, 139
Major League Wrestling, 255
Makropoulos, Georgiann, 16
Malenko, Dean, 16, 147, 238
Malenko, Joe, 16
Malenko, The Great, 16, 182-183
Mansfield, Eddy, 115
Maritimes, 49-55, 114, 129-131
Martinez, Pedro, 21
Martel, Rick, 75, 96, 147, 169
Martin, Frency, 96
Martin, Mad Dog, 96
Mauler, The Missouri, 54
Mayne, Lonnie (Moon Dog), 82-85
McCord, Dennis, 72-74
McDaniel, Wahoo, 98
McGraw, Bugsy, 115
McKenzie, Tex, 34, 173
McMahon, Linda, 160, 184, 199, 201, 205
McMahon, Shane, 125, 160, 183
McMahon, Stephanie, 160, 265
McMahon, Vincent J. (Sr), 21, 24, 26, 127-128, 137, 160, 163, 178
McMahon, Vincent K. (Jr.), 11, 152-157. 159-164, 167-170, 172, 174-182, 184-196, 197-206, 209-210, 219, 229-231, 233-235, 237, 241, 243-247, 254, 257, 264-266
McMichael, Steve, 147
Melby, Jim, 11
Meltzer, Dave, 172-176, 267
Memorial Hall (Kansas City), 111-112, 114
Mercado, Phil, 103
Michaels, Shawn, 184, 195, 266
Midnight Express, 147
Milano, Mario, 93
Milburn, Bob, 58-59
Miller, Brute, 96
Miller, Butch, 96
Miller, Ernest (The Cat), 220
Miller, Ron, 92-94, 96
Miller, Rudy, 36
Momota, Mitsuhiro, 64
Momoto, Yoshi, 64
*Monday Night RAW*, 182, 208, 210, 244
*Monday Nitro*, 208, 210, 213, 220, 224-225, 237-238, 240, 244
Monsoon, Gorilla, 21, 24, 26, 106, 127, 177

Moore, Archie, 25
Morales, Pedro, 116
Morgan, Ray, 13, 24
Morowski, Moose, 103
Morrell, Frank, 43, 89
Morrison, Blanche, 13
Morrison, James Mitchell, 13
Morrison, Pam, 8-9, 29, 256
Mortier, Hans, 21, 28
Mosca, Angelo, 125
Mould, Bob, 238
Mr. Hito (Adachi), 105
Muchnick, Sam, 108, 159
Mulligan, Blackjack, 69, 97-102, 117, 122
Municipal Auditorium (Nashville), 183
Muraco, Don, 127
Murdoch, Dick, 35, 56, 59, 61-63, 65, 68, 73, 81, 90-91, 93, 97, 99-103, 117, 127, 137, 145
Murdoch, Frankie Hill, 90
Murnick, Carl, 48
Murnick, Elliott, 48
Murnick, Joe, 43
Myers, Diana, 221, 243
Myers, Jim (see Steele, George)
Nagasaki, Kendo, 119-120, 130-131, 184
Nagashima, Shigeo, 190
Nailz, 192
Napolitano, George, 146
Nash, Kevin, 165, 212, 214-215, 220-221, 239, 245-246
Nassau Coliseum, 181
National Wrestling Alliance (NWA), 154-157, 159, 164, 171, 182
*National, The*, 175
Nead, Wilbur, 106
Negro, Ciclon, 56, 76-77
Neidhart, Jim, 106, 107
Nelson, Art, 41-42, 105, 119
Nelson, Willie, 170
New World Order (NWO), 212, 245
*No Mercy*, 230
Noble, Kay, 91
Nocco, Bill, 20
Norfolk Scope, 149
Norris, Chuck, 219
O'Connor, Pat, 53, 88, 105, 107-108
O'Day, Larry, 92-94, 96
Okerlund, Gene, 169, 255
Okuma, Motoshi, 64
Oliver, Rip, 126
Onita, Atsushi, 64
Orient Express, The, 184
Orlando Sports Stadium, 77
Orndorff, Paul, 207, 244
Outlaws, The, 35
Page, Diamond Dallas, 211, 216-217, 219-220
Page, Kimberly, 216
Park Center (Charlotte), 39, 42-43
Partlow, Sandy, 110
Patriots, The, 59, 63
Patterson, Pat, 125, 127, 153, 155, 160-164, 168-169, 171, 179, 187, 189-197, 217, 264, 266
Patterson, Thunderbolt, 98

Paul, Ronnie, 43-44
Perez, Alex, 56
Perez, Miguel, 21
Petrik, Jack, 148
Pfefer, Jack, 21
Philadelphia Arena, 16, 23
Philadelphia Civic Center, 145
Philadelphia Convention Hall, 19
Phillips, Mel, 191
Pillman, Brian, 147
Piper, Roddy, 127, 200
Piper's Pit, 122
Poffo, Angelo, 21
Poffo, Lanny, 189
Pomeroy, Eric, 53
Portz, Geoff, 103
Power Plant, The, 132, 222-224, 227, 240
Prater, Jerry, 123-124
Prichard, Bruce, 168, 193
Pulaski, Stan, 53
Purple Haze, The, 124
Race, Harley, 56, 63-64, 69, 74-76, 107-108, 124
Reagan, Ronald, 122
Red Rooster, The, 169
Rhodes, Dustin (see Runnels, Dustin)
Rhodes, Dusty, 35, 62, 93, 98, 111, 116-118, 122-123, 130-134, 136-137, 139-142, 144-145, 148-149, 169, 181-182, 227-228, 248-249, 261
Rich, Tommy, 98, 254
Richmond (VA) Fairgrounds, 43
Rickard, Steve, 96
Rikidozan, 64
Ringley, John, 48
Rittmann, Gary, 15
Rivera, Geraldo, 191
Road Warriors, 35, 137, 178-179, 261
Roberts, Jake (The Snake), 145
Roberts, Nick, 88
Robley, Phil, 44, 48
Rocca, Argentina, 21
Rodriguez, Alex, 259, 261
Rodriguez, Juan (Hawk), 20-21
Rogers, Buddy, 14, 21, 50, 234-235
Roma, Paul, 147
Romano, Tony, 43
Romero, Ricky, 57, 65, 68
Roop, Bob, 72-73
Rose, Pete, 219
Ross, Jim, 158, 197, 226
Roth, Ernie, 31
Rotuna, Mike, 119-120
Rougeau, Raymond, 189
*Royal Rumble*, 163-164, 168, 179-182
Royal, Gary, 136
Royal, Nelson, 136
Runnels, Dustin, 169, 182, 228
Russo, Vince, 196, 229-230, 232-234, 237-240, 242, 245, 247-248
Ryder, Bob, 218, 247
Sages, Doug, 190, 198
Sakurada, Mr. (Kazuo), 105
Sammartino, Bruno, 15, 24-26, 36-37, 92, 96, 178, 198
*San Angelo Standard Times*, 58

Sanders, Ron, 31-32
Santana, Tito, 62, 127, 233
Sapp, Bob, 224
Sapphire (Juanita Wright), 181
Sato, Akio, 64, 184-185
*Saturday Night's Main Event*, 163
Saturn, Perry, 220, 238
Savage, Randy, 145, 165, 180-181, 185, 220
Savoldi, Angelo, 23
Sawyer, Buzz, 98
Schiavone, Tony, 206, 209-210
Schiller, Harvey, 207, 227, 229-230, 234
Schmidt, Hans, 21, 33-34
Schneider, Stu, 234, 244
Scicluna, Baron, 21, 23-24, 26, 72, 178
Scott, George, 48, 102, 105, 117, 149
Selenkowitsch, Nico, 105, 107
Shadow, Red (Pedro Godoy), 33
Shane, Bobby, 72-74
Shango, Papa, 169
Sharpe, Ben, 64
Sharpe, Mike, 64
Sheik, The, 31-34, 37, 44, 88, 96, 98
Shire, Professor Roy, 14
Sicilians, The, 177
Siegel, Brad, 230-231, 234-240, 243-245
Simon, Larry (see Malenko, The Great)
Skaaland, Arnold, 23-24, 26, 32, 44, 177
Slater, Dick, 61, 72, 98, 138
Slatton, Don (The Lawman), 68, 88
Slaughter, Sgt., 116, 138, 175, 177
Sloan, Smasher, 21
Smoky Mountain Wrestling, 254
Snider, Duke, 258
Snuka, Jimmy, 116
Solie, Gordon, 124-125, 133
Solis, Merced, 127
Spectrum, The (Philadelphia PA), 145, 157
Spoiler, The, 115
Sportatorium (Dallas), 262
St. Clair, Tony, 103
Stanke, Siegfried, 65-67
*Starrcade '88*, 149
*Starrcade*, 48, 88, 154
Stasiak, Stan, 49, 126
Steele, George (The Animal), 24, 26, 164, 177-178, 233
Steinblock, Eddy, 103
Steiner, Scott, 234-235, 246-247
steroid trial, 194-199
Sting, 149, 154, 169, 225, 246
Stomper, The (Archie Gouldie), 53-54, 72, 77-80, 82, 84, 86
Strongbow, Chief Jay, 125, 177-178
Studd, John, 129
Sugiyama, Thunder, 64
Sullivan, John L., 37
Sullivan, Kevin, 103, 124-125, 207, 216-217, 219, 221, 224, 232, 236-239, 241, 245, 248-249, 255-256, 261
Sullivan, Nancy, 237-238
*Summerslam*, 168, 181
Sun Dome (Tampa), 119, 186
Super World of Sports (SWS), 194
Super, Lou, 19-20
*Survivor Series*, 157, 164

Swayze, Bruce, 72
Sweetan, Bob, 54
Sweetan, Freddie, 46-47, 53-54
Tanaka, Pat, 184
Tanaka, Professor, 20, 24
Taylor County Coliseum, 67
Taylor, Chris, 72
Taylor, Terry, 169, 173, 207, 222, 231, 240
Teal, Scott 10-11, 28, 143, 255
Tenryu, Genichiro, 184
Tharpe, Bruce, 11
Thatcher, Les, 11, 41, 74, 254-255
Thesz, Charlie, 149
Thesz, Lou, 56, 64, 149
Thornton, Chuck, 11
Thornton, Les, 96, 103
Tillet, Louie, 117
Tokyo Dome, 185
Tolos, Chris, 33
Torborg, Jeff, 259
Toshimitsu, Kitanoumi, 87
Total Nonstop Action (TNA), 247, 249
Traylor, Ray, 163
Trembley, Willie, 52
Trenton Armory, 16
Tsuruta, Tomomi (Jumbo), 64
*Tuesday in Texas*, 164
Turner, Ted, 86, 98, 148-149, 153, 159, 167, 204, 209, 244, 254
Tyler, Buzz, 110-111
Undertaker, 164, 185
USWA, 183
Vachon, Stan, 53
Valence, Jim, 20-21
Valentine, Greg, 189, 216
Valentine, Johnny, 15-16, 24, 55
Valiant, Johnny, 37
Varriale, Philip, 11, 255
Vettraino, Mike, 255
Vicious, Sid, 147
Vineland Speedway, 20, 32
Virgil (Mike Jones), 181-182
Von Erich, Fritz, 79-80, 99
Von Erich, Waldo, 92-93, 95
Von Hess, Karl, 14
Von Krupp, Otto, 16
Von Steiger, Karl, 56, 65-67, 74, 90-91
Wacholz, Kevin, 192
Wajima 136
Walt Disney World, 204-205
Waltman, Sean, 182-183, 220
WAR, 184
Ward, Fred, 87
Watson, Greg, 65
Watson, Whipper Billy, 65
Watts, Bill, 72, 102, 123, 133, 159, 179, 208, 217-218, 266
Weaver, Johnny, 41, 45-46, 54
West Texas State University, 59, 62
White Wolf, Billy, 138
Wild Samoan, Afa the, 127
William, Sweet, 96
Williams, Luke, 96
Windham, Barry, 62, 100-101, 145, 147
Wiskowski, Ed, 103
Wizard, The Grand, 31

World Championshp Wrestling (WCW), 11, 103, 132, 146, 163, 167, 182, 185, 204-215, 219-248, 263-264
World Wide Wrestling Federation (WWWF), 7, 15, 23, 54
World Wrestling Entertainment, 264
World Wrestling Federation (WWF), 116, 127, 145-146, 153-206, 264
*WrestleMania VII*, 175
*WrestleMania XIV*, 219
*WrestleMania XV*, 219
*WrestleMania XVI*, 219
*WrestleMania*, 159, 164, 168
wrestling bear, 85
*Wrestling from the Capitol Arena*, 13-14
*Wrestling Observer Newsletter*, 172-176
Wright, Alex, 103
Wright, Bearcat, 78
Wright, Stephen, 103
WTBS, 148
WWF drug program, 200
WWF sex scandal, 191-194
*WWF Superstars*, 172
*WWF Wrestling Challenge*, 163, 172
Yamamoto, Tojo, 195
Yeager, Steve, 259
Yokozuna, 169
Yother, Annette, 207
Young, Tommy, 27, 254
Zacko, Phil, 26, 177
Zahorian, Dr. George, 194
Zebra Kid, 17-18, 22, 178
Zinck, Al, 129
Zuma, Argentina, 21

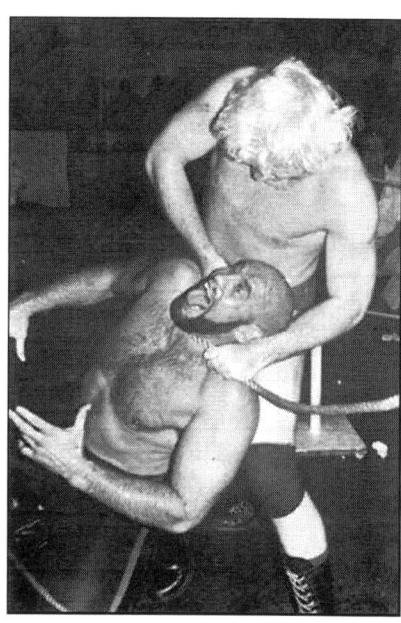

**THE END**

## Classic Arena Programs #1
## SLAM-O-GRAM, volume 1
### by Scott Teal

A full 28 years before Crowbar Press came into existence, Scott Teal introduced his first mainstream publication — SLAM-O-GRAM — a program sold at the wrestling matches in Tennessee, Alabama & Kentucky. The first issue was produced and sold on October 10, 1975, and 244 issues were published during the five years they were sold in arenas.

Copies of SLAM-O-GRAM programs are extremely rare and only a few wrestling enthusiasts have more than a handful in their collections. In fact, the first six issues were sold only in Huntsville, Alabama, so it's doubtful more than a few, if any, of those issues exist. Now, for the first time ever, they are being offered here in book format with each program being re-printed in its entirety.

## Florida Mat Wars • 1977
### by Robert Van Kavelaar, with Scott Teal

This is the first of a series of books that will take you back in time to a day when professional wrestling was king. Many of us remember waiting with anticipation for the newspaper to be delivered so we could check the sports page for the upcoming wrestling card or the results from the night before.

This volume, the first of many, contains all the known ads and results for 1977 that were published in the Florida territory, as well as feature articles, letters to the editor, and photo features that appeared in the newspapers in the days before professional wrestling became sports entertainment and no longer deemed worthy of being reported as a legitimate contest. Relive the memories through more than 900 newspaper clippings.

## Breaking Kayfabe
### by Jeff Bowdren

Since 2012, seven wrestling fans have been meeting with the wrestlers they idolized during the '70s and '80s. The group members, all of whom lived in South Florida and came from all walks of life, began referring to themselves as "The South Florida Marks."

One of the members, Jeff Bowdren, had been a wrestling fan since the early '70s. Since the first dinner he attended, he has taken notes and recorded 24 interviews filled with anecdotes, tales of the road, and wrestling history. This book is the product of his efforts.

**AVAILABLE AT www.crowbarpress.com**

### Through the Lens ... Through the Ropes #1
### Southeastern Championship Wrestling
Compiled by Scott Teal

Wrestling fans will treasure this beautiful collection of photos of the stars of Southeastern Championship Wrestling — Ron & Robert Fuller, Bob Armstrong, Ronnie Garvin, The Mongolian Stomper, Ron Wright, Joe Leduc, Bob Orton Jr., Don Carson, Jimmy Golden, and many others. The 321 photos include publicity stills, candid shots, and action photos from both TV and house shows, most being published for the first time. This is a book that belongs in every wrestling fan's library.

### The Solie Chronicles
by Robert Allyn, with Pamela S Allyn & Scott Teal

One of the most well-known pro-wrestling personalities wasn't a wrestler. He was a commentator and announcer named Gordon Solie. Wrestling fans of the '60s, '70s and '80s remember Gordon's legendary broadcasts on Championship Wrestling from Florida, Championship Wrestling from Georgia, and World Championship Wrestling. Gordon Solie made a major impact on the development of professional wrestling, national auto thrill show tours, stock car racing on Florida's Suncoast, and ultimately, as the host for the highest-rated show on the largest cable network in America.

The background material for this biography was found in Gordon's personal files and taken from interviews with 65 of the people who knew him the best, including Jim Ross, Lance Russell, Dory Funk Jr., Harley Race, Jack Brisco & Steve Keirn. It is written as a testament to a man who made his mark in many endeavors.

### BRUISER BRODY
by Emerson Murray

Today, more than 18 years after his death, pro wrestling fans still talk about Bruiser Brody with reverence and awe in their voice. Hardcore fans consider him to be the greatest brawler in the history of the sport. He also was one of the most unpredictable men ever to step into the ring, marching to his own drummer and refusing to bow to anyone. On any given night, he might or might not do what promoters asked of him. As a result, promoters hated him, but they also loved him because fans turned out in droves to see him.

This is the story of Bruiser Brody. No punches are pulled and the rulebook has been thrown out. This is THE definitive ... Bruiser Brody

### AVAILABLE AT www.crowbarpress.com

## Wrestling in the Garden
## The Battle for New York: Works, Shoots & Double-Crosses
### by Scott Teal & J Michael Kenyon

There has always been something special about attending an event in New York City — sporting events, theater, movies, concerts — and even though wrestling fans in the Northeast loved their local venues, when push came to shove, the one place they'd rather see wrestling than any other was Madison Square Garden. For many years, the Garden was considered to be the wrestling Mecca, and many great moments in wrestling history took place with those walls.

This book, the first in the "Great Cities of Wrestling" series, contains every wrestling event that took place in the Garden between 1875 and 2016. It is the definitive record of professional wrestling in Madison Square Garden ... The World's Most Famous Arena!

---

## The Greatest Wrestling in the History of Nashville, volume 1
### by Scott Teal & Don Luce

The second in the "Great Cities of Wrestling" series, this is the most detailed book every published on the wrestling history of any city in the world. This comprehensive work covers the matches in the ring and the events that took place behind the scenes from 1907, when big-time pro wrestling first made an appearance in Nashville, through 1960.

More than 2,000 wrestling shows and 9,688 matches from a day long gone with more than 550 illustrations and images. All this, plus TV match listings, attendance and gate figures, match stipulations, and much more. An incredible work that will be referred to over and over by both wrestling fans and historians alike.

---

## BRUISER
### by Richard Vicek, edited by Scott Teal

There have been several "Bruisers" in professional wrestling's history — Bruiser Brody, Don the Bruiser, Bruiser Bob Sweetan, to name the three most recognizable — but the name synonymous with pro wrestling for almost three decades was "Dick the Bruiser."

In all respects, Bruiser left an indelible mark in pro wrestling history that will never be matched in either longevity or significance. This book is a testament to the legacy he left behind.

**AVAILABLE AT www.crowbarpress.com**

## Inside Out
### How Corporate American Destroyed Professional Wrestling
by Ole Anderson, with Scott Teal

*"If I had realized that you people would be so damned stupid as to give the world champion $750,000, I would have made myself the champion."*
— Ole Anderson, to the executives at WCW and WTBS

Here, for the first time, Ole Anderson finally tells his story. The people who know him, know that Ole is never hesitant to speak his mind — and this book is no exception. Ole tells of his feuds behind the scenes in the halls and offices of corporate giant, Superstation WTBS. In Ole's own words, *"The wrestling matches may have been staged and scripted, but there was nothing 'fake' about the corporate and legal battles."*

This is a powerful story about a man who stood up to the establishment. His insight, humor, and colorful use of the English language makes this a "no-holds barred" book that you won't be able to put down.

## "Wrestlers Are Like Seagulls"
by James J. Dillon, with Scott Teal

For more than 40 years, James J. Dillon has been involved in the world of professional wrestling. Now he speaks candidly on all aspects of both his career and his personal life, including his time in the WWF as Vince McMahon's right-hand man. Never before has someone from McMahon's inner circle written a book with an insider's perspective of the company. From the highs of making big money, winning championship titles, rubbing elbows with top celebrities, and appearing on television every week, to the lows of filing for bankruptcy, extramarital affairs, divorces, and drug use, no stone is left unturned. In this book, there are truly "no holds barred."

## The Wrestling Archive Project, volume 1
by Scott Teal

Chock full of interviews with the true legends of pro wrestling, most of whom have never been interviewed by anyone else, this edition includes an interview with Buddy Colt, who had never been interviewed before. Also included are no-holds-barred interviews with Adrian Street, Mac McMurray, Benny McGuire, Dandy Jack Donovan, Dick Cardinal, Frank Martinez, Gene Dundee, Gene Lewis, Gorgeous George Grant, Ernie (Hangman) Moore, Joe Powell, Lord Littlebrook, Lou Thesz and Pepper Gomez.

**AVAILABLE AT www.crowbarpress.com**

## HOOKER
### by Lou Thesz, with Kit Bauman

This is Lou Thesz' story. In the late 1940s and well into the 1950s, he was the world heavyweight champion of the National Wrestling Alliance, its standard-bearer, and he carried those colors with dignity and class. "My gimmick was wrestling," he said, and it was evident to anyone who ever bought a ticket to see Lou Thesz that he was the real thing.

"Hooker" was something of a sensation among wrestling fans when it was first published in the 1990s because it was among the first accounts ever published by a major wrestling star that discussed the business with candor from the inside. Academics praised the book, too, for its clear depiction of an era and the rise of a cultural phenomenon.

---

## The Last Outlaw
### by Stan Hansen, with Scott Teal

Stan Hansen's account of his wrestling career is a veritable guidebook of pro wrestling in Japan. He educates and entertains with his stories about the promoters and their promotions, how the Japanese promoters operate their business behind the scenes, touring the country on the wrestling bus, the nightlife in the big cities, and how the sport in Japan differs from that in the U.S.

Stan also shares stories of his time in the U.S. and tells countless road tales about fellow wrestlers. He goes into detail about winning the AWA title and breaking Bruno Sammartino's neck. And what would a "Stan Hansen book" be without personal stories about the time he spent with Bruiser Brody: how they first met, the story behind their becoming a team, spending time in the evenings on the streets and in the clubs of Japan, and his own, personal insight into the "real" Bruiser Brody.

---

## The Hard Way
### by Don Fargo, with Scott Teal

As famous as he was for his ability to draw crowds to the arenas, Don Fargo probably was more famous for his hijinks behind the scenes. The stories about his pranks and wild lifestyle are talked about to this day by those who were witness to the events — dangling from the roof of the King Edward Hotel in New York, riding naked on the roofs of cars traveling at high speeds, nailing a certain body part to a table, and getting his hand stuck in ... well, let's just say, somewhere you wouldn't normally put your whole hand, and his problems with drugs and alcohol. You've never read a more entertaining life story than this one.

## AVAILABLE AT www.crowbarpress.com